**AA**

TOURING

# SCOTLAND

THE COMPLETE TOURING GUIDE

*Cover picture:*
*Loch Shiel and the Glenfinnan Monument, Highland.*

Produced by the Publishing Division of the Automobile Association
Editor Allen Stidwill
Designer Neil Roebuck
Picture Researcher Wyn Voysey
Index by D Hancock

Tours compiled and driven by the Publications Research Unit of
the Automobile Association.

Photographs by Woodmansterne Picture Library, Jarrolds Colour
Library, British Tourist Authority, J Hunter, J Allen Cash
Photolibrary, Spectrum Colour Library, AA Photolibrary, S & O
Mathews, Scottish Tourist Board, H Williams, D Hardley.

All maps by the Cartographic Department, Publishing Division of
the Automobile Association. Based on the Ordnance Survey Maps,
with the permission of the Controller of HM Stationery Office.
Crown Copyright Reserved.

Town plans produced by the AA's Cartographic Department.
©The Automobile Association.

Filmset by Senator Graphics, Great Suffolk St, London SE1
Printed and bound by New Interlitho SPA, Milan, Italy

Published by the Automobile Association, Fanum House,
Basing View, Basingstoke, Hampshire RG21 2EA

ISBN 0 86145 497 9
AA Reference 51907

Mighty snow-capped mountains tower over autumnal Loch Awe and the once isolated ruins of Kilchurn Castle, one of Scotland's finest baronial strongholds.

**Touring Scotland**

# CONTENTS

# INTRODUCTION

Scotland is one of the last great open space areas of Europe, famed for its moody Highland mountains, heather-covered hills, sparkling lochs and acres of tall green forests. It also harbours romantic castles, picturesque fishing ports, handsome towns and villages and a splendid capital city.

It is the land of choice malt whisky, of haunting bagpipes, tartan and tweed, of Highland Games and Gatherings, of winter sports and the ancient game of golf.

This book reveals these treasures and more through its carefully planned motoring tours which provide the ideal way to explore this fascinating land. Each self-contained circular tour can be completed within a day and includes magnificent colour pictures to give a foretaste of what is to come.

As well as the tours the book includes 15 pages of invaluable town plans to guide you around Scotland's popular towns. There is also a large scale, 3 miles to the inch atlas of the country.

*Touring Scotland* is just one in a series of six colourful *Regional Guides* which embrace the rich history and varied countryside of Britain. The other five guides in the series are: *Touring the West Country, Touring South and South East England, Touring Wales, Touring Central England and East Anglia* and *Touring the North Country.* The six regions covered by the series are shown on the adjacent map.

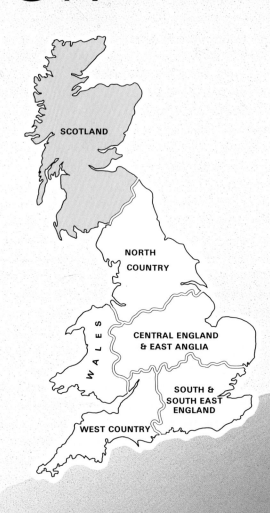

## ABOUT THE TOURS

The tours in this guide have been designed for clarity. Each tour occupies two pages and has a clear map accompanying the text. All the places described in the text are shown in **black** on the tour maps and are described as they occur on the road, linked in sequence by route directions. This precise wayfinding information is set in *italic*.

Castles, stately homes and other places of interest described in the tours are not necessarily open to the public or may be open only at certain times. It is therefore advisable to check the opening times of any place before planning a stop there. Properties administered by the National Trust, National Trust for Scotland and the Ancient Monument Scheme (NT, NTS and AM) are generally open most of the year, but this should be checked with the relevant organisation, as should precise opening times.

The Automobile Association's guide *Stately Homes, Museums, Castles and Gardens in Britain* is the most comprehensive annual publication of its kind. It describes over 2,000 places of interest, giving details of opening times and admission prices, including many listed in this book.

*History and magnificent scenery have made Glencoe one of the most celebrated glens in Scotland. Here faint echoes of bygone battles still linger around its remote and rugged landscape.*

## MAPS

| | |
|---|---|
| Main Tour Route | |
| Detour/Diversion from Main Tour Route | |
| Motorway | |
| Motorway Access | 2 |
| Motorway Service Area | S |
| Motorway and Junction Under Construction | |
| A-class Road | A68 |
| B-class Road | B700 |
| Unclassified Road | unclass |
| Dual Carriageway | A70 |
| Road Under Construction | = = = = |
| Airport | ✈ |
| Battlefield | ✕ |
| Bridge | ⌒ |
| Castle | ⊭ |
| Church as Route Landmark | † |
| Ferry | –Ⓥ– |
| Folly/Tower | 🮲 |
| Forestry Commission Land | ♠ |
| Gazetteer Placename | Zoo/Lydstep |
| Industrial Site (Old & New) | ⛏ |
| Level Crossing | LC |
| Lighthouse | 🯂 |
| Marshland | |
| Memorial/Monument | m |
| Miscellaneous Places of Interest & Route Landmarks | ■ |
| National Boundary | |
| National Trust Property | NT |
| National Trust for Scotland Property | NTS |
| Non-gazetteer Placenames | Thames/Astwood |
| Notable Religious Site | ✝ |
| Picnic Site | Ⓟ |
| Prehistoric Site | ᚼ |
| Racecourse | ⬭ |
| Radio/TV Mast | ⚊ |
| Railway (BR) with Station | |
| Railway (Special) with Station | ┼┼┼┼ |
| River & Lake | |
| Woodland Area | |
| Scenic Area | |
| Seaside Resort | ⚓ |
| Stately Home | 🏛 |
| Summit/Spot Height | KNOWE HILL 209 ▲ |
| | KNOWE HILL 209 ▲ |
| Viewpoint | ☀ |

## TEXT

| | |
|---|---|
| AM | Ancient Monument |
| c | *circa* |
| NT | National Trust |
| NTS | National Trust for Scotland |
| OACT | Open at Certain Times |
| PH | Public House |
| RSPB | Royal Society for the Protection of Birds |
| SP | Signpost (s) (ed) |

# HOW TO FIND THE TOURS

All the motor tours in the book are shown on the key map below and identified by the towns where they start. The tours are arranged in the book in alphabetical order by start town name. Page numbers are also given on page vii. Each tour begins at a well-known place, but it is possible to join or leave at any point if more convenient.

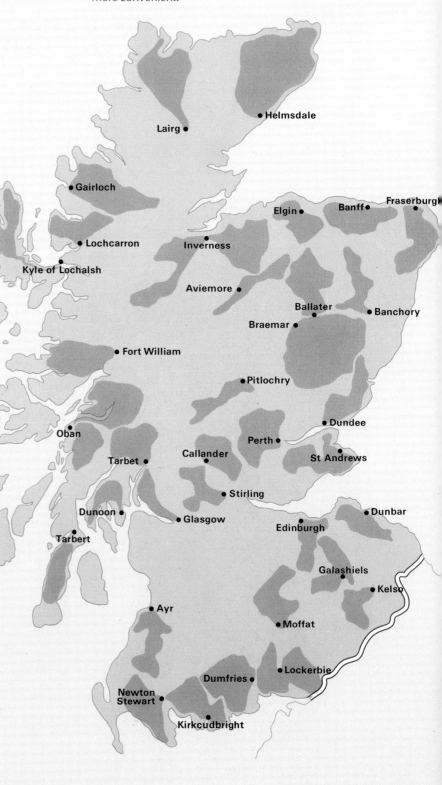

# TOURING
# SCOTLAND

## Motor Tours
## Pages 2-75

## AVIEMORE, Highland

In the 1960s the village of Aviemore, situated in the heart of the British winter sports area, became transformed into one of Scotland's major inland resorts. This amazing change was brought about by the building of the Aviemore Centre, a massive complex of shops, restaurants, luxury hotels, and entertainment facilities with a definite après-ski flavour. Superb sporting facilities include ice-rinks for skating and curling, a go-kart track, a dry ski slope, and a swimming pool. Various events are staged at the theatre and concert hall, and for people who dislike hotel rooms there are numerous well-appointed chalets. The local granite and timber of which the complex is built is in keeping with its site at the foot of the great rock of Craigellachie. Steam-hauled trains operate on a revived railway which runs along the Spey Valley to connect Aviemore with Boat of Garten, some 5 miles away. Another feature of the area is a 600-acre nature reserve.

*Leave Aviemore on the 'Perth' road B9152 and in 2 miles keep forward. Later skirt the shores of Loch Alvie and the village of Alvie.*

## ALVIE, Highland

Alvie Church is a homely focal point for this pleasant hamlet. Nearby Geal Charn Mor stands at 2,703ft and rewards anybody who climbs it with one of Scotland's finest views of the Cairngorm Mountains.
On Tor of Alvie Hill to the south is the Waterloo Cairn and Monument to the last Duke of Gordon.

*Continue through Kincraig to reach the Highland Wildlife Park.*

## HIGHLAND WILDLIFE PARK, Highland

This was opened in 1972 and is based on an interesting historic theme, to illustrate the wildlife that has existed in Britain from the ice ages to the present day. Among the inhabitants displayed in one of the most fascinating collections in the country are bears, wolves, lynx, wildcats, and European bison.

*Continue and in 3½ miles go forward on to the A86 to enter Kingussie.*

## KINGUSSIE, Highland

A popular pony-trekking centre surrounded by the wooded countryside of Strath Spey, Kingussie was chosen as the site for the superb Highland Folk Museum when it was moved from its place of foundation on Iona. Exhibits relate to the everyday life of the Scottish people and include farming implements, domestic tools, dress, tartans, relics of old crafts, and several much larger items such as a complete cottage furnished in traditional style, a mill

# BELOW THE CAIRNGORM SUMMITS

Here are the best winter-sports facilities in Britain, mountain walks that are unequalled elsewhere in the country, and the forested depths of beautiful Glen More. Superb views are afforded by ski lifts that operate all the year round, riding high above granite crags and tree-shrouded lochs.

Superb facilities for ski-ing exist around Aviemore, including a wide variety of nursery slopes and many more difficult runs.

from the Isle of Lewis, a traditional islander's black house, and a curious clack mill. A visit here will provide the type of understanding that can only enrich the tourist's enjoyment of Scotland in general, and the Highlands in particular. Some 2½ miles north-east of Kingussie, off the Aviemore road, is the 18th-century mansion of Balavil. This was built by James Macpherson, who was born in the area and later became a translator of Ossianic poetry.

*Before leaving Kingussie it is possible to take a detour from the main route by keeping forward on the A86 for 3 miles to Newtonmore.*

## NEWTONMORE, Highland

Highland ponies can be hired for rides into the bleak Monadhliath Mountains from a centre to the west of this town, which was the first place in Britain to offer pony-trekking as a recreation. Overlooking the site of a clan battle fought near by in 1386 is 2,350ft Craig Dhu, the ancient gathering place of the Clan Macpherson. Macpherson House Museum features clan history and relics of the 1745 Jacobite Rising.

*On the main tour, turn left on to the B970 SP 'Ruthven, Insh' and drive over a level crossing. Continue to Ruthven Barracks.*

## RUTHVEN BARRACKS, Highland

Built in 1719 and added to by General Wade 'the road builder' in 1734, these old barracks (AM) were adopted to house anti-Jacobite troops between the Risings of 1715 and 1745. They were captured and demolished by the followers of Bonnie Prince Charlie in 1746.

*Continue and in 1¾ miles cross the River Tromie at Tromie Bridge and turn left SP 'Kincraig'.*

## INSH, Highland

AA Celtic handbell that was once used to call people to worship is preserved in an 18th-century church above Loch Insh near Kincraig. It pre-dates the building by at least 1,000 years, and the site occupied by the church is even older.

*In 2½ miles keep forward with the 'Rothiemurchus' road and later cross the River Feshie at Feshiebridge.*

## FESHIEBRIDGE, Highland

Excellent all-weather footpaths extend along the Glen of Feshie towards Deeside from here. Some of the most scenic areas are where the valley penetrates the hill ranges of attractive Speyside.

*Continue along the B970 and drive through attractive Inshriach Forest to reach Rothiemurchus.*

## ROTHIEMURCHUS, Highland

At one time the woodland round this hamlet formed part of the primeval Caledonian Forest that covered most of the Scottish Highlands. Much of it is contained within the boundaries of Rothiemurchus Forest, which is accessible by attractive paths and tracks. Part of the area is protected as a nature reserve and there is a visitor centre.

*Just beyond Rothiemurchus it is possible to make a short detour from the main route by turning right on to an unclassified road and driving to Loch an Eilean.*

## LOCH AN EILEAN, Highland

Noted for its odd triple echo, this beautiful loch was once the bolthole of the Wolf of Badenoch, a clan leader who was notoriously bloodthirsty. The island ruins of his castle add a sinister note to the otherwise innocent enchantment of the lochside area.

*On the main tour, continue along the B970 to Inverdruie.*

## INVERDRUIE, Highland

Situated here is the Whisky Museum with an audio-visual display, museum, tasting room, shop and a visitor centre.

*Turn right for Coylumbridge.*

The splendid Cairngorm Mountains rise to the north of attractive Loch Morlich.

The wild cat is a fierce native of the Scottish Highlands.

## COYLUMBRIDGE, Highland

This ski resort on the River Druie is a key point of access to the peaks and valleys of the Cairngorms. A Forestry Commission road which starts here leads into the range, passing through Queen's Forest to the shores of Loch Morlich, where there is a youth hostel. After the recreational centre of Glenmore a further stretch of ski road ascends to the Cairngorms · carparks and chairlift terminals. Views from the carparks extend for miles over the Glen More Forest Park.

## GLEN MORE FOREST PARK, Highland

Some 3,300 acres of coniferous forest and 9,200 acres of mountainside make up this beautiful and often spectacular national forest park. At its heart is Loch Morlich, which lies in a hollow 1,000ft above sea level and has sandy beaches fringed by descendants of the old Caledonian pines that once covered the Highlands. Rock and heather take over where the trees stop, and all round the horizon are the serrated outlines of mountain peaks. Rare wildlife found nowhere else in Britain lives here, and species that are uncommon elsewhere abound. Walkers using the Forestry Commission trails may see the blue hare or stately red deer, the turkey-like capercaillie that was re-introduced to the Highlands several years ago, or the ptarmigan that never quite died out. Also here are grouse, golden eagles, the elusive osprey, and roe deer. Reindeer are being farmed in the area, so the walker who comes face to face with one of these magnificent creatures should not fear for his sanity.

*From Coylumbridge follow SP 'Nethy Bridge' along the B970 to continue along Strath Spey. After 6¼ miles a ½-mile detour can be taken from the main route by following an unclassified left turn to Boat of Garten.*

## BOAT OF GARTEN, Highland

The curious name of this village is derived from a ferry that used to cross the Spey from here before the present bridge was built in the 19th century. It is the northern terminus of a 5-mile steam hauled railway which runs along Strath Spey to the winter sports and recreation centre of Aviemore.

*On the main tour, continue along the B970 for a further ½ mile and turn right on to an unclassified road SP 'Loch Garten' to enter the Abernethy Forest. Continue to the banks of Loch Garten.*

## LOCH GARTEN, Highland

Visitors to the RSPB observation point here can watch many species of birds, including the rare osprey. *Pass Loch Garten and after ⅓ mile keep forward on to the 'Nethy Bridge' road. In 2⅓ miles turn right to rejoin the B970 and enter the resort of Nethy Bridge.*

## NETHY BRIDGE, Highland

Winter-sports enthusiasts come here for the ski-ing, and later in the year it is a popular centre for walkers and anglers. North of the village on the B970 are the ruins of Castle Roy, a great fortress that was a stronghold of the Comyn.

*Cross the River Nethy then turn right on to an unclassified road (no sign) and in ½ mile drive over crossroads SP 'Tomintoul'. Ascend onto moorland, and after 4½ miles turn right on to the A939 towards Tomintoul. Proceed, with the Hills of Cromdale on the left and the dark outlines of the Cairngorms to the right. Ascend to a road summit of 1,424ft, then descend to the Bridge of Brown. Climb again then descend and cross the Bridge of Avon, then turn left on to the B9136 SP 'Craigellachie'. Follow Strath Avon and in 8½ miles cross the River Livet at the hamlet of Glenlivet.*

## GLENLIVET, Grampian

Fine malt whisky has been distilled in this small village for many years, and although there is a modern distillery here (open to visitors) the method has not changed much.

*Beyond the Livet bridge turn left SP 'Whisky Trail' to join the B9008. After 4 miles reach the Delnashaugh Inn and turn left on to the A95 Grantown Road.*

## DELNASHAUGH INN, Grampian

Close to this famous landmark is Ballindalloch Castle, which was begun in the 16th century and bears the arms of the Macpherson-Grants. Beyond its picturesque grounds is the junction of the River Avon with the River Spey.

*After a short distance re-cross the*

River Avon, with the grounds of Ballindalloch Castle to the right, and continue to the hamlet of Toremore.

## TOREMORE, Highland

In 1960 the first distillery to be built in the Highlands this century was opened here. The building, which at the time was described as 'the most beautiful industrial structure in the Highlands', was designed by Professor Sir Albert Richardson.

*Continue along the south side of the Spey and pass through the hamlet of Cromdale. Continue to the resort of Grantown-on-Spey.*

## GRANTOWN-ON-SPEY, Highland

A local landowner planned this essentially residential resort in 1776, and the elegance of the 18th century has persisted to the present day. It is set in the lovely surroundings of Strath Spey and has become a major centre for anglers seeking the excellent Spey salmon. There is also considerable local involvement with the Scottish winter-sports industry. Castle Grant, a mansion that is the seat of the Earls of Seafield, stands about 2 miles north of the town.

*Leave Grantown on the 'Perth' road A95 and continue to Dulnain Bridge.*

Loch Garten is nationally famous as a breeding ground for the osprey.

*Continue on the A938 and follow the valley of the River Dulnain to Carrbridge. Here turn left on to the Aviemore road B9135 for the village.*

## CARRBRIDGE, Highland

The award-winning visitor cente in this Highland resort is claimed to be the finest in Europe. It offers all kinds of information about the Highlands, including an exciting audio-visual display that covers some 10,000 years of history. In winter Carrbridge is a popular ski-ing centre.

*Continue on the B9153 and in 2½ miles go forward on to the A95. Later take the B9152 to re-enter Aviemore.*

## AYR, Strath
As well as being a popular resort with miles of safe, sandy beach, this Royal Burgh is also a fishing and commercial port and flourishing centre of industry. Here the spirit of Burns is never very far away. The poet was christened at the Auld Kirk, his statue stands near the station, and relics of his life and work can be seen in the Tam O'Shanter Museum. Ayr's famous Twa Brigs over the River Ayr were built in the 13th and 18th centuries respectively, but the later structure has been replaced by a modern road bridge. The early crossing was renovated in 1910 and is now used by pedestrians only. The town's oldest building is 16th-century Loudon Hall, which was extensively restored in 1938, but earlier incomplete fragments, such as ancient St John's Towers can be seen elsewhere in the area. Ayr is well known for its fine parks and gardens and a fine racecourse. Landmarks of the town are the 126ft high steeple of the Town Hall and the 113ft-high Wallace Tower. Also of interest are the Maclaurin Art Gallery and Rozelle House Museum on the Alloway road.

*Leave Ayr on the A719 'Maidens' road and climb past Butlin's Holiday Camp to a height of over 300ft. Skirt Dunure, which lies to the right below the main road.*

## DUNURE, Strath
This attractive little fishing village is overlooked by a ruined castle on a clifftop site. During the 16th century the stronghold was notorious for the cruel treatment to prisoners and for the roasting alive of the Crown Factor of Crossraguel Abbey. Close by is an old dovecote in which pigeons were once raised to keep the castle supplied with fresh meat.

*Continue for 2 miles to reach the Electric Brae.*

## ELECTRIC BRAE, Strath
A curious optical illusion caused by

## THE LAND OF ROBERT BURNS
*Scotland's most famous poet was born and raised in this area of cliff-fringed coast and lovely river valleys. His characters still seem to populate the stern little towns, charming villages, and enchanting countryside between the sea and the beautiful reaches of wooded Glen Trool.*

Robert Burns was born in this cottage at Alloway in 1759. It now houses a commemorative museum.

the lie of the surrounding countryside makes the road through this area appear to be descending when it is actually climbing.

*In 2 miles turn right with the A719 and follow a wooded valley to the entrance of Culzean Castle.*

## CULZEAN CASTLE, Strath
An ancient tower that was once a Kennedy stronghold forms the centrepiece of this splendid castle (NTS), which was designed by the talented Robert Adam in 1777. Everything about the building prompts superlatives, but the Round Drawing Room and magnificent staircase are probably its finest features. Many of the rooms have beautifully decorated plaster ceilings. The grounds include the extensive Culzean Country Park.

## CULZEAN COUNTRY PARK, Strath
Scotland's first countryside park was created in the 565-acre grounds of Culzean Castle this century, but the lovely walled garden was established in 1783 and the buildings of the Home Farm were designed by Robert Adam while he was extending the castle. The farm has been adapted as a reception and interpretation centre for the park.

*Continue along the A719 to reach the village of Maidens.*

## MAIDENS, Strath
Just inland of this Maidenhead Bay resort is Shanter Farm, which was the home of Douglas Graham, the original of Burns' Tam O'Shanter. The bay has a good sand and shingle beach and a modern harbour for fishing and sailing.

*Leave Maidens on the A719 to reach the golf resort of Turnberry.*

## TURNBERRY, Strath
Traces of Turnberry Castle and also a lighthouse stand on Turnberry Point, an attractive promontory to the north of the resort's famous championship golf course. Legend

Views from the magnificent golf course at Turnberry extend past a lighthouse to distant Ailsa Craig.

has it that the castle was the birthplace of Robert the Bruce in 1247, and history records that he certainly landed here in 1307 to win his first battle against the English. On a clear day views extend to lonely Ailsa Craig, a rocky little island 12 miles away that rises to 1,110ft from the sea, and to the Isle of Arran.

*In Turnberry village turn left on to the A77 'Ayr' road to reach Kirkoswald.*

## KIRKOSWALD, Strath
Kirkoswald Churchyard contains the graves of two of Robert Burns' best loved characters, Tam O'Shanter and Souter Johnnie. In real life Tam was Douglas Graham of Shanter, who supplied grain to an Ayr brewery, and his crony 'Souter' was a village cobbler named John Davidson. Davidson's thatched 18th-century cottage (NTS) now houses a Burns' museum. There are life-size figures of these characters in the garden.

*From Kirkoswald continue along the A77 to reach Crossraguel Abbey.*

## CROSSRAGUEL ABBEY, Strath
Originally founded as a Cluniac monastery by the Earl of Carrick in the 13th century, this abbey (AM) was inhabited by the Benedictine order from 1244 to the 16th century. Many superb examples of 15th-century architecture can be seen amongst the extensive ruins.

*Continue along the A77 and enter the town of Maybole.*

## MAYBOLE Strath
Maybole was once the seat of the very powerful Kennedy family, who were the Earls of Cassillis. Their town house was 17th-century Maybole Castle, whose picturesque turret and oriel windows make a charming architectural contribution to the town's High Street. Nowadays it is used as administration offices for the Kennedy estates. Other family connexions exist with the Tollbooth, which was one of their mansions and incorporates fragments of a much older building.

*From Maybole turn right on to the B7023 'Crosshill' road and drive to Crosshill village. Turn right here with the B7023 'Dailly' road, then in 1 mile join the B741 and continue through the Water of Girvan valley. After 3 miles meet an unclassified left turn SP 'Barr'. A detour from the main route can be taken to Dailly by continuing along the B741 for 1 mile.*

## DAILLY, Strath
The 18th-century church in New Dailly features lairds' lofts, and the romantic 16th-century ruin of Dalquharran Castle stands to the north. Two miles south-west on the unclassified Old Dailly road are the Bargany Gardens (open), where fine displays of flowers and shrubs can be enjoyed.

Culzean Castle's Round Drawing Room is a superb example of Georgian elegance.

*On the main tour, take the unclassified road SP 'Barr' and drive through moorland for 5 miles, cross the River Stinchar and turn right to follow the river to Barr.*

### BARR, Strath
Changue Forest, part of the huge Galloway Forest Park, lies close to this little River Stinchar angling resort. Craigenreoch Hill rises to the south-east.

*Meet a T-junction and turn right then shortly turn left on to the B734 SP 'Barrhill'. In 6 miles meet the A714 and turn left SP 'Newton Stewart' to reach Pinwherry.*

### PINWHERRY, Strath
Ruins of a one-time Kennedy stronghold stand near the junction of the River Stinchar and the Duisk River at Pinwherry.

*Turn right with the A714 Barrhill road and cross the Duisk Water. Continue up the valley to Barrhill.*

### BARRHILL, Strath
Desolate, open moorland surrounds this pleasant little village, relieved only by the green banks of the Duisk valley.

*Continue along the A714 to Bargrennan and turn left on to an unclassified road SP 'Straiton'. Drive into the Galloway Forest Park.*

### GALLOWAY FOREST PARK, Dumf & Gall
A third of this huge 110,000-acre park is planted with trees, and its boundaries encompass five complete forests and 10 hills rising to over 2,000ft. Because this is a commercial enterprise as much as anything else, the predominant species of trees in the park are Douglas fir, Scots pine, Norwegian spruce, and other fast-growing conifers. This industrial aspect does not detract from its scenic value however, and each summer sees the arrival of more visitors to enjoy the tranquillity of its woodlands and exhilarating openness of those places that have not been planted.
One of the finest areas is Glen Trool Forest.

*Drive through Glentrool village and meet a right turn that offers a short detour from the main route to attractive Loch Trool.*

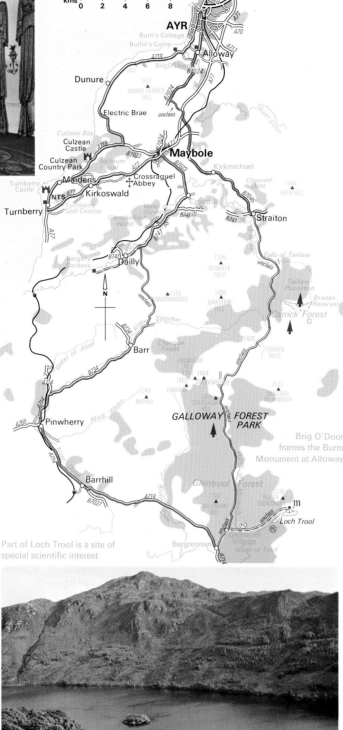

Part of Loch Trool is a site of special scientific interest.

### LOCH TROOL, Dumf & Gall
A campsite near the Martyr's Stone on the south-western side of this beautiful lake is the start of a 4½-mile circuit of its pleasantly wooded banks. Woodland and water-margin wild life can be seen. Above the northern shore a granite memorial records the defeat of an English force by Robert the Bruce at the eastern end of the loch in 1307.

Prominent to the north are the Rhinns of Kells and the Merrick, while Lamachan Hill rises to the south.

*On the main tour, continue through the forest park and in 8 miles branch right. Climb to a road summit of 1,420ft, then descend through the Tairlaw Plantation of Carrick Forest into the Girvan Valley. Drive to the village of Straiton.*

### STRAITON, Strath
A good pre-Reformation aisle can be seen in the restored church of this attractive little village, and the old mansion of Blairquhan (not open) stands west near the Water of Girvan. The glen of Lambdoughty Burn lies east of the Dalmellington road and is known for its lovely waterfalls.

*Go forward on to the Ayr road B7045 following the Water of Girvan to Kirkmichael. Continue with the B7045 and in 4 miles turn right on to the A77 then take the next turning left unclassified (no sign). In ¼ mile turn*

Brig O'Doon frames the Burns Monument at Alloway.

*right then in ½ mile turn right again into the B7024 SP 'Alloway'. Three miles farther cross the River Doon to enter Alloway.*

### ALLOWAY, Strath
The two-roomed clay and thatch cottage in which Scotland's national poet was born in 1759 contains many furnishings and domestic implements used in his day. Adjoining the cottage and set in pretty gardens, is the Burns Museum. This has an interesting exhibition of original manuscripts, a copy of the Kilmarnock edition of poems, and other of Burns' possessions, including his family Bible. The Auld Brig described by Burns still spans the River Doon here. It is possible that the bridge dates from the 13th century, and above it is the 19th-century Burns Monument. It was built to a fine design by Thomas Hamilton Junior with sculptures of characters in Burns' poems by a self-taught artist, James Thorn.
Bibles belonging to the poet and Highland Mary are kept inside the memorial. There is also a Land O'Burns Interpretation Centre. Situated in landscaped gardens, where audio-visual, multi-screen presentations show the life of Robert Burns. A roofless building near by is the haunted Kirk Alloway mentioned in one of his many works.
*From Alloway continue on to the B7024, and after 1½ miles join the A79 to re-enter Ayr.*

## BALLATER, Grampian

The Ballater Highland Games are internationally famous and have been drawing large audiences for over a hundred years. Traditionally held in August, they include many old Scottish sports and the arduous Hill Race to the summit of Craig Cailleach. The town itself is a popular summer resort, even without the attraction of the games, set in beautiful Grampian countryside. Lochnagar rises to 3,786ft in the south-west, and just north of the town the pretty Pass of Ballater is threaded by the old Deeside road as it passes beneath the flanks of Craig-an-Darroch. The long and lovely valley of Glen Muick lies south-west below 3,268ft Broad Cairn, and was a favourite of Queen Victoria. Edward VII bought the fine 18th-century house that stands 1 mile south-west of Ballater in Glen Muick while he was the Prince of Wales, and it is now used by HM the Queen Mother. To the east of Glen Muick is the Forest of Glentanar, which includes the 3,077ft bulk of Mount Keen.

*Leave Ballater on the A93 'Aberdeen' road and drive along the Dee Valley to the Cambus O'May Hotel, then in ½ mile turn left on to the A97 SP 'Huntly'. Drive past Lochs Kinord and Davan, then turn left again to remain on the A97. Pass through Logie Coldstone and climb through moorland, with the 2,862ft peak of Morven to the left to a road summit of 1,213ft, then descend to Deskry Water and later the River Don. Turn right with the A97. A 2½ mile detour can be taken from the main route to visit Strathdon by turning left here on to the B973.*

## STRATHDON, Grampian

Here the trout-rich River Don is joined by the Water of Nochty, which flows down from the Ladder Hills. The river and hill country round the village is particularly lovely, and the village itself is a charming place with a church spire that can be seen for miles around. A little to the south-west the Don is spanned by a fine 18th-century bridge, and to the south-east Colquhonnie Castle was begun in the 16th century but never completed. In mid-August Strathdon is usually the venue for the Lonach Highland Gathering.

*On the main route cross two river bridges and continue alongside the River Don. After 1¾ miles pass Glenbuchat Castle on the left.*

## GLENBUCHAT CASTLE, Grampian

Ruins of this ancient Z-plan tower house (exterior AM), considered one of the finest extant, form a major feature of lovely Castle Park. The building was erected in 1590 and is known for its variety of unusual architectural features.

*Continue to Glenkindie.*

## CASTLES OF THE LADDER HILLS

This is a place of large pine forests and purple moors, of windy summits and glens guarded by ancient castles that once symbolized the strength of their clans. Here in the picturesque valley of the Dee is Balmoral Castle, the private country home of the Royal Family.

Dufftown lies within easy reach of broad expanses of moorland.

## GLENKINDIE, Grampian

Close to Glenkindie House in the upper Don Valley is a remarkable weem, or ancient Pictish house. In a churchyard about 1 mile away on the other side of the river, near the remains of Towie Castle, is an ancient sculptured cross.

*Continue for 2¼ miles to pass the ruins of Kildrummy Castle on the left.*

## KILDRUMMY CASTLE, Grampian

Built in the 13th century and extensively repaired since, this ruined castle (AM) stands at 800ft above sea level and is guarded on two sides by precipitous ravines. It has seen more than its share of stormy Scottish history, and in 1306 was the scene of a famous and gallant defence by Sir

Balvenie Castle is one of the largest in north Scotland.

Nigel Bruce. The remains are extensive and the most complete of this period in Scotland. One of its great towers is almost equal in size to the superb example at Bothwell, and it preserves a complete layout of domestic buildings, hall, kitchen, solar, and a chapel with a triple lancet window. There is a Japanese Water Garden in the lovely grounds.

*Drive on to the hamlet of Mossat and turn left, then continue to Lumsden. Two miles further turn left on to the B9002 SP 'Dufftown' and pass Auchindoir Church, then Craig Castle, on the left.*

## AUCHINDOIR CHURCH, Grampian

One of Scotland's finest medieval churches, roofless but otherwise complete, can be seen here. The main features of the ruins (AM) are a carved 12th- or 13th-century doorway and an interesting Sacrament House.

## CRAIG CASTLE, Grampian

Patrick Gordon, who was killed on the battleground of Flodden Field in 1513, built the tower that first stood on this site 3 years before his death. It stands on the attractive waters of the Burn of Craig.

*From the castle climb across bleak moorland to 1,370ft and later turn left on to the A941. Gradually descend, passing through the hamlet of Cabrach into the upper valley of the River Deveron.*

## CABRACH, Grampian

The countryside round Cabrach, dominated by the 2,368ft Buck of Cabrach in the south-east, is a place of contrasts. Flourishing deer forests fringe barren moorlands, and the lonely source of the River Deveron is hidden in the heathy slopes of the surrounding hills.

*Continue along the A941 and drive alongside the River Deveron for a short distance before continuing over moorland. On the approach to Dufftown cross the River Fiddich and in 1½ miles reach an unclassified right turn that offers a ½-mile detour to Auchindoun Castle.*

## AUCHINDOUN CASTLE, Grampian

Prehistoric earthworks surround this ruined Gordon castle (AM), situated on a hilltop above the River Fiddich. It is thought that the stronghold was originally founded as early as the 11th century, but much of the existing structure was built by Thomas Cochrane in the reign of James III.

*On the main route, continue to Dufftown turning left then shortly left again for the town.*

## DUFFTOWN, Grampian

This pleasant town was laid out by James Duff, the 4th Earl of Fife, in 1817 in the form of a right-angle cross. In the middle of the square is a Tolbooth tower. The town has a small museum with items from Mortlach Kirk (AM) to the south. The area is well known for its many whisky distilleries, including the famous Glenfiddich plant (open).

*On the A941 just north of Dufftown are the ruins of Balvenie Castle.*

## BALVENIE CASTLE, Grampian

Originally built by the Comyn family, this great moated stronghold (AM) later came into the hands of the Black Douglases and subsequently the Atholls. It was the latter family who created the appearance of the building as it stands today, by demolishing the entire south-east front and replacing it with a 3-storey Renaissance tower house known as the Atholl Building. Edward I visited the castle in 1304, and it was occupied by the Duke of Cumberland in 1746.

*Leave Dufftown on the B9009 'Tomintoul road and follow Dullan Water through Glen Rinnes.*

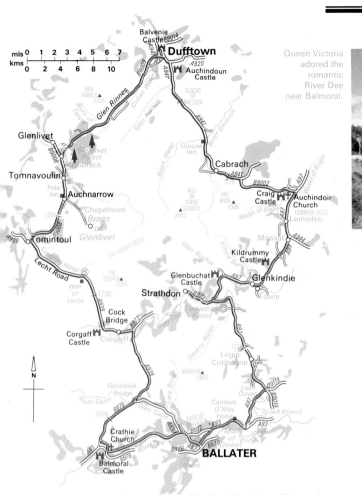

mls 0 1 2 3 4 5 6 7
kms 0 2 4 6 8 10

*Queen Victoria adored the romantic River Dee near Balmoral.*

*The Royal Family usually spends a summer holiday at Balmoral.*

## GLEN RINNES, Grampian
This lovely glen is surrounded by fine mountain scenery. Ben Rinnes rises to 2,755ft in the north-west, and the south is dominated by 2,563ft Corryhabbie Hill.

*Later pass Glenlivet Forest to reach Auchbreck (not signed). A 1¾-mile detour can be taken from here to visit the village of Glenlivet by turning right on to the B9008.*

## GLENLIVET, Grampian
Whisky has been distilled in this area for a great many years, and the famous Glenlivet distillery has been producing its fine unblended malt since 1824. Guided tours and a visitor centre are available. The Glen itself stretches south-east from the village towards the Ladder Hills and offers some good walks. Just south of the village are the remains of Blairfindy Castle, and a picturesque ruined bridge spans the Livet Water north at Bridgend.

*On the main route, keep left on to the B9008 (no SP). Proceed along Glen Livet and pass through Tomnavoulin before climbing to reach the Pole Inn at Auchnarrow.*

## AUCHNARROW, Grampian
Near Chapeltown in the Braes of Glenlivet, some 3½ miles south-east, is the old Scalen Seminary. This interesting Christian foundation was built in the mid-17th century and burned down during the Rising of 1745. Today its ruins form an interesting feature of the local landscape.

*Continue through forestry to a height of 1,285ft. Descend to crossroads and turn left on to the A939 'Braemar' road. A short detour from the main route into Tomintoul can be made by keeping forward here.*

## TOMINTOUL, Grampian
Claimed to be the highest village in the Highlands, Tomintoul is stretched out along a 1,160ft sandstone ridge between the Glen of Avon and the Conglass Water. It is also a winter skiing resort and in summer is popular with anglers, who come to fish here and south-west of the village, where the Avon is joined by the Water of Ailnack. There is a local museum in the square. The A939 road from Tomintoul to Grantown-on-Spey provides excellent views of the Grampian foothills.

*Continue along the A939 through a landscape that becomes bleak and desolate as the route skirts the Ladder Hills. Climb to a 2,090ft summit on the Lecht Road.*

## LECHT ROAD, Grampian
An old carved stone on the Well of Lecht commemorates the building of this military road by the 33rd Regiment under Lord Charles Hay in 1745. The road summit of 2,090ft is the second highest on any classified road in Britain but is still dwarfed by the surrounding mountains which have become a very popular winter sports area. During the winter deep snow often makes it impassable.

*Continue, and descend by a series of steps to Cock Bridge.*

## COCK BRIDGE, Grampian
This picturesque bridge carries the Lecht Road across the River Don and is situated 1,330ft above sea level.

*Continue with ruined Corgarff Castle on the right.*

## CORGARFF CASTLE, Grampian
The twice-burned 16th-century tower house (AM) of Corgarff played a large part in the 18th-century Jacobite Risings.

*In 2½ miles turn right with the A939 SP 'Braemar' and re-cross the River Don. Cross open moorland reaching the Glas-Choille summit, 1,138ft and descend to the fine old Gairnshiel Bridge. Cross the River Gairn and branch right with the B976, crossing further moorland, then after 5 miles reach Royal Deeside and a junction with the A93. Turn left on to the 'Aberdeen' road. After a short distance pass the road to Balmoral Castle on the right, across the River Dee and Crathie Church on the left.*

## BALMORAL CASTLE, Grampian
In 1852 Prince Albert bought this beautiful Royal Deeside estate for £31,000, and had the existing castle rebuilt in the romantic Scottish baronial style. Later Queen Victoria added Ballochbuie Forest to the grounds, and since 1855 Balmoral has been the private holiday home of the Royal Family. It is beautifully situated in a curve of the River Dee in the district of Mar, with Glen Gelder leading to the Balmoral Forest area and the White Mounth hills in the south. The glen provided a picturesque route for Queen Victoria and Prince Albert when they climbed Lochnagar on ponies in 1848. Appropriately, the Gaelic rendering of Balmoral is *Bouchmorale*, meaning Majestic Dwelling. The grounds, gardens and castle ballroom (works of art) are open in the early summer.

*Continue, and after a short distance pass Crathie Church on the left.*

## CRATHIE CHURCH, Grampian
Queen Victoria laid the foundation stone of this church in 1895, and the Royal Family attend services here when in residence at Balmoral. The grave of John Brown, Queen Victoria's personal retainer for many years, lies in the churchyard of the present building's ruined predecessor.

*Continue with the A93 alongside the River Dee and pass through attractive woodland on the return to Ballater.*

# BANCHORY TO HUNTLY

From wooded Deeside the route crosses the valley of the River Don, then over the Correen Hills and along the River Bogie to the magnificent castle at Huntly, formerly known as the Palace of Strathbogie. The return journey takes in Craigievar Castle, the loveliest and most perfectly-preserved of Scotland's castles.

## BANCHORY, Grampian
Banchory is a popular and well-favoured holiday town built of silvery granite and surrounded by forests of pine. The arrival of the railway brought new prosperity to Banchory and encouraged a great deal of new building in what had been little more than a village. Its history, however, stretches back to the 5th century, when St Ternan founded a monastery here on the banks of the Dee. The oldest part of the town, Kirkton, is at the east end. Here can be found the old churchyard of St Ternan's, although the church has long since disappeared. A 2-storeyed circular morthouse, built to guard against body snatchers, stands in the churchyard. Banchory has 3 parks and also boasts a most unusual local industry — a lavender farm and lavender-water distillery (OACT). Banchory Museum, in the Council Chamber, has an exhibition of local history and bygones.

*Leave Banchory on the A93 Aberdeen road and in ½ mile turn left on to the A980. In 2¼ miles turn left, skirting the Hill of Fare (1,545ft), to reach Torphins.*

## TORPHINS, Grampian
Torphins is a substantial little residential town which now quietly thrives on the tourist industry. Large, granite Learny House (not open) was built in 1898 by Colonel Francis Innes, and down a nearby side street is a row of old almshouses which the Colonel's father converted into a single residence for himself. A small entrance tower built as a porch and decorated with the Innes arms, has been added to it since.

*Turn right on to the B993 and in 3½ miles, at the junction with the B9119, turn left then right. In 4½ miles turn left on to the A944 Alford road. In 1¾ miles turn right to rejoin the B993. After 3¼ miles turn left to enter Monymusk.*

## MONYMUSK, Grampian
The great attraction in this village is the church. In 1170 the Earl of Mar built a priory here, but after the Reformation the priory chapel was turned into the parish church. This handsome building has a great square crenellated tower at one end, and is built of pinkish granite with facings of Kildrummy sandstone.

*Continue through the village and in 1 mile, at the crossroads, turn right, SP 'Chapel of Garioch', then cross the River Don and in ¼ mile turn left. In ¼ mile turn left again, SP 'Keig via Lord's Throat'. Follow this road for 6¼ miles, later climbing through the My Lord's Throat Pass, then turn right on to the B992. In 4 miles pass through Auchleven, then in 2¼ miles turn right on to the B9002. Go over a level-crossing then immediately turn left on to the B992 to enter Insch.*

## INSCH, Grampian
Now a large village, with a fine parish church at its centre dating from 1883, Insch was a burgh of barony in the 16th century. A lonely gable supporting an empty belfry in the churchyard is all that remains of the original church. At the base of the gable is an ancient stone marked with Pictish symbols and a small wheel cross, possibly even earlier than the date 1199 accredited to it.

*Pass the telephone box and turn left into Western Road. Shortly pass beneath Dunideer Castle.*

## DUNIDEER CASTLE, Grampian
The ruins of Dunideer Castle (not open) perched on an isolated conical hill 876ft high are an impressive landmark. They consist of a great wall with a rough arch in the middle and the remaining gable of a rectangular keep measuring 220ft by 90ft. Forming an outer ring around the castle are the remains of an Iron-Age vitrified fort — so called because the stones have been converted into a vitreous substance through the action of fire. This in turn is enclosed by a multiple earthwork, the origins of which are unknown.

The cattle bred in Scotland are said to produce the finest beef in the world

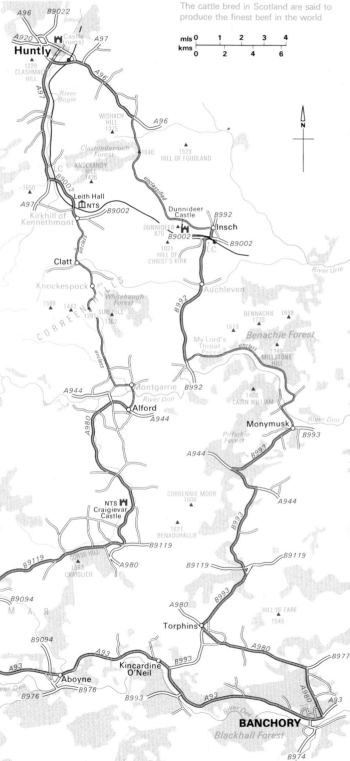

*At the junction with the A96, turn left, SP 'Huntly'. Continue for a further 4¾ miles, at the roundabout, take the 3rd exit for Huntly town centre.*

## HUNTLY, Grampian

This pleasant little market town is built on an 18th-century grid-iron pattern, based on 2 long, narrow, straight streets which intersect at the market place. From here Castle Street leads beneath the arch of the Gordon Schools — founded in 1839, and built on the site of the castle gate-towers — to the wooded drive of the magnificent castle (AM). This grew from a Norman fortress to a 17th-century Renaissance palace under the ownership of the powerful Gordons. After 1752 the family seat was moved to Gordon Castle, and Huntly was abandoned to fall into decay. Huntly Museum in the square displays exhibits of local historical interest.

*Leave on the A97, SP 'Rhynie', following the road southwards through Strathbogie. After 6 miles turn left on to the B9002 and in 1¾ miles pass (left) the entrance to Leith Hall.*

Craigievar Castle, which fortunately never saw action, represents the zenith of traditional Scottish architecture

## LEITH HALL, Grampian

James Leith, a member of a wealthy land-owning and shipping family, bought land here, and in 1649 his son laid the foundations of Leith Hall House (NTS) — a rectangular block, 4 storeys high and just one room deep. Domestic offices and stables were built in later years, and 50 years after their completion a new suite was added, which doubled the size of the house. A final wing, completely enclosing the courtyard, was added in 1868. The treasures within are not spectacular, but they chart the fortunes of a typical Scottish laird's family, including relics and keepsakes connected with Bonnie Prince Charlie, the Peninsula War, the Crimea, and the Indian Mutiny. In the grounds is a rock garden.

*In ¾ mile, at the end of Kirkhill of Kennethmont, turn right, SP 'Clatt'. In 2 miles enter Clatt.*

## CLATT, Grampian

The name of this little village is derived from 'cleith', which means concealed. This it is, for it hides away in the Gadie valley beneath the Correen Hills of the Garioch. The church is a plain building of 1799, rough-plastered, narrow and long. Within is a small, laird's gallery and an old stone font.

*Keep forward on the Knockespock road and in ½ mile bear right. Beyond Knockespock climb to cross the Correen Hills. In 4 miles turn left to reach Montgarrie. Here turn right then cross the River Don and continue to Alford.*

## ALFORD, Grampian

A thriving little town, Alford is the centre of a prosperous agricultural area where cattle markets are held and the local people come in from the country to meet. A hill west of the town was the scene of a famous victory by Montrose, supporter of Charles I, over Convenantor General Baillie in 1645. In Haughton Park is the Alford Valley Railway — 1½ miles of narrow-gauge are laid out through nature trails in delightful countryside.

*Turn right on to the A944 and in 1 mile keep forward on to the A980. After 5½ miles pass the entrance to Craigievar Castle.*

## CRAIGIEVAR CASTLE, Grampian

This isolated, romantic castle, set in a green, hilly countryside and surrounded by tall, mature trees, is one of Scotland's most picturesque buildings (NTS). The L-shaped tower house, built in 1626 by William Forbes, a wealthy Aberdeen merchant, rises up 7 storeys, smooth-walled and clean-lined, to a fairytale skyline of turrets. It has hardly altered since the day building was completed, and the magnificent plaster ceilings, the work of London craftsmen, remain intact. One of the bedrooms, called the 'Queen's' bedroom, has a most elaborate plaster ceiling and a splendid canopied bed. The great hall, overlooked by a charming minstrels' gallery, has a grand fireplace surmounted by an immense armorial tablet of the Royal Arms.

*In 2½ miles turn right on to the B9119, skirting the base of Corse Hill. In 3 miles the road starts to descend into Tarland.*

## TARLAND, Grampian

Tarland, lying in the middle of the Howe of Cromar, is an ancient market town where herds of pedigree cattle — Aberdeen Angus, British Friesian, Highland and Galloway — and valuable flocks of sheep, are bought and sold. Alastrean House, formerly the House of Cromar, passed from the Marquess of Aberdeen to the MacRobert family in 1934. Two sons of the family died fighting with the RAF in World War II, and in 1943 Lady MacRobert gave the house to the RAF as a guest and rest house for RAF officers.

*Continue on the B9119 for 3 miles then turn left at the crossroads, remaining on the B9119. At Dinnet, on Deeside, turn left on to the A93 and follow the river to Aboyne.*

## ABOYNE, Grampian

In 1650, Charles Gordon, 1st Earl of Aboyne, was granted a charter to build a burgh of barony close to Aboyne Castle (not open) and so began the history of this popular Deeside resort. Actually named Charlestown of Aboyne, the scattered village is grouped about a green, where the famous Aboyne Highland Games are held. Old Scots pines still grow in the built-up areas, creating a most pleasant shopping centre.

*Continue along the A93 to Kincardine O'Neil.*

## KINCARDINE O'NEIL, Grampian

This was once an important place, for here the Cairn-O'-Mount road, the main highway between Strathmore and Moray, crossed the River Dee. Thomas the Durval built a wooden bridge here in the 13th century, and before then there was a pass and a ferry. His son erected a church and a hospice for wayfarers; the church remains, roofless, standing among the old table-top tombs of the graveyard. In the 18th century the churchyard was used as a market place, the tombs serving as stalls. The present church dates from 1865.

*The final stretch back to Banchory runs alongside the river and through pleasant pine woods.*

# THE SCOTTISH RIVIERA

Crescents of firm sand backed by high sandstone cliffs arc between rocky headlands east of the sheltered Moray Firth. Busy resorts are interspersed with coastal villages and miles of empty shoreline, where local craftsmen come to gather the mineral serpentine for sculpting into souvenirs.

### BANFF, Grampian
Built on a series of cliff terraces rising high above the old harbour, this ancient seaport stands at the mouth of the River Deveron and is a popular holiday resort and sailing centre. Among its many fine buildings is the notable Duff House, built by William Adam in 1735 and eventually given to the town by the Duke of Fife. Its beautiful grounds now form a public park adjoining the Duff House Royal golf course. The 18th-century Town House incorporates an earlier tower, and the shaft of an old cross stands in the area known as Planestones. A few 17th-century houses and the remains of an old church can be seen elsewhere in the town, and an interesting cameo of local history is represented by the Biggar Fountain. This stands on the site of gallows where James Macpherson, a Highland freebooter in the 18th century, showed his contempt for authority by playing the fiddle as he was led to execution.
*Leave Banff on the A98 ''Inverness'' road and after 1¾ miles turn right on to the B9038 for Whitehills.*

### WHITEHILLS, Grampian
This little fishing village stands on a sandy and rocky bay sheltered by the scenic promontories of Stake Ness and Knock Head.
*At Whitehills turn left (no SP) on to the B9121 and in ½ mile at crossroads turn right on to the B9139 SP 'Portsoy'. In 3 miles reach Boyne Castle.*

### BOYNE CASTLE, Grampian
Beautiful woodland surrounds this picturesque ruin, which overlooks the Burn of Boyne. The stronghold dates from 1485 and was once held by the Ogilvie family.
*In 1¼ miles turn right on to the A98 to the village of Portsoy.*

### PORTSOY, Grampian
The prized Portsoy marble for which the area round this little resort and former fishing village is known is actually a variety of serpentine. When worked and polished the mineral reveals unsuspected shades of translucent green and pink. Louis XIV of France used it for two of the chimney pieces in the magnificent Palace of Versailles, and local craftsmen have been working it for centuries. Even today the area's shop windows are adorned with finely wrought serpentine paper weights, chessmen, and other small objects.

*Buckie boatyards produce some of the finest vessels in the Highlands.*

*Continue along the A98, parallel to the coast, and pass the fishing village and resort of Sandend. Continue to Cullen.*

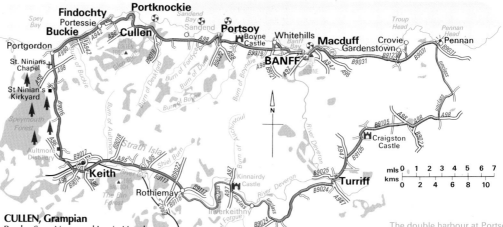

*The double harbour at Portsoy is characteristic of this part of the coast.*

### CULLEN, Grampian
Rocky Scar Nose and Logie Head extend out to sea on respective sides of this pleasant resort, sheltering the sandy beach and forming an attractive part of the local seascape. On the shore are three isolated rocks known as the Three Kings of Cullen. The town built on two levels, separated by attractive former railway viaducts offers many holiday facilities and preserves a number of good features. The original settlement was a mile inland around the 16th-century and later Cullen House (not open). Close by the house is St Mary's Church, which was founded by Robert the Bruce and became collegiate in 1543. Inside is the laird's pew of the Seafield line of Clan Grant, and a large monument to a member of the Ogilvy family.
*Continue along the A98 'Inverness' road and in 1¼ miles turn right on to the A942 for Portknockie.*

### PORTKNOCKIE, Grampian
During the late 19th century a deep water harbour was constructed to service the flourishing local herring industry, but nowadays the fishing has declined and the quays are almost deserted. Along the coast to the east of this picturesque little place is the spectacular Bow Fiddle Rock.
*Follow SP 'Inverness Coast Road' and pass the village of Findochty.*

### FINDOCHTY, Grampian
On each side of this attractive village is a rocky, empty coastline that makes excellent walking country. The beach at Findochty is of fine sand and is ideal for bathing.
*Continue to Portessie.*

### PORTESSIE, Grampian
Portessie is yet another of the many attractive little fishing villages for which this coastline is justly famous. It is unspoilt and retains many of its old cottages.
*Continue to Buckie.*

### BUCKIE, Grampian
High above the rooftops of this straggling port is the elegant and very prominent twin steeple of St Peter's Catholic Church, acting as a landmark from both sea and land. The harbour here is the busiest on the Moray Firth, and many of the town's long maritime associations are recorded in the Buckie Museum and Art Gallery. The town's war memorial is considered to be one of the finest in Scotland.
*Pass the harbour and turn right with the A990. Continue for 2 miles to Portgordon.*

## PORT GORDON, Grampian

The now disused grain exporting and fishing harbour here was built by the Duke of Richmond and Gordon in 1797.

*Turn left with the A990 and after 1¼ miles meet a junction with the A98. On the right is a building which is revered as the Banffshire Bethlehem.*

## ST NINIAN'S CHAPEL, Grampian

After John Knox's hysterical and often bloody Reformation, many Scots who had been Catholic changed to the Protestant faith under pressure from the new regime. In the old Banffshire area the influence of the Gordon Clan was such that the local people clung persistently to the traditional faith, even when the clan chiefs played them false and forsook the religion which they had supported for generations. Following the Jacobite Risings Scotland was swept by a wave of hatred against anything Catholic, and the 1,000 or so faithful in Banffshire were hounded from one secret church to the next until they were given an old cottage-cum-byre that had been converted for sheep. It was this property of the Laird of Tynet that served as their place of worship through the troubled times and became known as the Banffshire Bethlehem. Even today the white walls under a grey slate roof appear to be nothing more than a farm building, but the interior has been carefully restored and is still in use.

*Turn right then immediately left on to the Keith road B9016. In 1¾ miles a short detour can be made by turning right on to an unclassified road and driving for ½ mile to St Ninian's Kirkyard.*

## ST NINIAN'S KIRKYARD, Grampian

A decade or so after the Protestant Reformation, before the Jacobites created the need for such hideaways as the Banffshire Bethlehem, the faithful of this area built a new church in an ancient churchyard dedicated to St Ninian. This was the first Catholic place of worship to have been built since John Knox's religious crusade, but after the Jacobite Rising it was attacked by an armed band of Protestants and completely wrecked. Its site beside the Tynet Burn is marked by a cross raised to the memory of 18th-century Bishop Nicholson, who was the first Vicar Apostolic of Scotland.

*On the main route continue with the B9016 for 4¾ miles, meet a junction with the A96, then turn left on to the 'Aberdeen' road. In 1 mile turn left on to the A95 and continue to the town of Keith.*

## KEITH, Grampian

Narrow lanes criss-crossing between the three parallel main streets of this Strath Isla market centre give it a quaint, timeless character all of its own. It stands on the River Isla,

The seashore near Gardenstown is picturesque but rocky and precipitous.

which is spanned by two bridges connecting the town with its close neighbour Fife of Keith. The early crossing dates from 1609 and the later from 1770. At one time Keith was famous for its fair, but nowadays it is better known as the site of the Strathisla Distillery. This was founded in 1785 and is the oldest working malt whisky distillery in Scotland.

*Leave Keith on the A95 SP 'Banff' and follow Strath Isla. After 5 miles turn right on to the B9117 with SP 'Rothiemay'. In 2½ miles turn right then immediately left, and after ¾ mile follow the B9118 to Rothiemay.*

## ROTHIEMAY, Grampian

Remains of Rothiemay Castle stand beyond the River Deveron in fine gardens, and the river itself is spanned here by a fine old bridge. A monument at Milltown of Rothiemay commemorates James Ferguson, an early 18th-century astronomer.

*Continue forward on an unclassified road, cross the River Deveron, and turn left. Continue along a narrow road through the well-wooded countryside of the Deveron Valley, and after 5½ miles turn right on to the A97 'Huntly' road. In ½ mile turn left on to an unclassified road SP 'Inverkeithny'. After 1½ miles keep left and descend to Inverkeithny*

*Macduff harbour is the base for the town's important herring fleet.*

hamlet, at the junction of the Burn of Forgue and the River Deveron. Climb above the river, then leave the valley and cross open country to a junction with the B9024. Turn left on to the 'Turriff' road and in 6 miles turn left again on to the A947 towards 'Banff' for Turriff.

## TURRIFF, Grampian

In 1639 this thriving little market town was the scene of the Trot of Turriff, when Covenanters met Royalists in battle. A church of the Knights Templar stood here, and the old Market Cross was re-erected in 1865. Turriff stands on a plateau overlooking the confluence of the Deveron and the Water of Idoch and is the centre of a district particularly rich in castles and tower houses. Pleasant woodland to the east of the town surrounds the great tower house of Delgatie Castle (open by written application only) a seat of the Clan Hay that has been in the family's possession for nearly 700 years. It was founded by the Hays of Delgatie in the 13th century and shows alterations up to the 16th century. Inside are various relics and pictures, but among its best features are its fine painted ceilings of c1590. Towie Barclay Castle (open by appointment only) built around 1587 is completely Gothic and medieval in inspiration and consists of a single high rib-vaulted chamber in two bays.

*Stay on the A947 'Banff' road and in 2 miles turn right on to the B9105 towards 'Fraserburgh'. After 2½ miles pass Craigston Castle on the right.*

## CRAIGSTON CASTLE, Grampian

Remarkable woodcarvings are preserved in this early 17th-century castle, which was built by John Urquhart and has hardly been altered since (not open).

*Continue through Buchan countryside and in 3½ miles turn right on to the A98. In another 2½ miles turn left on to an unclassified road SP 'New Aberdour'. After another 2½ miles turn left again towards 'Pennan', then continue along a winding road to meet a junction with the B9031 at the coast. Drive over the crossroads and descend steeply into the village of Pennan.*

## PENNAN, Grampian

Pennan Head dominates the rocky and precipitous shore of Pennan Bay, and the pretty Troup Burn joins the sea near the village. Farther west is the bold outline of Troup Head. The village itself has housed generations of fishermen and is typical of many along this coast.

*Return to the B9031 and turn right towards 'Banff'. Continue along a hilly road with occasional coastal views. Short detours from the main route towards the coast lead to the attractive villages of Crovie and Gardenstown.*

## CROVIE, Grampian

Crovie Head shelters this community, which stands at the base of high red cliffs on Gamrie Bay.

## GARDENSTOWN, Grampian

Picturesque cottages and houses rise in tiers above the lovely old harbour of Gardenstown, a fishing village on the shores of Gamrie Bay. To the west near Mhor Head, on the Hill of Gamrie Mhor, is a ruined church that was founded to commemorate a local victory over the Danes. The date given for this event is recorded on the gable of the building as 1004, but it is unlikely that the existing structure is as early as that. West and east of the village are ranges of spectacular cliffs.

*On the main route, continue for 8¾ miles (from Pennan) and turn right on to the A98 towards 'Inverness'. Continue to Macduff.*

## MACDUFF, Grampian

Steep streets of attractive houses lead down to a superb harbour in Macduff, an important Banff Bay town known for its fishing industry. It has one of the most pleasing waterfronts in Scotland, very picturesque and bustling with activity and very fine views of the area can be enjoyed from the war memorial on top of the Hill of Doune.

*Cross the River Deveron and return along the A98 to Banff.*

### BRAEMAR, Grampian

The royal and ancient Highland Games for which Braemar is most famous are held in early September every year. Tradition has it that the originator of the Gathering was King Malcolm Canmore, who ruled much of Scotland at the time of the Norman invasion. He called the clans to the Braes of Mar so that he might 'by keen and fair contest, select his hardier soldiers and fleetest messengers'. Visitors, often including the Queen and other members of the Royal Family, come from all over the world to listen to the piping and to watch the athletic events, which culminate in tossing the caber. Braemar itself is a pretty little place, with a number of guest houses and hotels. One of these, the Invercauld Arms, stands on the spot where, in 1715, the Standard was raised which marked the beginning of the blood-thirsty futile Jacobite rebellions. Opposite the Invercauld Galleries is the house where Robert Louis Stevenson wrote *Treasure Island* in 1881. Braemar Castle (OACT) was originally built by the Earl of Mar in 1628, but after the Jacobite Rising of 1715 it became a barracks for English troops, who were moved here in an attempt to keep the Highlanders in check. During the latter part of the 18th century the castle was strengthened and extended.

*Leave on the A93 Perth road and proceed along Glen Clunie, gradually ascending to the Cairnwell Pass.*

### CAIRNWELL PASS, Tayside & Grampian

The summit of this awe-inspiring pass reaches to 2,199ft, making it the highest classified road in Britain. Glenshee, of which the Cairnwell Pass forms part, has been one of the most important mountain passes in Scotland since as early as Roman times. The Glenshee Chairlift, to the west of the pass, runs to the summit of the 3,059ft Cairnwell Mountain.

*Continue down Glen Beag to Spittal of Glenshee.*

### SPITTAL OF GLENSHEE, Tayside

Until recently no more than a scattered community in the wild heart of the Grampian Mountains, Spittal of Glenshee is now a flourishing ski-centre, complete with hotel, ski-school and ski-hire shop. Its peculiar name is derived from the hospital that once stood here and provided shelter for travellers in the remote Highlands.

*Continue on the A93, following Glen Shee for 5¼ miles, then turn sharp left on to the B951, SP 'Kirriemuir, Glenisla'. Shortly cross the Shee Water and in ¼ mile, at Cray, bear right. In 2½ miles bear right again into Glen Isla. In 4 miles enter Kirkton of Glenisla.*

# THE GRAMPIAN MOUNTAINS

Beautiful Highland scenery greets the traveller at every turn in the glens and mountains of Grampian. At Balmoral the Royal Family spend their holidays and every year thousands follow suit — to see the Highland Games and Pipers at Braemar, to ski, to walk, to climb and to admire.

Left: Glen Isla, 20 miles long, forms a natural route into the lonely Grampians

### KIRKTON OF GLENISLA, Tayside

Exceptional Highland scenery stretches many miles north of this attractive village. Nearly 12,000 acres are covered by the plantations of the Braes of Angus Forest, which was established in 1945. Boating and other water sports can be enjoyed on the Blackwater Reservoir, 3 miles east of the village. Glen Isla itself runs northwards through increasingly splendid countryside towards Caenlochan Forest, parts of which are the National Nature Reserve.

*Continue on the B951 and in 1½ miles leave the glen to enter the Melgam Water valley. Shortly pass the Loch of Lintrathen, and 3½ miles farther enter Kirkton of Kingoldrum. Continue on the B951 and in 3 miles turn left on to the A926 and shortly sharp right to enter Kirriemuir.*

### KIRRIEMUIR, Tayside

Peter Pan's creator, Sir James Barrie, was born in Kirriemuir in 1860. In his novels he called the town Thrums, and in the suburb of Southmuir is the cottage in which Barrie described *A Window in Thrums.* His birthplace, 9 Brechin Road, is a modest 2-storey cottage that has been transformed into a museum (NTS) containing original manuscripts, momentoes and some of the original furnishings. In a pavilion behind the cemetery of New Church, where Barrie is buried, is a camera obscura (OACT), which gives panoramic views of the surrounding scenery.

*Leave on the B957, SP 'Brechin', and after 5½ miles cross the River South Esk to reach Tannadice. In 1½ miles turn left on to the A94. In 5½ miles turn right on to the A935, SP 'Brechin', for Brechin.*

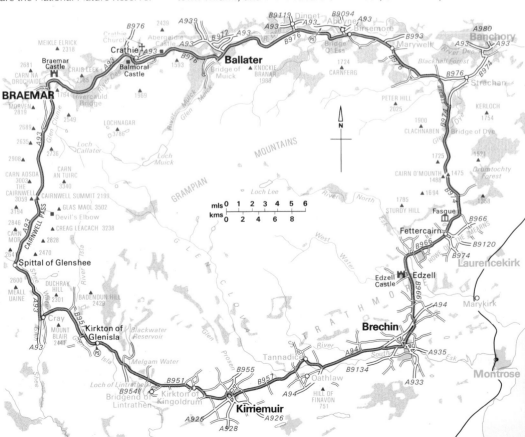

*Leave on the B974 Strachan Banchory road. After 4 miles the road starts the long climb (1 in 5 in places, with hairpin bends) to the summit which, at 1,475ft, is a fine viewpoint. Descend towards Deeside and later cross the Bridge of Dye (1680). In 2 miles, at AA Box 753, turn left, SP 'Aboyne'. After 2¼ miles turn left on to the B976, rejoining the Dee valley after 6 miles. In 3 miles, at Birsemore, keep forward, SP 'Ballater', and continue for 11¼ miles to the edge of Ballater.*

### BALLATER, Grampian

Ballater was not established until 1770, when a Farquharson laird decided to cater for the tide of people who came to try the mineral wells discovered at Pannanich, 2 miles south-east. Although the wells no longer flourish, the town is still a popular holiday centre. There are numerous sporting facilities in the area, and the Ballater Highland Games are a highlight every August.

*At the edge of the town keep forward on the B976, SP 'Balmoral', and in ½ mile bear right to cross the River Muick, SP 'Breamar'. In 5½ miles pass (right) Abergeldie Castle (not open), residence of King Edward VII whilst Prince of Wales. In 2 miles pass the entrance to Balmoral Castle.*

### BALMORAL CASTLE & CRATHIE CHURCH, Grampian

Queen Victoria spent her first holiday at Balmoral in 1848, and instantly fell in love with the house and its surroundings. Prince Albert purchased the estate in 1852 and immediately set about transforming the original castle into a large Scottish baronial-style mansion. Today Balmoral remains the much-loved holiday home of the Royal Family. Although the castle is not open to the public, the grounds are open for several months during the summer. Crathie Church stands across the Dee from Balmoral, and is the church used by the Royal Family when they are staying at the castle. Queen Victoria laid the foundation stone of the present church in 1895, and it contains several memorials to members of the Royal Family. In the churchyard is a monument to John Brown, Queen Victoria's famous servant.

*After crossing the River Dee turn left at the edge of Crathie on to the A93. Follow the north bank of the Dee, passing through more pine forests with fine views of the most eastern Cairngorm Mountains. Later recross the River Dee at Invercauld Bridge and after 2¼ miles pass the entrance (right) to Braemar Castle (see Braemar) before the return to Braemar.*

### BRECHIN, Tayside

Many buildings of local red sandstone give the old streets of this town a pleasing and harmonious character. A background of green hills rising towards the eastern Grampians, and the sparkling waters of the River South Esk, add to the charm of the setting. Brechin Cathedral, which now serves only as the parish church as it is no longer the

bishop's seat, was originally built in about 1170, but was entirely restored from 1900 onwards. The 87ft-high round tower (AM) attached to the church is Brechin's greatest treasure. Thought to date from the 10th or 11th century, it has functioned both as a

watchtower and as a place of refuge during periods of danger and unrest. Near the church is 18th-century Brechin Castle (not open), the seat of the Earl of Dalhousie, which stands on the site of a very much earlier fortification.

*Leave on the B996, SP 'Aberdeen'. In 2 miles turn right on to the A94, then in ¼ mile turn left on to the B966. In 3½ miles enter Edzell.*

### EDZELL, Tayside

Set on the River North Esk in the fertile Howe of Mearns, Edzell is a neat little village whose origins go back to the 16th century, but which was largely rebuilt in 1839. Edzell Castle (AM), lying a mile west of the village, was once said to be the finest castle in Angus. Its oldest part is the 16th-century tower house, to which a large quadrangular mansion was added a few years later. In 1602 Sir David Lindsay, Lord Edzell, added the castle's most famous feature, the extraordinary walled garden. The wall itself is unique in Britain, being decorated with a wealth of heraldic and symbolic motifs.

*Continue on the B966 to Fettercairn.*

### FETTERCAIRN, Grampian

In 1861 Queen Victoria and Prince Albert paid an incognito visit to Fettercairn, and 3 years later the imposing turreted arch which forms an entrance to the village was built to commemorate the occasion. In the picturesque little square is part of the town cross from the ancient town and royal residence of Kincardine. Of Kincardine itself nothing survives except the neglected churchyard of a small chapel. North of the village is Fasque, a large mansion (OACT) which has been the home of the Gladstone family since 1829. The contents of the house reflect the lives of the family, who included William Gladstone, 4 times Prime Minister of Britain.

# WHERE ROB ROY LIES

Deep lochs and dour mountains, swift-flowing and bubbling streams, glittering waterfalls and hillsides covered in dark green pine — all the elements of a highland landscape within a day's drive. In these picturesque surroundings the romantic life of Rob Roy unfolded, his deeds the subject of many a legend and ballad.

## CALLANDER, Central
Almost English-looking meadows flank the River Teith as it flows toward the town, whose main street and simple square are surrounded in turn by Regency-style houses, some with picturesque first floor bow-windows which overhang the pavement below. This comfortable town was originally built by the Commissioners for the Forfeited Estates on the Drummond lands after the 18th-century Jacobite risings. Callander is especially fortunate in having several beauty spots within reach of the walker, such as the Falls of Bracklinn, the Pass of Leny and its Falls, and Ben Ledi. In the town is the fascinating Kilmahog Woollen Mill, which at one time was famous for its handwoven blankets and tweed. Parts of the old structure are preserved along with an old water wheel which is still in working order and traditional woollens can be bought in the shop. Callander is better known as 'Tannochbrae' in the BBC series *Dr Finlay's Casebook*.

*Leave on the A84 Stirling road and pass in 6¾ miles (left) the road to the Doune Motor Museum.*

## DOUNE MOTOR MUSEUM, Central
An attractive 16th-century house Newton Doune, houses the Doune Motor Museum (OACT), where vintage and post-vintage cars are displayed and motor racing hill climbs are held.

*Shortly turn left on to the A820, SP 'Dunblane', to enter Doune.*

## DOUNE, Central
This proud, old-fashioned town took its importance from the castle, which was once a royal palace and is still the property of the Earls of Moray. At the western end of Doune is the small, triangular market place, an old mercat cross at its centre, where cattle and sheep fairs were held. The double-arched bridge was built in 1535 by the wealthy Robert Spittal, tailor to James IV. Doune was long famous for the manufacture of pistols, and today they are highly prized by collectors. Sporrans were also made here, but after the rebellion of 1745 Highland dress was banned. Cotton-milling became

the new industry of Doune at Deanston Mills half a mile away, where there is also a distillery. Doune Castle is one of the best preserved medieval castles in Scotland open to the public. It stands at the junction of the Rivers Ardoch and Teith. Two great keeps are connected by low buildings, which include the great hall, to make one side of a quadrangle, and the other 3 sides are enclosed by massive 40ft walls, 8ft thick and capped by a parapet and wall-walk. Dating from the early 15th century, the castle was built by the Dukes of Albany, and passed into the hands of the Stuarts of Doune, Earls of Moray, in the 16th century.

*From Doune a detour can be made to visit Scotland's Safari Park at Blair Drummond House 2 miles south. Turn right, following SP 'Stirling A84', and shortly cross the River Teith. In 2¾ miles, at the crossroads, turn left for Blair Drummond House.*

## BLAIR DRUMMOND HOUSE, Central
Two lairds of Blair Drummond have, through their own initiative, brought repute to this ancient property. A celebrated judge, Henry Home, married the

Drummond heiress in 1741, and when his wife came into property in 1767 he carried out a scheme to convert soggy peat land into fine arable land. He built a series of sluices and channels which eventually led down to the River Forth. The peat was cut out and dumped into the channels which periodically flooded and so washed the peat away. The project created 1,500 acres of fine agricultural land, which is still farmed today. Today the park around the house has been turned into a wildlife safari park by the joint efforts of the present laird, a neighbouring laird, and Chipperfield's Circus. This popular park features wild lions, giraffes, buffalo, eland, zebras, camels and elephants among its collection, which wander freely about 100 acres of woodland tended by gamekeepers.

*Return to Doune and on entering the town turn right on to the A820 Dunblane road and in 3¼ miles enter Dunblane. On reaching the A9 turn right, SP 'Stirling', and in 1 mile, at the roundabout, take the 1st exit. SP 'Bridge of Allan' and 'Stirling'. Off the B824 to the right lies Keir House Gardens. The main tour continues to Bridge of Allan.*

During the summer months salmon may be seen leaping up the rapids of the Falls of Leny — a popular beauty spot

Loch Earn is a well-known yachting and water-skiing centre

Left: Rob Roy's grave at Balquhidder

## KEIR HOUSE GARDENS, Central
Sir William Stirling Maxwell laid out these 40 acres of woodland and formal gardens (OACT) around Keir House in the 1860s, and the layout remains largely true to the original plan. Special features include a yew tree-house, a water garden and a pond which was cleared and replanted in the 1960s, magnificent rhododendrons, flowering shrubs and herbaceous borders. Perhaps the most important element in these beautiful gardens is the trees; an arboretum of rare conifers and a woodland of large rare trees draw enthusiasts from all over the world.

## BRIDGE OF ALLAN, Central
For 150 years this was a spa town, and the fine villas found here date from about 1810 when the properties of the mineral waters of the Arthog springs were discovered. The baths and pump room which were built still stand. The small town now benefits from its proximity to Stirling University.

*At the end of the town turn left, SP 'Sheriffmuir', passing the grounds of Stirling University then, on the ascent, bear right. Ascend onto the edge of the Ochil Hills, later crossing the Wharry Burn. Shortly keep forward on the Blackford road to cross Sheriff Muir, reaching a height of 1,031ft. In ¾ mile, on the descent, turn left, SP 'Greenloaning'. At the A9 turn left then right, SP 'Braco', and in ¼ mile right again on to the A822 for Braco.*

## BRACO, Tayside
In the grounds of Ardoch House (not open) lie the substantial and exceptionally well-preserved remains of a Roman fort. Coins have been found here, and this, with the Roman Great Camp to the north-west, could house 40,000 troops at any one time.

*Continue on the A822, cross the River Knaik and in ¾ mile turn left on to the B827, SP 'Comrie', to follow the river through moorland before descending to Comrie.*

## COMRIE, Tayside
The Earn, the Lednock, the Ruchill Waters and the glens of Lednock and Arthog, all meet at Comrie, which stands on the Highland Boundary Fault — the 20,000ft-deep fracture in the earth which divides the Highlands from the Lowlands. Comrie therefore has more recorded earthquake tremors than anywhere else in Britain, although none have caused more damage than cracks in the walls of a few houses. It is possible that the New Year custom of the Flambeaux procession is in some way connected with the tremors — a torchlight procession parades around the town, and there is dancing around a bonfire, ostensibly to drive away evil spirits. All around the town wooded hills rise, and there are delightful walks to the Devil's Cauldron, Spout Falls, and other waterfalls at Glen Turret and Glen Boltachan.

*Leave on the A85 Crianlarich road and continue to St Fillans.*

## ST FILLANS, Tayside
Set at the eastern tip of the long and beautiful Loch Earn, St Fillans is a favourite haunt of those who love fishing, sailing, mountaineering, walking, or just admiring scenery. To the south rises wooded Dunfillan Hill (2,011ft) on top of which perches a rock known as St Fillans Chair, a site once fortified by the Picts.

*Beyond the village the road takes the north bank of Loch Earn and at the western end stands the village of Lochearnhead.*

## LOCHEARNHEAD, Central
Lochearnhead, gazing eastwards from the green slopes above Loch Earn at the foot of Glen Ogle, is a pleasing, scattered village, with ample hotels for the many tourists who come here to enjoy the water-skiing and yachting available on the loch. The surrounding country, ablaze with wild nasturtiums in the summer, offers fine hill-walking.

*Turn left on to the A84 Stirling road and proceed to Kingshouse. From here a detour can be made to Balquhidder and Loch Voil by turning right on to the unclassified road.*

## BALQUHIDDER, Central
Salmon, trout and the rare char live in the cold waters of Loch Voil, and at its eastern end stands the 2 churches of Balquhidder (pronounced Balwhidder). One is mid-19th century, and now a roofless ruin. However, in the churchyard is the grave of the great Scottish hero, Rob Roy. He was born into the MacGregor clan in 1660, and inherited the chieftainship. He was a staunch Jacobite and a great rebel who was outlawed after the failure of the rebellion of 1715. Although a man of action, Rob Roy died peaceably at Kirton, Balquhidder, in 1740, aged about 80 years old. Sir Walter Scott in his novel *Rob Roy*, describes the legends, stories and fact which accompany this charismatic figure.

*From Kingshouse continue on the A84 southwards into the thickly forested Strathyre.*

## STRATHYRE, Central
Strathyre, a village in the Strath of the same name through which flows the River Balraig, has 2 functions — to cater for the visitor, and to act as a forestry centre for Strathyre Forest. It has always attracted tourists (Wordsworth stayed here in 1803) and is a convenient touring centre for the southern Highlands. The Forestry Commission established Strathyre Forest in the 1930s, and now the entire valley is clothed in dark pines, although in 1968 80,000 trees were blown down in a fearsome storm; however, 8,000,000 survived, which gives an idea of the extent of the forest. The Strathyre Forest Centre contains a museum, demonstration room and exhibition room, where information of forest trails and walks can be found.

*A mile south of the village the road reaches the eastern shore of Loch Lubnaig.*

## LOCH LUBNAIG, Central
A place of poetical beauty, Loch Lubnaig stands at the foot of Ben Ledi (2,883ft) and stretches 5 miles north to south. Near its head are the remains of a crannog, or artificial island refuge. From the road the view to the opposite side makes a fine spectacle, the great mountain clothed in trees with streams pouring down the steep side in numerous waterfalls. St Bride's derelict churchyard stands, where the loch pours out as the River Leny, overgrown and romantic, on a most beautiful site. A mile below, in the Pass of Leny, are the Falls of Leny — actually a series of rapids rather than a waterfall.

*At the southern end of the loch the road enters the narrow Pass of Leny before the return to Callander.*

# QUEEN OF THE SOUTH

From Dumfries, where Robert Burns, Scotland's national poet, made his final home, travel on to visit the romantic ruins of Sweetheart Abbey, the riches of Maxwelton House, a glorious garden on the shores of the Solway Firth and the sylvan expanses of the Forest of Ae.

### DUMFRIES, Dumf & Gall
Queen of the South is the title of this ancient burgh with its old red sandstone buildings and well-tended parks beside the broad waters of the River Nith. The town received its first charter in 1393 from Robert III, and it was here that Robert the Bruce assassinated the Red Comyn, the representative of the English Crown, in 1306, so precipitating the Wars of Independence. Bruce declared himself King of Scotland shortly afterwards, and soon returned to Dumfries to capture the castle in his first victory over Edward I. The remains of the castle (AM) lie in wooded parkland at Castledykes. Dumfries' centre point and landmark is the Mid Steeple. This was built in 1707 to act as a court house, prison and administrative centre. Robert Burns is Dumfries' hero. He lived in the town from 1791, until his death in 1796, in a house in Mill Vennel, now called Burns Street. His house is open to the public and contains many precious relics of this celebrated national poet. The Globe Inn, Burns' favourite pub, also holds tangible memories of him, including the chair he used to sit in and a window pane on which the poet is believed to have scratched some verse with a diamond. Dumfries Burgh Museum is an 18th-century windmill that had a camera obscura built into it in 1836 which projects a living panorama of the town on to a table. The museum specialises in local history and personalities of the past. At one end of the medieval stone bridge over the Nith is Old Bridge House. Here each room has been furnished to illustrate a period of history — it has, for example, an 1850s kitchen and a Victorian child's room. Below the old bridge is the Caul — a weir built to power the riverside grain mills in the 18th century.

*Leave on the A75 Stranraer road and cross the Buccleuch Street bridge into the adjoining town of Maxwelltown. In ½ mile turn left on to the A710, SP 'New Abbey' and 'Solway Coast', and in 6½ miles enter New Abbey.*

### NEW ABBEY, Dumf & Gall
The slopes of Criffel (1,866ft) tower above the picturesque village of New Abbey with its low, whitewashed cottages and charming 18th-century water-mill

on the banks of the New Abbey Burn. However, it is Sweetheart Abbey that dominates the village. A great precinct wall, built of giant boulders, enclose some 30 acres in which stand the hauntingly-beautiful ruins of this Cistercian abbey (AM). It was founded in the 13th century by Lady Devorgilla, wife of John Balliol, regent of Scotland. The good lady was buried in front of the high altar in 1289 with the embalmed heart of her husband, in whose memory she built the abbey. Her devotion is thought to have given the abbey its name. The ruins from the 13th and 14th centuries consist of a 90ft central tower, much of the nave and transepts, and a choir with a huge rose window, all built of red sandstone.

*Continue on the A710, passing through Kirkbean, and Mainsriddle and at Caulkerbush keep forward, SP 'Rockcliffe'. At Colvend, next to White Lock, a short detour can be made to Rockcliffe by turning left on to an unclassified road.*

### ROCKCLIFFE, Dumf & Gall
This quiet resort on the Rough Firth was more dangerous in the 18th century when smugglers of wine and tobacco used the narrow inlets and bays nearby for their illegal, but prosperous, trade. Today the bays and the mild climate are enjoyed by tourists. A hill walk to nearby Kippford passes the Mote of Mark (NTS), an ancient hill fort occupied C AD600. It overlooks another NTS property, Rough Island, a 20-acre bird sanctuary which can be reached by foot over sands at low tide from Rockcliffe.

Above: Mid Steeple, behind the statue, was a courthouse and prison until 1867

Right: the roofless red sandstone ruins of Sweetheart Abbey

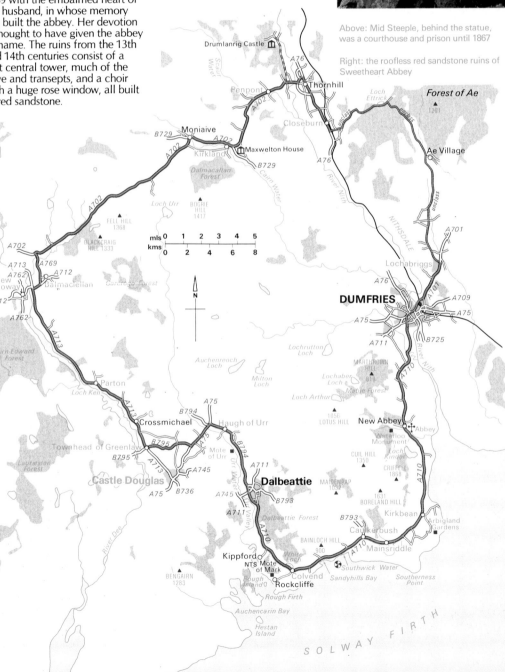

*Continue on the A710 Dalbeattie road through Colvend and past the wooded hills of Dalbeattie Forest. After 2¼ miles a 2nd detour can be made by turning left to Kippford.*

## KIPPFORD, Dumf & Gall
A village of whitewashed cottages on the rugged and beautiful estuary of the Urr — the Rough Firth. In days gone by its livelihood was gained from fishing and smuggling, but in this century tourism and yachting provide the villagers with a living. There is also a 9-hole golf course here.

*The main tour continues on the A710 through the Urr valley to Dalbeattie.*

The tiny village of Kippford is a popular holiday resort on the Solway Firth

## DALBEATTIE, Dumf & Gall
Lying in the wooded valley of the Urr, Dalbeattie is built of the shiny grey stone which brought it wealth and prosperity in the 19th century. This granite was used for building all over the world, and even today stone chips from the Craignair quarries are used for road surfacing, but the once crowded harbour is now deserted.

*At the crossroads go forward on to the B794 Haugh of Urr road. Follow the Urr Water northwards and pass, after 2½ miles, the Motte of Urr across the valley. Bear left into Haugh of Urr then keep forward and in 1 mile turn left on to the A75 Stranraer road. In 1¾ miles turn right on to the B795, SP 'Laurieston'. At Townhead of Greenlaw turn right on to the A713, SP 'Ayr', to Crossmichael.*

## CROSSMICHAEL, Dumf & Gall
Crossmichael owes its name to the Cross of St Michael which once stood here and where the Michaelmas Fair was held at Christmas. In the churchyard lies the martyr's grave of 'William Graham, shot dead by a party of Claverhouse's troop, for his adherence to Scotland's Reformation Covenants, 1682.' The River Dee widens here to form a reservoir, of which Loch Ken is now an extension.

*Continue alongside the shores of Loch Ken to pass through Parton and in 6½ miles turn right on to the A712 Corsock and Crocketford road. In ½ mile turn left on to the A769 (no SP), and 2 miles further turn right on to the A702 for Moniaive.*

## MONIAIVE, Dumf & Gall
Cairn Water is formed here by the confluence of the Craigdarroch and Dalwhat waters and the Castlefairn Burn. The village itself was chartered as a burgh in 1636, though all that remains of such grandeur is the 17th-century mercat cross that still stands as the centrepiece. James Renwick, the last Covenanter to be executed, was born in Moniaive, and died in Edinburgh in 1688 at the age of 26.

*Turn right, SP 'Thornhill', and cross the river bridge then turn right again. In 2¼ miles a short detour can be made to Maxwelton House by turning right on to the B729, then turning left after 1 mile.*

## MAXWELTON HOUSE, Dumf & Gall
During the 14th and 15th centuries the house (OACT) was the stronghold of the Earls of Glencairn. In the 17th century it became the home of the Lauries, one of whom, Annie Laurie, is immortalised in the famous Scottish ballad named after her. The author was Douglas of Fingland, deemed by Annie's father to be an undesirable suitor. The house has recently been restored and contains an interesting museum of early agricultural and domestic life.

*The main tour continues along the A702 to Penpont. 1 mile beyond the village an unclassified road to the left leads to Drumlanrig Castle.*

## DRUMLANRIG CASTLE, Dumf & Gall
William Douglas, 1st Earl of Queensberry, built this magnificent house (OACT) of rose-red sandstone between 1679 and 1691. The vast formal gardens he laid out have disappeared, but the house remains, grandiose and impressive. Richly decorated within, it is filled with world famous art treasures, including a Rembrandt painting, outstanding silver, and superb furniture given to the house by Charles II. A carved winged heart surmounted by a crown frequently occurs on the stonework and this, with the word 'FORWARD', is the Douglas Crest. It originated thus: when Robert Bruce died in 1329 without achieving his ambition of going on a crusade to the Holy Land, his embalmed heart was entrusted to Sir James, 'The Black Douglas', who went to Spain to fight the muslims. As Sir James, mortally wounded in battle, fell, he threw the silver casket containing the heart at the unbelievers, shouting, 'Forward, Brave Heart'. After 13 generations the Douglas line died out, and the house and title went to the Dukes of Buccleuch in 1810, who own the house today.

*The main tour continues over the River Nith then bears left and shortly right. At the T-junction turn right on to the A76, SP 'Dumfries', for Thornhill.*

## THORNHILL, Dumf & Gall
This small town on an attractive stretch of the River Nith is known as the 'ducal village', because of its long association with the Dukes of Queensberry and Buccleuch. North Drumlanrig street has an avenue of lime trees planted in the 19th century by the 6th Duke of Buccleuch, and a tall column crowned by a statue of a winged horse — the emblem of the Queensberrys — stands in the town centre. Drumlanrig Castle is closely associated with both families.

*Follow the Dumfries road south and ¾ mile beyond Closeburn turn left, SP 'Loch Ettrick'. In ¾ mile turn left again to reach Loch Ettrick. Shortly beyond it turn right, SP 'Ae', to enter the Forest of Ae. In 4 miles, at the crossroads, branch right to skirt (left) the village of Ae.*

## AE, Dumf & Gall
Set in the Forest of Ae, the village was built by the Forestry Commission in 1947 to house its workers. Experiments carried out here have given rise to notable advances in forestry techniques; trees can now be grown well above the normal tree line and can be planted in peat bogs — thought previously to be impossible. The forest itself is mainly sitka spruce, with some larch, Scots pine and Norway spruce. Ornamental trees have been planted along the road from Closeburn, and nature trails and marked walks have been laid out, beginning from the picnic area on the banks of the Water of Ae. Roe and fallow deer live in the forest, and the sparrow hawk may sometimes be seen.

*Continue through open countryside and in 3¾ miles, at the crossroads, keep forward. In 2½ miles at Locharbriggs turn right on to the A701 for the return to Dumfries.*

## DUNBAR, Lothian

An old fishing port which became a royal burgh in 1370, Dunbar lies between the fishing grounds of the North North Sea and the rich farmland of its hinterland, renowned for the redness of its soil in which grows the Dunbar Red potato. The town's long civic history is epitomised by the Town House. This features a 6-sided tower, dates from 1620, and is said to be the oldest public building in Scotland to have been in continuous use; the old market cross stands close by. The parish church, situated on high ground with a tower 180ft high, is a landmark for local fishermen. Much of the town's history is tied up with its castle, another landmark, high up on a rocky headland. The castle was eventually destroyed by the Regent Moray after the Battle of Carberry, which resulted in the downfall of Mary, Queen of Scots. Close to the town a country park of some 1600 acres conserves the natural beauty of the area. It is named after conservationist John Muir, born in Dunbar in the mid 19th-century.

*Leave on the A1087 Berwick road shortly passing through the hamlet of Broxburn. In 1 mile turn left on to the A1 and continue south-east, passing close to the cliff-edge on the approach to Cockburnspath.*

## COCKBURNSPATH, Borders

Cockburnspath lies on the edge of the Lammermuir Hills near the rocky North Sea coast. The pretty 14th-century church has a distinctive round 16th-century beacon-tower and the early 17th-century mercat cross is crowned by a stone thistle. Just to the east of the village is the sandy beach of Pease Bay, which lies at the edge of the steep Pease Dean valley. Spanning this is a bridge nearly 130ft high and 300ft long which was built in 1786.

*½ mile south of the village turn right off the A1 on to an unclassified road, SP 'Abbey St Bathans'. Follow SP 'Preston' and 'Duns', and later turn right on to the A6112 for Preston. Turn right into the village and at the end turn right again on to the B6355. Shortly cross the Whiteadder Water and in ¾ mile turn right. Later recross the Whiteadder at Ellemford Bridge and follow its valley to Cranshaws.*

## CRANSHAWS, Borders

At the heart of the Lammermuir Hills, set beside the Whiteadder Water, the hamlet of Cranshaws possesses probably the best preserved of the Border pele towers. It has been identified as Ravenswood of Sir Walter Scott's *The Bride of Lammermoor;* Scott heard the original story from his great aunt Margaret Sirenton, who almost certainly knew the Cranshaws.

*Continue on the B6355 to Gifford.*

## DUNBAR AND THE LAMMERMUIR HILLS

Bounded to the north by a rocky coast dotted with pleasant villages and seaside resorts overlooking the Firth of Forth, this corner of Lothian is dominated by the great rolling summits of the windswept Lammermuir Hills which shelter such treasures as Dunbar Castle and Haddington's abbey church.

Above: the remains of Dirleton Castle date from the 13th century when it was built by the Norman de Vaux family

## GIFFORD, Lothian

This neat, well-planned, 18th-century village once had many small industries, notably linen-weaving and papermaking — Scottish banknotes were printed on Gifford paper in the early 18th century. Today, however, the industry has gone, nor are the village's 3 annual livestock fairs held any more. It has become a charming, old-world backwater, ideal as a walking and pony-trekking centre for the Lammermuir Hills.

*Turn right on to the B6369 and in 4¼ miles turn right again on to the A6137 to enter Haddington. Shortly turn left, SP 'Edinburgh', to reach the town centre.*

## HADDINGTON, Lothian

Haddington is one of the country's most beautifully restored and preserved towns, and an outstanding example of Scottish burghal architecture. It has a distinct medieval street plan and many buildings are scheduled as special architectural or historic interest. The best illustration of the

kind of extensive restoration undertaken is the Parish Church of St Mary. This red sandstone church, known as the Lamp of the Lothians, was built in the 14th century to replace an earlier church. By 1540 it became known as an important collegiate church, but shortly after this period of prosperity fighting between the English, Scots and French came to the town and the church and town were severely damaged. The citizens of Haddington have, through various societies, rebuilt the chancel and completely restored this building where John Knox worshipped as a boy. Other notable buildings include the Town House, which like many other houses here, was designed by the famous architect William Adam. Poldrate Mill, a 3-storey corn-mill with an undershot water-wheel, is now an arts and community centre and 17th-century Haddington House, the oldest domestic building in the town, is now used as a library, meeting rooms and administrative centre for the Collegiate College.

*Leave on the B6471 Edinburgh road and in 1½ miles turn left on to the A1. In 2¼ miles pass through Gladsmuir then in ¼ mile, at the crossroads, turn right on to the B6363. In 2 miles turn right on to the A198 into Longniddry. Shortly bear left with the A198 to reach Gosford Bay and skirt the grounds of Gosford House (not open). In 1 mile enter Aberlady.*

Below: Preston Mill, now restored, is one of the oldest and smallest watermills left in Scotland

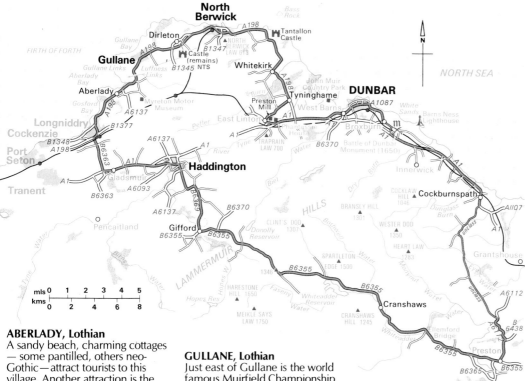

## TANTALLON CASTLE, Lothian

Perched upon a headland, defended by 100ft-high cliffs on 3 sides and by a moat on the other, Tantallon Castle (AM) was a stronghold for the Douglas clan for centuries. An old saying hereabouts likened an impossible task to 'knocking down Tantallon or building a bridge to Bass'. Built in 1375 Tantallon was however, knocked down after a siege by James V in 1528, and General Monk reduced it to rubble after heavy bombardment in 1651. Walls, towers and earthworks survive, and a 17th-century dovecot stands between the 2 inner ditches.

*In 2¾ miles enter Whitekirk.*

## WHITEKIRK, Lothian

A massive square tower topped by a wooden spire was the target of suffragettes in 1914 — the church was completely gutted and although arson was suspected, it was never proved. National subscription, however, enabled it to be rebuilt in 1971, and the church remains one of the finest examples of Gothic parochial architecture in Scotland. A long, narrow, bare building behind the church is one of the last tithe barns in Scotland, and it is said monks from Holyrood in Edinburgh stored grain here.

*Turn left and shortly pass through the grounds of the Tyninghame Estate on the approach to Tyninghame.*

## TYNINGHAME, Lothian

A delightful estate village, Tyninghame is built of the characteristic local red sandstone. The first church here, however, was founded by St Baldred (who died in 756), but was destroyed by Anlaf the Dane in 941. Today the remains, 2 12th-century Norman arches, are used as the burial chapel of the Earls of Haddington, who own nearby Tyninghame Manor (not open).

*Turn right on to the B1407 and in 1½ miles pass Preston Mill.*

## PRESTON MILL, Lothian

Preston Mill (NTS) is the only watermill surviving on the Tyne now; for centuries there were several grain mills along the river. The 16th-century mill has been restored to working order, and is complete with all its attendant outhouses, tools and machinery. The buildings, which include the curious conical roof of the drying kiln, provide a scene much favoured as a subject by artists.

*Turn left into East Linton then bear left, SP 'Dunbar', to cross the River Tyne and shortly turn left (next to Phantassie House (not open) on to the A1. In 3 miles, at the roundabout, take the A1087 for the return through West Barns to Dunbar.*

## ABERLADY, Lothian

A sandy beach, charming cottages — some pantilled, others neo-Gothic—attract tourists to this village. Another attraction is the nature reserve where all 5 species of Tern can be seen in one place (many species of birds have been recorded here). A collection of historic motor cars dating from 1896, motorcycles from 1903 and many other types of vehicle, are displayed in the Myreton Motor Museum (OACT) on the outskirts of the village.

*Turn left then bear right and skirt the inlet of Aberlady Bay before crossing the Luffness and Gullane Golf Links to enter Gullane.*

## GULLANE, Lothian

Just east of Gullane is the world famous Muirfield Championship Golf Course, headquarters of the oldest golf club in the world. The view over the Firth of Forth from Gullane Hill reaches over the water to the Fife coast, and beyond that to the distant Lomond and Ochil Hills. The 12th-century Church of St Andrew is now a roofless ruin — it is said James VI dismissed the last vicar for smoking tobacco.

*Continue on the A198 to Dirleton, turning left on to the B1345 to enter the village.*

## DIRLETON, Lothian

This is claimed by many to be the most beautiful village in Scotland. Three sides of a green are lined by 17th- and 18th-century houses, the fourth side is taken up by the castle (AM) and its grounds; trees surround it all and complete a scene of well-matured unity. The castle last stood seige against Cromwell's troops, and was rendered indefensible by General Lambert in 1650. Today it is surrounded by flower gardens. The castle's own gardens are hemmed in by ancient yew trees, and include a 17th-century bowling green, still in use, and a 16th-century circular dovecot.

*At the end of the village turn left to rejoin the A198, shortly entering North Berwick, and keep forward on the B1346 for the sea-front.*

## NORTH BERWICK, Lothian

An ancient burgh, fishing village, and popular resort, North Berwick boasts 2 golf courses and 2 sandy beaches which are divided by an attractive harbour with a heated open-air swimming pool set into the rocks beside it. The ruins of a 12th-century church can be explored near the harbour, a place where, in 1591, it is said the devil appeared before a group of local witches and wizards. This story is related in the local records of the witches' trial. Boats from North Berwick take visitors around the fascinating Firth of Forth islands which stand just off the coast.

*Follow SP 'Berwick B1346' and shortly rejoin the A198. In ¾ mile, at the roundabout, take the 1st exit. In 2 miles pass (left) the track leading to Tantallon Castle.*

### DUNDEE, Tayside
One of the largest cities in Scotland, Dundee covers some 20 square miles of hillside above the north bank of the Firth of Tay. Clashes between English and Scottish forces punctuate its history. Its strong seafaring tradition dates back to when local men went whaling to Iceland and the north as early as the 12th century. The only surviving gate of the strong walls that protected the town in medieval times is the Cowgate Port. One of the oldest buildings is 15th-century St Mary's Tower, the only surviving part of St Mary's Church, now a viewpoint and museum (temporarily closed). Also of interest are the Mills Observatory (open), and the comprehensive local collections shown in the City Museum and Art Gallery. Exhibits relating to natural history and geology can be seen in the Barrack Street Museum. Victoria Dock contains Captain Scott's HMS *Discovery* and the 19th-century HMS *Unicorn*, the only floating wooden warship in the country. Nearby Camperdown Park comprises 400 acres of landscaped gardens around the neo-classical Camperdown House. Nowadays Dundee is an important centre of industry, with 35 acres of dockland and a reputation for fine jam made with fruit from the fertile Carse of Gowrie. The renowned Dundee marmalade was first made by Mrs Keiller in 1797 and is still enjoyed on breakfast tables throughout the world.

*Before leaving Dundee on the main route it is possible to make a 4-mile detour: leave the city on the A930 and drive to Broughty Ferry.*

### BROUGHTY FERRY, Tayside
Originally an old fishing village and ferry terminus, Broughty Ferry has developed into a residential suburb of Dundee and is a popular holiday resort. Broughty Castle (AM), a 15th-century castle rebuilt as an estuary fort in the 19th century, stands on a rocky headland and houses a fascinating whaling museum. Claypotts Castle (AM) is one of the most complete examples of an old tower house in existence, the dates on the tower of the latter are 1569 and 1588, and it still has its roof.

*On the main tour, leave Dundee on the A92 with SP 'Aberdeen', and drive through agricultural country to Muirdrum. A short detour can be made from the main route to Carnoustie by turning right on to the A930 and continuing for 2 miles.*

### CARNOUSTIE, Tayside
Carnoustie is a popular holiday resort with sandy beaches and a championship golf course considered one of the best in the world. There is also another good course here, the Buddon Links course which has fine coastal views.

*On the main route, continue with the A92 and in 5 miles turn right under a railway bridge to enter Arbroath.*

## ON THE ANGUS COAST
Fishing ports and popular holiday resorts fringe the surprisingly gentle North Sea coast of old Angus, where weathered cliffs of red sandstone guard sandy bays and narrow rock strands. Inland are the rugged heights of the Grampian Mountains and the fertile Howe of Mearns.

### ARBROATH, Tayside
Best known for its smokies, delicious haddock flavoured and browned by smoke from an oak fire, this fishing port has a harbour at the mouth of the Brothock Water and has become a popular holiday resort. Various recreational facilities supplement the natural advantages of good sands and safe bathing, and the local countryside offers pleasant walks. Distinctive red sandstone cliffs known for their caves fringe the beach to the north-east. The town itself has been a Royal Burgh since 1599 and has an important place in Scottish history. After the Battle of Bannockburn, in 1320 Robert the Bruce signed Scotland's Declaration of Independence at Arbroath Abbey Considerable 13th-century remains (AM) of this important foundation have survived.

*Continue along the A92 'Aberdeen' road to a point just north of the town. A short detour can be made by turning left on to an unclassified road and driving to St Vigeans.*

### ST VIGEANS, Tayside
One of the finest collections of early-Christian and medieval memorial stones in Scotland is housed in St Vigeans' Cottage Museum (AM). Many of these beautiful monuments take the form of Celtic crosses, invariably carved with elaborate interlacing decorations on the front and groups of animals, figures, and symbols on the back.

*On the main route, continue along the A92 for ¾ mile to a point where another detour can be made, this time by turning right on to an unclassified road and driving to Auchmithie.*

### AUCHMITHIE, Tayside
Perched on a rocky sandstone cliff 150ft above a sandy beach, this precarious and exceptionally picturesque little fishing community can trace its history back to the 11th century. The cliffs extend north-east to impressive Red Head and Lang Craig, which overlook Lunan Bay. Dickmont's Den and the Forbidden Cave are just two notable examples of the many caves in the area.

*On the main route, continue along the A92 to Inverkeilor.*

### INVERKEILOR, Tayside
A tiny place remarkably unspoilt, its notable attractions include its church which contains a good 17th-century pew, and the 15th-century and later pile of Ethie Castle standing two miles to the south-east. Remarkable singing sands, whose grains vibrate against each other when walked on, lie to the east on Lunan Bay.

*From Inverkeilor a 2¼-mile detour can be made to Lunan by turning right on to an unclassified road, driving for 1½ miles to a T-junction, and turning left to Lunan.*

A superb view of the city can be enjoyed from Dundee Law.

### LUNAN, Tayside
Ruined Red Castle stands beside the sandhills in Lunan Bay. It may have been built to counter raids from Danish pirates in the 15th century, but an earlier fort on the site was given by Robert the Bruce to his son-in-law in 1328.

*On the main route, leave Inverkeilor on the A92 to cross Lunan Water. Continue, later enjoying views into the Montrose Basin before crossing the River South Esk to enter the town of Montrose.*

### MONTROSE, Tayside
Here the South Esk River forms a 2-mile square tidal lagoon known as the Montrose Basin, which is popular with many different species of wader all the year round and is a wintering place for pink-footed Arctic geese. The town itself is a pleasant market and holiday centre popular with sailors, golfers, and anglers. A fine sandy beach is complemented by a grassy belt that parallels the spacious High Street and is known as The Links. Leading from the High Street to the town's charming old heart are narrow, twisting 18th-century closes lined by quaint old houses.

*Beyond Montrose keep forward with the A937 SP 'Laurencekirk'. Continue for 4½ miles and turn right under a railway bridge before crossing the River North Esk to reach Marykirk.*

### MARYKIRK, Grampian
Marykirk is well situated at the edge of the Vale of Strathmore, near the point where it merges with the Mearns country, and is a good touring centre for these lovely districts. Its own villagescape is enhanced by the North Esk River.

*Turn left on to the B974 SP 'Fettercairn', reach a junction with the A94, then turn right and left to stay on the B974. Continue for 3¼ miles and turn right on to the B966 for Fettercairn.*

### FETTERCAIRN, Grampian
Set in woods and fields at the edge of the Howe of Mearns, this 18th-century village boasts a great 19th-century royal arch that was built to commemorate an incognito visit made by Queen Victoria and Prince Albert. The village square has a 17th-century cross which is notched to show the length of the Scottish ell, a measurement that is roughly the same as the English yard. It remains to be seen if the memory of the yard will remain as strong as this in the age of metrication. Fettercairn House dates from the 17th century and was erected by the 1st Earl of Middleton, who was Lord High Commissioner to the Scottish Parliament. About 1 mile south-west of Fettercairn is 16th-century Balbegno Castle (not open).

*Leave Fettercairn on the B966 'Edzell' road. In 3½ miles it is possible to make a detour from the main route, adding 31 miles to the tour, by turning right on to an unclassified road and driving to beautiful Glen Esk.*

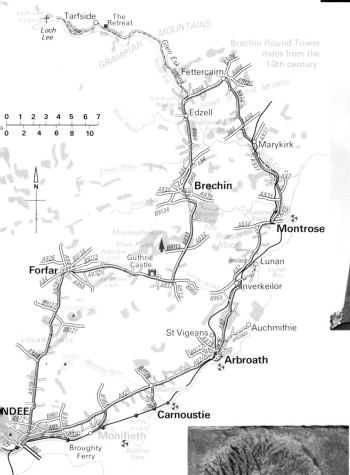

Brechin Round Tower dates from the 10th century.

The Medicine Well at Montrose was a popular 18th-century spa

The River North Esk enters the Howe of Mearns at Gannochy.

### GLEN ESK, Tayside

The road through the superb scenery of long Glen Esk accompanies the River North Esk into the fastness of the Grampian Mountains. It is a truly memorable drive for anybody who has the time to take it. The following route instructions and entries detail the countryside from end to end.

*On the detour, follow the unclassified road for 9¼ miles to reach The Retreat.*

### THE RETREAT, Tayside

This one-time shooting lodge is now a museum of local country life and handicrafts.

*Still on the detour, continue to Tarfside.*

### TARFSIDE, Tayside

Beautifully set in the foothills of the Eastern Grampians, this highly attractive village stands near the confluence of the North Esk River and the Water of Tarf. Mount Battock rises to 2,555ft in the north-east.

*Still on the detour, continue to Loch Lee Church and the end of the Glen Esk road.*

### LOCH LEE, Tayside

Shortly before reaching the end of this lovely glen the road passes the picturesque ruins of Invermark Castle. At the end of the glen, south-west of the little local church, is the lovely expanse of Loch Lee. Queen Victoria and Prince Albert climbed the 3,077ft bulk of Mount Keen, which rises to the north-west of the glen, in 1861. Their visit is commemorated by the Queen's Well beside the Mounth Track, which follows a lovely route cross-country to Aboyne.

*If the detour has been taken, rejoin the main route by returning along the entire length of Glen Esk to the B966. On the main tour, continue along the B966 and cross the River North Esk before reaching Edzell.*

### EDZELL, Tayside

From the south this little inland resort is approached through a fine 19th-century arch raised to the memory of the 13th Earl of Dalhousie. Early 16th-century Edzell Castle (AM) lies to the west of the main village and was visited by Mary Queen of Scots in 1562. One of its major features is a fine 17th-century garden surrounded by a wall which displays unique heraldic and symbolic decoration. The village itself lies between the lovely countryside of Strathmore and the fertile Howe of Mearns, which is situated just west of the North Esk River.

*Continue for 3¼ miles and meet the A94 'Perth' road. Turn right here, then in ¼ mile turn left on to the B966 for the town of Brechin.*

### BRECHIN, Tayside

Rising steeply from the banks of the South Esk River, this lovely old cathedral town of red-sandstone buildings stands against a backdrop of hills that gradually rise to the great dark chain of the Eastern Grampians. The old cathedral dates from the 12th century and parts of the original building still exist as proof of the foundation's great antiquity. It was partly rebuilt in the 19th century, but the lovely Maison Dieu Chapel (AM) is preserved as a particularly fine example of 13th-century workmanship. Attached to the church is an 87ft-high round tower (AM) that dates from the 10th or 11th century, with the addition of a spire in the 14th century, and is one of only two such examples existing in Scotland. The other is at Abernethy, and both buildings are similar in shape and decoration to those built by the Celts in Ireland. They were generally used as watchtowers and places of refuge for whole villages. Brechin Castle, the seat of the earls of Dalhousie, was rebuilt in 1711.

*Follow SP 'Arbroath' to leave Brechin on the A933 and cross the River South Esk. Skirt the private Kinnaird deer park and Montreathmont Moor Forest, then after 7 miles meet the A932 and turn right SP 'Forfar'. Continue for 1¾ miles and pass the grounds of inhabited Guthrie Castle on the right.*

### GUTHRIE CASTLE, Tayside

Very occasionally open to the public, this castle has been the home of the Guthrie family ever since it was built by Sir David Guthrie in 1468. The lovely Spring Garden is best seen in early spring.

*Continue on the A932, passing Balgavies Loch and the larger Rescobie Loch, and enter Forfar.*

### FORFAR, Tayside

Forfar lies in charming surroundings in the flat Howe of Angus, between the little Lochs Forfar and Fithie at the north-east end of the Vale of Strathmore. In the 11th century there was a Royal residence here, and an ancient octagonal turret marks the site of the castle where King Malcolm conferred surnames and titles on the Scottish nobility at a parliament in 1057. The castle itself was destroyed many years later by Robert the Bruce. His son was buried near Loch Fithie in Restenneth Priory (AM), a 12th-century foundation in beautiful surroundings. Forfar's Town House preserves a gruesome pronged bridle that was used to silence victims before and during execution, and is associated with so-called witches who were burned here during the 17th century. Forfar is perhaps best known for the 'Forfar Bridie', a half-moon shaped meat and onion pastry.

*Leave Forfar on the A929 'Dundee' road, passing through agricultural country and crossing the low Sidlaw Hills on the return to Dundee.*

# THE COWAL PENINSULA

Bordered by the waters of Loch Fyne, the Firth of Clyde and the Kyles of Bute, the Cowal Peninsula is a natural holiday ground for nearby Glasgow. Yet despite its popularity, this wooded, hilly country retains a remoteness and wildness surprising for a place so near Scotland's largest city.

**DUNOON, Strathclyde**
By the terms of the charter of 1471 the Campbells had to pay a fee of 'one red rose when asked for' to the crown for the keepership of Dunoon Castle. Traces of the old 13th-century castle can be seen on Castle Hill above the pier where, in 1646, the Marquess of Argyll brought 200 prisoners and had them massacred and thrown into mass graves after a raid by the Campbells on Lamont territories. The present castle, Castle House, was built as a villa in 1822 for James Ewing, Provost of Glasgow, and is now used for municipal purposes. At the foot of Castle Hill is a statue of Burns' sweetheart, 'Highland Mary', who was born near Dunoon on the site of the farm at Auchnamore. Up until the beginning of the 19th century, when tourism became a fashion, Dunoon remained a quiet village, but now it is a thriving holiday resort. It boasts 2 fine bays which are popular with yachtsmen. At the end of August the Cowal Highland Gathering is staged in the town's sports stadium, after which the stirring March of a Thousand Pipers takes place in the streets.

*Leave Dunoon on the A815 following the shoreline through Kirn to Hunter's Quay.*

**HUNTER'S QUAY, Strathclyde**
Hunter's Quay, the headquarters of the Royal Clyde Yacht Club (the first to be founded in Scotland), stands at the entrance of Holy Loch. Its busiest time is in July when the Clyde Yachting Fortnight takes place. The name of this little resort comes from the Hunter family, of Hafton House, which stands north-west of the town. The loch is said to take its name from an incident which occurred during the building of Glasgow Cathedral. A ship loaded with earth from the Holy Land, which was to be laid beneath the foundations, became stranded here. Today the loch is used by the Polaris submarines.

*Continue on the A815 into the village of Holy Loch and in 2 miles enter Sandbank.*

**SANDBANK, Strathclyde**
Sandbank, set in beautiful countryside on the banks of Holy Loch, is a popular holiday resort. Several Americas Cup challengers have been built in the shipyards in this little town and the tradition of boat-building here is a long and famous one.

*Turn right, remaining on the A815 and in 1½ miles bear right. At the head of the loch cross the River Eachaig and enter Strath Eachaig, passing in 2 miles the entrance to the Younger Botanic Garden, which occupies the valley.*

Right: Dunoon's pier, from which steam cruises can be taken to nearby waters

Below: the Kyles of Bute separate the Isle of Bute from the mainland

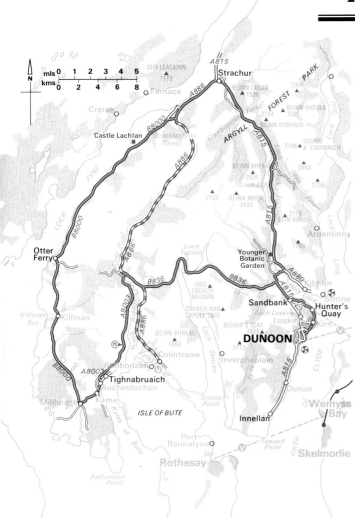

## YOUNGER BOTANIC GARDEN, Strathclyde

An impressive avenue of 130ft-high sequoias leads from the entrance of the gardens to Benmore House, which is now used as an adventure centre for Glaswegian children. The trees were planted by James D. Duncan, a wealthy sugar refiner, who owned the Benmore estate in the latter half of the 19th-century, and planted some 6 million trees between 1870 and 1883. The last private owner, H. G. Younger of the Scottish brewing family, donated the gardens and woodlands (OACT) to the nation in 1928. It is now an annexe of the Royal Botanic Gardens, Edinburgh. Apart from conifers and hardwoods, the botanic gardens offer beautifully laid-out flower beds and shrubberies, and among the less usual plants is the Chilean fire bush. The Golden Gates at the rear of the park were originally made for the Great Exhibition of 1851, and were brought here by James Duncan.

## ARGYLL FOREST PARK, Strathclyde

In 1935 the Argyll Forest Park was created, the first of its kind in Britain, 10 years before the Dower Report advocated the formation of the larger National Parks. It consists of large stretches of forest, mountain and moorland;

some 60,000 acres in all. It is ideal country for the keen walker or rambler, and the astonishing variety of animals and plants can be appreciated by everyone. The tour takes in the southern part of the park between Dunoon and Loch Ech, known as Benmore Forest.

*Continue on the A815 for 6½ miles with views to the left of Beinn Mhor (2,433ft) before entering Strachur.*

## STRACHUR, Strathclyde

Lying near the shores of Loch Fyne, which reaches a depth of some 600ft here, Strachur has become a small but popular resort. It was originally the seat of the McArthur Campbells, whose mansion, Strachur Park (not open), dates from about 1783. Nearby Argyll Forest Park provides Strachur with an important saw-milling and wood-working industry.

*Turn left on to the A886, SP 'Colintraive', to follow the shores of Loch Fyne. Ater 3½ miles turn right on to the B8000 Otter Ferry road (a short cut, saving 19 miles, can be taken by continuing on the A886 through Glendaruel). Descending through Strathlachan, the road rejoins Loch Fyne with views of Castle Lachlan to the right.*

## CASTLE LACHLAN, Strathclyde

Overlooking the waters of Loch Fyne this ruined tower is possibly part-12th or 13th-century, but dates mostly from the 16th century. It was destroyed after the defeat of the Scots at Culloden.

*Continue along the shores of Loch Fyne to Otter Ferry.*

## OTTER FERRY, Strathclyde

Otter Ferry sits at the shoreward end of a mile-long sand spit, which stretches out into Loch Fyne. This little township takes its name from its position — oitr means sand spit in Gaelic. Across the loch rise the green rounded hills of Knapdale.

*Turn left and continue through Kilfinan and in 6¼ miles, at Millhouse crossroads, turn sharp left. At the edge of Kames turn left. Shortly pass through Auchenlochan and in ¼ mile turn left on to the A8003 Glendaruel road. For the centre of Tighnabruaich keep forward on the B8000.*

## TIGHNABRUAICH, Strathclyde

Cruise steamers call at the pier here, which reaches out into the Kyles of Bute, the Isle of Bute being only half a mile away across the water. Tighnabruaich means house on the brea, and is a reminder of the days when one solitary house stood here. Nowadays Tighnabruaich is a popular little resort. Two miles away is the Tighnabruaich Wildlife Centre and Forest Trail. A feature here are the photo-safari hides which overlook a small lochan, where wild ducks, roe deer, Soay sheep and blue hare may be viewed.

*Climb out of Tighnabruaich on the A8003 to pass high above the Kyles of Bute.*

## ISLE OF BUTE, Strathclyde

The Isle of Bute, a 15 mile-long island, dovetails into the cloven coastline of the Cowal Peninsula, from which it is separated by the beautiful stretches of water known as the Kyles of Bute. Where now a car ferry crosses from Colintraive on the mainland to Rhubodach on

the island, cattle were made to swim in the days when there was no ferry. The northern half of the island is hilly, the south flatter and more fertile. The main town is Rothesay, a favourite resort, with sandy bays and the remains of a 13th-century castle (AM), surrounded by a deep moat. The fortress was destroyed by Cromwell in the 17th century. Also of interest is ruined St Mary's Chapel and the Bute Museum where the island's past is recorded.

*Continue past the shores of Loch Riddon. Later descend to the River Ruel at the head of the Loch and in 1½ miles turn right on to the A886. In 1½ miles turn left on to the B836. For a detour to Colintraive (5¼ miles), where the car ferry leaves for Rhubadach on the Isle of Bute, continue on the A886. The main tour continues on the B836 passing round the head of Loch Striven, before skirting Loch Tarsan reservoir. After passing through Glen Lean return to Holy Loch and turn right on to the A815. At Sandbank turn left, returning along the Clyde shores through Hunter's Quay to Dunoon.*

*A short excursion can be made to Innellan by taking the A815 southwards out of Dunoon.*

## INNELLAN, Strathclyde

This Cowal Peninsula holiday resort has a climate so mild that palm trees grow in some of the gardens. A steamer pier links Innellan with Wemyss Bay across the Firth of Clyde, and there is also a fine view of Clyde shipping from here. Delightful villas, built on terraces at the turn of the century by wealthy Greenock merchants, enjoy the view. The road through Innellan continues past Toward Point and round to the remote settlement of Inverchaolain on the shores of Loch Striven. Ruined Castle Toward is passed before this last outpost of civilisation is reached, and shows a good 15th-century tower, 3 storeys high, backed by the 165ft-high Bishop's Seat.

*Tighnabruaich — a small resort with a steamer pier facing the Isle of Bute*

## EDINBURGH, Lothian

Scotland's finest city and its capital since 1437, Edinburgh stands on seven hills between the waters of the Firth of Forth and the 2,000ft summits of the Pentlands. Until 200 years ago this great centre of culture and learning was little more than a cluster of houses along the Royal Mile, a cobbled slope that followed a windy ridge from Castle Hill to the Palace of Holyroodhouse. The foremost building here is the castle (AM), which overlooks the picturesque streets of the Old Town from its lofty summit and has a history that stretches back at least 1,000 years. Its old name *Duneadain*, meaning Fort on a Slope, aptly describes its site on Castle Rock and refers to a previous stronghold that may have had iron-age origins. Many of Edinburgh's oldest buildings stand on even older sites along the Royal Mile, which has been admirably restored in recent years and has a distinctive aura of age. Canongate Tolbooth dates from 1591, 15th-century John Knox's house was built by goldsmiths to Mary Queen of Scots, and 17th-century Gladstone's Land features rooms decorated with fine tempera paintings (all open). Lady Stair's House is a restored 17th-century building housing a museum, and off Canongate is 16th- and 17th-century Holyroodhouse (AM) – Scotland's finest royal palace. Ruins of the 12th-century Chapel Royal foundation adjoin the palace. Here and there the splendour of the city is relieved by more down-to-earth domestic architecture, like the old White Horse Inn and the mercat cross. The 14th-century stronghold of Craigmillar Castle is associated with Mary Queen of Scots, and the 17th- to 19th-century Parliament House is where the Scottish parliaments met before the Union of 1707. Famous George Heriot's School dates from 1628 and was founded by the Jingling Geordie of Scott's *Fortunes of Nigel*. Near the Castle Mound are the Royal Scottish Academy and the National Gallery of Scotland, where many fine paintings by artists from various schools can be seen, and in Chambers Street the Royal Museum of Scotland exhibits one of the most comprehensive general displays in Britain. The National Library of Scotland comes close to Oxford's famous Bodleian in the richness of its contents, and the museum of the Scottish Records House, Charlotte Square. There are many other fascinating museums, galleries, workshops, and studios in the city, most of which will be listed in the local guides. Every year since 1947 Edinburgh's concert halls, theatres, galleries, and public halls have opened their doors to the arts of the world in the International Festival, a cultural extravaganza that takes place in late summer.

Among the other features of particular note are the Royal Observatory Visitor Centre at Blackford Hill, whose wide range of different astronomical exhibits

# THE CITY ON SEVEN HILLS

Seven hilltops guarded by a massive castle carry Edinburgh, the Athens of the North. Just a few miles from its ancient heart are the rugged cliffs of the wild North Sea coast and the breathtaking scenery of mountains that were old before much of Britain was formed.

Edinburgh Castle stands high on a rock that may once have been the site of an iron-age hillfort.

include discoveries in the exploration of the Universe, whilst The Scottish National Zoological Park, one of the finest zoos in Europe set in eighty acres of grounds, contains a superb collection of mammals, birds and reptiles. The Zoo offers a further bonus with its magnificent panoramic views of Edinburgh and the surrounding countryside.

*Leave Edinburgh city centre with SP 'Galashiels' and in 2 miles drive forward onto the A701 SP 'Peebles'. Drive through Straiton and Bilston then in 1 mile turn left on the B7003 SP 'Roslin'.*

## ROSLIN, Lothian

Scott mentioned this former mining village's famous Rosslyn Chapel in the *Lay of the Last Minstrel*. It was founded in 1446 by William Sinclair and contains many fine stone carvings, including the exquisite Prentice Pillar. Nearby Roslin Castle overlooks the North Esk River and picturesque Roslin Glen.

*On the main route, continue to Rosewell, meet a T-junction, and turn right on to the A6094. In 2¼ miles turn left on to an unclassified road and cross Cauldhall Moor. In 1¾ miles meet crossroads and turn left on to the B6372, then 1¾ miles farther turn right on to an unclassified road SP 'Peebles'. In 1¼ miles pass a left turn leading to Gladhouse Reservoir.*

## GLADHOUSE RESERVOIR, Lothian

This attractive reservoir is set amid beautiful scenery below the summits of the Moorfoot Hills.

*On the main route, continue for 3 miles and descend, then turn left on to the A703 to reach Eddleston.*

## EDDLESTON, Borders

This tiny hamlet lies in the valley of the Eddleston Water, with the 2,137ft summit of Blackhope Scar rising from the Moorfoot range to the east. On the Peebles road to the south of the village is a memorial to George Meikle Kemp, who served as an apprentice here in the 19th century and later designed the famous Scott Monument in Edinburgh.

*At Eddleston turn right with SP 'Lyne via Eldons' and climb an unclassified road to 900ft. Descend and in 1¼ miles bear left. A short detour from the main route to visit Lyne can be made by bearing right, then driving for ½ mile and turning right to continue along the A72.*

## LYNE, Borders

One of the smallest churches in Scotland can be seen here. Inside are a pulpit and two pews of Dutch workmanship. Close by are the remains of a Roman camp of AD 83.

*On the main route, continue for ½ mile and turn left on to the A72 SP 'Peebles', driving alongside the Lyne Water and the River Tweed. In 1¾ miles a detour can be taken from the main route by turning right on to an unclassified road and crossing the Tweed to follow Manor Water to the village of Manor.*

## MANOR, Borders

Made famous by Scott's work *The Black Dwarf*, this small village stands at the foot of the long and beautiful Manor Valley. A little churchyard near Manor Water preserves the tomb of David Richie, on whom Scott modelled his Black Dwarf or Bowed Davie character.

*On the main tour, continue along the A72 and after a short distance pass Neidpath Castle on the right.*

## NEIDPATH CASTLE, Borders

Originally a stronghold of the Fraser family, this 15th-century castle (open) is beautifully positioned above the River Tweed and is an attractive feature of the local countryside.

*Proceed along the A72 to Peebles.*

## PEEBLES, Borders

Anglers come here to fish for the great Tweed salmon, but this attractive old Royal Burgh also offers facilities for golf, tennis, and pony-trekking. It has been the home of such famous people as the author Robert Louis Stevenson and Mungo Park, whose exploration helped to open up Africa. William Chambers and his brother Robert, publishers of the first Chambers' encyclopaedias and dictionaries, were born here and donated the Chambers Institute, a library, and a museum to the town. Relics of the town's history include the ruins of 13th-century Cross Kirk and the old shaft of a former parish cross. Old local inns include the 17th-century Cross Keys and early 19th-century Tontine. The woodlands of the Glentress Forest lap the outskirts of Peebles.

## GLENTRESS FOREST, Borders

One of the first state forests to be established in Scotland, the Glentress comprises over 2,000 acres of fast-growing conifers such as Douglas fir, Norway spruce, and Sitka spruce.

*Continue along the A72 SP 'Galashiels' to Innerleithen.*

Edinburgh's Charlotte Square is a gem of Georgian architecture.

Traquair House has seen centuries of beer-brewing.

Neidpath Castle was restored after severe damage by Cromwell's artillery.

### INNERLEITHEN, Borders
Sir Walter Scott popularized this small wool town in his novel *Ronan's Well*. To the south is the fine mansion of Traquair House (open), which can trace its history back to the 10th century and is the oldest inhabited house in Scotland. In its time it has played host to 27 English and Scottish monarchs, and its interior is packed with treasures and relics from many generations. A unique 18th-century brewhouse here is licensed to sell its own beer, and the grounds feature attractive woodland walks.

*A detour from the main route can be taken by keeping forward on the A72 and driving to Walkerburn.*

### WALKERBURN, Borders
This Tweed Valley village was created in 1854 by the Ballantyne family as a weaving centre. They established a woollen mill here which was able to process raw wool to finished cloth in the one location. Today it is the home of the Scottish Museum of Wool Textiles. Here the fascinating history of the woollen industry is revealed, showing how it evolved from a cottage industry, through the Industrial Revolution, to the present day. Spinning demonstrations can be seen in the old weaver's cottage and a number of hand and power operated weaving machines are on display. A history of the art of dyemaking is of particular interest as are the examples of early wool and cloth patterns including tartans and shepherd check.

*On the main route, leave Innerleithen by turning left on to the B709 SP 'Heriot' and drive alongside Leithen Water for 4 miles. Leave the main river behind and climb to a road summit of 1,250ft over a narrow pass, then descend to the Dewar Burn. In 2 miles drive forward on to the B7007 and follow a gradual ascent to a 1,324ft summit at the back of the Moorfoot Scarp. In good weather views from here take in the Pentland Hills, the 1,900ft summits of Scald Law and Carnethy, Arthur's Seat in Edinburgh, and the waters of the Firth of Forth. In 3¼ miles turn right on to the A7 SP 'Galashiels'. Continue along the A7 for 1¼ miles and turn left on to the B6367 SP 'Pathhead'. Continue to Crichton.*

Peebles enjoys a delightful setting by the salmon-rich River Tweed.

### CRICHTON, Lothian
Crichton Castle (AM) stands south-west of the actual village and is more elaborate than is usual in Scotland. It overlooks the River Tyne from a high and desolate site, and the Italianate lines that were the legacy of the Earl of Bothwell in the 16th century are certainly out of keeping with the dour practicality of conventional castle design. The medieval church features a quaint bellcote.

*Turn left, then right along the B6367 to Pathhead.*

### PATHHEAD, Lothian
Close to this little village are two fine houses. Oxenfoord Castle stands beyond the Tyne Water and now serves as a school, and 18th-century Preston Hall which dates from 1791.

*At Pathhead turn right on to the A68 then left SP 'Haddngton' to rejoin the B6367. In 2 miles turn right on to the A6093. In 1 mile a detour can be taken from the main route by turning left on to the B6371 for Ormiston.*

### ORMISTON, Lothian
Situated on the Tyne Water, this village boasts a fine 15th-century cross (AM) mounted on steps.

*On the main route, continue along the A6093 to Pencaitland.*

### PENCAITLAND, Lothian
This village is divided into two parts. Wester Pencaitland has an old mercat cross, and Easter Pencaitland is centred on a notable 13th-century church.

*Meet crossroads and turn left on to the B6355 SP 'Tranet', then take the next turning right on to the B6363 SP 'Longniddry'. In 3 miles a detour can be taken to the village of Gladsmuir by meeting crossroads and turning right on to the A1.*

### GLADSMUIR, Lothian
In early times this area was notorious for witchcraft, but the village is more famous for its associations with the Battle of Prestonpans in 1745.

*On the main route, drive over the crossroads on the B6363 and continue to Longniddry.*

### LONGNIDDRY, Lothian
Between 1643 and 1647 John Knox, the religious reformer, was a tutor here. The village itself is attractively sited just inland from the coast.

*Turn right on to the A198 and follow SP 'North Berwick'. In 1 mile meet a T-junction and turn left on to the B1348 to Cockenzie and Port Seton.*

### COCKENZIE AND PORT SETON, Lothian
A large power station makes an unsightly blemish on the otherwise attractive appearance of Cockenzie, a quaint little fishing village close to the resort of Seton. Features of the latter include 2 miles of sandy beach, a fine 14th-century collegiate church (AM), and Robert Adam's Seton Castle of 1790.

*After 2 miles pass the site of the Battle of Prestonpans on the approach to Prestonpans.*

### BATTLE SITE OF PRESTONPANS, Lothian
In 1745 the forces of Prince Charles Edward defeated Sir John Cope's entire army here in an astonishing 10 minutes.

### PRESTONPANS, Lothian
Former prosperity is evident in this town's splendid 17th-century mercat cross (AM), Hamilton House (NT), and several other notable survivors from that period. The name Prestonpans originated from a salt-extraction industry operated by the monastic community from Newbattle Abbey in the 12th century.

*Drive for 1½ miles beyond Prestonpans, meet a roundabout, and take the 3rd exit on to the A1. Return to Edinburgh through Musselburgh.*

### MUSSELBURGH, Lothian
This manufacturing town on the sandy Esk estuary has a 16th-century Tolbooth which preserves an ancient clock given by the Dutch in 1496. Jacobean Pinkie House (open) incorporates a 14th-century tower but mainly dates from c1590. A fine painted ceiling can be seen in the Long Gallery, and the building now forms part of Loretto School.

## BETWEEN THE MORAY FIRTH AND STRATH SPEY

Castles and cathedrals, beaches and bays, an enigmatic monument made by the ancient Scots, and one of the most beautiful bridges in Britain are all encountered on this tour through the forests and valleys of the old county of Morayshire.

### ELGIN, Grampian

Set in a richly fertile agricultural district known for hundreds of years as the Garden of Moray, Elgin stands on the meandering loops of the River Lossie and retains many of its fine old 18th- and 19th-century buildings. Its greatest treasure is the ruined cathedral (AM), founded by Andrew, Bishop of Moray in 1224, which stands today as one of the most beautiful ecclesiastical buildings in Scotland. Despite centuries of neglect and vandalism a great deal of 13th-century work survives in the cathedral, notably in the choir. The Panns Gate, or East Gate, is the only surviving gate from the cathedral precincts, and a wing of the 16th-century Bishop's House (AM) still stands. Other notable buildings in the town include St Giles Church, a classical structure dating from 1828, the Greyfriars Chapel, which incorporates fragments from an abbey founded by Alexander II. The town museum displays collections of fossils and prehistoric artefacts. At the west end of the town is Lady Hill, crowned by a 19th-century statue to the Duke of Gordon.

*Leave Elgin on the A941, SP 'Lossiemouth'.*

### LOSSIEMOUTH, Grampian

Long, sandy beaches and a host of recreational facilities make this prosperous fishing village popular with holidaymakers. James Ramsay MacDonald, Britain's first Labour Prime Minister, was born here in 1866. Fascinating caves and rocks may be found 2 miles west at Covesea, where there is also a lighthouse.

*From the seafront follow the B9040, SP 'Hopeman, Burghhead'. After 5½ miles, for a detour to Duffus, take the B9012 on the left.*

The pleasant, open countryside around Craigellachie is characterised by large conifer plantations. Ben Aigan rises to 1,544ft in the distance

### DUFFUS, Grampian

A couple of miles south-east of Duffus is one of the finest examples of a motte-and-bailey castle (AM) in Scotland. Its earthen mound is surmounted by the remains of a 14th-century tower which eventually collapsed because the mound could not support its massive weight. Nearly 8 acres are enclosed by the castle's precinct ditch. Duffus Church (AM) retains the base of a 14th-century tower, a vaulted 16th-century porch and a number of interesting tomb-stones. Also of the 14th-century is the village's tall parish cross (AM).

The main tour continues on the B9040 to Hopeman. Continue on the B9012 and after 1½ miles, a turning (right) leads to Burghead.

### BURGHEAD, Grampian

This busy little port stands on a headland still protected by the ramparts of an ancient hill fort. Within the fortifications is the so-called Roman Well (AM), which is neither Roman nor a well. It is a rock-cut chamber approached down a flight of steps at the bottom of which is a cistern surrounded by a ledge. The structure is unique and is thought to be an early Christian baptistry. Burghead's museum has displays which illustrate the archaeology of the Laich of Moray. An extremely ancient ceremony called Burning the Clavie is enacted in the village on 11 January, the old New Year's Day. A lighted tar barrel is first paraded round the burgh, then cast from the top of Dourie Hill to ward off evil spirits.

*The main tour continues on the A9089 Forres road to Kinloss. The B9011 (right) leads to Findhorn.*

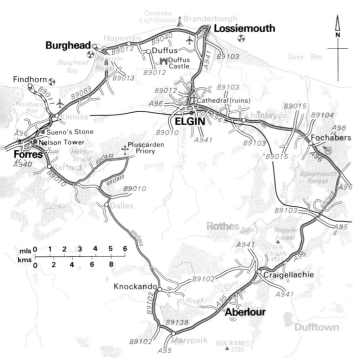

## SUENO'S STONE, Grampian

One of the most remarkable monuments (AM) of its kind in Europe, this slender, 20ft-high sandstone pillar is sculpted on all 4 of its faces. On one of the 2 broad sides is a tall cross surrounded by elaborately carved figures, and on the other are groups of figures depicting hunting and fighting scenes. The stone possibly commemorates victory of Sueno, son of the King of Denmark, over Malcolm III, which would date the stone at 1008.

*Turn right on to the A96 to enter Forres.*

## FORRES, Grampian

Beautiful Highland scenery surrounds this ancient royal burgh. The town's royal connections can be traced back to the 10th century, and it is especially associated with characters immortalised in Shakespeare's play *Macbeth*. King Duncan held his court at Forres in the early 11th century, and it was here that Macbeth and Banquo were confronted by the 3 'weird sisters'. The town's standing as a royal residence was brought to an untimely end when the Wolf of Badenoch burned it in 1390. Today Forres is a quiet little town, with only a castle mound to serve as a tangible reminder of its famous past. It is marked by a tall granite memorial to Dr Thomson, who died in the Crimean War tending the wounded. In the Falconer Museum is a splendid collection of fossils, many of them recovered from Culbin Sands. Nelson Tower, built on Cluny Hill in 1806 to commemorate Lord Nelson, serves as a splendid viewpoint from which to enjoy the lovely countryside along the River Findhorn.

*Leave Forres on the B9010, SP 'Dallas'. After 4½ miles branch left, SP 'Elgin', to reach Pluscarden Priory.*

## PLUSCARDEN PRIORY, Grampian

Overlooked from the north by the dark mass of Monaughty Forest, Pluscarden Priory stands beside the Black Burn. Originally founded by King Alexander II in 1230, the priory was deserted from 1560 to 1948, when it was re-colonised by monks from Prinknash Abbey near Gloucester. Through the labour of the monks and many charitable gifts, the priory has been restored and is now the hub of a thriving community. Visitors — who are made very welcome — enter the priory through a door in the 13th-century tower and can see ancient wall-paintings, modern stained glass, and the lovely Lady Chapel, which has been preserved almost intact.

## FINDHORN, Grampian

Findhorn Bay was formed by the River Findhorn as it tried to find a way through the drifting expanses of the Culbin Sands. Formerly the largest area of dunes in Britain, much of Culbin Sands was stabilised and afforested by the Forestry Commission between 1922 and 1966. Beyond the forest is The Bar, where marshes and dunes combine to form a haven for myriads of birds and a great variety of wild flowers. The village is a popular seaside resort, ideal for bathing and fishing. Findhorn is world-famous for the Findhorn Foundation, which was begun in 1962 as a community devoted to bringing fertility to the barren sands by spiritual methods. It has now grown into a highly successful and efficient enterprise, complete with pottery, weaving, candle-making shops and a printer.

*The main tour continues on the B9011 to Sueno's Stone.*

*Continue towards Elgin then after ¼ mile, at the church, turn right. After 3¼ miles turn left to rejoin the B9010, then in 1 mile turn right, SP 'Knockando', to reach Dallas. At the end of the village turn left and cross the River Lossie. The scenery becomes increasingly wild and desolate on the long run down to Knockando.*

## KNOCKANDO, Grampian

The church here has an internal gallery, and ancient carved slabs can be seen in the churchyard. To the south, beyond the beautiful Spey valley, is the 2,755ft peak of Ben Rinnes. Elchies Forest, to the north of the village, covers some 3,500 acres and forms the main mass of Craigellachie Forest.

*Turn right on to the B9102, SP 'Grantown'. After 3 miles turn left on to the B9138, SP 'Marypark'. Cross the River Spey, then at Marypark turn left on to the A95 and later enter Aberlour.*

## ABERLOUR, Grampian

Correctly named Charlestown of Aberlour, from its founder Charles Grant of Aberlour, this long village was planned in 1812 and retains its pleasing uniformity of style. A footpath leads from the village to a pretty footbridge over the Spey. Many riverside, woodland and hill walks start from the village, which is also a noted salmon angling centre.

*Continue to Craigellachie.*

## CRAIGELLACHIE, Grampian

Thomas Telford's graceful bridge over the Spey lends distinction to this lovely village. It was built in 1812 at the foot of a precipitious crag called Craigellachie Rock. Part of the crag had to be blasted away to make an approach road to the bridge, which is a single iron span with twin stone towers at either end. The bridge survived devastating floods in 1829, but the southern bank was swept away.

*Continue on the A95 Keith road and after 6½ miles, at a crossroads, go forward on to an unclassified road. After 3¾ miles turn left on to the A96 to reach Fochabers.*

## FOCHABERS, Grampian

In 1798 Fochabers was built in its present position after the original village had been demolished so that Gordon Castle could be enlarged. Much of the castle itself, which stands to the north and was once one of the biggest buildings in Scotland, has now been demolished. Speymouth Forest stretches away to the east, and has several car parks, picnic sites and forest walks. Some of the pine trees on the hills above Fochabers were planted over 200 years ago by the Dukes of Gordon.

*Continue on the A96 Inverness road and pass through Lhanbryde before returning to Elgin.*

A window depicting the Visitation in the public chapel of Pluscarden Priory

# ROAD TO THE ISLES

*Reminders of Bonnie Prince Charlie and the ill-fated Jacobite Rising are everywhere in the west Highland countryside. Ben Nevis towers over lochs and glens, moors and hillsides, known for the bloody battles and long-drawn-out feuds enacted there in the past.*

Snow-capped Ben Nevis forms a popular excursion from Fort William. On a clear day views from the summit extend for 150 miles.

### FORT WILLIAM, Highland
The first fort built here was a wattle-and-daub structure erected by General Monk in 1655, but the town takes its name from a stone stronghold that replaced it by order of William III. It was besieged by Jacobites in the Rising of 1715, but they failed to take it and General Wade was commissioned to strengthen it. His engineering talents were proved in 1745, when the second Jacobite Rising failed to capture it. The fort was garrisoned until the mid 19th century, by which time its redundancy was obvious and it was demolished to make way for the railway. Relics from these and earlier days can be seen in the West Highland Museum including a curious picture of Prince Charles Edward that can only be seen in its reflection on a curved and polished surface. The town itself is a major resort and touring centre for the West Highlands, situated near the west end of Glen More and the head of Loch Linnhe. Towering above the town is the massive bulk of Ben Nevis, while the comparatively low summit of 942ft Cow Hill affords lovely views into lower Glen Nevis. One of the major features of the local landscape is the white quartzite peak of Sgurr a' Mhaim, which rises like a snow-capped Alp to the south, while north-east of the town another is an aluminium smelting works which makes use of hydro-electric power.

### BEN NEVIS, Highland
An enormous expanse of countryside round Fort William and the Lochaber area, including a large part of Glen More, is dominated by 4,408ft Ben Nevis. It is the highest mountain in the British Isles, and round its south and west flanks is Glen Nevis, one of the most beautiful valleys in Scotland. At the far end of the glen the River Nevis rushes through a steep wooded gorge, but closer to Fort William its waters can be crossed to reach a mountain path starting at Achintee Farm. The mountain can be climbed from here, but the path is only suitable for properly equipped walkers. The energetic explorer will find many enchanting and often impressive natural features to reward his efforts, such as the Allt Coire Eaghainn waterfalls plunging from their hidden corrie, the waterfall of Steall in its wild setting at the end of Glen Nevis, and the spectacular narrow arrête that links the Ben with the upper slopes of Carn Mor Dearg.

*From Fort Wiliam follow SP 'Inverness' to take the A82 northwards out of the town and pass Inverlochy Castle.*

### INVERLOCHY CASTLE, Highland
Thought to date from the 13th century, this ruined Comyn stronghold (AM) stands by the River Lochy and is well-preserved. The largest of its circular towers is named after the family and has massive 10ft-thick walls enclosing rooms that are a full 20ft across. A Civil War battle between a royalist force led by the Marquess of Montrose and a Covenanters' army under the command of the Duke of Argyll took place near here in 1645.

*Beyond the castle turn left to join the A830 'Mallaig' road — the famous Road to the Isles. At one time this was notoriously difficult, but has been much improved. Cross the River Lochy, then the Caledonian Canal, and enter Banavie.*

### BANAVIE, Highland
Telford came here in the 19th century to build a chain of eight locks, known as Nepture's Staircase, on the Caledonian Canal, and his brilliance in solving difficult civil engineering problems can still be seen.
*Continue to Corpach.*

### CORPACH, Highland
A little to the west of Corpach is Kilmallie Churchyard, where an obelisk was raised to Colonel John Cameron after he fell in the Battle of Quatre Bras during the Waterloo Campaign of 1815. The town is well-known for the large paper and pulp mill.
*Continue along the A830 and follow the picturesque shore of Loch Eil to Kinlocheil.*

### KINLOCHEIL, Highland
Nowadays this is a peaceful little place, but it must have been full of tension when Prince Charles Edward came here after unfurling his father's standard at Glenfinnan in 1745.
*Continue to Glenfinnan.*

### GLENFINNAN, Highland
More than 1,000 clansmen mustered here under the Stuart banner to begin the second Jacobite Rising in 1745. The place where the standard is said to have been unfurled is marked by a tall castellated tower (NTS) with an inner staircase leading to a 19th-century statue of a Highlander at the top. There is also a visitor centre. Each year Highland games are held on the site in memory of those who died for Bonnie Prince Charlie. Views from here extend along 18-mile Loch Shiel.

### LOCH SHIEL, Highland
Many visitors consider Loch Shiel to be the most picturesque expanse of fresh water in the Highlands. At its north end it is framed by spectacular mountain scenery, and parallel ranges of rocky hills border Glen Finnan to the north of the '45 Rising monument. Below the massive bulk of Ben Resipol are the narrows of the loch and the little island of Eilean Fhionain, which used to be a burial ground many centuries ago.

*Continue, then pass Loch Eilt on the way to Lochailort.*

### LOCHAILORT, Highland
Situated in a lovely position at the head of the sea loch Ailort, this village stands against a backdrop of high hills in which 2,877ft Rois Bheinn is prominent. At the seaward end of the loch is the tiny island of Eilean nan Gobhar, where the French ship that brought Bonnie Prince Charlie anchored in July of 1745.

*From Lochailort a 39-mile detour can be taken to Mallaig by continuing along the A830 alongside Loch Ailort, then Loch nan Uamh.*

### LOCH NAN UAMH, Highland
Worth visiting for its own sake, this picturesque loch is best known for its associations with Bonnie Prince Charlie and the Jacobite Rising of 1745. Borrodale House was the scene of a fateful meeting when the whole issue of the Jacobite cause came into question, and although it was burnt after the Battle of Culloden it still preserves much of its original structure. After the '45 Rising had degenerated into a disorganized bloodbath the Prince returned to Loch nan Uamh with a fortune on his head, and he had to hide in the woods of Glen Beasdale before escaping to the isolation of the Outer Hebrides.

*Still on the detour, continue to Arisaig with views across the Sound of Arisaig to the little islands of Rhum and Eigg.*

Wild Loch Shiel echoes with memories of Bonnie Prince Charlie at Glenfinnan.

## ARISAIG, Highland
A memorial clock in the Roman Catholic church here commemorates the most revered of all Scots Gaelic poets, Alisdair MacMhaigstir Alasdair, who took part in the Rising of 1745. South-east are the gardens of Arisaig House Hotel.

*Still on the detour, continue to Morar*

## MORAR, Highland
Loch Morar is the deepest inland water in Britain, and the Falls of Morar have been harnessed in a local hydro-electric scheme on the River Morar. The white sands of a bay formed by the river's estuary are famous. The hamlet itself is situated on a narrow neck of land between the loch and the Sound of Sleat.

*Continue on the detour to Mallaig.*

## MALLAIG, Highland
Facing the Isle of Skye from the rocky shores of north Morar, this major fishing port stands at the western end of the Road to the Isles and is the mainland terminus of the islands' ferry. Cars can be taken from here to Armadale, on Skye.

*On the main route, at Lochailort turn left on to the A861 SP 'Ardgour' and follow the eastern shore of the loch and the Sound of Arisaig. Later turn south to reach Loch Moidart and Kinlochmoidart.*

## KINLOCHMOIDART, Highland
Here, where the River Moidart flows through woodland to the head of Loch Moidart, survive 5 of the 7 beech trees planted to commemorate 7 local men who were among Bonnie Prince Charlie's most constant companions.

*Continue along the A861 and after 6 miles reach an unclassified right turn. A detour can be made from the main route to Castle Tioram here.*

## CASTLE TIORAM, Highland
One of the most romantic and beautifully situated ruins in the Western Highlands, this 13th-century castle is perched on a spit of land that becomes isolated when the tide rises. It was built by the Macdonalds of Clanranald who, after they realized that the 1715 Rising was doomed to failure, burned it rather than let it fall into enemy hands.

*Continue on the A861 to Acharacle.*

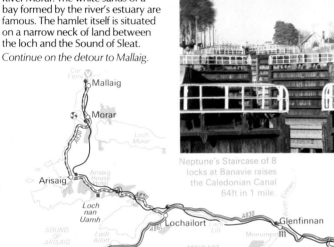

Neptune's Staircase of 8 locks at Banavie raises the Caledonian Canal 64ft in 1 mile.

## ACHARACLE, Highland
This little angling resort stands on the west tip of Loch Shiel.

*Continue to Salen*

## SALEN, Highland
The small fishing resort of Salen stands on Loch Sunart, a narrow ribbon of sea that separates Ardnamurchan from the traditionally MacLean territory of the Morvern district. It is little more than a cluster of cottages round a hotel, but its surroundings are a superb mixture of mountain, moorland, and pine plantations.

## LOCH SUNART, Highland
At the head of this beautiful sea loch is an amphitheatre of hills where the Ardgour and Morvern districts meet.

*A 50-mile detour can be made from Salen to Kilchoan and Ardnamurchan Point: take the B8007 (a narrow, winding road) west along the loch and drive inland through the Ardnamurchan Peninsula, returning to the coast at Kilchoan. To reach Ardnamurchan Point and lighthouse (a further 6 miles) continue along the B8007 for another 4 miles and turn left on to an unclassified road to Ardnamurchan Point.*

## KILCHOAN AND ARDNAMURCHAN POINT, Highland
Situated on the rocky Ardnamurchan coast, this remote little village has a pier that is the starting point of a passenger ferry to Tobermory, on the Island of Mull. Ardnamurchan Point, the most westerly point in mainland Britain, is a wild and lonely area populated by seabirds.

*On the main tour, leave Salen and continue along the A861 SP 'Strontian' beside the northern shore of Loch Sunart to the village of Strontian.*

## STRONTIAN, Highland
Strontium, a rare mineral that used to be mined in the district, is named after this village. To the north the River Strontian carves its way between the mountains of Sunart and Ardgour before emerging from its glen to join Loch Sunart in an area that used to be mined for lead. Close by is the Ariundle Forest nature reserve, one of the few places where the true Scottish wildcat survives.

*Keep right and continue along the A861 through Glen Tarbert. Later pass through Inversanda to reach the shores of lovely Loch Linnhe.*

## LOCH LINNHE, Highland
Situated at the extreme west end of the Great Glen, or Glen More, Loch Linnhe is divided into the Inner and Outer Loch by the Corran Narrows. Loch Leven joins it beyond the Narrows, which are crossed by a car ferry between Ardgour and Corran.

*Continue along the west shore of Loch Linnhe to Ardgour.*

## ARDGOUR, Highland
This name applies generally to a wild and rugged district between Loch Shiel and Loch Linnhe, and particularly to a small village on the Corran Narrows.

*From the ferry point at the Ardgour Hotel the main route crosses the narrows by the Corran Ferry and at Corran turn left on to the A82 for the return to Fort William. A detour (23 miles) by way of the west shore of Loch Linnhe and Loch Eil can be made by keeping forward with the A861 to Camusnagaul.*

## CAMUSNAGAUL, Highland
Excellent views extend over Loch Linnhe to Fort William that ever-popular resort with tourists and climbers alike, dominated by the towering summit of Ben Nevis. Close by the loch bends west to become Loch Eil.

*Continue along the A861 to follow the shore of Loch Eil, then round the head of the loch and turn right on to the A830 for Kinlocheil and the return to Fort William.*

During the season Mallaig harbour is packed with fishing boats.

# THE ROCKY NORTH SEA COAST

Many of the villages on this tour were founded by
enlightened landlords of the 18th and 19th centuries in an
attempt to encourage new industry and better the lot of
their tenants. Inland, weaving was introduced, and on the
coast harbours were built. The neat, tidy towns and
villages remain, but the cottage looms have gone and
North Sea oil dominates the area's future.

### FRASERBURGH, Grampian
Alexander Fraser, 7th Laird of
Philorth, was granted a charter in
1546 which enabled him to build a
harbour and from this grew
Fraserburgh. The old town huddles
around the harbour complex, with
all its attendant warehousing,
boatbuilding, fish processing, cold
storage and other maritime
industries. On Kinnaird Head
overlooking the town stands a
16th-century castle. The massive
whitewashed keep has walls 6ft
thick, and is 4 storeys high — the
roof has been made flat and the
caphouse for the turnpike stair
converted into a lighthouse. About
50yds away stands an original
tower known as the Wine Tower.
Its purpose is unknown, but it has
2 storeys connected only by a
trapdoor and dates from c 1560.

*Follow the A98 Inverness road for
¾ mile then turn right on to the
B9031, SP 'Rosehearty'.*

### ROSEHEARTY, Grampian
Rosehearty, a sturdily-built fishing
village, stands on old
Aberdeenshire's northern-most
point. It was allegedly founded in
the 14th-century by shipwrecked
Danes. The streets are regularly set
out with brightly-painted cottages.
The oldest building here is the
Dower House of Pitsligo, which
dates from 1573 and now stands,
sadly, as a roofless shell.

*Continue on the B9031, SP 'New
Aberdour'. In 2½ miles turn left on
to the B9032, SP 'Rathen'. In 1½
miles, at the crossroads, turn right
on to the A98 then in ¼ mile turn
left on to an unclassified road, SP
'Strichen'. In 4¼ miles turn right on
to the A981 for Strichen.*

### STRICHEN, Grampian
Lord Strichen of Session laid out
this little plain stone town in 1766,
in an attempt to provide better
housing and employment for his
tenants: today it is a thriving
community. A stream, crossed by
several little bridges, flows along
one side of the village.

*At the far end of Strichen turn
right, SP 'New Deer', pass under a
bridge, then branch left on to an
unclassified road, SP 'Old Deer'.
After 4 miles turn left on to the
A950, then 1¾ miles further turn
right on to the B9030, SP
'Auchnagatt', to enter Old Deer.*

Right: traditional fishing boats in the
harbour at Peterhead

Below: Pitmedden Gardens had fallen
into ruins until acquired by the NTS in
1952 who recreated them exactly as they
would have been in the 17th century

### OLD DEER, Grampian
This small village lying in the
wooded valley of the South Water
of the Agie was an important
ecclesiastical centre long ago. Its
history begins in AD520, when St
Dristan, a Pict, established a
monastery beside the river. By the
end of the 12th century this first
foundation dwindled, and the
buildings became ruined.
However, in 1218 William Comyn
founded a new Cistercian abbey
(AM) on the opposite banks of the
River Agie, which became the
administrative centre of the area.
The ruins which remain of this
latter community comprise the
church, cloister, kitchen, refectory,
warming room, abbot's house and
infirmary.

*Continue on the B9030 to
Stuartfield.*

### STUARTFIELD, Grampian
In 1772 John Burnett, Laird of
Crichie, created this village and
named it in honour of his
grandfather, Captain John Stuart.
At this time landowners were

becoming increasingly aware of
their tenants welfare and it was
built specifically as a weaving
community — each house
possessing its own loom.

*Continue on the B9030 and at the
end of the village bear right. At
Auchnagatt turn right on to the
A948, then cross the bridge and
turn left on to an unclassified road
(no SP). In 2 miles keep forward on
the Methlick road and in 3½ miles
turn left on to the B922 to
Methlick.*

### METHLICK, Grampian
Methlick has rather grander
buildings than most of its
neighbours, and among these are
the Beaton public hall of 1908,
and the fine Gothic parish church
with gabled clock tower, which
stands on its own green.

*Continue on the B9170 Old
Meldrum road. After 2¾ miles
turn left on to the B999, SP
'Tarves'. 1¾ miles farther, at a
crossroads, turn left to reach
Tarves.*

### TARVES, Grampian
Set on a slight ridge, Tarves is
centred around what used to be a
small green, but is now covered
with tarmac. At one end stand the
old church and a war memorial
cross. In the church is the tomb of
the Forbes family, which William
Forbes built in 1589; it is a splendid
Gothic piece with Renaissance
trimmings. Arched recesses
contain beautiful carved figures of
William and his wife —
enlightened and popular people
who endowed a poorhouse for
paupers in the village.

*Continue on the B999 passing a
road (right) to Tolquhon Castle.*

### TOLQUHON CASTLE, Grampian
In a remote position in a
pleasantly-wooded dell stands
handsome Tolquhon (AM), a
courtyard castle that was
originally just a single keep, built
by the Prestons of Craigmillar in
the 13th century. The castle
passed to the Forbes family by
marriage in 1420. In 1584-9
William Forbes had architect
Thomas Leiper build the large
quadrangular mansion and
gatehouse seen today. It has inner
and outer courts with both circular
and square towers; one of them,
Preston Tower, was built in the
15th century by the 1st Forbes
Laird, Sir John.

*Return to the B999, cross over the
A920, and pass (right) the entrance
to Pitmedden Gardens.*

### PITMEDDEN GARDENS,
Grampian
Here are the magnificent formal
gardens first laid out by Sir
Alexander Seton, who inherited
Pitmedden (NTS) in 1675. They
are laid out on 2 levels — to the
north an upper garden with
terraces and to the south the
Great Garden. This consists of 4
parterres; 2 are replicas of designs
known to have existed in Charles
I's garden in 1647. The parterres
are separated by lawns and yew
and box hedges, and each garden
has a fountain.

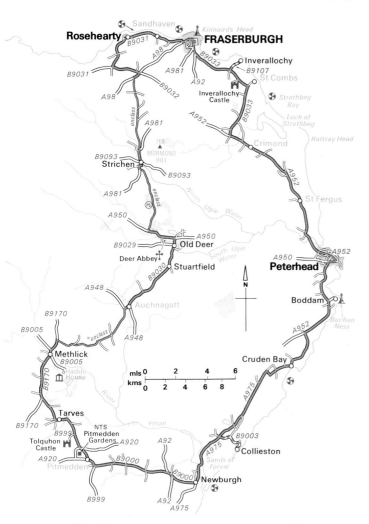

*Continue on the A975, SP 'Cruden Bay'. In 3½ miles (right) is the B9003 leading to Collieston.*

### COLLIESTON, Grampian
Picturesque Collieston perches upon clifftops around a deep rocky bay known as St Catherine's Dub; so called because in 1594 a Flemish galleon, called the *St Catherine,* was wrecked here. The indented coastline with its many caves made Collieston as popular with smugglers in the past as it is with holidaymakers today.

*Continue north on the A975 to Cruden Bay.*

### CRUDEN BAY, Grampian
A small town and its fishing harbour, Port Errol, lie in a bay with 2 miles of sands flanked by links, which have helped to make Cruden Bay a renowned golfing centre. The 19th Earl of Errol created the harbour in the 19th century to take advantage of the fishing grounds and coastal trade along the coast. Today, the pleasant fishermen's cottages make delightful holiday homes, and the golf course is as popular as ever.

*Continue on the A975 Peterhead road. After 2¾ miles turn right on to the A952 and then in 2½ miles pass the B9108 (right) leading to Boddam.*

### BODDAM, Grampian
Buchan Ness is the most easterly point of the Scottish mainland, and by it stands the pink granite village of Boddam, overlooking its large double harbour. It is a fishing port, though not as prosperous as it once was, and has a large school and a 130ft-tall lighthouse which was built by Robert Stevenson in 1827.

*Continue on the A952 to Peterhead.*

### PETERHEAD, Grampian
George Keith, 5th Earl of Marishal, founded Peterhead in 1593 with 56 inhabitants. Since then the town has prospered to become a sizeable place clustered around the harbour. For a while at the end of the 18th century, it was a popular spa town, but this was short lived and when the whaling industry was in full swing Peterhead became Scotland's whaling 'capital'. When this declined the herring boom followed, now replaced by more modern fish-processing plants. Peterhead's latest main concern is oil, and a huge harbour has been built to accommodate North Sea oil vessels. The Arbuthnot Museum and Art Gallery (OACT) specialises in local exhibits, especially those connected with the fishing industry.

*Leave Peterhead on the A952, SP 'Fraserburgh', to pass through Saint Fergus and Crimond. 1½ miles beyond Crimond turn right on to the B9033, SP 'St Combs'. After 3¼ miles turn left, SP 'Fraserburgh', then 1½ miles farther pass the B9107 (right) leading to Inverallochy.*

### INVERALLOCHY, Grampian
This is a small, typical fishing village with close-set rows of cottages packed gable-end towards the narrow streets. There is no harbour — the boats were landed on a shingly beach — and now the fishermen work out of Fraserburgh. Inverallochy Castle is a crumbling ruin (not open), consisting of a lofty tower and remnants of a curtain wall 30ft high. It was an important stronghold of the notorious Comyn family.

*Continue on the B9033 and then the A92 for the return to Fraserburgh.*

*From Pitmedden village continue on the B999 Aberdeen road, then in ½ mile turn left on to the B9000, SP 'Newburgh'. In 5 miles turn right on to the A92 then turn left to rejoin the B9000 for Newburgh.*

View from Boddam Lighthouse of the coast to the south of Peterhead

### NEWBURGH, Grampian
A large village and once a busy fishing port, Newburgh stands at the mouth of the Ythan estuary — the largest on the Aberdeen coast. Although the river which flows through it is not much more than a stream, when the tide is in the waterway stretches 700 yards across.

# IN WESTER ROSS

This is the gentler corner of Wester Ross where Loch Maree, dotted with pine-clad islands, the sandy bays of Gairloch and the unexpected lushness of Inverewe Gardens soften the harsh landscape of the Torridon rocks that are millions of years old.

Above: beautiful Loch Maree above which soars the 3,217ft snow-speckled mass of Ben Slioch

Left: the River Dromas and the Falls of Measach in Corrieshalloch Gorge

Leave Gairloch on the A832 Kinlochewe road and follow the River Kerry past the Gairloch Dam and through Slattadale Forest to the shore of Loch Maree.

## GAIRLOCH, Highland

This village resort on Loch Gairloch has distant views of the Outer Hebrides and the bay provides good fishing and bathing from sandy beaches; boating facilities are also available. Gairloch was once a fishing hamlet dependent on the sea for its livelihood, and fish are still landed here; big salmon in the morning, and in the evening, the little fleet brings home catches of whitefish, prawns, lobsters and crabs. Freshwater trout can be had in the several lochs within easy walking distance of the village. There are hotels and guesthouses here to cater for the visitor, as well as a 9-hole golf course — unusual in this part of north-west Scotland. The most imposing building here is Flowerdale House (not open), an 18th-century mansion which stands between the hotel and the pier. It was once the seat of the Mackenzies of Gairloch.

## LOCH MAREE, Highland

This is the largest entirely natural loch in Scotland, for Loch Maree has not yet been dammed or altered in the interests of hydro-electricity. The loch has great visual impact, nearly always viewed as a sweeping whole, a primeval landscape of sombre colours, water, wind and rock. There were great forests hereabouts of ancient oak, but these were destroyed when charcoal burners from the south, banned by Elizabeth I from felling trees in England, came north in search of fuel for their primitive iron-foundries which used local bog-iron to fulfil the demand for metal for canons and firearms. The loch has many wooded islands, among these the Isle of Maree, made famous by Saint Maelrubha who set up his cell here in the 7th century. The island is associated with Druids, as well as Celtic Christianity, and the Druids sacred oaks still grow beside the Christians' holy holly trees. Special powers connected with this place were said to cure lunacy. Salmon and trout are highly prized in this loch, and the whole area is a valuable refuge for wildlife, including black-throated and red-throated divers and golden eagles. At Anancaun there is a Field Station in which there is an Information Centre where a pamphlet can be obtained describing a nature trail taking one hour, which serves as a splendid introduction to the wildlife of Loch Maree.

Beyond Loch Maree pass through Kinlochewe and continue to Achnasheen (see tour 82) then follow Strath Bran to reach Gorstan. Here turn left on to the A835 Ullapool road. Later pass the shores of Loch Glascarnoch.

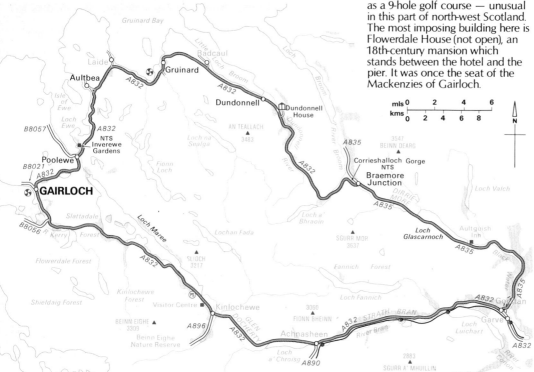

## LOCH GLASCARNOCH, Highland
This is a 'new' loch created by the Scottish Hydro-Electric Board as part of their Conon valley scheme. The waters are held back by a 2,670ft-long, 92ft-high dam. A tunnel carries the water 5 miles, dropping 550ft, to Mossford Power Station on Loch Luichart.

*Continue along the A835 to Braemore Junction.*

## BRAEMORE JUNCTION, Highland
The junction is between the Dundonell and Ullapool roads which converge on their way to Inverness. The breathtaking mountain scenery is typical of the route; to the north-east rise the vertical cliffs of 3,041ft Seana Bhraigh between the forests of Inverlach and Freevater. Southwards brood the remote Fannich Mountains, among them 3,673ft Sgurr Mor, overlooking cold, glassy Loch Fannich.

*Turn left on to the A832, SP 'Gairloch', and shortly pass the entrance to Corrieshalloch Gorge.*

## CORRIESHALLOCH GORGE, Highland
Over countless years water has tumbled into this 200ft box canyon, gradually wearing down the hard metamorphic rocks to create this spectacular and dramatic gorge (NTS). The river itself plunges in a long white plume 150ft over the Falls of Measach. In the crags and crannies in the walls of the canyon grow flora of the Highlands, elsewhere made scarce by the introduction of sheep, which eat it, and the extensive burning during the last century. Five species of fern grow here among plants with charming names such as hairgrass, mountain sorrel, woodmillet, goat willow and bird cherry. Below the falls is a suspension bridge with a viewing platform. The bridge was built by Sir John Fowler (1817-98), joint designer of the Forth Railway Bridge.

*The A832 climbs on to higher ground and later follows the Dundonnell River. To visit Dundonnell House turn right on to an unclassified road and cross over the river.*

## DUNDONNELL HOUSE, Highland
The gardens (OACT) of this 18th-century house are particularly fine. Numerous rare plants and shrubs can be seen, with Chinese and Japanese varieties predominating. There is also a colourful collection of exotic birds in the gardens.

*The main tour continues on the A832 to Dundonnell.*

## DUNDONNELL, Highland
The road to Dundonnell is known as 'destitution road', for it was built as a relief scheme, giving employment to crofters who were suffering terrible hardship as a result of the potato famine in 1847. Dundonnell itself is a climbing centre which lies at the head of Little Loch Broom, in the comparatively lush valley of Strath Beg; above tower the peaks of 3,484ft An Teallach. The name of this bleak mountain means The Forge, and refers to the smokelike mists which seem to perpetually shroud its peak.

*Continue alongside Little Loch Broom before rounding a headland to reach Gruinard.*

## GRUINARD, Highland
The scenery here, is, as often is the case in the Highlands, the outstanding feature. Stattic Point and Rumore Promontory reach with long arms to virtually enclose the islanded bay, and a long strip of golden sand arcs alongside the shore, closely followed by the road. From Gruinard Hill there are views of An Teallach, Ben More Coigeach, and towards the horizon the hills of Sutherland. Gruinard Island has a rather sad story. During World War II scientists came here to experiment with germ warfare; the result is that the island is infected with anthrax and landing on it is prohibited.

*Continue along the coast to the hamlet of Laide. Here turn inland and later rejoin the coast again near the outskirts of Aultbea.*

## AULTBEA, Highlands
Aultbea stands on the shores of Loch Ewe, a safe anchorage used extensively during both world wars by the Home Fleet. It was because of this that Sir Winston Churchill visited Aultbea in his capacity as 1st Lord of the Admiralty in 1939. Today the loch is being further developed by NATO (North Atlantic Treaty Organisation). Aultbea itself is a small crofting village, sheltered to some extent by the Isle of Ewe opposite. Today the inhabitants are wage earners, but in the past their croftlands — cultivated strips salvaged by back-breaking labour from this most hostile of landscapes — had to support entire communities with only a little fishing to supplement the family income. Today income is boosted by another kind of catch — tourists.

*Remain on the Gairloch road alongside Loch Ewe. In nearly 6 miles pass the entrance to Inverewe Gardens.*

## INVEREWE GARDENS, Highland
This is a truly unexpected delight, a magnificent garden (NTS) of 24 acres in which some 2,500 species of plants, trees and shrubs grow — some of them sub-tropical — on a Highland headland. When Osgood Mackenzie inherited the estate in 1861, this headland of Torridon sandstone had no more growing on its peat hags than some heather, crowberry and 2 dwarf willows. He began planting in 1865, first Corsican and Scots pines to act as a windshield, then gradually as these trees grew, he planted others in their shelter, as well as an astonishing variety of plants. Soil was carried manually in creels — large baskets — to provide a topsoil. Today, through his careful planning and experimentation, the gardens nurture, in subtly-designed surroundings, plants from such far-flung countries as Japan, Tasmania, Chile and South Africa.

*Continue into the village of Poolewe.*

## POOLEWE, Highland
Situated at the head of Loch Ewe, Poolewe is a centre for the excellent salmon and trout fishing to be had in the loch and river. There are 2 hotels to cater for visitors, as well as camping and caravan sites. Stunning views down the entire length of Loch Maree are much photographed and very memorable.

*At Poolewe turn inland and pass through rugged country before the return to Gairloch.*

Gruinard Bay is a popular feeding ground for many rare birds

# SIR WALTER SCOTT'S COUNTRY

This is where Scott, the great romantic novelist, chose to live; first at Ashiesteel House, and then at Abbotsford, where the wrote the *Waverley* novels. Scott was fascinated by Scottish history, and in these borderlands reflecting centuries of clan feuds and Anglo-Scottish rivalry he found much to inspire him.

## GALASHIELS, Borders

Galashiels was granted a charter in 1599. A pageant that is still celebrated and illustrates the town's history is the 'Braw Lads' gathering in early summer. The focal point for this event is the Mercat Cross, dating from 1695. Woollen mills have operated in the town since 1622, but the industrialisation of the 19th century brought both the industry and the town to the forefront. The Scottish College of Textiles, founded here in 1909, is the centre of wool studies in Scotland. In the town centre in front of the clock tower is the splendid war memorial, designed by Robert Lorimer — a statue of a mounted Border Reiver or moss-trooper — a bandit who raided the borderlands between the 16th and 18th centuries. Old Gala House, new headquarters of the Galashiels Art Club, dating from the 15th and 17th centuries, is one of the oldest buildings in the town and houses a unique 17th-century Scottish painted ceiling.

*Leave on the B6374 Melrose Road for Lowood, passing in 1½ miles, at Langlee, a tablet recording Sir Walter Scott's last journey from Italy to Abbotsford House shortly before his death. In 1½ miles go forward on to the B6360. Pass through Gattonside and in 2¼ miles follow SP 'Edinburgh' to join the A68 for Lauder.*

## LAUDER, Borders

Old Berwickshire's only royal burgh, Lauder, was granted its charter in 1502, although it claims to have been a burgh since William the Lion's reign. Situated on the Leader Water in Lauderdale, the town is an excellent angling centre. The Lauder Common Riding, held late summer, is one of the oldest horse riding festivals in the country.

*Continue on the A68 Edinburgh road through the broad valley. In 2 miles reach the famous Soutra Hill viewpoint (1,130ft). On the descent pass Fala village, and in 1¼ miles turn left on to the B645. In 2½ miles at Tynehead go forward on to the B6367 and 1¼ miles further turn left on to the A7, SP 'Galashiels'. Shortly enter the Gala Water valley and follow it to Stow.*

## STOW, Borders

The area around Stow is steeped in early history, and legend tells how King Arthur routed the Saxons here then built a church in thanksgiving. The old church of St Mary's was first consecrated in 1242 but is now a ruin, and the modern church which has replaced it, a pleasing 19th-century Gothic building, bears a 140ft-high spire. Opposite, a packhorse bridge dating from 1655, spans the Gala Water. These bridges are extremely rare, and are known as packhorse bridges because of the low parapets built to prevent heavily laden packhorses falling into the river.

*Continue on the A7 and in 3¾ miles turn right on to the B710 for Clovenfords.*

## CLOVENFORDS, Borders

Sir Walter Scott frequently stayed at Clovenfords, although the inn he used has now been replaced. The great novelist stayed here on visits while he was Sheriff of Selkirk, before he bought nearby Ashiesteel where he lived from 1804 to 1812, and wrote *Marmion*, *Lady of the Lake* and *The Lady of the Last Minstrel*. Wordsworth also stayed here in 1803.

*At the crossroads turn right on to the A72. Descend to the Tweed valley and turn right. Ashiesteel House can be seen across the river at this point. Continue for 5 miles to Walkerburn.*

## WALKERBURN, Borders

This village was created by Henry Ballantyne in 1854, when he and his sons built the first wool mill in which new wool went in one end, and finished cloth came out the other. He was the 7th generation of weavers in his family, and the 12th generation continue the business today. The Scottish Museum of Wool Textiles (OACT) is sited here, which illustrates the history of spinning and weaving from its beginnings to the present day.

*Continue on the A72 and in 2 miles enter Innerleithen.*

## INNERLEITHEN, Borders

Innerleithen was no more than a hamlet before 1790, when Alexander Brodie — a Traquair blacksmith who made his fortune in London — built the first wool mill here, a step which has developed into an important wool, spinning and knitwear industry. The early 19th century saw the growth of Innerleithen as a spa town because the mineral spring called Doo's Well was thought to have curative properties similar to the waters at Harrogate. Lord Traquair supplied a pump room in 1824, along with reading rooms and a verandah. Border games are held in the town annually, and a pageant known as the Cleikum Ceremony has been performed since 1900; it represents St Ronan ridding the town of the devil.

*Turn left on to the B709, and shortly cross the River Tweed, in ½ mile pass (right) the entrance to Traquair House.*

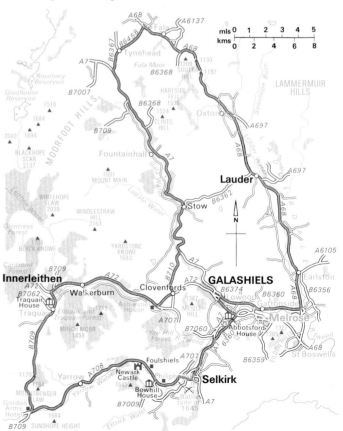

## TRAQUAIR HOUSE, Borders

Traquair House (OACT) is said to
be the oldest inhabited house in
Scotland. It was originally a
hunting lodge for Scottish kings;
the first recorded royal visit was
made in 1107. The oldest part of
the house contains the remains of
a 14th-century pele tower but the
present house was mainly built in
the 16th century, although the
entrance porch was added during
the last century. Twenty-seven
monarchs have stayed here over
the years, including Mary, Queen
of Scots. Examples of her
embroidery are among the
delightful treasures within the
house, but of all these the visitor
must not miss the Brew House,
where the potent Traquair Ale is
traditionally brewed in the old
vats.

*Continue through Traquair village
up the narrow valley of the
Paddock Burn to a summit of
1,170ft before descending to the
Gordon Arms Hotel on the Yarrow
Water. At the crossroads turn left
on to the A708 and in 9 miles pass
(left) Foulshiels.*

## FOULSHIELS, Borders

On the banks of the Yarrow Water
stands Foulshiels, where the
celebrated explorer Mungo Park
was born in 1771. He studied
medicine at Edinburgh and
became an assistant ship's surgeon
on the *Worcester,* bound for
Sumatra. He joined the African
Association in 1795 and set out on
a journey which lasted 19 months,
and included his capture by an
African chief and his subsequent
escape. He returned to Peebles

and settled as a doctor, but in
1805 the wanderlust overcame
him again and he once more set
off into the African interior where
he met his death in a fight with
natives on the Niger.

*To the right, on the opposite side
of the river, stands Newark Castle.*

## NEWARK CASTLE, Borders

This massive Border stronghold
crowning the steep banks of the
River Yarrow, was built during the
mid 15th century. Though now a
ruin, it was a royal hunting-seat, as
the surrounding Ettrick Forest was
famous for its abundance of
game. In 1548 the castle was the
scene of a seige by the English
under Lord Grey, and in 1645 100
men in Montrose's army were
executed here after the Battle of
Philiphaugh.

*In 1¼ miles pass (right) the B7039
which leads to Bowhill House.*

## BOWHILL HOUSE, Borders

Sir Walter Scott called it Sweet
Bowhill, for this great, rambling
house (OACT) has an easygoing,
comfortable atmosphere
attributable, perhaps, to those who
lived here. However, it was the 4th
and 5th Dukes of Buccleuch who
left their mark most distinctly. The
former was a close friend of Sir
Walter Scott, and the latter was a
notable agriculturist and among
the most enlightened of Victorian

landowners. Yet despite the
impression of a family home these
2 congenial men imparted to the
house, it contains many art
treasures worthy of a museum or
art gallery. Among these are 3
superb Mortlake tapestries, works
by the painter Lely and artists of
the Van Dyck School, and
beautiful French furniture. There
are also many curious relics of
history, such as the white linen
shirt in which the Duke of
Montrose was executed.

*In 2 miles bear right, then turn right
to cross Ettrick Water into Selkirk.*

## SELKIRK, Borders

Selkirk's position on the
borderlands put it in the front line
of Anglo-Scottish wars for 3
centuries, but in 1513 the town
was burned by the English forces
after the Battle of Flodden. A
statue of a standard-bearer,
representing the sole survivor of
this defeat, stands in the market
place and the town hall, with its
100ft spire, still sounds a nightly
curfew. Halliwells House
museum, in the town's oldest
surviving building recreates its
past roll as a house and
ironmongers shop.

*Leave Selkirk on the A7 Galashiels
road and in 2¾ miles turn right on
to the B6360 for Abbotsford.
Follow the River Tweed to
Abbotsford House.*

## ABBOTSFORD HOUSE, Borders

In 1811 Sir Walter Scott was
successful enough in his writing to
buy a modest farmhouse and farm
of about 110 acres in this
countryside he loved so much.
Here the *Waverley* novels were
written, bringing sufficient wealth
to enable Scott to knock down the
farmhouse and build Abbotsford
House (OACT) in 1822. The house
is of Tudor design and covered in
Gothic detail which sparked off
the distinctive baronial style seen
in so many Victorian houses.
Ruskin condemned it, Queen
Victoria referred to it as rather
gloomy, but Scott loved it. His
personality dominates the house
with its dark panelling, moulded
ceilings and great pseudo-
medieval firegrates. Scott's study is
just as he kept it. Gifts from the
great, including Goethe's
medallion portrait, keep company
with the fascinating objects Scott
collected himself — an engraved
tumbler which belonged to Robert
Burns and a lock of hair belonging
to Prince Charles Edward, are
among his treasures.

*In ½ mile, at the roundabout, take
the A6091 for the return to
Galashiels. Cross the River Tweed
and at the next roundabout take
the A7 for the town centre.*

## GLASGOW, Strathclyde

Glasgow owed its tremendous growth to the Industrial Revolution, during which time it became one of the major ship building and heavy engineering centres in the world. The centre of the city contains many gracious and imposing Victorian buildings, including, in George Square, the palatial City Chambers (OACT), which were opened by Queen Victoria in 1888. Glasgow Cathedral stands on the site of a church built in AD534 by St Mungo — the traditional founder of the city. A good deal of 12th and 13th century work survives in the cathedral, especially in the magnificent crypt, which now serves as Glasgow's parish church. The city is richly endowed with museums, art galleries, parks and gardens. The Glasgow Art Gallery and Museum, in Kelvingrove, contains the finest municipal art collection in the United Kingdom as well as extensive collections covering archaeology and natural history; Pollok House is a lovely 18th-century mansion, set in beautiful gardens, which houses paintings by such artists as El Greco, Goya and William Blake. Haggs Castle, in St Andrew's Drive, was built in 1585 and is now a museum, created especially for children, whose theme is the exploration of time. One of Glasgow's most famous buildings is the School of Art (OACT). It was designed in a brilliantly original style, by C.R. Macintosh and completed in 1909. Other museums in Glasgow include the Royal Fusilier's Regimental Museum, the Hunterian and the Peoples Palace, which contains a visual record of the people and life of Glasgow, and the Transport Museum. Of Glasgow's hundreds of acres of splendid parks and gardens perhaps the most exciting is the Botanic Gardens. The astonishing Burrell Collection — with its paintings, pottery porcelain, precious metalwork, stained glass, etc — is housed in a special gallery in Pollok Country Park.

*Leave Glasgow on the A82 Great Western Road, SP 'Dumbarton Crianlarich'. In 12 miles follow SP 'Crianlarich' to skirt Dumbarton. Cross the Leven Valley and pass Alexandria. At the roundabout junction with the A811, at the end of the by-pass, turn off to visit Balloch.*

## BALLOCH, Strathclyde

Its position on the banks of Loch Lomond has made this little village popular with holidaymakers and yachtsmen. Balloch Castle Country Park (OACT) is an extensive area of grassland surrounded with woods which includes among its attractions a walled garden and a nature trail. From the village a visit can be made to Cameron Loch Lomond Wildlife Park.

# THE GARDEN OF GLASGOW

Within a few short miles of Scotland's largest city and seaport is the natural beauty of the loch country, the queen of which is Loch Lomond, largest of Britain's waters — and one of the prettiest. Glasgow too has its treasures; buildings, museums and art galleries which rank among the best in the world.

Glasgow Cathedral is the only complete medieval cathedral in Scotland

## CAMERON LOCH LOMOND, WILDLIFE PARK, Strathclyde

Among the many creatures which roam the parkland here are bears, bison, yak and deer. Also in the park is a childrens' zoo, a waterfowl sanctuary and numerous leisure facilities. Cameron House (OACT) is a beautiful and historic family home that is particularly associated with the 18th-century novelist Tobias Smollett.

*The main tour continues northwards, on the A82, SP 'Crianlarich', to Rossdhu House.*

## ROSSDHU HOUSE, Strathclyde

This charming Georgian mansion (not open) is the home of the chiefs of Clan Colquhoun. It was built near the loch-side site of the original 15th-century castle, and the grounds include a sweep of beach that is ideal for picnics and walks.

*Continue on the A82, passing Loch Lomond on the right.*

## LOCH LOMOND, Strathclyde

Often described as the Queen of Scottish Lakes, Loch Lomond is the largest area of land-locked water in Britain and stretches some 23 miles from Ardlui in the north down to Balloch in the south. The tremendous beauty of the loch is enhanced by the many islands which are dotted across its southern waters. Five of the islands form part of the Loch Lomond National Nature Reserve.

*Continue to Luss.*

## LUSS, Strathclyde

Luss is beautifully set at the mouth of Glen Luss and looks over a group of wooded islands towards the distinctive summit of 3,192ft Ben Lomond. Sir James Colquhoun built the church in 1875 in memory of his father, who drowned in the loch. In the churchyard is an ancient effigy of St Kessog, one of many missionary saints who lived in the Loch Lomond area during the 5th and 6th centuries, and an ancient stone font.

*Continue north on the A82 turning left on to the A83 at Tarbet, then continue to Arrochar.*

## ARROCHAR, Strathclyde

This little touring and yachting centre is set at the head of Loch Long and makes a superb base from which to visit the rugged mountains and wooded expanses of the Argyll Forest Park. Away to the north-west is 2,891ft Ben Arthur, popularly known as the Cobbler from its Gaelic name An Gobaileach; and to the west, in the heart of Ardgarten Forest, is 2,580ft Brack.

*Turn sharp left on to the A814, SP 'Helensburgh', to pass Loch Long.*

## LOCH LONG, Strathclyde

Stretching like a long, thin finger from the Clyde estuary up to Arrochar, this sea loch is increasingly popular with yachtsmen from Glasgow. The whole of its western shore is bounded by the huge Argyll Forest Park (see page 23), which includes the line of hills known as Argyll's Bowling Green.

*Continue along the A814 past Garelochhead.*

## GARELOCHHEAD, Strathclyde

Yachts and many other pleasure craft ply up and down Gare Loch during the holiday season, and large ships are frequently to be seen laid up in the loch's waters. Garelochhead itself is a well-known resort with a green backdrop bordered by the long ridges of Argyll's Bowling Green. Away to the east is a range of lonely hills whose highest point is 2,339ft Beinn Chaorach.

*For a detour to the Rosneath Peninsula (adds 29 miles if Coulport is visited) turn right on to the B833, SP 'Kilcreggan'.*

Inset: Loch Long, over 17 miles long and one of the deepest lochs in Scotland, is used for submarine trials

## KILCREGGAN, Strathclyde

Situated at the tip of the Rosneath Peninsula, where many Clyde businessmen have their homes, Kilcreggan is linked by ferry to Gourock, across the Clyde estuary. The peninsula figures in Sir Walter Scott's novel *The Heart of Midlothian,* in which Knockderry Castle, 3 miles north-west of Kilcreggan, is called Knock Dunder. The road which runs round the tip of the Rosneath Peninsula ends at Coulport, which stands on the east shore of Loch Long and looks across to the Cowal Peninsula and Argyll Forest Park.

*The main tour continues on the A814 Helensburgh road from Garelochhead to Rhu.*

## RHU, Strathclyde

A notorious smuggling centre during the 18th and 19th centuries, Rhu is now used by respectable yachtsmen. Henry Bell, who launched the pioneer Clyde steamboat *Comet* in 1812, is buried in the churchyard. Glenarn Gardens (OACT), on the outskirts

Helensburgh was developed on the lower Clyde in about 1776 by Sir James Colquhoun

of the village, contain a large variety of shrubs and are particularly notable for their remarkable collection of rhododendrons.

*Continue along the A814 to Helensburgh.*

## HELENSBURGH, Strathclyde

The flywheel from the *Comet,* Europe's first steam-driven ship, along with an anvil used in its construction, are preserved in Helensburgh's Hermitage Park. Henry Bell, who designed and built the craft, is commemorated by an obelisk in the town. Another famous inventor, John Logie Baird, who pioneered television, was born here. Helensburgh is set in magnificent mountain scenery, and the road which leads northwards into Glen Fruin is particularly notable.

*Continue on the A814 to Dumbarton.*

## DUMBARTON, Strathclyde

Dumbarton Rock, a magnificent 240ft crag rising above the

confluence of the Rivers Leven and Clyde, has dominated Dumbarton's history since at least as early as the 5th century. It was at the centre of the independent kingdom of Strathclyde, and a royal castle stood on the rock until the Middle Ages. Little survives of the medieval castle, but considerable portions of the fortifications built during the 17th and 18th centuries still stand (AM). Preserved in the castle is a sundial presented to the town by Mary, Queen of Scots during her brief stay at the castle in 1548. One of the oldest buildings in the town is Glencairn House, which dates from 1623. Boat-building, which included the construction of the famous clipper *Cutty Sark,* was once the town's principal industry, but today Dumbarton is mainly concerned with the blending and bottling of whisky.

*Leave on the A814 Glasgow road and in 2 miles turn right on to the A82. In 11 miles re-enter Glasgow along the Great Western Road.*

## NORTH TO DUNNET HEAD

The rocky, wave-torn headland of Dunnet Head extends far into the stormy Pentland Firth to become the northernmost point on the British mainland. Along the coast are rocky cliffs and small sandy bays where seals bask in the sun, high dunes hiding smothered villages, and ferry points for the Orkneys.

The small port of Helmsdale is famous for its lobsters.

**HELMSDALE, Highland**
This small fishing town at the mouth of the River Helmsdale has a natural harbour which offers a safe anchorage and sandy beaches.

*Leave Helmsdale on the A9 'Wick' road and climb on to moorland before descending steeply to the village of Berriedale.*

**BERRIEDALE, Highland**
Red-deer antlers decorate the post office and old smithy of this pleasant village, which is situated at the mouth of Berridale Water. Remains of a 14th-century castle stand here, and the house of Langwell stands in fine gardens where a variety of plants grow in exposed conditions (gardens only open). Langwell Water rises on a distant slope of the 2,313ft Morven and meets Berriedale Water here.

*Ascend from Berriedale and continue, with good views along the rocky coast. Pass Dunbeath Castle on the right and descend to Dunbeath.*

**DUNBEATH, Highland**
This scattered fishing village probably derives its name from an ancient Pictish broch which lies about ½ mile north-west and is called Dun Beath. The castle of the same name (not open) perches on a lofty promontory 1 mile south and, despite having been enlarged in the 19th century, retains much of its original 15th-century work. It was besieged and captured by Jacobites during the Risings. To the north-east of Dunbeath is the Lhaidhay Croft Museum in an early 19th-century Caithness longhouse.

*Continue to Latheronwheel.*

**LATHERONWHEEL, Highland**
Latheronwheel is the residential half of a partnership with its sister community of Latheron and has a small but attractive harbour at the bottom of a steep lane.

*Continue to Latheron.*

**LATHERON, Highland**
Sister village of Latheronwheel, Latheron is at the centre of a district which is well known for its ancient remains. A homestead of early Iron-Age date is the latest of several ruins recently excavated about 1 mile north at The Wag. A hill above the local church is surmounted by a tower which houses the church bell.

*Proceed to Lybster.*

**LYBSTER, Highland**
This is the largest of several attractive fishing villages that manage to make a living on this wild and rocky coast. Its church, built with locally dressed flagstones, has a west door and chancel entrance that are typical of an ancient design used in the area. A road east of the village leads to The Grey Cairns of Camster (AM), which are two chambered tombs from the prehistoric megalithic period.

*Continue to Mid Clyth.*

**MID CLYTH, Highland**
Appropriately named the Hill of Many Stones (AM), the slopes behind this village feature 22 prehistoric rows containing 192 stones. They are unique in Scotland, but similar structures exist elsewhere.

*Continue along the A9 to Thrumster.*

**THRUMSTER, Highland**
Many prehistoric remains survive in the area round Thrumster, particularly in the vicinity of Loch Yarrows. These include brochs, cairns, and various scattered stones, and there is a standing stone just south of the village school.

*Continue to Wick.*

**WICK, Highland**
Situated on Wick Bay at the mouth of the Wick River, this ancient Royal Burgh is a market town and fishing port with two good harbours. One of these was initially designed by Thomas Telford and later improved by Stephenson. Wick is famous for the Caithness Glassworks (open) and there is also a town Heritage Centre. The ruined Castle of Old Wick (AM), also known as Castle Oliphant, stands 1½ miles south-east. Close by are the curious rock stacks known as Brig O'Tram and Brough.

*A detour can be made from the main route by leaving Wick on the unclassified Ackergill Street and*

*driving 3 miles, passing Wick Airport and the castles of Girnigoe and Sinclair to reach Noss Head.*

**CASTLE GIRNIGOE AND CASTLE SINCLAIR, Highland**
Close together in a striking situation at Noss Head are these two picturesquely ruined castles, both abandoned in the mid 17th century.

*On the main route, leave Wick on the A9 SP 'John O' Groats' for Reiss.*

**REISS, Highland**
Reiss stands at a road junction a little inland from Sinclair's Bay, which has one of the longest stretches of sand on this coast. On the shore is modernized Ackergill Tower, which claims to be one of Scotland's oldest inhabited castles.

*Turn right with the main road and skirt Sinclair's Bay to the right. Continue to Keiss.*

**KEISS, Highland**
The remains of the 16th-century Keiss Castle stand on the coast to the north of this Sinclair's Bay fishing village, near its modern replacement.

*Continue to Freswick.*

**FRESWICK, Highland**
The transition from land to sea near this village is a gentle affair of green slopes and broad sands around Freswick Bay. Close by are the ruins of 15th-century Bucholly Castle.

*Continue along the A9. On the approach to John O' Groats a short detour can be made from the main route by taking an unclassified right turn to Duncansby Head.*

**DUNCANSBY HEAD, Highland**
Here, at the extreme north-eastern point of the Scottish mainland, spectacular sandstone cliffs soar to over 200ft above the sea in a massive display of strength that must have alarmed would-be invaders in times past. Remains of an ancient watch tower still stand on the head, close to a lighthouse, and the great chasm of Long Geo runs inland from the sea.

*On the main tour, continue to the end of the A9 at John O' Groats.*

**JOHN O' GROATS, Highland**
The shortest distance by road between this village and Land's End in Cornwall is exactly 877 miles. Its name is derived from that of a Dutchman who came to Scotland in the 15th century, and its beach is famous for the attractive little seashells known as Groatie Buckies.

*Return along the A9 for ½ mile and turn right on to the A836 SP 'Thurso'. After 2 miles a detour can be made from the main route along an unclassified left turn to Canisbay.*

**CANISBAY, Highland**
The most 18th-century church in this village contains a number of interesting monuments, including one to members of the de Groot family. Jan de Groot gave his name to John O' Groats.

*Berriedale Water flows through a long valley to join the sea.*

The stacks of Duncansby rise to the south of John O' Groats.

A salmon leap is provided at the Bridge of Forss.

*On the main tour, continue along the A836 to reach Mey, with views over the Pentland Firth to the right. Various access roads lead to the shoreline from the tour route.*

## MEY, Highland
Grey seals are a common sight in the little coastal bays of the Pentland Firth, and views across the water from this village take in the distant Orkneys. One of the best vantage points in the area is in the gardens (open occasionally) of the Castle of Mey, famous as the summer residence of HM the Queen Mother since 1952. The building dates from the mid 16th century.
*Proceed to Dunnet.*

## DUNNET, Highland
Dunnet Church has a saddleback tower and is thought to date from the 14th century. The village itself overlooks Dunnet Bay to the south. St John's Loch, nearby, is popular with trout fishermen.

*A detour can be made from the main route at Dunnet by turning right on to the B855 to reach Dunnet Head.*

## DUNNET HEAD, Highland
Fine views from this, the most northerly point in Britain, extend across the rough seas of the Pentland Firth to the Orkneys and the 450ft rock stack of the Old Man of Hoy. A lighthouse stands on the headland.
*On the main route, skirt the sands of Dunnet Bay to reach Castletown.*

## CASTLETOWN, Highland
This village was founded in 1824 to house workers employed in a nearby quarry once famous worldwide for its paving stones. It has a picturesque little harbour and

stands close to the 2-mile long sands of Dunnet Bay.

*Continue to Thurso.*

## THURSO, Highland
An expanding resort and residential town on the sandy shores of Thurso Bay, this charming place is the most northerly town on the British mainland. It stands on the River Thurso, which is well known for its salmon and flows into the bay between the craggy cliffs of Holborn Head and Clardon Head. Close to the harbour are well-restored houses dating from the 17th and 18th centuries, and ruined St Peter's Church stands on a site occupied since the Vikings. The remains that stand here today are of a 17th-century building. Thurso's interesting museum maintains good collections of plants and fossils, and boasts a lovely little Runic cross. Roofless Thurso Castle, birthplace of the 18th-century statistician and agriculturalist Sir John Sinclair, stands ½ mile north-east of the town. Beyond this is Harold's Tower, which was erected over the 12th-

century grave of Harold, Earl of Caithness, and has subsequently been used as the clan's burial place. Sir William Smith, founder of the Boys' Brigade, was born at Pennyland in 1854.
*Leave by the A836 'Tongue' road and after a short distance reach the A882 junction. This offers a detour to Scrabster.*

## SCRABSTER, Highland
A ferry from Stromness in the Orkneys crosses the Pentland Firth to Scrabster, which stands on sandy Thurso Bay and is sheltered in the north-east by the remarkable Holborn Head. This headland is split from top to bottom by several chasms, the largest of which is open to the sea and spanned by two natural rock arches. Near by the precipitous rock of Clett rises 150ft from the sea.

*On the main tour, continue along the A836 to reach Dounreay.*

## DOUNREAY POWER STATION, Highland
The world's first prototype fast-breeder reactor was constructed at

the experimental nuclear power station here in the 1950s. A visitor centre with guided tours of the plant is open from May to September.

*Continue to Reay.*

## REAY, Highland
Situated near the head of Sandside Bay, this village has a good 18th-century church that can be considered typical of the area. It has an external staircase leading to the belfry, and there is a carved Celtic cross slab in the churchyard. The bay's broad sands, appreciated by the holiday-maker today, were the death of the old village that was overwhelmed by them in the 18th century.

*Continue and in 4½ miles turn left on to the A897 'Helmsdale' road to enter Strath Halladale. Pass through the small angling resort of Forsinard and cross bleak moorland. Leave by passing little Loch an Ruathair to reach the edge of Kinbrace village.*

## KINBRACE, Highland
Two burns meet near this lonely crofting village to form the River Helmsdale, and the local countryside is rich in prehistoric remains. Several chambered cairns can be seen near the Kinbrace Burn. In 1877 the 3rd Duke of Sutherland devised a local reclamation scheme to increase his holding of arable land.

*Continue along the A897 beside the River Helmsdale and pass through the Strath of Kildonan to reach Kildonan.*

## KILDONAN, Highland
At some time in the 19th century small quantities of gold dust were found in Kildonan Burn, but the minor gold rush that resulted from the discovery fizzled out when efforts to extract it failed. Prehistoric rows of stone stand north-west on Leirable Hill.

*Descend through the Strath of Kildonan and return to Helmsdale.*

# FROM THE CAPITAL OF THE HIGHLANDS

Close to Inverness are some of Scotland's best-known features. The Moray Firth offers sheltered boating and fishing, Loch Ness broods with mystery in the bottom of the Great Glen, and the engineering prowess of the 19th century is proved by the locks and cuts of the Caledonian Canal.

**INVERNESS, Highland**

Inverness, often referred to as the capital of the Highlands, is situated amid beautiful scenery with views across the Beauly and Inverness Firths. Buildings of interest include the early Victorian castle commanding a fine position overlooking River Ness, with a monument to Flora MacDonald; the High Church, parts of which date from the 13th century; Cromwell's citadel clock-tower; 16th-century Abertarff House, northern headquarters of the NTS; An Comunn Gaidhealach, the headquarters of the Gaelic Language Organisation with a permanent exhibition and sales centre on Highland culture; 19th-century St Andrew's Cathedral; the 130ft high Tolbooth Steeple of 1791, and Dunbar's Hospital, an almshouse of 1668. Also of interest are the Library, Museum and Art Gallery, the modern Eden Court Theatre and the Gothic-style Town House. A good viewpoint is at the cemetery on Tomnahurich Hill between the river and canal. Craig

Phadraig, to the west, is crowned by a vitrified fort. North of the town is the impressive Kessock bridge, carrying the A9 over the Beauly Firth. It has an overall length of 3,260ft, main span of 744ft and height above high water of 90ft.

*On the main tour, leave Inverness by the A862 SP 'Beauly' and after 1 mile cross the Caledonian Canal.*

**CALEDONIAN CANAL**

Created in the 19th century to provide passage between the Irish and North Seas, this 60½-mile waterway along the remarkable Great Glen uses 22 miles of canal to link lochs and virtually split Scotland in two. Without it the sailing boats of the day would have had to risk the passage round Cape Wrath.

*Continue along the A862 to skirt the south shore of Beauly Firth, and after 7 miles a detour to Moniack Castle can be made by turning left on to an unclassified road then in ½ mile turning left again and taking the next turning right.*

**MONIACK CASTLE, Highland**
This former Lovat stronghold (open)

*Urquhart Castle was ruined before 1715.*

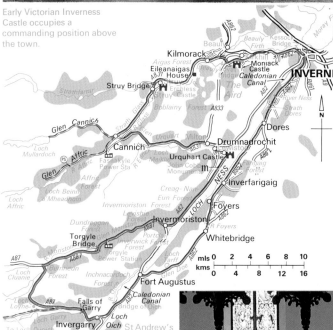

*Early Victorian Inverness Castle occupies a commanding position above the town.*

*St Andrew's Cathedral was built in 1866-69 at a cost of £20,000*

is now a major wine-making centre.
*On the main route continue on the A862 and in 3 miles cross the River Beauly at Lovat Bridge then branch left on to the A831 SP 'Cannich' and continue to Kilmorack.*

**KILMORACK, Highland**
South-east of this village is 19th-century Beaufort Castle, seat of the Chief of Clan Fraser. Near by are the ruins of an earlier stronghold. Although the castle is not open to the public it can be seen from foot and bridle paths that cross the Beauly River.

*Continue along thickly wooded river banks and reach Crask of Aigas. Just past this hamlet, on the other side of the River Beauly, is Eileanaigas House.*

**EILEANAIGAS HOUSE, Highland**
Situated in lovely gardens between two arms of the River Beauly, this house (not open) was the home of Lord Lovat in 1697 and that of Victorian prime minister Robert Peel. It is also associated with the Sobiéski brothers, who claimed direct descendancy from Prince Charles Edward.

*Continue along the Beauly Valley, passing Erchless Castle before crossing Struy Bridge.*

**STRUY BRIDGE, Highland**
Near this bridge the River Farrar joins the Glass to form the Beauly River. Beautiful walks along Glen Strathfarrar penetrate deep into mountain country from here, eventually reaching the lovely expanse of Loch Monar.

*Continue through Struy and along Strath Glass to reach Cannich.*

**CANNICH, Highland**
Cannich is a charming stone-built Highland village in a beautiful woodland setting at the south end of Strath Glass. The area is popular with walkers.

*Pleasant detours from Cannich lead through Glen Cannich and Glen Affric, each of which is penetrated by about 10 miles of road. At the end of each glen turn round and return to the main route in Cannich.*

### GLEN CANNICH, Highland
The woodland scenery in this glen is outstanding. After passing under the slopes of 2,120ft Beinn a'Chairein the road enters densely forested hill country and follows the River Cannich to tiny Loch Carrie. After skirting the banks of Carrie the road reaches Loch Mullardoch, an attractive water which backs up behind the main dam of the Cannich hydro-electric scheme.

### GLEN AFFRIC, Highland
In many ways Glen Affric is very much like its neighbour Cannich. After the hamlet of Fasnakyle, where a power station is situated, the road passes the Dog Fall and emerges amid birch and pine trees that surround Loch Beinn a'Mheadhoin. Magnificent scenery accompanies the road as it nears its end by the isolated expanse of Loch Affric, with 3,401ft Sgurr na Lapaich rising above the water.

*On the main tour, continue along the A831 'Drumnadrochit' road to climb away from Strath Glass and enter Glen Urquhart. Pass Loch Meiklie and follow the River Enrick between pine-clad slopes, through Milton to Drumnadrochit.*

### DRUMNADROCHIT, Highland
Situated on the River Enrick and the west side of Loch Ness, this village is a popular centre for walking, angling, climbing, and pony-trekking. The Official Loch Ness Monster Exhibition located here has exhibits and audio-visual displays and now includes the International House of Heraldry and also glass-blowing.

*Turn right on to the A82 SP 'Fort William' and in 2¼ miles enter the Great Glen and pass Urquhart Castle on the left.*

### URQUHART CASTLE, Highland
Ruined Urquhart Castle overlooks Loch Ness from a lonely promontory and is one of the largest castles in Scotland. It dates from the 14th century and has had a long and violent history. Many sightings of the Loch Ness Monster have been reported from this part of the loch.

### LOCH NESS, Highland
One of a chain of lochs connected by the Caledonian Canal in the Great Glen, Loch Ness extends 24 miles from near Inverness to Fort Augustus and in places is over 700ft deep. It is world famous as the reported home of the Loch Ness Monster or Nessie as it has become known. Sightings of the creature have been reported since the 7th century, but these have swelled from a trickle to a flood since the road along the wooded west shore was opened in 1933. Investigation is hampered by the almost opaque quality of the water, which is stained brown by the peat-laden streams that feed the loch.

*Continue to Invermoriston.*

### INVERMORISTON, Highland
This small town at the east end of Glen Moriston faces Loch Ness and is bordered to the north by the Hills of Invermoriston.

*Turn right on to the A887 'Kyle of Lochalsh' road, enter wooded Glen Moriston, and climb gradually beside the river to cross Torgyle Bridge.*

### TORGYLE BRIDGE, Highland
The reach of the River Moriston spanned by this bridge is known for its fine rapids. Torgyle Power Station can be seen to the left.

*Continue through the glen to meet the 'Fort William' road and turn left on to the A87. Climb on to bare mountains beside Loch Loyne, and continue with spectacular views before passing an AA viewpoint and descending beside Loch Garry. Here a single-track road to the right leads 22 miles west to Loch Quoich and Kinloch Hourn, passing through some of the wildest scenery in Scotland. On the tour, continue along the A87 to pass the Falls of Garry.*

### FALLS OF GARRY, Highland
At the east end of Loch Garry the River Garry plunges over rocks and ledges in a series of beautiful waterfalls. It is now part of a hydro-electric scheme. The forests to the west of this area can be explored by means of planned walks, nature trails, and woodland paths.

*Beautiful Glen Moriston forms part of a large hydro-electric scheme.*

*Proceed to Invergarry.*

### INVERGARRY, Highland
South of this little hamlet, on the shores of Loch Oich, are the impressive ruins of Invergarry Castle. It was once the seat of the MacDonells of Glengarry and replaced castles destroyed in 1654 and 1689. Bonnie Prince Charlie stayed here before and after the battle of Culloden, and the 'Butcher' Duke of Cumberland had the building burned in reprisal. Just north of the ruins the River Garry flows into Loch Oich, and the whole area is framed by spectacular Highland mountain scenery.

*Turn left on to the A82, skirting the north end of Loch Oich.*

### LOCH OICH, Highland
Small but beautiful, this is the highest of the Great Glen lochs in the Caledonian Canal chain. Bonnie Prince Charlie rallied his clansmen at Aberchalder Lodge, near the north end, before crossing the Corriveyairack Pass on his way to Edinburgh and England. The road that runs along the east shores of the loch was built by General Wade as a military way.

*Telford spent from 1803 to 1847 building the Caledonian Canal.*

*Continue to Fort Augustus, crossing the Caledonian Canal.*

### FORT AUGUSTUS, Highland
Wooded hill country surrounds this hamlet, which stands at the south-west end of Loch Ness in the Great Glen. It takes its name from a Hanoverian outpost that was built against the Jacobite Highlanders after the first Rising in 1715. General Wade built the first fort in 1730 and it was named after William Augustus, the Duke of Cumberland, who was later to become known as the Butcher of Culloden. In the second Rising of 1745 the Highlanders actually captured the fort and managed to hold it until the Prince's defeat at Culloden marked the end of the Jacobite cause. The site of the fort is now occupied by a 19th-century abbey and a Catholic boys' school. The Great Glen Exhibition in Fort Augustus relates the history and traditions of the area.

*Turn right on to the B862 'Whitebridge, Dores' road and follow a former military road which eventually leads to Inverness. Climb steeply through Glen Doe and enjoy magnificent scenery to the north, then pass Loch Tarff and pass through forested areas to reach Whitebridge.*

### WHITEBRIDGE, Highland
Here the River Foyers is joined by the River Fechlin, which flows from remote Loch Killin in the hills rising to the south-east.

*Proceed for 1 mile and turn left on to the B852 SP 'Foyers'. Descend through woodland to the east shore of Loch Ness to reach Foyers.*

### FOYERS, Highland
This village on the eastern shores of Loch Ness is best known for the beautiful Falls of Foyers. The uppermost of these drops 30ft and the lower 90ft, but their scenic impact was considerably reduced when they were starved of water by the opening of Britain's first hydro-electric scheme in 1896.

*Continue alongside Loch Ness, with fine mountain views to the west, and reach Inverfarigaig.*

### INVERFARIGAIG, Highland
A permanent Forestry Commission display and several marked trails have been provided here to help the public understand the industry and wildlife of the area.

*Continue to Dores.*

### DORES, Highland
Dores stands in Strath Dores at the point where it meets Loch Ness and is well situated for walking and angling. Aldourie Castle lies 2 miles north off the B862 and has a seat of the Frazers since 1750. The first castle was built here in 1626, but the earliest work evident today dates from the 18th century.

*Join the B862 and follow Strath Dores, then the River Ness, for the return to Inverness.*

# CAPITAL OF THE HIGHLANDS

Between Loch Ness and the cold North Sea lies Inverness, now dubbed Capital of the Highlands. South and east is a land of high mountains and deep glens, glamorous ski-resorts and bleak battlefields — among them Culloden, where Bonnie Prince Charlie was finally defeated.

The house on Culloden Moor that is reputed to have been used by the Duke of Cumberland during Culloden

## INVERNESS, Highland
King David I proclaimed Inverness a royal burgh in the 12th century, and it is he who first built a stone keep on Castle Hill. The present castle was built in 1834, and is now a courthouse and administrative centre (Inverness is the headquarters of the Highland Region). Within is an exhibition illustrating the history of the Gael, a Highland craft shop and an information centre. A statue of Flora MacDonald stands on the castle esplanade. Erected in 1899, it looks towards the hiding place where she hid Bonnie Prince Charlie after his defeat in 1746. Little of the old town which huddled under David's royal castle is left, and the town centre is a new development of the 1960s. Reminders of the past do remain, such as Abertarff House, the headquarters of the National Trust for Scotland. This dates from 1593 and has a rare turnpike stair — a medieval spiral staircase. The Tolbooth Steeple in Church Street, built in 1791, is where dangerous criminals were kept. St Andrew's Cathedral, with its fine carved columns, is also worth a visit. Inverness, a city of much greenery and many trees, sits astride the River Ness which flows between tree-lined banks and deserves the title Capital of the Highlands.

*Leave on the A9 Perth road then shortly turn left, SP 'Croy', on to the B9006 to reach Culloden Moor.*

## CULLODEN MOOR, Highland
Upon this field (NTS) on 16 April, 1746 the Jacobite cause was finally quelled and the English finally conquered the Scots. The Jacobite army had retreated from England and returned to the Highlands, where the English army, under the Duke of Cumberland, caught up with them. The night before the battle Bonnie Prince Charlie had attempted a surprise attack on the English, but before they were within 2 miles of the camp the English sounded the alert — they had been discovered. They returned to Culloden House where they were billeted, only to find Cumberland hot on their heels and ready for battle the next morning. After the Jacobite's crushing defeat, Cumberland took no prisoners and gave no quarter; the wounded were murdered, prisoners shot, retreating Jacobites chased and cut down. This, and the reign of terror created by Cumberland in the aftermath, earned him the nickname 'Butcher' Cumberland. Prince Charles escaped, eventually to France, but his followers were persecuted to destruction. Today the battlefield is marked by a cairn erected in 1881 which stands 20ft high. Old Leanach Cottage, which survived the battle that had raged around it, is now a museum, housing a display of historical maps and relics of the battle; other features of the field are pointed out here, and a topographical battle plan shows how the battle was fought. There is also a Trust Visitor Centre with a museum and an exhibition.

¼ mile beyond the Visitor Centre turn right, SP 'Clava Cairns'. At the next crossroads the road ahead leads to Clava Cairns and Standing Stones (AM) dated at 1800-1500 BC. The Cairns were originally domed and used as burial chambers, and are among the most complete in Scotland. The main tour continues on the B851 Daviot road. After 3¾ miles turn left on to the A9, SP 'Perth'. In 9 miles an unclassified road (right) leads to Tomatin.

## TOMATIN, Highland
This Strath Dearn village is situated on the River Findhorn, which has its source in the lonely wilderness of the Monadhliath range of mountains, to the south-west. The district has many distilleries, the peaty streams providing water ideal for the brewing of whisky. The streams and rivers also attract large numbers of anglers, for whom Tomatin caters admirably. The village was once a royal hunting ground belonging to Inverness Castle.

*Later pass Slochd Mor (1,332ft) and 3½ miles farther branch left on to the A938, SP 'Grantown', to reach Carrbridge.*

## CARRBRIDGE, Highland
Carrbridge is a popular skiing resort in the Cairngorms, and here the tourist season is a long one — skiing in the winter, fishing and touring in the summer — so there are several hotels and guesthouses. The Landmark Visitor Centre here provides a superb introduction to the area. A multi-screen slide show tells, in sound and vision, the story of the Highlands from the last Ice Age to the present day, and in the evenings film shows are given, often about natural hisory. Also to

be found here is a craft and book shop, a nature trail and an open-air sculpture park, the whole complex beautifully set in delightful countryside beside a small lochan.

*Continue on the A938 and after 1¾ miles turn left on to the B9007, SP 'Forres'. After 6¾ miles turn right, SP 'Lochindorb', to reach Lochindorb Castle.*

## LOCHINDORB CASTLE, Highland
The ruins of Lochinbord Castle lie on a small island in a loch of the same name, 969ft above sea level, in the middle of desolate Dava Moor. The castle was a hunting seat for the powerful Comyns, and was occupied for 3 months by Edward I in 1303 during his Scottish campaign. During the latter half of the 14th century it became a stronghold of the Wolf of Badenoch, who terrorised the surrounding countryside, and is notorious for his burning of Elgin Cathedral in 1390. The castle was destroyed during the reign of James II.

*Continue along the unclassified road and after 3¼ miles turn left on to the A939, then turn right on to the A940 to reach Forres.*

## FORRES, Grampian
This is the ancient burgh where King Duncan held court and, in Shakespeare's play *Macbeth*, the place to which Macbeth and Banquo were travelling when they met the 3 'weird sisters'. See also page 27.

*Continue on the A96 Inverness road to Brodie.*

## BRODIE, Grampian
The land belongs to the Brodie of Brodie, whose family is one of the oldest untitled families in Britain, and has owned the lands here since the 11th century. It is

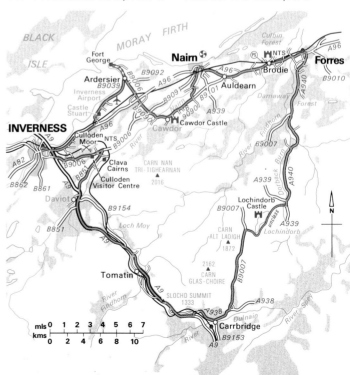

Inverness's Victorian castle occupies the same strategic site as its predecessor

Scottish courtesy to call the head of the family simply 'Brodie'. The castle (NTS), which stands north of the village dates from the 15th century with 16th-century additions. It was burnt down in 1645 by Lord Gordon on behalf of Montrose during the campaign for Charles I. However, some parts survived and were rebuilt, then added to again in 1840. There is a magnificent private collection of Dutch, Flemish and English paintings in the castle.

*Continue on the A96 Inverness road to Auldearn.*

### AULDEARN, Highland
Auldearn is chiefly remembered for a battle fought here in 1645 between Montrose, for Charles I, and the Covenanters. Montrose defeated the enemy, who outnumbered his force 2 to 1, by what is considered his most brilliant tactical display. A royal castle once stood here, but now all that overlooks the battlefield is the peaceful 17th-century Doocot of Broath (NTS) — a circular dovecot which must have housed a considerable number of birds within its superb masonry.

*Continue on the A96 to Nairn.*

### NAIRN, Highland
Nairn is a popular resort on the Moray Firth, sometimes referred to as the Brighton of the North. It is easy to see what has made this town so popular, with its surprisingly dry and sunny climate, splendidly wooded countryside and dramatic river valleys around it. There are also fine sands with good bathing and 3 golf courses. The harbour was built to plans by Thomas Telford in 1820, but has since been enlarged.

*Leave on the B9090, SP 'Cawdor', and after 2¾ miles turn right to reach Cawdor Castle.*

### CAWDOR CASTLE, Highland
A great castle (OACT) dominates the little village of Cawdor gathered at its feet. The tower keep of the castle dates from 1454, although there is some stone work which dates back to 1386. This once stood on its own, surrounded by a dry ditch and entered by a drawbridge and portcullis. The tower is 4-storeys high with turrets at each corner. In the 16th century a curtain wall and extra living space was added, and in the 17th century the north and west wings were enlarged, giving the castle the shape and form seen today. It was inhabited by the Thanes of Cawdor until 1510, and then by the Campbells of Cawdor until the 1745 uprising.

*Continue on the B9090 and after 1¼ miles turn right, SP 'Inverness'. After ¾ mile, at a crossroads, go forward, SP 'Ardersier', and after 3½ miles reach Ardersier.*

### ARDERSIER, Highland
Known as Ardersier, the village is often called Campbelltown because these lands were acquired by the Campbells of Cawdor in 1574. A charter of 1623 enabled them to erect a burgh of barony called Campbelltown, which was to have a weekly market. The Campbells intended great things for their burgh, but it never became more than a village. It had a small fishing industry, and for a long time was a charming, quiet fishing village. However, in recent years the oil industry has changed all that, and Ardersier is widely known as the base for the construction at Whiteness Head of huge platforms for the oil fields under the North Sea.

*Continue on the B9006 to Fort George.*

The old kitchen, complete with its original utensils, at Cawdor Castle

### FORT GEORGE, Highland
Considered to be the finest example of late artillery fortification in Europe, Fort George (OACT) was built to replace an earlier fort of the same name which had been blown up by the Jacobites in 1746. The architect was Robert Adam, and the irregular polygonal shape was erected between 1748-63 at a cost of £160,000. It covers 12 acres, and stands on a narrow spit of land where Inner and Outer Loch Moray meet. Today the fort is garrisoned by the Queen's Own Highlanders, but the Regimental Museum and some parts of the fort are open to the public, and is rather more pleasant than the grim exterior might suggest.

*The main tour continues from Ardersier on the B9039 and passes, after 4 miles, Castle Stuart. In ¾ mile turn right on to the A96 for the return to Inverness.*

# SIR WALTER SCOTT'S COUNTRY

A romantic glow cast by the great novels of Sir Walter Scott suffuses the wild and beautiful landscapes of the Border country. High in the Eildon Hills is the viewpoint from which he drew particular inspiration, and all round are tiny hamlets, remote castles, and the magnificent ruins of ancient abbeys.

Some of the original architectural splendour is preserved in ruined Melrose Abbey.

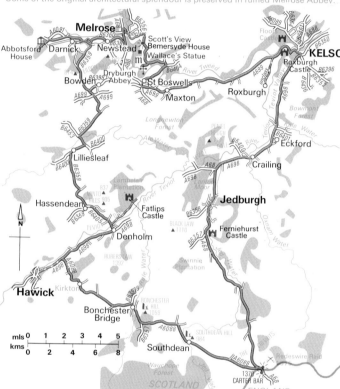

### KELSO, Borders
This bustling Border town was described by Sir Walter Scott, who once lived here, as 'the most beautiful, if not the most romantic, village in Scotland'. Its abbey (AM) was the largest and most splendid of all the Border abbeys. Fine Norman workmanship can be seen in the surviving fragments of the abbey church. The cobbled town square features the elegant Town House of 1816, and John Rennie built the town's splendid Tweed Bridge in 1803. Not far from the bridge is the distinctive Turret House (NTS, not open). Floors Castle (open), home of the Duke and Duchess of Roxburgh, stands about 1 mile to the north-west of the town.

*Leave Kelso on the A699 'St Boswells' and 'Selkirk' road, cross the River Tweed, and turn right. Cross the Teviot and in 1/4 mile reach Roxburgh Castle.*

### ROXBURGH CASTLE, Borders
Roxburgh's Royal Burgh was a major town in the 13th century, but the town has completely disappeared and only the castle mound remains.

### ROXBURGH, Borders
Roxburgh's famous name now belongs to a small hamlet lying 2 1/2 miles south-west of the castle site, on the banks of the River Teviot.

*From Roxburgh Castle drive on the A699 for 7 miles to reach Maxton.*

### MAXTON, Borders
Maxton Church has been considerably altered and restored, but originally dates back to the 12th century. A curious old cross shaft in the village marks the spot where the men of the barony assembled for war. A ruined tower remains from an old seat of the Ker family.

*From Maxton continue on the A699 for 1 1/2 miles and meet the A68. Turn right, then right again on to the B6404 to enter St Boswells.*

### ST BOSWELLS, Borders
Once a famous centre for livestock sales, this village faces across a 40-acre common to St Boswells Green, centre of the Buccleuch Hunt.

*Continue on the B6404 and in 1 mile cross the River Tweed. In 1/4 mile turn left on to the B6356 SP 'Dryburgh', then drive through pleasant riverside scenery and in 1 1/4 miles reach Dryburgh Abbey.*

### DRYBURGH ABBEY, Borders
One of a famous group of 12th-century Border monasteries founded by David I, Dryburgh (AM) was repeatedly attacked by the English and badly damaged in 1544. The cloister buildings have survived in a remarkably complete state, and though the church itself has not fared so well its west front, parts of the nave, and the chapter house can still be seen. This is the resting place of Sir Walter Scott.

*Return along the B6356 and in 1/2 mile turn left to pass the Wallace Statue.*

### WALLACE STATUE, Borders
This massive statue to Sir William Wallace overlooks magnificent Tweed Valley scenery.

*Proceed on the B6356 to reach Bemersyde House on the left.*

### BEMERSYDE HOUSE, Borders
Traditional home of the Haig family, this house (not open) was frequently visited by Sir Walter Scott. It incorporates an ancient tower which was burned in a raid during 1545.

*In 1/4 mile turn left, then in 1/2 mile reach Scott's View.*

### SCOTT'S VIEW, Borders
This AA viewpoint on Bemersyde Hill faces west across the winding Tweed to the three conical peaks of the distinctive Eildon Hills.

*In 1/2 mile drive forward on to an unclassified road SP 'Melrose' and descend through woodland to cross Leader Water. In 1/4 mile turn right SP 'Jedburgh' and meet the A68. Turn left to cross the River Tweed, then immediately right to join the B6361. Continue to reach Newstead.*

### NEWSTEAD, Borders
Standing on the south bank of the River Tweed, this old-world village faces across the water to the slopes of Leaderfoot Hill. To the east of the village, a Roman-style altar marks the site of the Roman army camp of Trimontium.

*Continue on the B6361 to Melrose.*

According to legend the Eildon Hills were cleft into three by a wizard.

### MELROSE, Borders
Border raids in the 14th and 16th centuries destroyed most of David I's beautiful Cistercian abbey (AM) at Melrose. Parts of the nave and choir remain, but the most spectacular survivals are the red sandstone windows with their rich tracery. The heart of Robert Bruce is buried somewhere within the abbey. A nearby museum of carved stones and treasures from the abbey and the Trimontium Fort is contained in the 15th-century Commendator's House. The town preserves a 17th-century cross with the arms of Scotland.

*From Melrose follow SP 'Galashiels' to join the A6091 and after 1/4 mile reach the B6494 left turn leading to Darnick. This can be taken as a detour.*

### DARNICK, Borders
The romantic Tweed-side setting of old Darnick Tower (not open) belies its turbulent past. Originally built in 1425, it was burned by the English, and rebuilt in 1569.

*On the main route, continue along the A6091 SP 'Galashiels' and keep forward over 2 roundabouts, taking the B6360 to reach Abbotsford House.*

## ABBOTSFORD HOUSE, Borders

Internationally famous as the home of Sir Walter Scott, this fine building (open) was designed by the writer himself and he died here in 1832. It has been preserved in his memory, and the library contains a staggering collection of some 20,000 rare books.

*Return to Melrose, meet a roundabout, and turn right on to the B6359 SP 'Lilliesleaf' and 'Hawick'. Ascend to a 814ft road summit, with views ahead of the Cheviots. After 3 miles meet the B6398 on the left, which leads to Bowden.*

Scott's writing materials are preserved at Abbotsford House.

## BOWDEN, Borders

A Conservation Area, features of Bowden are a laird's loft in the 17th-century church and the 16th-century market cross which serves as a war memorial.

*On the main tour, continue with the B6359 and drive forward over the crossroads with the A699 and continue for 3 miles. Turn left to cross Ale Water, then right on to the B6359 and proceed to Lilliesleaf.*

## LILLIESLEAF, Borders

The parish church in this little village was built in 1771, but since then has been considerably extended. Some 2 miles south-west is a 19th-century tower on an old motte.

*Leaving Lilliesleaf turn left with the B6359 SP 'Denholm'. Proceed to Hassendean.*

## HASSENDEAN, Borders

The song *Jack o'Hazeldean* is associated with this small village.

*In Hassendean turn left on to the B6405, passing the twin peaks of the Minto Hills. In 1¾ miles reach an unclassified left turn that offers a detour to Fatlips Castle.*

## FATLIPS CASTLE, Borders

High on the summit of the steep Minto Crags stand the ruins of this curiously-named castle, which was built in the 16th century for the Lockhart family.

*On the main route, continue along the B6405 and cross the River Teviot to enter Denholm.*

This typically ornate entrance hall was part of Sir Walter Scott's design for his home, Abbotsford House.

## DENHOLM, Borders

Two literary figures were born in this small River Teviot village. James Murray (original editor of the *Oxford English Dictionary*) and Scott's poet friend John Leyden. Westgate Hall is an attractive 17th-century building near the village green, and Text House is the weird creation of a local eccentric, Dr Haddon.

*In Denholm meet the junction with the A698 and turn right SP 'Hawick'. After 3½ miles turn left on to the A6088 SP 'Bonchester Bridge, Newcastle'. A detour from the main route can be made by keeping forward on the A698 to the old woollen town of Hawick.*

## HAWICK, Borders

John Hardie, a pioneer of Hawick's woollen industry, is buried in St Mary's Churchyard. The rebuilt church dates from the 13th century, and in Moat Park is probably the motte of a Norman castle. The battle of Flodden Field was a disaster for Hawick in 1513, when nearly all the men of the town were killed; they are commemorated by the Horse monument in the High Street. Wilton Lodge Museum and Art Gallery features the growth of the town's woollen industry.

*On the main tour, continue along the A6088 through Kirkton to reach Bonchester Bridge.*

## BONCHESTER BRIDGE, Borders

Rule Water flows under this bridge and beneath the slopes of 1,059ft Bonchester Hill, eventually to join the Teviot farther north. Wauchope Forest lies to the south.

*Continue on the A6088, passing Bonchester Hill on the left, to reach Southdean.*

## SOUTHDEAN, Borders

Souden Kirk stands in ruins to the south of Southdean, a little village beside the Jed Water. The building was a church in the 13th century, and the meeting place for Scottish leaders before the battle of Otterburn in 1388. A superb miniature altar only 9¼ inches long with fine carved crosses has been excavated from the site.

Jedburgh Abbey, although damaged and burned by the English, retains enough of its character to make it one of Scotland's finest medieval buildings.

*Continue on the A6088 and ascend to the A68. Continue to Carter Bar.*

## CARTER BAR, Borders

Scotland meets England at this 1,370ft viewpoint in the Cheviot Hills. Lush pastures and trim plantations spread out to the north, with the Eildon Hills in the distance, and the Roman camp and earthworks of Chew Green lie to the east. The lonely tree-clad Rede Valley and Border Forest Park provide a wild southerly prospect.

*Return along the A68 SP 'Jedburgh' and descend to the wooded valley of Jed Water to reach Ferniehurst Castle.*

## FERNIEHURST CASTLE, Borders

Scene of frequent Border skirmishes, this fine 16th-century castle was once the seat of the Border family of Ker. Their arms can still be seen on panels in the castle, but the most impressive part of the interior is the huge fireplace in the great hall. In today's more peaceful times the castle serves as a youth hostel.

*Continue along the A68 to Jedburgh.*

## JEDBURGH, Borders

A popular walking, climbing and riding centre, Jedburgh stands as a gateway to Scotland. Its finest attraction is the abbey (AM), which is roofless and in ruins but nevertheless magnificent. It was one of David I's Border abbeys and was burned in 1523. Mary Queen of Scots is associated with the town, and the 16th-century Mary Queen of Scots' House is now a museum devoted to her life. The castle at the top of Castlegate is a 19th-century construction on the site of the 12th-century stronghold built by Scottish kings. Inside, rooms have been constructed to show the 'reformed' system of the early 19th century. The medieval custom of Candlemas Ba' takes place in Jedburgh every Shrove Tuesday, when a game of handball is played through the streets between Uppies born above the mercat cross — and Downies, born below it.

*Leave Jedburgh on the A68 SP 'Edinburgh' and in 2 miles meet the A698. Turn right for Crailing.*

## CRAILING, Borders

The fine Regency mansion of Crailing House (not open) is the main feature of this pleasant small village.

*Continue on the A698 and in 1 mile meet an unclassified road on the right. A short detour can be taken along this road to Eckford.*

## ECKFORD, Borders

A pair of 18th-century jougs – iron collars used to punish wrongdoers – is preserved in the church. An old watch-house stands in the churchyard to guard against body-snatching, once a common crime.

*On the main tour, continue along the A698 and re-enter Kelso.*

## KIRKCUDBRIGHT, Dumf & Gall

This ancient burgh stands in the heart of an area known as the Stewartry and was once a bustling port. Much of the local history is displayed in the Stewartry Museum, and the town is dominated by the handsome ruins of 16th-century Maclellan's Castle (AM). Close to the 17th-century mercat cross is the old Tollbooth, once a prison for John Paul Jones. A fine collection of pictures by E A Hornel can be seen in 18th-century Broughton House (gardens and library open). South of the town the wooded peninsula of St Mary's Isle separates the Dee estuary from Manxman's Lake.

*Leave Kirkcudbright on the A755 SP 'Gatehouse of Fleet' and cross the River Dee. In 6½ miles turn right then left across the A75 to join the B727. Skirt the Fleet Forest and enter Gatehouse of Fleet.*

## GATEHOUSE OF FLEET, Dumf & Gall

This town was the inspiration for Scott's otherwise fictitious town Kippletringham, in *Guy Mannering*. In the town is a huge granite clock tower of 1871, and the local countryside includes isolated moorland where the poet Burns once composed some of his works. To the north-west the Water of Fleet runs through a beautiful glen, and south are the contrasting features of Fleet Bay and deciduous Fleet Forest. Cally Palace Hotel, close to the town in fine parkland, was designed by architect Robert Mylne in 1763.

*Go forward on the B796, and after 1 mile turn right on to the Stranraer road A75. After a short distance pass the ruins of Cardoness Castle to the right.*

## CARDONESS CASTLE, Dumf & Gall

This section of the drive follows one of the most beautiful roads in the south of Scotland. The picturesque ruins of the 15th-century tower house at Cardoness (AM) stand in a superb situation overlooking Fleet Bay, Murray's Isles (NT), and the Islands of Fleet.

*Continue, and in ¾ mile reach an unclassified right turn that can be followed for a detour to the hamlet of Anwoth.*

## ANWOTH, Dumf & Gall

Anwoth Church is a ruined 17th-century building which has retained a number of good features, including a medieval bell. In the churchyard are a cross from the dark ages and the remarkable 8ft-high tomb of a member of the Gordon family who was buried here in the 17th century.

*On the main route, continue along the A75 to follow the scenic coastline, passing below Barholm Castle to the right.*

# AMONG THE GALLOWAY HILLS

North of the empty beaches and bird-haunted estuaries of the Solway Firth are high forests, secret little lochs hidden between ridged outriders of the Galloway Hills, and dozens of green river valleys carved through hill flanks to the sea.

## BARHOLM CASTLE, Dumf & Gall

Close to the main road below this ruined tower (not open) is Dirk Hatteraick's Cave, the hiding place of the smuggler captain in Scott's *Guy Mannering*. The castle itself was once a place of refuge for the religious reformer John Knox, and is beautifully set overlooking Wigtown Bay.

*Continue, and after a short distance pass Carsluith Castle to the left.*

## CARSLUITH CASTLE, Dumf & Gall

An unusual feature of this roofless 16th-century tower house (AM) is its L-shaped plan, brought about by the

Kirkcudbright used to be one of Scotland's major ports, but it gradually declined in the 17th century. Today it is a small harbour at the mouth of the Dee.

addition of a staircase wing in 1568.

*Continue along the A75 to Creetown.*

## CREETOWN, Dumf & Gall

This former granite port overlooks the Cree estuary and the wide expanse of Wigtown Sands. The Gem Rock Museum here has gemstones and minerals from all over the world. To the north-east the Moneypool Burn runs through a charmingly wooded valley.

*Continue through Creetown and after 3½ miles reach the hamlet of Palnure.*

Cardoness Castle is a well-preserved tower house on the Big Water of Fleet.

## PALNURE, Dumf & Gall

A charming and worthwhile excursion can be made from this village to follow the clear Palnure Burn to Bargaly Glen. To the north-east rises Cairnsmore of Fleet (2,331ft) which is associated with John Buchan's spy novel *The Thirty-Nine Steps*.

*Continue on the A75, and in 3 miles at a roundabout take 3rd exit A714 to enter Newton Stewart.*

## NEWTON STEWART, Dumf & Gall

In the 18th century this lovely Galloway market town was a centre for the weaving, spinning, and carpet-making industries. Nowadays these local skills can be seen in the production of mohair rugs and scarves at the Glencree Mill (open). Between Newton Stewart and Minnigaff the River Cree is spanned by a fine granite bridge built in 1813 by John Rennie. Galloway Forest Park, famous for its many historical and archaeological sites as well as for its great natural beauty, lies to the north.

*Leave Newton Stewart with SP 'New Galloway (A712)', cross the Cree Bridge, and pass the edge of Minnigaff. In 1 mile turn left on to the A712 'New Galloway' road. Continue through attractive woodlands of the Galloway Forest Park, with splendid views of the high Galloway Hills to the north and south, along the A712 to reach Murray's Monument.*

## MURRAY'S MONUMENT, Dumf & Gall

This obelisk commemorates Dr Alexander Murray, who grew up near by as a shepherd boy and eventually became Professor of Oriental Languages in Edinburgh University. Near the monument the Grey Mare's Tail burn plunges in two waterfalls. Nearby on the crags of Talnotry an interesting wild goat park can be seen from the road.

*Continue along the A712 and after 4½ miles reach the shores of Clatteringshaws Loch.*

## CLATTERINGSHAWS LOCH, Dumf & Gall

Part of the Galloway power scheme, this great reservoir was created by the obstruction of the Black Water of Dee. On the eastern shore are the battle site of Rapploch Moss, where a granite boulder (NTS) marks the spot where Robert the Bruce defeated an English force in 1307, and the Galloway Deer Museum. The River Dee runs from the loch to join the sea at Kirkcudbright, and the views in this area are magical. To the right of the main road is the 1,616ft Black Craig of Dee, and the Fell of Fleet rises to 1,554ft in the south.

*Continue along the A712 and after 6 miles enter New Galloway.*

## NEW GALLOWAY, Dumf & Gall
This noted angling centre on the River Ken is Scotland's smallest Royal Burgh. Kells Churchyard, sited a little to the north of New Galloway, features the grave of a Covenanter who was shot in 1685. Also here is the curious but attractive Adam and Eve Stone.

*Turn right on to the Kirkcudbright road A762 and after 1 mile pass Kenmure Castle on the left.*

## DALBEATTIE, Dumf & Gall
In the 19th century the shiny grey granite of which this lovely place is built was shipped from quays on the Urr Water to all parts of the world. South of the town are the green ranks of Dalbeattie Forest, while 2½ miles north is the Mote of Urr—one of the finest Saxon fortifications anywhere in Britain.

*Leave Dalbeattie by returning along the A711 and re-cross the Urr Water, then turn left SP 'Auchencairn' and continue along the A711 to Palnackie.*

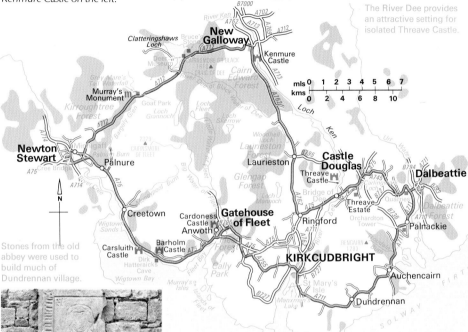

The River Dee provides an attractive setting for isolated Threave Castle.

Stones from the old abbey were used to build much of Dundrennan village.

Dalbeattie's quarries are famous for superb granite.

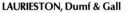

## KENMURE CASTLE, Dumf & Gall
A little of the original 16th- and 17th-century work can still be seen in the ruins of this Gordon family stronghold, but most of the structure is more recent than that. The hero of Sir Walter Scott's poem *Young Lochinvar* sprang from this family.

*After a short distance reach the shores of Loch Ken.*

## LOCH KEN, Dumf & Gall
Formed by damming the rivers Ken and Dee, this reservoir is partly bordered by rich woodland and is a picturesque addition to the landscape. Some 5 miles south-east of New Galloway the Black Water of Dee enters the loch after flowing through the lovely woodlands of Cairn Edward Forest.

*Continue along the A762 and skirt the shores of Woodhall Loch to reach the hamlet of Laurieston.*

## LAURIESTON, Dumf & Gall
The works of writer S R Crockett are based on this area, and there is a monument to him in the village. Coniferous Laurieston Forest lies to the west, and south-west the waters of Loch Mannoch are overlooked by the Glengap Forest.

*Continue through attractive hill country to Ringford.*

## RINGFORD, Dumf & Gall
During his bloody campaign of persecution the notorious Sir Robert Grierson of Lairg murdered five Covenanters here in 1685. A memorial to the victims stands 2 miles north of the village, on the tour route.

*Turn left on to the A75 'Dumfries' road. In 4 miles, shortly after crossing the River Dee, reach a track that leads left to Kelton Mains for Threave Castle.*

## THREAVE CASTLE, Dumf & Gall
Built in the 1360s by Archibald the Grim, 3rd Earl of Douglas, this castle (AM) is beautifully sited on an island in the River Dee. The locally-forged and nationally famous Mons Meg cannon was used by James II to overcome the rebellious Douglas family here in 1455; this impressive piece of ordnance can now be seen in Edinburgh Castle. In 1640 the stronghold was captured by Covenanters, who sacked it and vandalized its interior.

*Continue along the A75 towards Castle Douglas. Before the tour route enters this town it passes an unclassified right turn which offers a short diversion to the Threave Estate.*

## THREAVE ESTATE, Dumf & Gall
Threave Estate includes the house and grounds, and is the National Trust for Scotland's School of Practical Gardening. The house is not open to the public, but the Wildfowl Refuge and lovely gardens are. Visitors flock here in the spring to see the estate's vast and very beautiful display of daffodils.

*On the main route, pass alongside Carlingwark Loch and enter Castle Douglas.*

## CASTLE DOUGLAS, Dumf & Gall
Once the commercial capital of its county, this pleasant old town is beautifully sited near the shores of Loch Carlingwark. In 1765 the loch was drained, revealing the remains of several prehistoric lake-dwellings known as crannogs, and a number of Bronze-Age artefacts.

*At the far end turn right on to the A745 'Dalbeattie' road and after 5 miles descend past granite quarries then turn left on to the A711. Cross the Urr Water to reach Dalbeattie.*

## PALNACKIE, Dumf & Gall
This attractive whitewashed village stands on the Urr Water north of the Rough Firth, which is an inlet of the Solway Firth. About 1 mile south on an unclassified road is 16th-century Orchardton Tower (AM), one of only two circular tower houses existing in the whole of Scotland.

*Continue on the A711 to Auchencairn.*

## AUCHENCAIRN, Dumf & Gall
A short way offshore from this Auchencairn Bay village is Hestan Island, which was featured as the Isle of Rathan in S R Crockett's book *Raiders*. It is the site of a lighthouse.

*Continue on the A711 to Dundrennan.*

## DUNDRENNAN, Dumf & Gall
Stone from the ruins of 12th-century Dundrennan Abbey (AM) was used to build many of the houses in this village. The foundation itself has sad associations with Mary Queen of Scots, for it was here that she spent her last night on Scottish soil before sailing from Port Mary to England and eventual imprisonment. The port is south of Dundrennan.

*Continue along the A711 for the return to Kirkcudbright.*

## KYLE OF LOCHALSH, Highland
This busy fishing and shipping village stands at the west end of Loch Alsh and is the railhead on a line from Inverness. It is also the main ferry stage for Skye, and the shores of that beautiful island lie just a few hundred yards away across the Kyle Akin waters. Fine views from Kyle of Lochalsh encompass the Cuillin range on Skye, the Crowlin Islands, and Raasay to the west. East is the vast Balmacara Estate (NTS).

*Take the Skye ferry across the narrow strait to Kyleakin.*

## KYLEAKIN, Highland
Ruined Castle Moil stands on the shore a little to the east of this small fishing and car-ferry port. It is thought that its small Highland keep may have been built by the daughter of a Norwegian king but it is known to have served as a lookout post and fortress against Norse raiders for centuries. During most of this time it was a stronghold of the Mackinnons of Strath. Behind the village is the 2,396ft bulk of Beinn na Cailleach.

*Drive along the A850 and pass through Breakish to reach Broadford.*

## BROADFORD, Highland
Broadford is a convenient touring centre for south Skye. It stands by Broadford Bay on a junction of roads from the ferry ports of Armadale, Kylerhea, and Kyleakin, overlooked by the granite screes of the Red Hills. Prominent in the range is 2,400ft Beinn na Caillich, the site of the largest hill cairn in Scotland. Tradition has it that a Norwegian princess was buried here, where the winds of Norway could blow over her grave, in the 13th century. Offshore to the west is the Island of Scalpay.

*From Broadford a detour can be made along the A881 to reach Torrin and Elgol.*

## TORRIN, Highland
In front of this crofting township is Loch Slapin, and the majestic Red Cuillin range rises in the north-east. Across the loch on the Strathaird peninsula is the great Black Cuillin peak of 3,044ft Bla Bheinn and a precipitous rocky ridge known as Clach Glas. The latter is popular with experienced rock climbers.

*Still on the detour, continue to Elgol.*

## ELGOL, Highland
Magnificent views from this Loch Scavaig hamlet extend north to the Cuillins and south to the mountainous little islands of Canna, Rhum, and Eigg. Motor-boat trips can be taken from here to Loch Coruisk, which lies amongst the wild Cuillin peaks in a landscape of lochs and mountains more scenic than any other in the British Isles. The loch can also be reached by way of footpaths, one of which runs along the lovely and mountainous north shore of Loch Scavaig.

## THE ISLE OF MIST
History and legend join hands in the misty no-man's land that is Skye's romantic, often turbulent, past. Old castles guard the shoreline, and some of the most spectacular mountains in Scotland encircle the magical scenery of hidden inlets and unsuspected lochs.

*On the main drive, continue on the Portree road, and skirt the island of Scalpay then Loch Ainort with views of 2,649ft Garbh-bheinn to the left.*

*Castle Moil at Kyleakin commands breathtaking views up Loch Alsh.*

## CUILLIN HILLS, Highland
Unrivalled for scenic splendour anywhere in Britain, the Black and Red Cuillins are the most famous landscape features of this outstanding island. A 6-mile arc of black peaks, 15 of which exceed 3,000ft in height, curves across the south-west part of the island as the Black Cuillin range; on the other side of Glen Sligachan, in spectacular contrast to its jagged neighbours, are the softly rounded summits and glowing pink granite of the Red Cuillins. The black peak of 3,309ft Alasdair and rough pinnacled mass of 3,167ft Sgurr nan Gillean attract experienced climbers, while the determined walker heads for the fastnesses of hidden corries and surprising little valleys in the red hills. Both ranges are prone to sudden mists and can be deadly, even to experienced people. Local advice

should be sought before attempting to explore either.

*Ascend from Loch Ainort with Red Cuillin summit of 2,542ft Glamaig to the left of the road. Later descend with views of the island of Raasay on the right to reach Sconser.*

## SCONSER, Highland
Parts of an inn where Dr Johnson and Boswell stayed while visiting the island in 1773 have been incorporated in the Sconser Lodge Hotel. The hamlet itself is sited at the mouth of Loch Sligachan.

*Proceed to Sligachan.*

## SLIGACHAN, Highland
Well known for its salmon and sea trout, this hamlet stands on the River Sligachan near the head of the loch of the same name. The U-shaped glacial valley of Glen Sligachan extends south into the Black Cuillins, with the 3,167ft peak of Sgurr nan Gillean prominent to the left. Several high peaks and spectacular Loch Coruisk can be reached via a path through the glen.

*Drive north along Glen Varragill and descend to Portree Loch to reach the harbour town of Portree.*

## PORTREE, Highland
Skye's pleasant little capital town of whitewashed houses stands on Portree Bay, which is sheltered by high cliffs on three sides. Well situated as a touring centre for the island, the town has a charming harbour and receives all kinds of light boat traffic at its pier. Opposite, across the Sound of Raasay, is the wooded island of Raasay. This isolated place is of particular interest to botanists and geologists.

*Turn right on to the A855 and later pass the reservoirs of Loch Fada and Loch Leathan, both of which are incorporated in a hydro-electric scheme. To the left are the Trotternish Ridge and the precipices of The Storr.*

*Portree offers a pleasant harbour for steamers to Raasay.*

## THE STORR, Highland
Extending the length of the wild Trotternish peninsula of Skye, a 10-mile backbone of rock is dominated by the 2,360ft conical peak of The Storr. Here is a grand and disturbing landscape of sudden cliffs and jagged crags, where the Old Man of Storr pinnacle rises to 160ft like a giant's tower in a child's story. It has posed a challenge for centuries, but was not climbed until 1955. The Storr lochs are harnessed to a hydro-electric scheme.

*Continue, passing Lealt Falls and the well-known Kilt Rock near Loch Mealt, to reach Staffin.*

## STAFFIN, Highland
Opposite this village in the curve of sandy Staffin Bay is the gull-populated isolation of Staffin Island. One mile south-east is the Kilt Rock, so named because its columnar and horizontal beds of basalt suggest the pleats in a Highland kilt.

*Continue, passing the Quiraing on the left.*

The Cuillin Hills form Skye's most dramatic aspect.

Dunvegan Castle is steeped in legend.

Gaunt ruins of Duntulm Castle stand exposed on the headland.

### QUIRAING, Highland
This strange wilderness of rocks is one of the most peculiar sights on Skye. It is a remarkable group of stone stacks and pinnacles bearing such descriptive names as Needle Rock, The Table, and The Prison, including a grassy natural amphitheatre and a rugged group known as Leac nan Fionn.

*Continue and skirt Flodigarry.*

### FLODIGARRY, Highland
Flora Macdonald, known for her part in Bonnie Prince Charlie's escape after the collapse of the Jacobite cause at Culloden, spent the early years of her marriage here. She escorted the Prince, disguised as her maid, from Benbecula in the Outer Hebrides to Portree. Her house adjoins a local hotel.

*Continue to Duntulm.*

### DUNTULM, Highland
Crumbling Duntulm Castle dates from the 15th century and was once the seat of the Macdonalds of Sleat and Trotternish. The promontory of Rubha Hunish extends beyond the shore of Score Bay north of Duntulm, and views north-west across the waters of the Minch encompass the mountainous Outer Hebridean island of Harris.

*Continue along the coast road to Flora Macdonald's burial place and the Skye Cottage Museum.*

### SKYE COTTAGE MUSEUM AND FLORA MACDONALD MONUMENT, Highland
Traditional Highland furniture and relics from the island's past can be seen in the four well-restored crofters cottages here. This type of dwelling

and the Black Houses were traditional amongst the islands, though few good examples now survive. Close by is the old burial ground of the Macdonalds, Martins, Macarthurs, and Nicolsons. In 1790 Flora Macdonald was buried here, wrapped in a sheet in which Bonnie Prince Charlie had slept at Kingsburgh. Over her grave is a great Iona cross inscribed by Dr Johnson.

*Proceed beyond Kilmuir and descend Idrigill Hill, with fine views over Uig Bay. Turn left on to the A856 for Uig.*

### UIG, Highland
Situated on a fine bay, this picturesque little hamlet of scattered crofts faces across Loch Snizort and its islands to the Vaternish peninsula. The steamer pier is used by car ferries to the Outer Hebrides. In 1746 Flora Macdonald and Bonnie Prince Charlie landed here after a much more difficult and dangerous voyage from those islands.

*Continue to Kensaleyre on the shore of Loch Eyre, an inlet of Loch Snizort Beag, and in another ½ mile turn right on to the B8036. After another 1¾ miles meet a T-junction and turn right on to the A850 to follow the shores of Loch Snizort Beag and Loch Greshornish to Edinbane. To the right of the road are views of the Outer Hebrides. Continue to Dunvegan.*

### DUNVEGAN, Highland
Dunvegan Castle north of the village is the seat of the Macleod chiefs. Dating from the 15th to 19th centuries, it is claimed to be the oldest continuously inhabited castle in Scotland. Views from the ramparts extend across island-studded Dunvegan Loch to the distant ranges of Harris. Its greatest treasure is a fragment of silk which is known as the fairy flag and was probably woven on the Island of Rhodes in the 7th century. According to tradition a fairy gave the flag, and various magical properties, to the 4th clan chief in the 14th century. Other relics include the great broadsword of the 7th chief, the ancient Dunvegan Cup of Irish silver that was given to the 11th chief, and various items related

to Bonnie Prince Charlie. Features of the building itself include a 15th-century dungeon with a high slit window opening on to the kitchen stairs, no doubt as an additional torture for the hungry prisoners. South-west of Dunvegan is a pair of flat-topped basalt mountains known as Macleod's Tables.

*From Dunvegan take the A863 'Sligachan' road, which affords good views of the Cuillins ahead, and on the approach to Struan pass Dun Beag on the left.*

### DUN BEAG, Highland
Extensive remains of a 2,000-year-old Pictish broch stand here. Once a 40ft look-out post and refuge, the ruins include 12ft-thick walls, several rooms, and parts of a stone staircase.

*Cross high ground above Loch Harport and descend to Glen Drynoch. A detour can be made from the main route here by turning right on to the B8009 and driving first to Carbost, then to Port-na-Long.*

### CARBOST, Highland
The well-known Talisker Whisky Distillery is sited here, on the west shores of Loch Harport.

*Still on the detour, continue to Port-na-Long.*

### PORT-NA-LONG, Highland
This tiny weaving village has become famous for Harris Tweed.

*On the main route, continue to Sligachan and turn right on to the A850 for the return to Kyleakin, where the ferry is taken back to Kyle of Lochalsh on the mainland.*

## LAIRG, Highland
Many of the roads which cross the wild landscapes of the far north-west of Scotland converge at this little village. It is a thriving community with shops, and a market that is particularly busy during the lamb sales. Anglers come here to take advantage of the fishing on Loch Shin, which stretches away to the north-west. At certain times of the year salmon can be seen leaping through a narrow gorge at the spectacular Falls of Shin, 5 miles south of Lairg.

*Leave Lairg on the A836, SP 'Tongue'. After 9 miles enter the North Dalchork Forest, then pass the Crask Inn and follow Strath Vagastie to Altnaharra.*

## ALTNAHARRA, Highland
This angling resort, which consists of little more than a hotel and a cluster of houses, is situated in Strath Naver at the western tip of Loch Naver. It is overlooked from the south by the great mass of Ben Klibreck, whose highest peak reaches 3,154ft. Until the early 19th century, over 1,000 people made their livings on the fertile lands alongside Loch Naver. They were forced to leave their homes during the infamous land 'clearances', when landlords evicted their tenants to free their land for sheep farming and deer hunting, which they found to be more profitable. The homeless peasants settled on the desolate coast where they could eke a meagre living from the sea. The tumbled ruins of their villages can still be seen, as can remains left by earlier builders. Near Klibreck Farm, at the south-west end of the loch, are prehistoric hut circles and a Celtic cross, and further along the loch are the remains of a broch (an ancient stone tower)

# AN ANGLER'S PARADISE
This land at the northernmost tip of our island is a fisherman's dream, with numerous lochs and fast-flowing rivers offering some of the best sport in the country. Great mountains of stark, bare rock, deep valleys and cold lochs create an almost lunar landscape — the work of the great glaciers of the last Ice Age.

Kyle of Durness is one of the 3 sea lochs that split the northernmost tip of Scotland into 3 great headlands

known as Dun Creagach. A lovely but narrow road runs north-west from Altnaharra passing lonely Loch na Meadie and reaching Strath More near its junction with Glen Golly.

*The main tour continues along the Tongue road through more barren country to reach the shore of Loch Loyal. Beyond the loch there is a short climb on to higher ground before the descent towards the Kyle of Tongue. On reaching the A838 turn left for Tongue.*

## TONGUE, Highland
Tongue is set beside the sandy shores of the large sea loch called the Kyle of Tongue. On the headland, where the little Allt an Rhian stream enters the kyle, are the ruins of Castle Varrich. This is thought to have been the fortress of an 11th-century Norse king and later became a Mackay stronghold. The kyle was bridged to the north of Tongue in recent years, by means of a causeway, saving a long detour round the head of the loch. During the 1745 Rebellion the naval ship *HMS Hazard* was captured by Jacobites, who renamed it the *Prince Charles,* and loaded it with supplies and money. The vessel was pursued by navy

ships and eventually ran ashore in the Kyle of Tongue. Prince Charles sent a large force to retrieve his lost cash, but both money and men were captured. To the south of Tongue is the mighty granite peak of 2,504ft Ben Loyal, from whose summit there are dramatic views of large areas of northern Scotland.

*Leave on the A838 Durness road and cross the Kyle of Tongue by a causeway. After 8½ miles the tour runs alongside Loch Eriboll before reaching Eriboll.*

## ERIBOLL, Highland
Wild and beautiful Loch Eriboll stretches far into the mountains of north-west Scotland, and the tiny cluster of houses that is Eriboll village clings to the hillside on its eastern side. King Haco of Norway anchored his fleet here in 1263, and was frightened and dismayed by the eclipse of the sun which occured while he was there. The loch was a point of assembly for allied warships during World War II. Seals can sometimes be seen feeding in Loch Hope, which lies to the east of Eriboll.

*Continue around Loch Eriboll and after 14 miles pass (right) the footpath to Smoo Cave.*

## SMOO CAVE, Highland
One of the most dramatic natural features in northern Scotland, Smoo Cave, is approached from a clifftop path which begins near the little settlement of Lerinmore. Its entrance is over 30ft high and 130ft wide, and the main chamber is 200ft long. Beyond is a second chamber into which the Allt Smoo stream plummets 80ft down a sheer rock face into a deep pool. Beyond this again is yet another chamber. The first cave is easily accessible, but the 2 further caves can only be reached by experts. The name Smoo is probably derived from the old Norse word, smjuga, which means cleft.

*Continue to Durness.*

## DURNESS, Highland
Set on the hillsides above Sango Bay, Durness is the most north-western village in Britain. It is a neat and well-ordered community that has preserved its crofting traditions in the face of increasingly heavy odds. The name of Durness is thought to be derived from the Viking for Cape of the Wild Beasts — after the wolves which once plagued the area. Limestone cliffs, pocked by small caves and inlets, enclose the white sands of Sango Bay. Away to the north-west are the desolate lands which culminate in Cape Wrath, the extreme north-western point of the Scottish mainland. Although no public road leads to the cape, mini-buses carry visitors to it from the Kyle of Durness Ferry in the summer months. On this wild coast are the cliffs of Clo Mor, at 900ft the highest in Britain.

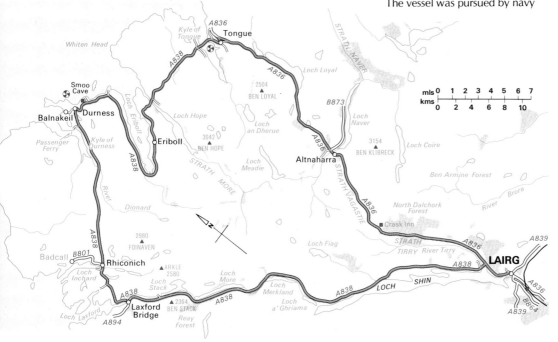

*A short detour to the north-west of Durness can be made to visit Balnakeil.*

### BALNAKEIL, Highland

On the road to this remote hamlet is Balnakeil Craft Village, a community of artists and craftsmen who established themselves in disused service-buildings during 1964. Visitors are made welcome at the pottery and art gallery. Balnakeil itself has roots which go back to the very beginning of British Christianity, but tangible remains, in the shape of a ruined monastery, date back only to 1619. The headland beyond Balnakeil has spectacular cliff scenery, especially at Flirium, where the strangely-contorted rock formations are a haven for puffins.

*From Durness the main tour heads southwards along the Scourie road and after 1 ¾ miles passes the turning for the Kyle of Durness Ferry (right). Continue through barren, mountainous countryside to Rhiconich.*

### RHICONICH, Highland

A coaching inn once stood in this tiny hamlet at the head of Loch Inchard. It is surrounded by an extrordinary landscape of stark rocks littered with innumerable lochs and lochans. This almost lunar scene is formed from some of the most ancient rocks in the world. Views to the south-east encompass the bleak expanses of the Forest of Reay, a largely uninhabited land of bogs and craggy hills that was once the hunting ground of the chiefs of the Clan MacKay. Foinaven, whose highest peak reaches to 2,980ft, dominates this awesome scene.

*Remain on the A838 to Laxford Bridge.*

### LAXFORD BRIDGE, Highland

This scattering of cottages at the head of Loch Laxford is at the heart of what has been called a fisherman's paradise; indeed, lax is the Norse for salmon. To the east, beneath the conical peak of 2,346ft Ben Stack, is Loch Stach, one of the finest fishing lochs in Scotland. Wildlife of many other kinds, including black-throated divers, otters, pine martens and red deer, can often be seen in and around the loch.

*Turn left on to the Lairg road. Later pass beneath Ben Stack and follow the waters of Loch Stack. Pass a further succession of lochs before the long run alongside Loch Shin.*

### LOCH SHIN, Highland

Desolate Highland scenery surrounds this rather featureless loch. It is 17 miles long and its waters are used to produce hydro-electricity. A large dam near Lairg has raised the water level more than 30ft. Major engineering works needed to make the system work efficiently included the construction of a 2½ mile-long tunnel to bring water into the loch from Glen Cassley, and another tunnel, 5 miles long, which carries water to a generating station at Inveran. The highest mountain in the old county of Sutherland, 3,273ft Ben More Assynt, rises to the north-west.

*Near the far end of the loch turn right on to the A836 for the return to Lairg.*

## LOCHCARRON, Highland

Perhaps the most pleasant village in all of Wester Ross, Lochcarron lies scattered along 4 or 5 miles of road; bright, neat houses with bright, neat gardens look over the loch towards the ranks of mountains beyond. The part of the village by the old harbour is called Slumbay, which means Safe Bay, a name harking back to the days when hundreds of boats would shelter in Loch Carron when herring were plentiful. The main part of the village, known as Jeantown, grew up in the 19th century, although the commercial herring fishing died away by the turn of the century. This beautifully-placed village has several guest houses and shops, and is a delightful, quiet place for those who enjoy boating and fishing and walking.

*Leave Lochcarron on the A896, SP 'Applecross and Shieldaig'. Ascend on to higher ground and later descend to the shore of Loch Kishorn. In 1½ miles turn left, SP 'Applecross'. Cross the mountains via the 'Pass of the Cattle', a fine viewpoint at 2,053ft, and descend to Applecross.*

## APPLECROSS, Highland

Applecross is one of the most inaccessible places in Scotland and can only be reached by a tortuous road which zig-zags up from sea-level to 2,054ft. St Maelrhuba founded one of the earliest Christian churches in the north here. He came here in 673 from Ireland, and went about his missionary work throughout the Applecross Peninsula until his death in 722. The saint is said to have been buried in the old churchyard some 1,000 years before the present church was built and the people of Applecross used to carry a pinch of soil taken from near his grave as a safeguard on long or dangerous journeys. Applecross was also a place of sanctuary for fugitives hundreds of years after the saint's death. The church was delapidated for many years until the West Highland School of Adventure had it completely restored to act as a chapel for the school, which is based at the former shooting-lodge of Harefield. The main part of the village lies on the east side of the bay, and was built by crofters at a time when, inland, the estates were being made into deer parks where wealthy landlords could shoot deer. It is little more than a line of houses called The Street, overlooking the sea.

*Leave on the unclassified Shieldaig road, and follow the coast through remote, rugged country with views across the Inner Sound to the islands of Skye, Raasay and Rona. Beyond Fearnmore the tour turns eastwards alongside Loch Torridon. On reaching the A896 turn left for Shieldaig.*

## THE APPLECROSS PENINSULA

Shaped like a fish's tail, the peninsula has a unique beauty — one of strong bare rock and wide skies. There are no fences or apparent restrictions, and the fishing and crofting hamlets of this sparsely populated region seem to belong to another, less hurried age.

## SHIELDAIG, Highland

A bright, tidy village which looks westward over the bay of Loch Shieldaig towards the lofty hills of North Applecross. The village was created solely for the purpose of encouraging young men to settle here as fishermen and provide a steady supply of manpower for the Royal Navy, if and when needed. Official grants were provided for boat-building, there were guaranteed prices set for the fish caught, duty-free salt was supplied for the curing of the fish, and plenty of land was provided for the tenants on which to build and grow food. Perhaps most important of all, a new road was constructed, giving Shieldaig access to the outside world. The people prospered for many years, until the estates passed to the Duchess of Leeds, who had no interest in her tenants and seemed to consider them less important than sheep. Poverty came to Shieldaig when all their special privileges were stripped away. By the 1860s only one boat remained and the villagers were so poor that they could not operate it.

*Follow the Torridon road to Annat.*

## ANNAT, Highland

This scattered settlement is approached along a pleasant road above which lie unexpected banks of rhododendrons and pine trees. There are old houses here with sheep pens beside the rocky seashore, and the strips of cultivated land beside the road are tended much as they have been since the days when these crofts were self-sufficient.

*Continue on the A896 and after 1 mile (left) is the road for Torridon.*

Above: Shieldaig village between the loch and high mountain of the same name

Right: Loch Torridon

## TORRIDON, Highland

'Glen Torridon, its loch and the mountains on either side exhibit more beauty than any other district of Scotland, including Skye'. So said W. H. Murray in his assessment of the Highland landscape, which he made for the National Trust for Scotland in 1961. The mouth of the great sea loch of Torridon faces the north-east of Skye, and as it progresses inland it splits into upper Loch Torridon and Loch Shieldaig. At the north end rise red sandstone mountains, some capped with white quartzite, which make an unforgettable sight when caught in the rays of sunset. One of these is Liathach (3,456ft) and beneath its precipitous scree slopes is Torridon village, which stands at the head of the loch. The sandstone from which this impressive range is sculpted is 750 million years old. Some 16,000 acres of the Torridon area is owned by the National Trust for Scotland and apart from its splendidly rugged scenery, which is of especial interest to geologists, it is also valued for its wildlife. Here live the red and roe deer, mountain goats, the rare golden eagle, the mountain hare and the wildcat. Near Torridon village is a Trust Visitor Centre, where there is a red deer museum and an audio-visual presentation of local wildlife.

*Leave Torridon on the A896 Kinlochewe road, and follow Glen Torridon. Later skirt the Beinn Eighe Nature Reserve.*

## BEINN EIGHE NATURE RESERVE, Highland

Established in 1951, the first National Nature Reserve to be declared in Britain, Beinn Eighe Nature Reserve covers over 10,000 acres, and includes the woodlands of Coille na Gas-Leitire, Kinlochewe Forest and 3,309ft Ben Eighe. Coille na Gas-Leitire — meaning Wood on Grey Slopes — is a remnant of the Caledonian Forest which at one time spread right across the Highlands. These woods are used as a study area for the re-establishment of the ancient woodlands, and, of course, are an important haven for wildlife. Pine marten, wild cat, otter, fox, deer, golden eagle, buzzard and falcon all live here, although some of them are rarely glimpsed.

*Continue to Kinlochewe.*

## KINLOCHEWE, Highland

This small, scattered village lies at the head of beautiful Loch Maree, dominated by the mountain of Slioch, the 'spear', which rises 3,217ft. There is a hotel here which is a splendid base for those who

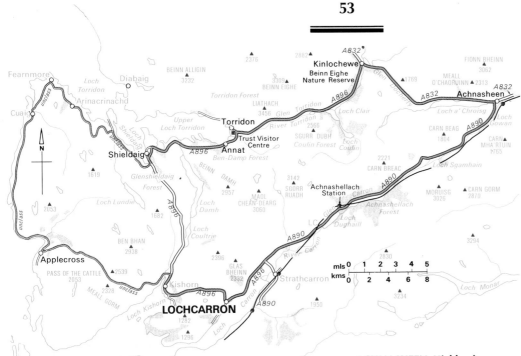

station. The area roundabout is used in the production of hydro-electricity.

*Leave on the A890, SP 'Kyle of Lochalsh'. Cross open moorland then pass Lochs Gowan and Sgamhain. Enter the Achnashellach Forest and follow the River Carron before reaching Achnashellach railway station.*

### ACHNASHELLACH STATION, Highland
Behind Achnashellach railway station a track follows the River Lair to a narrow gorge where the river crashes over waterfalls. Beyond, the track leads to Coire Lair, where the river's source lies. To go further (8 miles) follow the footpath to Lochs Coulin and Clair and so to Glen Torridon. This walk is exceptional — the views from Coulin Woods to Beinn Eighe and Liathall, their feet reflected in the lochs, is not to be missed, for the countryside is the finest in Wester Ross.

*Continue on the A890 then keep forward on to the A896 for the return to Lochcarron.*

enjoy magnificent mountain scenery, hill-walking, climbing or fishing — the latter is excellent, with sea trout, brown trout and salmon being the best catches.

*Turn right on to the A832, SP 'Achnasheen'. The tour then follows Glen Docherty and later runs alongside Loch a'Chrosg to reach Achnasheen.*

### ACHNASHEEN, Highland
Achnasheen lies between Strath Bran and Glen Carron, dominated to the north by the 3,060ft granite peak of Fionn Bhein. It is a little hamlet in which the hotel is actually part of the old railway

# BORDER VALES AND MARSHES

This lonely, unpopulated land was the scene of border strife and bloody warfare for many centuries, but it was also the inspiration for some of Burns' poetry and the goal of eloping couples. The peace of its river-threaded dales and gentle grandeur of its hills belies its turbulent history.

## LOCKERBIE, Dumf & Gall

In the late 17th century this pleasant little town was a major centre for horse and lamb trading. Lamb Hill takes its name from a market that has been held here since 1680, and everywhere there are signs of Lockerbie's agricultural affiliations. However, it has not always been as peaceful as it seems today. In 1593 one of the last Border family feuds ended in a fierce battle at which the Johnstones killed Lord Maxwell and some 700 of his followers. Wealth from the China tea trade came to local landowners and manifested itself in several great mansions that appeared in the area.

*From Lockerbie follow signs Glasgow to join the A74 and drive through Annandale. In 7 miles cross Johnstonebridge.*

## JOHNSTONEBRIDGE, Dumf & Gall

This picturesque bridge spans the River Annan, which flows south through the lovely countryside of the Annandale valley.

*In 6 miles turn left on to an unclassified road for Beattock.*

## BEATTOCK, Dumf & Gall

Beattock stands in hilly country on the Evan Water, in lovely Upper Annandale. Close by are four prehistoric forts, and farther north along the Evan Valley, on the way to the famous Beattock road and railway summits, are the picturesquely ruined towers of Blacklaw, Mellingshaw, and Raecleuch.

*Turn left, pass under a railway bridge, and in 1 mile turn right on to the A701 'Dumfries' road. Continue to the hamlet of St Ann's and cross the Kinnel Water.*

## ST ANN'S, Dumf & Gall

The bridge here dates from c1800, and the picturesque ruins of Lochwood Tower from 1592. A little to the north-west of the hamlet are the lovely Raehills Glens.

*Continue to Amisfield Town.*

## AMISFIELD TOWN, Dumf & Gall

Amisfield Tower 1 mile north-west is the ancestral home of the Charteris family, who have been associated with the area since the 12th century. It was built in the 16th century and is one of the best and most beautiful buildings of its type in Scotland.

*Continue through Locharbriggs to Dumfries in Lower Nithsdale.*

## DUMFRIES, Dumf & Gall

Affectionately known as Queen of the South by the Scots, this ancient Royal Burgh was combined with its sister community of Maxwelltown in 1929. The two districts are linked by five bridges across the River Nith, and they hold much of their history in common. The central point of the town is an 18th-century complex of buildings known as Mid Steeple, comprising the old municipal buildings, courthouse, and prison. An inscribed tablet of distances on the

*Ruthwell Cross, housed in a special apse, has been exceptionally well preserved since the 8th century.*

wall of the building is a reminder of times when Scottish cattle drovers herded their animals the length of England to reach the lucrative markets of London. The 15th- and 16th-century remains of Lincluden College (AM), including the fine collegiate church and provost's house, can be seen just outside the town. Relics from this and other periods of the burgh's history are preserved in Dumfries Museum. Many famous people have visited or lived in the town, but it is the two Roberts who are best remembered. Robert the Bruce changed the course of Scottish history when he stabbed the Red Comyn in the former Greyfriars monastery, and

*Devorgilla's Bridge, which was built in 1426, is one of five that span the River Nith at Dumfries.*

some 500 years later in 1791 the poet Robert Burns made his home here. Burns wrote some of his most famous songs while living in the town, and the house where he died has been made into a Burns Museum in his honour. On display are personal possessions and some of his manuscripts, and the road in which the house stands has been renamed Burns Street. Other relics associated with the poet can be seen in the Hole in The Wa' Tavern and the Globe Inn. The family grave and mausoleum are together in St Michael's Churchyard. There is a Burn's interpretation centre at the Old Town Mill.

*At the roundabout turn right SP 'Stranraer' then shortly turn left SP 'Carlisle' and drive alongside the River Nith. At the end turn left then right, SP 'Glencaple' on to the B725 and continue along the B725 to Glencaple.*

**GLENCAPE, Dumf & Gall**
In his novel *Guy Mannering* Sir Walter Scott refers to this little Nith-estuary village as Portanferry. To the local people it is the Auld Quay.

*Continue alongside the Nith estuary, with 1,868ft Criffell prominent across the water to the right, after 3 miles the ruins and estate of Caerlaverock Castle lie ¼ mile to the right.*

**CAERLAVEROCK CASTLE & NATURE RESERVE, Dumf & Gall**
A fortified building has stood here since the early 13th century, but the triangular structure (AM) that now occupies the site owes most of its existence to the 15th century. As a Maxwell stronghold Caerlaverock had a stormy history. In 1638 a fine Renaissance-style block was put up but in 1640 the castle was seriously damaged in a 13-week siege by victorious Covenanters and it became a ruin. The Maxwell crest and motto can still be seen between two splendid towers over the gateway. The estate is now part of a 13,000 acre nature reserve with outstanding hide facilities and an observatory tower. The saltmarsh and sandy foreshore between the River Nith and Lochar Water is the winter haunt of the barnacle goose and other wildfowl.

*Continue to Bankend and turn right SP 'Ruthwell'. Cross flat and often marshy countryside, and after $4\frac{3}{4}$ miles turn right on to the B724. After $\frac{1}{2}$ mile an unclassified left turn offers a detour to Ruthwell Church. (Ruthwell village lies to the right).*

Robert Burns is commemorated in Dumfries, where he died in 1796.

**RUTHWELL, Dumf & Gall**
The 18ft cross at Ruthwell Church dates from the 8th century and is one of the most remarkable dark-age monuments (AM) to have survived in Europe. This archaeological treasure is preserved in a special apse and is heavily inscribed with early written phrases in the Northumbrian dialect of English. These make up the *Dream of the Rood*, which may have been written by the Saxon poet Caedmon; other inscriptions on the cross are in Runic characters. At Ruthwell village is the Duncan Savings Bank Museum.

Until 1940 English couples could be married in Scotland without their parents' consent. The blacksmith's shop at Gretna Green preserves the anvil over which the ceremony was performed.

*Continues along the B724 to the village of Cummertrees.*

**CUMMERTREES, Dumf & Gall**
Scott describes the district around this village in *Redgauntlet*. The full effect of the Solway Firth's notorious spring tides can be observed from nearby Powfoot.

*Continue for 3 miles and turn right on to the A75 to enter Annan.*

**ANNAN, Dumf & Gall**
Sited on the River Annan and the Solway Firth, this pleasant touring centre is noted for its shrimps and is within easy reach of beautiful countryside. Famous names connected with the town include Robert Stevenson, who built the fine bridge in 1826 and Thomas Carlyle who attended the old grammar school and later described it as Hinterschlag Gymnasium in his *Sartor Resartus*. North of Annan are the cooling towers of the Chapelcross Nuclear Power Station.

*Cross the River Annan, meet traffic lights, and turn left on to the B722 'Eaglesfield' road. In 2 miles turn left again on to an unclassified road SP 'Ecclefechan', then after 2½ miles cross the Mein Water and turn right to Ecclefechan. Turn right on to the B725 to enter the village.*

**ECCLEFECHAN, Dumf & Gall**
The Arched House (NTS) was the birthplace in 1795 of the writer and philosopher Thomas Carlyle, and now contains a collection of his personal possessions. Both he and his parents are buried in the village churchyard.

*In Ecclefechan turn right and in ½ mile join the A74 'Carlisle' road. After 2½ miles pass a junction where a detour to Kirtlebridge can be taken.*

**KIRTLEBRIDGE, Dumf & Gall**
Close to Kirtle Water, a little to the south-east of Kirtlebridge, are several old towers. The one known as Robgill was built in the 16th century and now forms part of a recent mansion, and the ancient Irving stronghold of Bonshaw Tower still has its ancient clan bell. About ½ mile south-east is the fine Merkland Cross, an interesting wayside monument that dates from the 15th century.

*On the main route, continue along the A74 and after 2 miles reach a junction where a short detour to Kirkpatrick Fleming can be taken.*

**KIRKPATRICK FLEMING, Dumf & Gall**
A cave which lies to the west of this village is popularly held to be the place where Robert the Bruce was given a lesson in perseverance by a spider. The event is also claimed by several other places in Scotland and Northern Ireland.

*On the main route, continue along the A74 and after $3\frac{1}{2}$ miles branch left on to an unclassified road SP 'Gretna Green' to reach Springfield.*

**SPRINGFIELD, Dumf & Gall**
Founded by weavers in 1791, this village became famous for elopement marriages that were performed here in the 19th century.

*A short detour can be taken from the main route here by turning right for Gretna Green.*

**GRETNA GREEN, Dumb & Gall**
For 100 years Gretna Hall and the smithy at Gretna Green were the first places over the Scottish border where runaway lovers could be married without parental consent. Clandestine marriages of this nature were prevented in England by an 18th-century law, but in Scotland it was only necessary for the couple to make a witnessed declaration that they wished to become man and wife. A law passed in 1856 made it a requirement that either the man or woman should have lived in Scotland for a minimum of three weeks, and more legislation in 1940 prevented the village smith from performing the ceremony.

*On the main route, continue along the unclassified 'Longtown' road into England and cross Solway Moss. In 1542 the Moss was the site of a battle in which the Scots were defeated by the English. After $\frac{3}{4}$ mile turn left on to the A6071 and later join the A7 to enter Longtown.*

**LONGTOWN, Cumbria**
At one time the main Carlisle to Glasgow road ran through Longtown, but this was superseded when the present A74 was built by way of Sark Bridge in 1830. To the north is Netherby Hall, made famous by the romantic elopement of the Graham heiress with Lochinvar in Sir Walter Scott's *Marmion*.

*Return via the A7 and turn right SP 'Galashiels'. Follow the River Esk and return to Scotland at Scots Dyke. In ½ mile turn right on to the B720 for the village of Canonbie.*

**CANONBIE, Dumf & Gall**
Before the Scots Dyke was built in 1552 the Debateable Land, an area close to Canonbie between the Rivers Sark and Esk, was held by anybody who had the force of arms to do so. The dyke formed an effective new boundary and put an end to the troubles. The village itself stands 2 miles from this new border and was once the site of an important priory. It was also a coaching stop, and an interesting old inn has survived from those days. Liddesdale, to the north-east is associated with Scott's novels.

*Turn right on to the B6357, cross the bridge then turn left with the B720. Later rejoin the A7. Continue through the wooded, narrowing valley of Eskdale to Langholm.*

**LANGHOLM, Dumf & Gall**
This angling resort and wool centre stands at the junction of Wauchope Water and the River Esk, with the lovely Ewes Water flowing in from the north. An annual border-riding ceremony that was instituted in the 19th century still takes place in the town. A monument to General Sir John Malcolm stands on 1,163ft Whita Hill, which rises to the east. The forbears of Neil Armstrong, the first man to walk on the moon, came from this area.

*Leave the town on the B709 'Eskdalemuir' road and in 2 miles reach Craigcleuch.*

**CRAIGCLEUCH, Dumb & Gall**
The Scottish Explorers' Museum has hundreds of colonial artefacts housed in a baronial mansion.

*Continue along the B709 to Bentpath.*

**BENTPATH, Dumf & Gall**
The brilliant engineer Thomas Telford was born in a shepherd's cottage near Glendinning Farm in 1757; his tablet stands ½ mile beyond the hamlet.

*After 2 miles turn right and cross the River Esk then climb into the Castle O'er Forest. Proceed to Eskdalemuir.*

**ESKDALEMUIR, Dumf & Gall**
This hamlet is on an important junction of roads in an area that abounds with prehistoric remains.

*Cross the river and turn right then left on to the B723 for Lockerbie.*

## MOFFAT, Dumf & Gall

Moffat lies in the deep valley of the River Annan, overshadowed by the steep Lowther Hills. This is sheepfarming country, its importance celebrated by the conspicuous bronze ram that stands proudly on top of the Colvin fountain at the end of the town's broad High Street. In the 17th century sulphur springs were discovered a short distance away from Moffat, and it remained popular as a spa throughout the 18th and 19th centuries. Holiday-makers today find it an ideal base from which to explore the beauties of Annandale. Famous people associated with Moffat include road engineer John Macadam, who was buried in the churchyard in 1836, and James Macpherson, who launched his Ossianic Fragments at Moffat House, now an hotel, in 1759. These fragments purported to be ancient Gaelic poems which Macpherson claimed to have discovered, to the great excitement of the literary world of his day, but later their authenticity was disputed in a storm of controversy.

*Follow SP 'Selkirk A708', and shortly enter the valley of the Moffat Water. After the Craigieburn Plantation the valley narrows considerably, with hills rising to over 2,100ft on both sides. Near the summit of the climb pass (left) the Grey Mare's Tail waterfall.*

## GREY MARE'S TAIL, Dumf & Gall

Emptying out of Loch Skene, the Tail Burn cascades 200ft over the rockface in a breathtaking fall of white water aptly christened the Grey Mare's Tail. There are 2 other falls with the same name in the south-west, but neither is as magnificent as this one. The countryside around the burn, now owned by the National Trust for Scotland, is famous for its profusion and variety of flowering plants, and goats inhabit the rocky hillsides.

*After reaching 1,100ft the route descends to Loch of the Lowes and Tibbie Shiel's Inn.*

## TIBBIE SHIEL'S INN, Borders

St Mary's Loch, set among a superb landscape of steep hills, is joined to the tiny Loch of the Lowes by a neck of land on which, strategically placed, stands Tibbie Shiel's, a famous fishermen's inn. Nearby is the statue of the Ettrick Shepherd, as the vernacular poet James Hogg (1770-1835) was known. Many of his poems describe St Mary's Loch.

*Continue alongside St Mary's Loch for 1½ miles then cross the Megget Water and shortly turn left, SP 'Tweedsmuir', along the Megget Water valley. The road ascends to a 1483ft summit at the Megget Stone before descending steeply to the shores of Talla Reservoir. Continue to Tweedsmuir.*

## TWEEDDALE AND CLYDEDALE

Scotland's great Lowlands rivers, the Tweed and the Clyde, roll majestically east and west through the green hills of the wild Borders country, where centuries of family feuds and bitter skirmishes with the marauding English found their most lyrical expression in the haunting sadness of the Border Ballads.

Talla Reservoir, completed in 1905, provides Edinburgh with its water and the angler with brown trout

## TWEEDSMUIR, Borders

This delightful village with its single-arched stone bridge spanning the River Tweed, was made famous by John Buchan, best known for his novel of adventure The Thirty Nine Steps. Many of the exciting episodes described in his books are set in the wild Borders country of his boyhood home. When, as Governor General of Canada (1935), he was raised to the peerage, he chose the title of Baron Tweedsmuir. This was strong Covenanting country and several victims of the 17th-century persecution of the staunchly Presbyterian Covenanters lie buried in the graveyard of Tweedsmuir Church.

*Turn right on to the A701 Edinburgh road and descend through Tweeddale. After 7 miles turn right on to the B712 Peebles road. Shortly enter Drumelzier.*

## RIVER TWEED, Borders

The source of the Tweed lies close to that of the other great Lowland river, the Clyde. Instead of flowing westwards, however, it makes its way eastwards and for some distance is used as the border with England, flowing out to the North Sea at Berwick, 97 miles away. The Tweed has inspired many of the most beautiful Border ballads and the works of some of the most famous of Scotland's writers, in particular Sir Walter Scott. Many weaving towns are scattered through the valley, but the world-renowned cloth obtained its name through a Sassenach misunderstanding. Londoners read the local technical term 'tweel' as tweed, and the name has stuck ever since. Salmon, sea trout and brown trout all live in the river.

## DRUMELZIER, Borders

High above Tweeddale, north-east of the village, the ruins of Thines Castle, destroyed by James VI in 1592, and by tradition the burial place of the Arthurian wizard Merlin, overlook the confluence of the River Tweed and Drumelzier Burn.

*In 2 miles pass (right) the grounds of Dawyck House (not open) and Arboretum.*

## DAWYCK BOTANIC GARDEN, Borders

These beautiful gardens (OACT) specialising in trees and flowering shurbs, were created in the 18th century by Sir James Naesmyth, acting on the advice of his teacher, the great Swedish botanist Linnaeus, to whom we owe the scientific classification of plants. Sir James is credited with being the first person to introduce the larch to Scotland (1725). The gardens are famous for their rhododendrons, magnificent Douglas firs, pinetum and avenues of lime trees and silver firs.

*Cross the River Tweed and in 2 miles reach Stobo.*

## STOBO, Borders

In the barrel-vaulted porch of Stobo's Norman church are preserved a set of jougs, the Scottish equivalent of stocks. These were a type of iron collar in which wrongdoers were confined.

*In 2½ miles cross the Lyne Water then turn left on to the A72, SP 'Glasgow'. Follow the Lyne Water and then Tarth Water for 6½ miles then keep left, SP 'Biggar'. In 5½ miles enter Skirling.*

## SKIRLING, Borders

A wealth of wrought iron work decorates Skirling's houses, attractively arranged around the village green. Scattered here and there are painted figures of beasts and birds. The idea was Lord Carmichael's who built his own house here and died in 1926.

*Continue on the A72 and in 2 miles turn left on to the A702 to enter Biggar.*

## BIGGAR, Strathclyde

The crowning in July every year of the Fleming Queen commemorates Mary Fleming, one of the 'Queen's 4 Marys' of the folk song, who was born at Boghall Castle, now ruined. Mary Fleming, Mary Seton, Mary Beaton and Mary Livingstone were all Ladies-in-Waiting to Mary, Queen of Scots. Biggar's broad main street lies alongside Biggar Water, ending at Cadger's Bridge, which has preserved this name ever since William Wallace, hero of the 13th-century Scottish Wars of Independence, crossed it disguised as a cadger (pedlar) to lead his army to victory over the English at a battle south of the town. The Gladstone Court Museum, a

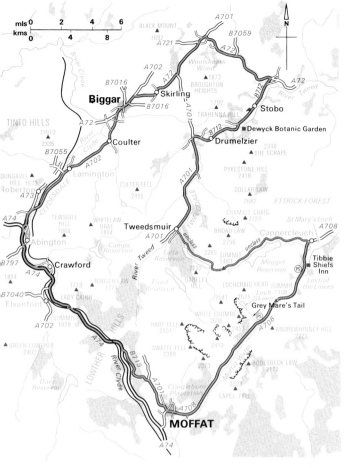

converted 19th-century coachworks, has a fascinating reconstruction of an old-world village street, complete with authentic shop signs and advertisements. Among the premises on display are an old bank and telephone exchange. An outdoor extension will eventually house agricultural buildings and a Victorian gasworks. The museum is named after William Gladstone, whose family came from this area.

*Keep forward on the A702, SP 'Carlisle', entering the Clyde valley. After 3 miles pass through Coulter.*

## COULTER, Strathclyde
This pretty village stands beside the Coulter water, well shaded by trees. By the former railway station, Coulter Motte Hill is an early medieval castle mound and would originally have had a moat and a timber tower and palisade. Tinto Hill rises up to 2,335ft in the distance.

*Across the valley to the right there are further views of Tinto as the tour approaches Lamington. Shortly beyond Lamington the road joins the River Clyde and the electrified Glasgow railway line, running alongside the latter for 3 miles before crossing the valley and turning left on to the A73. In 1¼ miles turn left to join the A74.*

## RIVER CLYDE, Strathclyde
The Clyde rises as a mountain stream in the hills south-west of Crawford and flows westwards for 106 miles. In its upper reaches the

Clyde is famed for its limpid waters, populated by the wary brown trout. The stream is so clear that local anglers would only use horse-hair lines because gut and nylon were held to be too coarse, and the fish would not rise to the bait. The fertile Clyde valley is the home of the celebrated Clydesdale heavy horses, and is also noted for its fruit orchards.

*Follow the railway and river up the valley to Crawford.*

## CRAWFORD, Strathclyde
On the opposite bank of the Clyde from the village, Crawford Castle (not open) has stood as guardian since the 13th century, when it belonged to the powerful Border family — the Lindsays. It was restored and reconstructed in the 17th century when it passed into the hands of the Douglases. Crawford makes an excellent centre from which to explore the green lowland hills. The curious stone pillar in the village street was, in fact, destined to be a tombstone for the Cranston family who ran the last mailcoach in the area.

*In 9 miles, on the winding descent through the forested Lower Hills, branch left on to the B719 Moffat road. Climb again through woodland before descending into the upper Annan valley and turning right on to the A701 for the return to Moffat.*

Grey Mare's Tail waterfall cascades down 200ft into Moffat Water

# THE MACHARS OF WIGTOWNSHIRE

Along the coast from Newton Stewart breathtaking views of the Isle of Man and over the Solway Firth to the distant mountains of the Lake District introduce the sandy rock-strewn shores of the lovely Bay of Luce and, inland, across the lonely moors and the high hills of Galloway.

**NEWTON STEWART, Dumf & Gall**
The mountainous wooded landscape of the distant Galloway Hills provides the magnificent setting of this busy little market town. Newton Stewart grew up around an ancient ford and was founded by William Stewart, son of the Earl of Galloway, in 1677. He gave the town its name and obtained its charter as a burgh of barony from Charles II. In the next century it was bought by Sir William Douglas, who established the weaving industry and attempted unsuccessfully to change the name to Newton Douglas. Many of the old houses lining the attractive main street stand so close to the river that they look almost Venetian. The 5-arched granite bridge over the Cree, that connects Newton

Stewart to the neighbouring village of Minnigaff, was built in 1813 by the famous engineer John Rennie.

*From the bypass roundabout at the south end of the town follow SP 'Wigtown A714'.*

**WIGTOWN, Dumf & Gall**
Where Wigtown's broad main street opens out into a spacious green, cattle were once herded for safety at night. The more ornate of the town's 2 mercat crosses was erected in 1816 to commemorate the Battle of Waterloo; the other, incorporating a sundial, is older and dates from 1738. In the churchyard and on the crest of Windy Hill, the highest point in the town, stand memorials to the 5 Wigtown Martyrs; 3 men and 2 women, executed in 1685 for adhering to their Presbyterian faith. The women, Margaret

McLauchlan, aged 63, and the 18-year-old Margaret Wilson suffered a terrible fate: they were tied to stakes in the estuary and slowly drowned by the incoming tide.

*Turn right through the Square and pass the memorial, then turn left, SP 'Whithorn', for Bladnoch.*

Roland, Lord of Galloway, founded Glenluce Abbey in 1190 as a Cistercian house and daughter house of Dundrennan Abbey

Port William overlooking Luce Bay

**BLADNOCH, Dumf & Gall**
Bladnoch Water runs by the little village and out to the sea above Baldoon Sands. Overlooking the estuary stands ruined Baldoon Castle, home in 1669 of David Dunbar on whom Sir Walter Scott modelled the bridegroom in his tragic novel *The Bride of Lammermoor*. The events on which he based his story were true: Lady Dalrymple, wife of Lord Stair of Glenluce, obliged her daughter Janet to marry Dunbar although she loved the penniless Lord Rutherford. The marriage took place at Glenluce, but Dunbar had scarcely arrived home with his young wife when she fell ill and died within the month.

*Turn left and cross the River Bladnoch and in 1¼ miles go forward on to the A746. A mile beyond Kirkinner branch left on to the B7004, SP 'Garlieston'. In 4 miles reach the edge of Garlieston and turn right, SP 'Whithorn', (for the village centre turn left).*

**GARLIESTON, Dumf & Gall**
Founded in the 18th century by Lord Garlies, 7th Earl of Galloway, the village, with its pretty cottages, peaceful bowling green and old mill, lies at the head of a delightful bay on the east coast of the Machars peninsula. The bay is sheltered by the low, rocky promontory of Eggerness Point and at low tide all the upper part of the beach is left high and dry, revealing a multitude of delightful rock pools to explore.

*In ½ mile turn left and in 4 miles further turn left on to the A746 for Whithorn.*

**WHITHORN, Dumf & Gall**
In the bleak countrysde of the Machars lies one of the earliest centres of Christianity in Britain. St Ninian landed on this remote western shore in AD397 and built his simple oratory at Whithorn —

the name comes from hwit aern, meaning 'white house'. The priory, today in ruins, was founded in the 12th century by Fergus, Lord of Galloway, and soon became a place of pilgrimage, being visited by many of the Scottish sovereigns. The last royal visitor, before the priory was finally dissolved, was Mary, Queen of Scots in 1563. The entrance to the priory lies through a graceful 17th-century gateway, emblazoned with the royal coat of arms, known as the Pend. The town museum contains a notable collection of early Christian relics, including the Latinus Stone dating from the 5th century.

*From the southern end of the main street a detour to Isle of Whithorn can be made by turning left on to the A750.*

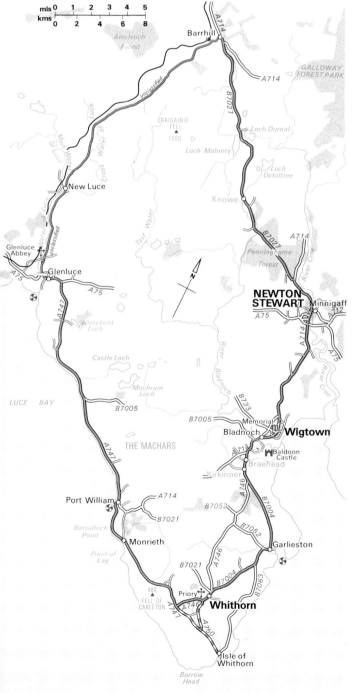

### ISLE OF WHITHORN, Dumf & Gall

This quiet, lonely little village, perched almost on the tip of the peninsula, lays claim to be the most southerly village in Scotland. The isle has long been joined to the mainland by a causeway. On a rocky headland looking out to sea stands a ruined 12th-century chapel dedicated to St Ninian. This was originally thought to be the site of his oratory, but excavation has shown that Whithorn Priory is the more likely place. In St Ninian's Cave further round the coast numbers of crosses and other relics dating from the Celtic period have been found, showing that the cave was used as a hermitage for Whithorn Priory.

*From here the detour returns along the A750 for 1½ miles then goes forward on to the A747 Port William road across windswept countryside. The main tour from Whithorn continues on the A746 Port William road and in 1½ miles turns right on to the A747 for Monreith.*

### MONREITH, Dumf & Gall

In earlier times the splendid sands of Monreith Bay saw the secret landing of many a cargo of contraband from Ireland or the Isle of Man run in by local smugglers. The strangest landing however occurred in 1760, when villagers were astonished to find on the shore the body of a French naval officer in full dress uniform, wrapped in a velvet carpet. He was identified as Captain Thurot, commander of a French squadron that had captured Carrickfergus Castle, only to be defeated by the British in the Bay of Luce.

*Follow the coast round Barsallock Point to Port William.*

### PORT WILLIAM, Dumf & Gall

A seaside village whose pretty cottages look out across Luce Bay, Port William was founded beside an attractive sandy beach in 1770 by Sir William Maxwell whose family home, Monreith House, stands a little way inland beside the White Loch of Myrton.

*At the roundabout take the 1st exit, SP 'Glenluce'. Continue along the coast for 10 miles, with views across Luce Bay, then turn inland across a stretch of bleak Machars countryside. Later turn left on to the A75, SP 'Stranraer', into Glenluce.*

### GLENLUCE, Dumf & Gall

Glenluce, one of the prettiest villages in the region, lies on the east bank of the Water of Luce, surrounded by lovely wooded countryside. The Castle of Park, built in 1590 by Thomas Hay, looks down over the village, where, in 1654, a famous poltergeist took up residence in a weaver's cottage and defied all efforts at exorcism for 4 years, at the end of which time the phenomenon mysteriously ceased.

*At the end of the village, on a sharp left-hand bend beneath the railway viaduct, take the 2nd unclassified road to the right, SP 'Glenluce Abbey'. In 1¼ miles pass Glenluce Abbey.*

### GLENLUCE ABBEY, Dumf & Gall

Founded in 1190, the ruined abbey (AM) occupies a superb site in the beautiful Vale of Luce. Its vaulted 15th-century chapter house remains almost intact and, for its period, a remarkably efficient medieval drainage system has been excavated. This consists of skilfully jointed stone channels and interlocking earthenware pipes that could still be functional today. The abbey is associated with the 13th-century wizard Michael Scott, who is said to have stopped an outbreak of plague in the area by luring it to the abbey and walling it up, thus starving it to death. A little to the east of this site stand the gaunt remains of Carscreugh Castle, home of Janet Dalrymple, whose tragic death in 1669 inspired Sir Walter Scott to make her the heroine, Lucy Ashton, of *The Bride of Lammermoor*.

*Continue alongside the Water of Luce for 4 miles to New Luce.*

### NEW LUCE, Dumf & Gall

The village, known as the 'capital' of the moors district of Galloway, lies high up in the Vale of Luce at the point where the Cross Water and the Main Water of Luce join forces to form the Water of Luce. Behind the village rises a bleak expanse of moorland.

*Keep forward SP 'Barrhill' on to a narrow, hilly road crossing bleak moorland. Later rejoin, and then turn right to cross the Cross Water of Luce, following the Ayr-Stranraer railway line on the opposite side of the valley. Several miles after leaving the railway enter the Arecleoch Forest (Forestry Commission) before descending into the Duisk valley and Barrhill.*

### BARRHILL, Strathclyde

In the days of the stagecoach this remote village on the River Duisk was a welcome staging post on the road from Girvan to Newton Stewart. Two roads meet at Barrhill and take a separate path across the lonely moors, merging again just outside Newton Stewart. The more northerly one crosses the fringe of Galloway Forest Park; the other ascends to 3 high mountain lakes, Lochs Dornal, Ochiltree and Maberry.

*Turn right on to the A714 and at the end of the village right again on to the B7027, SP 'Newton Stewart via Knowe'. This road passes through open moorland with many lochs and rivers and fine views of the high Galloway Hills to the east. At Challoch turn right on to the A714 for the return to Newton Stewart.*

# STRONGHOLDS IN THE HIGHLANDS

High above the fishing quays of Oban is an unfinished replica of the Colosseum, a fascinating folly built to relieve unemployment. Inland are the castles and towers of the Campbells and MacDougalls, grim ruins of serious intent in the spectacular loch and mountain scenery of the Highlands.

Carnassarie Castle has been in ruins since the Argyll rebellion of 1685.

## OBAN, Strath

In the 200 years of its existence Oban has become a major centre in the West Highlands. Its busy port offers ferry services to the islands of Lismore, Mull, Colonsay, Coll, and some of the Outer Hebrides, making the town a thriving tourist resort. One of its most remarkable buildings is McCaig's Folly, which was begun in 1897 to relieve local unemployment but never finished. It was intended to be a replica of Rome's Colosseum and to house a museum and art gallery. The inside courtyard is landscaped, and the folly shines bravely in floodlights that bathe the summit of Battery Hill at night. Oban's museum is housed in Corran Hall, and the little granite St Columba's Cathedral near by was built by Sir Gilbert Scott. The Island of Kerrera stands just offshore from Oban and features the ruined MacDougall stronghold of Gylan Castle. The town is a popular golfing resort, and the fine 18-hole course lies to the east. Macdonald's Mill, ½ mile south of the town centre on the A816, mounts a fascinating display of the story of spinning and weaving. The Caithness Glassworks is also of interest with demonstrations of paperweight making. On the shore north of the town is the ruined 12th- or 13th-century McDougall stronghold of Dunollie Castle. A modern mansion nearby contains Robert Bruce's Brooch of Lorne.

*Leave Oban on the A816 'Campbeltown' road and after 4½ miles join the shores of Loch Feochan. In 2¾ miles reach a junction with the* B844. *A detour can be made to Seil by turning right here and driving to Kilninver.*

## KILNINVER, Strath

This small village on Loch Feochan faces north-west across the wide Firth of Lorne to the mountainous Island of Mull.

*Turn right with the B844, and cross a bridge. In 4 miles reach Clachan Bridge.*

## CLACHAN BRIDGE, Strath

Telford built this attractive hump-backed bridge in 1792. It spans Seil Sound, a narrow arm of the Atlantic to link with the island of Seil.

*Cross the bridge onto the island of Seil and continue to Balvicar. Here turn right for Easdale.*

## ISLAND OF SEIL, Strath

Slate used to be quarried here and on the much smaller island of Easdale. Of interest are the An Cala Garden (open), and the Easdale Island Folk Museum records the quarrying industry there. Luing Island to the south of Seil is accessible via the Cuan Ferry.

*On the main tour continue along the A816. In 2½ miles a detour can be made to Loch Scammadale by turning left on to an unclassified road through Glen Euchar to reach lovely Loch Scammadale.*

## LOCH SCAMMADALE, Strath

This attractive loch lies in Glen Euchar, surrounded by hills.

*On the main tour, continue along the A816 and drive through wooded Glen Gallain. Descend to reach Kilmelford.*

## KILMELFORD, Strath

This quiet angling village stands near the head of Loch Melfort which is sheltered by islands in the Firth of Lorne. The Pass of Melfort, north of the village off the A816, is a picturesque area which includes a small hydro-electric dam.

*From Kilmelford continue along the A816 to follow the shores of Loch Melfort and reach Arduaine Gardens.*

## ARDUAINE GARDENS, Strath

Many rare trees and shrubs have been collected in theis 21-acre garden (open), which is especially famed for its spring displays of rhododendrons and azaleas. The attractive layout includes water and rock gardens, and superb views extend over Loch Melfort and the Sound of Jura.

*Oban's busy port serves as the gateway to the Western Isles.*

*Continue on the A816 for 3½ miles. A detour from the main route to Craignish Castle can be taken here: turn right on to the B8002 and drive alongside Loch Craignish through Ardfern to Craignish Castle.*

## CRAIGNISH CASTLE, Strath

The 16th-century keep of Craignish Castle (not open) stands amid a fine rhododendron garden facing the Sound of Jura.

*On the main tour, continue along the A816 to reach Kintraw.*

## KINTRAW, Strath

This attractive little hamlet offers magnificent views of the beautiful sea loch of Craignish, with its scattered islands.

*Proceed on the A816 to the junction with the B840. Ahead along the A816 a road to the right, after ¼ mile leads to Carnassarie Castle.*

## CARNASSARIE CASTLE, Strath

Ruined Carnassarie Castle (AM) stands high on a hill about 1 mile north of the village of Kilmartin. It was built for the Bishop of the Isles in the 16th century, but was captured and partially blown up during the Duke of Argyll's ill-fated rebellion in 1685.

*On the main route turn left on to the B840 and proceed to Ford, passing Loch Ederline to the right.*

## FORD, Strath

Sandwiched between huge Loch Awe and tiny Loch Ederline, Ford is a small angling resort. The surrounding countryside is ideal for walking.

*At the Ford Hotel go forward on to an unclassified road SP 'Dalavich' with Loch Awe on the right.*

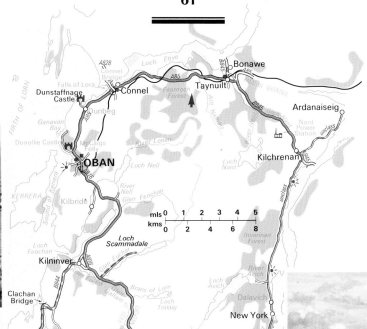

This isolated standing stone near Kintraw, stark against a background of hills, is thought to be of bronze-age date.

## LOCH AWE, Strath

The Campbells of Inveraray had many occasions to be grateful for the protection given against attack from the north by this long natural moat. Reminders of its part in Scotland's turbulent history are scattered along the shores of the loch today. Ruins of a castle stand near Fincharn at the southern end, and the wooded islet of Fraoch Eilean in the north conceals remains of another. Early religious stirrings are recalled by ancient chapels built on some of Loch Awe's islands by holy men seeking isolation. In the south is the Innis-Sherrich Chapel, which was dedicated to St Findoc c1257 and stands near several 14th- or 15th-century carved slabs. Another foundation can be seen on Inishail, in the north. Today the loch forms part of Scotland's largest hydro-electric scheme and is a paradise for anglers and walkers. The lovely countryside of Inverliever Forest borders the loch and features several marked nature trails, some of which lead to notable viewpoints. At its northern end the loch is dominated by the twin peaks of 3,689ft Ben Cruachan.

*Continue through Inverliever Forest to reach New York.*

## NEW YORK, Strath

A marked contrast to its famous namesake, this tiny hamlet faces across the peaceful expanse of Loch Awe to an ancient chapel at Portinnisherrich.

*Leave New York and continue to the new forestry village of Dalavich, then after a short distance cross the River Avich. Continue through Inverinan Forest, meet the B845, and turn left to enter Kilchrenan.*

## KILCHRENAN, Strath

A granite block in the churchyard here commemorates 13th-century Mac Cailean Mor, clan hero and founder of the Argyll fortunes.

*At Kilchrenan a detour can be taken from the main route to visit the gardens at Ardanaiseig by turning right on to an unclassified road.*

## ARDANAISEIG GARDENS, Strath

Superb views of Loch Awe can be enjoyed from these beautiful gardens (open), which are full of rare shrubs and trees. In the early part of the year banks of rhododendrons and azaleas burst into a magnificent display of colour.

Telford's unusual Clachan Bridge is known as the 'Bridge over the Atlantic' because it actually spans a creek of that ocean.

## TAYNUILT, Strath

Taynuilt is a small resort at the foot of Glen Nant, facing the lovely waters of Loch Etive. Ben Cruachan rises magnificently in the east, and the situation enjoyed by the village affords marvellous views of the mountains which overlook Upper Loch Etive. Lord Nelson is somewhat unexpectedly commemorated by a standing stone in the village.

*A detour can be made from the main route to visit Bonawe: in Taynuilt village turn right on to the B845, then after ⅓ mile turn right again on to an unclassified road and enter Bonawe.*

*On the main tour, continue on the B845 from Kilchrenan SP 'Taynuilt' and drive through Glen Nant. Meet the A85 and turn left to reach Taynuilt.*

## BONAWE, Strath

During the 18th century a thriving iron industry developed in the unlikely Highland setting of picturesque Bonawe. The furnace, casting house, and workmen's cottages (all AM) used at that time have all been painstakingly restored.

*On the main tour, continue along the A85 and later follow the shores of Loch Etive to reach Connel.*

## CONNEL, Strath

Cantilevered Connel Bridge is the largest of its kind in Europe, after the Forth Bridge, and is a splendid example of its type. Beside the bridge is a remarkable sea-cataract known as the Falls of Lora.

*Continue on the A85 to Dunbeg for an unclassified right turn leading to Dunstaffnage Castle.*

## DUNSTAFFNAGE CASTLE, Strath

The castle (AM) on a bay north-east of Oban is a ruined four-sided 13th-century Campbell stronghold with a gatehouse, two round towers and walls 10ft thick. It was once the prison of Flora MacDonald.
The chapel near the castle was the burial place of the Campbells.

*Continue on the A85 to re-enter the port of Oban.*

Loch Etive is a sea loch of quiet seclusion and home of many seabirds.

# GLENCOE AND THE PASS OF BRANDER

*A corner of Scotland steeped in a history as wild and dramatic as the landscape in which it took place: Glencoe and the Pass of Brander — scenes of bloody warfare; Dunstaffnage Castle, where the Stone of Destiny first rested on Scottish soil; and from this century the subterranean power station beneath Ben Cruachan.*

Oban, easily accessible by sea and land, is a busy fishing port and market town

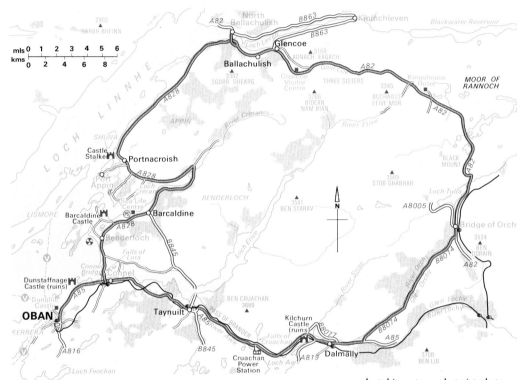

### OBAN, Strathclyde

Oban, situated at the centre of Scotland's western seaboard, is at the hub of the tourist industry. There are sea trips from the bustling harbour to the many nearby islands along the coast, such as Mull, Tiree, Coll, Barra and South Uist. The town has many hotels and guesthouses, for it is a beautiful and romantic place in its own right, looking over an almost landlocked bay and surrounded by hills and mountains in every direction. A strange relic of yesteryear stands on top of Oban Hill and dominates the townscape. This is McCaig's Folly. McCaig was a wealthy banker, who began building this Colosseum-like structure to help solve the local unemployment problem, and to provide a museum which would also serve as a memorial to his family. Unfortunately he died before its completion and the scheme was abandoned; today it remains an empty shell. The Corran Hall on the esplanade houses a museum and the country library, and is also the venue for much traditional dancing and music. Macdonald's Mill (OACT) houses an exhibiton called the Story of Spinning and Weaving, and demonstrations of this ancient craft are given on the premises. On the northern outskirts of Oban stands ruined Dunollie Castle (not open) which belonged to the MacDougalls, an ancient and powerful family who once owned as much as a third of Scotland.

*Leave Oban on the A85, SP 'Connel' and 'Crianlarich', and continue to Taynuilt.*

### TAYNUILT, Strathclyde

This small resort lies at the point where the Pass of Brander meets Loch Etive, overlooked by the impressive and beautiful Ben Cruachan (3,689ft). Near Muckairn Church stands a large stone of unknown antiquity, re-erected here by workmen to commemorate Lord Nelson in 1805, the year of Trafalgar. It was the first of the many monuments to be raised in Nelson's honour all over Britain.

*Remain on the Crianlarich road and enter the Pass of Brander, then continue alongside Loch Awe to Cruachan Power Station.*

### CRUACHAN POWER STATION, Strathclyde

Above the Pass of Brander towers 3,689ft-high Ben Cruachan. In the shoulder of the mountain lies the Corrie Reservoir and at its foot Loch Awe. During the day water from the Corrie drives the turbines of the power station (OACT) housed in a man-made cave the size of Coventry Cathedral 1,000ft beneath the mountain. At night water is pumped back up the mountain from Loch Awe, to replenish the head of water in the reservoir. Visitors are taken into the power station via a tunnel nearly a mile long, carved out of solid granite.

*Continue on the A85 to the village of Lochawe. At the north-east extremity of Loch Awe is Kilchurn Castle.*

### KILCHURN CASTLE, Strathclyde

This was the seat of the Glenorchy Campbells and at one time stood on an island, but as Loch Awe has dropped its water level by 10ft, the castle (AM) is now surrounded by marshland instead. The keep is 15th century, 3 storeys high and surmounted by a parapet and wall-walk. The north and west extensions were added a century later. There are round towers at 3 corners of the courtyard with extensive lean-to buildings where the troops were housed. Strangely, there is only one entrance to the castle, and to reach the courtyard the soldiers had to tramp through the kitchen.

*The tour enters the Strath of Orchy to reach Dalmally.*

### DALMALLY, Strathclyde

Dalmally is a pleasant place scattered over the floor of a wooded valley, where the River Orchy flows into Loch Awe. The large hotel here, formerly an ancient inn, is particularly popular with anglers, who come here for the excellent sport provided by the river, the loch, and the many streams hereabouts. Opposite the hotel is a strangely-twisted stone known as Bruce's Stone. Bruce passed through the village twice; once in 1306 after his defeat at Methven, and again in 1308 before his victory at the Pass of Brander.

*In 2¼ miles turn left on to the B8074 and follow a single track road through Glen Orchy. After 10 miles turn left on to the A82 for Bridge of Orchy. Beyond the village pass Loch Tulla and climb on to the Moor of Rannoch.*

### MOOR OF RANNOCH, Strathclyde & Tayside

Famous as the largest moor in Scotland, the Moor of Rannoch is an exhilaratingly desolate area of some 60 square miles of bog, moor, lochans and mountains. A railway crosses the moor, and as the peat over which it travels is often boggy and up to 20ft deep, the line used to be supported on brushwood. The north-east corner of the moor is a Nature Reserve, where several rare species of bog flora grow, and a patient observer may be rewarded by the sight of red deer or a lone golden eagle.

The menacing crags that tower up above Glencoe provide some of the most famous rock and ice climbs in Britain

*Beyond the Moor of Rannoch the tour enters the Pass of Glencoe.*

### GLENCOE, Highland

Both history and magnificent scenery have made Glencoe one of the most celebrated glens in Scotland. It drops some 10 miles from the Moor of Rannoch to the saltwater Loch Leven, a total descent of about 1,100ft. Great rocky mountains rise on either side — Bidean nam Bian (3,766ft) is the highest summit in Argyll. Some 14,500 acres of the countryside are now owned by the National Trust for Scotland, but this does not include the lower part of the valley where the notorious massacre of the Macdonalds occurred in 1692. After the Jacobite Rising of 1689, William III pardoned all clan chiefs, provided they signed an oath of allegiance by January 1692. Maclean of Glencoe was prevented from signing by his old rivals the Campbells. As a result soldiers under Campbell of Glenlyons were billeted on the MacDonalds as a punishment. They were entertained and fed for 12 days during this, an exceptionally hard winter. However on the 12th day, under government orders, the Campbell soldiers rose and slew men, women and children without warning. Some escaped only to perish on the freezing hillsides. A monument in the form of a tall Celtic cross beside the Bridge of Coe at Carnoch commemorates the dead chief and his people. Close to the site of the massacre is a Visitor Centre, which provides a Ranger Naturalist Service. In the main street of Glencoe itself is the Glencoe and North Lorn Folk Museum (OACT) housed in 2 heather-thatched cottages, which displays Macdonald relics, local domestic and agricultural exhibits, Jacobite relics, costumes and embroidery.

*Gradually descend through the Glen to the edge of Glencoe village and follow the shoreline of Loch Leven past Ballachulish.*

### BALLACHULISH, Highland

This scattered village at the sea entrance to Loch Leven was the scene of a notorious murder trial known as the Appin murder case. A granite memorial near the new bridge over the loch marks the spot where James Stewart of the Glen was wrongly hanged for the shooting of Colin Roy Campbell of Glenure — 11 of the jury were Campbells. The identity of the true murderer was never discovered. Slate used to be quarried nearby, and Ballachulish is mainly composed of stone quarrymen's cottages.

*In 1¾ miles, at the roundabout, take the A828, SP 'Oban', and pass beneath the Ballachulish Bridge. Continue southwards and follow Loch Linnhe to reach Portnacroish.*

### PORTNACROISH, Strathclyde

This little community at the western edge of the Strath of Appin takes its name from the episcopal Church of St Cross. Upon a wooded rise nearby stands a monument commemmorating the Battle of Stalc between the 1st Stewart of Appin and a Campbell, MacDougall and Macfarlane alliance. The Stewart's victory here avenged the murder of his father, slain at his second wedding. The battle was fought in 1468, and the Hollow of Treachery, close by, is where the slaughter took place.

*Opposite Portnacroish is Castle Stalker.*

### CASTLE STALKER, Strathclyde

Artists and photographers delight in recording the image of this strong and tall rectangular keep stood upon its tiny rock at the mouth of Loch Laich. It dates from the 15th century, although the upper parts were altered in 1631. It has 9ft-thick walls, is 4 storeys high, and is topped by a parapet and a wall-walk. The basement is vaulted, and there is a dungeon reached only by a trap door at the foot of the stairway. The castle (OACT) was erected by Duncan Stewart the 2nd of Appin, later made Chamberlain of the Isles by James IV, who used it as a hunting lodge.

*Continue on the A828 around Loch Creran to Barcaldine.*

### BARCALDINE, Strathclyde

South-west of the hamlet is the Sea Life Centre, where the largest collection of marine life in Britain is kept on display in a way designed to enable a greater understanding of the underwater world. Further along the shores of Loch Creran is Barcaldine Castle. (open by appointment). This baronial-style 16th-century castle, commanding magnificent views over Loch Cleran to Glencoe, was built by Duncan Campbell of Glenorchy. It remained in that family's hands until 1842 when it was sold. It was later bought back, roofless, and restored by the family between 1896 and 1910, and is still lived in to this day. It is an L-shaped tower-house of 3 storeys, with a stair tower and 4 angle-towers at the corners.

*Remain on the A828 to Benderloch, then in 2½ miles cross Loch Etive by the Connel Bridge and at the A85 turn left. 1½ miles farther, across Dunstaffnage Bay (right), stands Dunstaffnage Castle.*

### DUNSTAFFNAGE CASTLE, Strathclyde

Almost islanded on its high promontory, Dunstaffnage (AM) stands in an excellent strategic position at the mouth of Loch Etive. This was the first resting place on Scottish soil of the Stone of Destiny when it first arrived from Ireland. In the 9th century the stone was removed to Scone, where kings of Scotland were crowned on it for many years. Robert the Bruce took the castle after his victory over the MacDougall clan at the Pass of Brander in 1308, and it was given to the Campbells. In the 15th century Alexander II had the castle enlarged in preparation for his attack on the Norsemen occupying the Hebrides. Flora MacDonald was held captive here in 1746, but the castle has not been lived in since 1810, when it was destroyed in a fire.

*Continue on the A85 for the return to Oban.*

Ben Cruachan rises up behind Loch Etive — a narrow sea loch stretching from the Firth of Lorne to the foot of Glen Etive

# THE SIDLAW AND OCHIL HILLS

*Scott immortalized the wild beauty of the countryside round Perth in his novels, and his praise is as justified today as it was then. Here the flanks of the Sidlaw and Ochil Hills sweep down to deep wooded straths, or valleys, where the enchantment of running water is never far away.*

## PERTH, Tayside

Once known as St Johnstoun, the fair city of Perth is an old Royal Burgh set at the head of the Tay estuary between the meadows of the North and South Inch. In early times the area attracted the attention of English forces, and the town was taken and fortified by Edward I in 1298. Its single year as the capital of Scotland ended with the murder of James I at a former Blackfriars monastery in 1437. In 1559 John Knox effectively started the Protestant Reformation here with his emotive sermon against church idolatry. Cromwell's parliamentarian army took the city a little under a century later, and it came into the Jacobites' hands in the Risings of the 18th century. One of the most important buildings to have survived all this turmoil is famous St John's Kirk, a fine medieval and later church that has been attended by many members of English and Scottish royalty. Perth's associations with Sir Walter Scott are numerous. The 14th-century heroine of the *Fair Maid of Perth*, Catherine Glover, lived in a house on the site where the present Fair Maid of Perth's House now stands (open). Also of interest are the Perth museum and art gallery, and the regimental museum of the Black Watch, which is housed in Balhousie Castle. A survival of early industry exists in the city's 19th-century dye- and glassworks, and the bridge which spans the Tay here was built by Smeaton in 1771.

*Before the main route begins it is possible to take a short detour on the A85 SP 'Crianlarich', to Huntingtower Castle.*

## HUNTINGTOWER CASTLE, Tayside

Formerly known as Ruthven Castle, this great stronghold (AM) has a permanent place in Scottish history as the site of the Raid of Ruthven. In 1582 the 16-year-old James VI came here at the invitation of the Earl of Gowrie, ostensibly to hunt. When he tried to leave he found himself prevented by Protestant nobles, who demanded the dismissal of the young king's favourites. The conspirators held the young king for a year while they wielded power in his place. The 15th-century mansion that stands here today has been restored and contains fine painted wooden ceilings.

*On the main route, follow SP 'Braemar' across the River Tay to leave Perth on the A93, and in 2 miles pass the grounds of Scone Palace.*

## SCONE PALACE, Tayside

Scone Palace, the home of the Earl of Mansfield, is a 19th-century mansion that stands on the site of the old Abbey of Scone. This was founded c1114 by Alexander I, and before it was destroyed by a mob of John Knox's reformers in 1559 it was the coronation place of all the Scottish kings up to James I. By tradition the kings were crowned on a stone that was brought to the ancient mote-hill of Scone by Kenneth Macalpine in the 9th century. This, identified with both Jacob's Pillow at Bethel and the Stone of Destiny at Tara in Ireland, was removed from the site and placed under the Coronation Chair of Westminster Abbey by Edward I in 1297. This token of conquest did little to improve relations between the two countries. The present mansion (open) contains various relics and objects of art.

*Continue to Old Scone.*

## OLD SCONE, Tayside

As the abbey developed it attracted a little satellite community that grew into the village of Scone. In 1805 this was moved by the Earl of Mansfield to improve the landscape, and only the village cross and graveyard remain to mark its old site.

*Continue through Guildtown, then after 1½ miles reach Stobhall.*

Kinnoul Hill rises steeply above the Tay to the south-east of Perth, and provides outstanding views over the valley.

## STOBHALL, Tayside

This picturesque group of buildings (not open) is centred on a courtyard and was once the home of the Drummond family. It is picturesquely sited on the banks of the Tay and comprises the house, chapel, and tower. Much of the structure dates from the 15th century.

*Later cross the Bridge of Isla to reach the grounds of Meikleour House, continue alongside the fine beech hedge that follows the estate boundary, and at the end turn left on to an unclassified road for Meikleour.*

Meikleour Mercat Cross dates from 1698.

## MEIKLEOUR, Tayside

The 600-yard beech hedge passed on the way to this charming old-world village belongs to the local manor house and was planted in 1746. A focal point of the village is the mercat cross of 1698, opposite which is an old place of punishment known as the Jougs Stone.

*Join the A984 'Dunkeld' road and drive through Spittalfield to Caputh.*

## CAPUTH, Tayside

An attractive bridge spans the salmon-rich Tay here, and across the river to the west is 16th-century and later Murthly Castle (not open) in grounds which feature huge specimens of Sitka spruce and Douglas fir. Some 3 miles east is the Roman camp of Inchtuthill.

*Continue, driving through attractive and well-wooded Strath Tay to reach the town of Dunkeld.*

## DUNKELD, Tayside

Telford spanned the Tay with a fine bridge here in 1809, but this delightful small town is best known for the lovely ruins of its ancient cathedral (AM). It was founded in the 9th century, was desecrated in 1560, and considerably damaged in the 17th-century Battle of Dunkeld.

Nowadays the 14th-century choir has been restored and is in use as the parish church. East of the town is the Loch of Lowes Wildlife Reserve, where a variety of species can be watched from special hides, and 1 mile south-west is the restored 18th-century folly of Ossian's Hall. Near by the River Braan plunges over a rocky lip as the Falls of Braan, close to Hermitage Bridge (NTS).

*Leave Dunkeld on the 'Crieff' road and cross the River Tay into Little Dunkeld. Turn right then left on to the A822 and ascend. After 7½ miles turn left to join the A22, then continue to Amulree.*

Weaving is one of several cottage industries which still thrive in Scotland.

### AMULREE, Tayside
The lovely countryside around Glen Quaich and Loch Freuchie, and in Glens Cichill and Almond, can be explored from here.

*Enter Glen Almond and follow one of General Wade's military roads through lonely Sma' Glen.*

### GLEN ALMOND, Tayside
Rugged and mountainous at its beginning near Loch Tay, this beautiful glen gradually widens out to become a broad fertile valley after Newton Bridge. One of its many interesting features is a large prehistoric burial cairn.

### SMA' GLEN, Tayside
Heatherclad Sma' Glen is a famous beauty spot that has attracted generations of admiring visitors. A partly-vitrified fort tops 1,520ft Dun Mor on the east side, and below it between the river and the road is a glaciated boulder known as Ossian's Stone, possibly named after Ossian the 3rd-century bard and warrior.

*Continue to Gilmerton skirting the fine park of Monzie Castle.*

### GILMERTON, Tayside
Some 5½ miles east of this little village are sparse traces of 13th-century Inchaffray Abbey.

*Turn right on to the A85 and continue to Crieff.*

### CRIEFF, Tayside
Beautifully situated in a hillside position overlooking Strath Earn, Crieff is a popular touring centre in one of Tayside's most scenic areas. To the north of the town the River Earn is joined by Turret Water, which flows from lovely Loch Turret and plunges downhill in a series of picturesque waterfalls. The town itself is old, with many interesting features. Close to the Town Hall is an octagonal cross of 1688, and the old Market Cross incorporates a 10th-century cross-slab made of red sandstone and decorated with Celtic patterns. Iron stocks that were last used in 1816 are kept in the 17th-century Tolbooth. About 4 miles south-east of the town is the ruin of 17th-century Innerpeffray Castle, and near by in Innerpeffray Library (open) is one of Scotland's oldest and most valuable collections of books.

*Leave Crieff on the A822 'Stirling' road, and in 2 miles reach the grounds of Drummond Castle on the right.*

### DRUMMOND CASTLE, Tayside
Built by the 1st Lord Drummond in 1491, this fine castle has been considerably altered over the centuries and shows the work of several periods. The formal gardens (open) are laid out in the form of St Andrew's Cross.

*Continue to Muthill.*

### MUTHILL, Tayside
Surviving fragments of Muthill's abandoned church (AM) include a splendid Romanesque tower that dates at least from the 12th century. Other remains are mostly of 15th-century date.

*In 1¾ miles turn left on to the A823 SP 'Dunfermline'. In 3 miles a detour can be made from the main route by turning left on to an unclassified road and continuing to Tullibardine.*

The elegant Long Gallery is the highlight of the 19th-century palace at Scone.

### TULLIBARDINE, Tayside
Founded in 1446, the collegiate chapel (AM) at Tullibardine is one of the few in Scotland to have been finished and left unaltered.

*On the main route, continue for 1 mile and pass the entrance to Gleneagles Hotel.*

### GLENEAGLES HOTEL, Tayside
Gleneagles is situated on moorland near Auchterarder and is one of the best-known golfing resorts in Scotland, a country famed for its excellent courses.

*Cross the A9 and follow the A823 through Glen Eagles, drive into the heart of the Ochil Hills and enter Glen Devon to reach the village of the same name.*

### GLENDEVON, Tayside
An excellent touring base for exploring the lovely glen from which it takes its name, this village stands on a road that affords fine views north over Strath Earn to distant ranges of mountains.

*After 2 miles turn left on to the B934 towards Dunning, then re-cross the Ochil Hills for Dunning.*

Famous roadbuilder and soldier General Wade constructed the highway through Sma' Glen.

### DUNNING, Tayside
The church in this pretty village has been rebuilt but retains a typical 13th-century tower.

*In Dunning turn right with the B934, then keep left and follow SP 'Perth'. In 1¾ miles turn right with SP 'Bridge of Earn' on to the B935, then immediately keep left and continue to Forteviot.*

### FORTEVIOT, Tayside
This village stands just south of an attractive confluence where the Water of May joins the River Earn. It was once a Pictish capital. To the north 19th-century Dupplin Castle stands in wooded grounds east of Dupplin Loch, and the splendid early-Christian Dupplin Cross can be seen close to Bank Farm on the summit of The Earn.

*Continue to Forgandenny.*

### FORGANDENNY, Tayside
Culteuchar Hill, also known as Castle Law, rises to a 1,028ft summit south of this village and preserves the remains of an old fort.

*Continue to Bridge of Earn.*

### BRIDGE OF EARN, Tayside
This village stands in the wide Strath of Earn and fragments of its original medieval bridge can still be seen, and the 16th-century mansion of Balmanno lies 2½ miles south-east. Fine views are available from nearby Moncrieffe Hill.

*At Bridge of Earn turn left on to the A912 'Perth' road, then cross the River Earn and turn right on to an unclassified road towards Rhynd. In 2⅓ miles meet a T-junction and turn left, then after 1 mile reach a track that leads to the right for Elcho Castle.*

### ELCHO CASTLE, Tayside
More accurately a fortified mansion, ruined Elcho Castle (AM) was the ancestral seat of the earls of Wemyss and is noted for its tower-like wings. It dates from the 16th century.

*Continue, with views of the River Tay and city of Perth from the road. Meet a junction with the A912, turn right, and return to Perth.*

# GLEN LYON LANDSCAPES

On either side of the River Lyon's lovely and often spectacular glen are the wooded flanks and high rugged summits of the Breadalbane Mountains. Below them are the beautiful reaches of Loch Tay, attractive lochside villages in small river valleys, and the cascades and falls of numerous streams.

**PITLOCHRY, Tayside**
Fine woodland graces the countryside round this attractive little resort and touring centre. It lies in the lovely valley of the River Tummel and is the site of a huge hydro-electric power station that, although built for obvious economic and practical reasons, has turned out to be a popular and unusual tourist attraction. When the station was built the river was blocked to form the artificial Loch Faskally, and a fish ladder had to be included to help springing salmon follow the old course of the river to their spawning beds in its upper reaches. Visitors can watch the brave efforts of these fish from an observation chamber in the exhibition centre. Various plays and concerts are staged at the Pitlochry Festival Theatre, also known as the Theatre in the Hills, during the summer months.

*Leave Pitlochry on the A924 'Perth' road and in ½ mile turn right on to an unclassified road SP 'Festival Theatre'. Cross the Aldour Bridge and turn right with SP 'Foss' on to a narrow road. Pass the theatre and in ¼ mile turn right on to the Inverness road A9. In*

*¾ mile turn right again on to an unclassified road and proceed alongside Loch Faskally and pass the Clunie Memorial Arch.*

**CLUNIE MEMORIAL ARCH, Tayside**
A bronze, horseshoe-shaped memorial at the end of the 2-mile water conduit between Loch Tummel and the Clunie generating station, this arch is the same shape as the conduit and commemorates men who died during its construction in 1946.

*Continue alongside Loch Faskally to reach the Linn of Tummel.*

**LINN OF TUMMEL, Tayside**
Once known as the Falls of Tummel, the Linn of Tummel (NTS) is a well-known feature where running water lends its own particular enchantment to lovely countryside. The name of the area was changed when the raising of the water level in Loch Faskally reduced the height and impressiveness of the waterfall. Walks starting from the Linn can be taken alongside the River Garry to

*Queen Victoria was particularly attracted to the beauty of Loch Tummel.*

Meall Luaidhe, to the south of Bridge of Balgie, rises to 2,558ft.

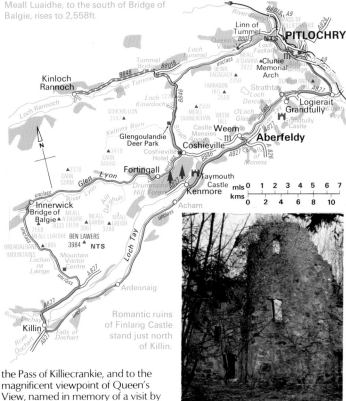

the Pass of Killiecrankie, and to the magnificent viewpoint of Queen's View, named in memory of a visit by Queen Victoria.

*Continue through magnificent scenery along the south bank of the River Tummel and Loch Tummel. After 12 miles turn left on to the B846 SP 'Aberfeldy'. A detour from the main route can be made to Kinloch Rannoch by turning right to stay with the B846; follow the River Tummel to Kinloch Rannoch.*

**KINLOCH RANNOCH, Tayside**
Situated in an area of great scenic beauty, this little angling resort stands on the River Tummel at the east end of lovely Loch Rannoch. Magnificent views extend from the village to distant peaks that guard the entrance to Glencoe, and on the southern shores of the loch the famous Black Wood of Rannoch recalls the primeval Caledonian pine forests that covered the Highlands.

*On the main drive, continue along the B846 'Aberfeldy' road and climb out of the Tummel Valley to a road summit of over 1,270ft above Loch Kinnardochy. There are good views*

to the right of the 3,547ft quartzite peak of Schiehallion. On the descent pass the Glengoulandie Deer Park on the right.

**GLENGOULANDIE DEER PARK, Tayside**
Red deer, Highland cattle and endangered species can be seen here in natural surroundings.

*Continue along the B846 and descend through the valley of the Keltney Burn to reach the Coshieville Hotel.*

**COSHIEVILLE, Tayside**
An old inn from which this area and its hotel take their names once stood at the junction of roads from Aberfeldy, Fortingall, and Rannoch. It was a favourite stopping-off place for 18th-century cattle drovers on their way to Falkirk and Crieff.

*Turn right on to an unclassified road and continue to Fortingall.*

Romantic ruins of Finlarig Castle stand just north of Killin.

## FORTINGALL, Tayside

Old thatched cottages and the attractive River Lyon are the main scenic features of this lovely little village, which is separated from the north end of Loch Tay by the wooded bulk of Drummond Hill. A huge yew standing in the local churchyard is thought to be the oldest living tree in Britain. Its girth was measured at 56ft in 1772, and the village tends its one remaining live stem with great care. Earthworks to the south-west of the village are often referred to as the Roman outpost of *Praetorium*, but they are more likely to have survived from a medieval fortified homestead. According to legend Pontius Pilate was born in the area.

*Drive for ¼ mile beyond Fortingall and turn right SP 'Glen Lyon' to follow the River Lyon into its valley.*

## GLEN LYON, Tayside

Measuring a full 32 miles in extent, this is the longest and one of the loveliest glens in Scotland. Its Gaelic name means Crooked Glen of Stones, and there is a tradition that the heroic Fingal of Celtic mythology had twelve castles here. Some of the castle, may be explained by the Iron Age ring forts that survive in the area.

*Continue through Glen Lyon to Innerwick (not signed).*

## INNERWICK, Tayside

Isolated amongst the picturesque hills of Glen Lyon, this lonely village has a church which preserves an ancient bell.

*Continue, and after 1 mile at Glen Lyon Post Office turn left (no signs) and cross the Bridge of Balgie.*

## BRIDGE OF BALGIE, Tayside

The attractive Bridge of Balgie is situated on the Glen Lyon road at a point where it meets the steep (1 in 6) mountain road to Killin.

*Continue along the narrow Glen Lyon road and ascend through moorland to 1,805ft as the route crosses the Breadalbane Mountains. Descend, with views to the right of Lochan na Lairige and to the left of Ben Lawers.*

## BEN LAWERS, Tayside

At 3,984ft this grand old mountain of the Breadalbane district is the highest for many miles around. About 8,000 acres of its flanks and summit are protected by the National Trust for Scotland, and the abnormally large number of Alpine plant species growing on its lower slopes makes it an area of considerable scientific interest. Views from the summit, which can be reached quite easily, extend over the whole of the Breadalbane country and much of the Grampian range. Local history and details of the area's many outstanding features can be studied at the visitors' centre (NTS).

*Continue past the Ben Lawers Mountain Visitor Centre, then after 2 miles turn right to join the A827 along the north side of Loch Tay.*

Killin, on the River Dochart, is dominated by Ben Lawers.

## LOCH TAY, Tayside

Overlooked at its western end by Ben Lawers and surrounded on all sides by breathtaking scenery, this superb loch was a favourite place of the poet Sir Walter Scott. He composed a beautiful word picture that captures the essence of its loveliness in his poem the *Fair Maid of Perth*. Below Ben Lawers the 120-mile-long River Tay flows towards Aberfeldy, carrying the greatest volume of water of any British river and providing an inland route for the famous Tay salmon.

*Continue along the A827 to Killin.*

## KILLIN, Central

During spring and summer this all-year-round resort offers fishing and walking, while in the winter months it provides après-ski facilities for people who come here to ski on the slopes of Ben Lawers. The village is situated at the eastern end of mountain-encircled Glen Lochay, on the excellent game-fishing Rivers Dochart and Lochay. One of two small islands near Dochart Bridge adjacent to the attractive Falls of Dochart is the traditional burial ground of the Clan MacNab, and their 17th-century seat of Kinnell House faces the village from the south side of the river.

In its grounds is a well-defined circle of standing stones. Just north of Killin is ruined Finlarig Castle, a one-time Campbell stronghold described by Scott in his *Fair Maid of Perth*.

*At the end of Killin cross the River Dochart, then turn right and take the next turning left on to an unclassified road SP 'Ardeonaig'. Continue along the south side of Loch Tay and pass through the hamlets of Ardeonaig and later Acharn. In 1½ miles go forward on to the A827 SP 'Aberfeldy'. To the left of the route at this point is the small resort of Kenmore.*

## KENMORE, Tayside

Robert Burns admired the lovely views from an 18th-century bridge that spans the Tay here, where the river leaves Loch Tay, and set his impressions down in verse. This little snippet of local history is recorded in the parlour of the hotel, a venerable establishment first licensed over 400 years ago. William and Dorothy Wordsworth left their beloved Lake District long enough to visit Kenmore, and nowadays the village is a charming and popular resort.

Salmon fishermen flock to the River Tay at Kenmore, a village praised by the poet Robert Burns.

*Continue along the A827 in the Tay Valley, with views of Drummond Hill Forest and Taymouth Castle on the left.*

## TAYMOUTH CASTLE, Tayside

Once the seat of the Breadalbanes, Taymouth Castle was visited by Queen Victoria in 1842. The present building dates from the early 19th century and houses a school.

*Proceed on the A827 to Aberfeldy.*

## ABERFELDY, Tayside

A 5-arched bridge that spans the River Tay in this little market town and touring centre was built by General Wade in 1733. The General built roads and bridges all over Scotland after the Rising of 1715, so that troops could be rushed to trouble spots with the minimum loss of time. Of all his works this bridge at Aberfeldy is thought to be among the finest still standing.

*At Aberfeldy turn left on to the B846 SP 'Kinloch Rannoch'. Cross Wade's military bridge and proceed to Weem.*

## WEEM, Tayside

Weem Hotel, said to date back to 1527, displays a sign commemorating a visit by General Wade in 1733. Castle Menzies (open) stands in fine grounds just west of the village. This 16th-century stronghold was the clan's chief seat and is is now the Clan Centre. Monuments to the Menzies can be seen in the local church. Overlooking the village is the 800ft-high viewpoint of the Rock of Weem.

*Turn right on to an unclassified road SP 'Strathtay', and follow the north bank of the river to Strathtay. A detour from the main route can be made here by turning right to cross the Tay and driving into Grandtully.*

## GRANDTULLY, Tayside

Grandtully Castle (not open), 2 miles south-west dates from the 16th century and is the ancestral home of the Stuarts of Innermeath. Canoe slaloms are held in the village, which is pronounced Grantly.

*On the main route, keep straight on for 1¼ miles and turn left to join the A827 'Ballinluig' road. Continue to Logierait.*

## LOGIERAIT, Tayside

Interesting sculptured stones can be seen in the churchyard here, plus reminders of the macabre body-snatching exploits of Burke and Hare in the shape of several mortsafes. These were once placed over new graves and locked. At one time the crime was common in Britain.

*At Logierait turn left on to an unclassified road for Dunfallandy. Follow the west bank of the River Tummel for 4 miles, then turn right to re-cross the Aldour Bridge. On the far side of the bridge turn left on to the A924 and re-enter Pitlochry.*

# BETWEEN THE FORTH AND TAY

This narrow tongue of land between the Firth of Forth and Firth of Tay offers a contrasting landscape of exposed shores and sheltered estuaries. Here the rich farmlands of the Howe of Fife climb towards the high landward barrier of the Lomond and Ochil Hills.

St Andrews Castle.

## ST ANDREWS, Fife
Historically this ancient Royal Burgh is one of the most significant places in Scotland. The cathedral (AM), which was founded in 1160, had grown to become Scotland's largest church by the time the finishing touches were made in 1318. Sparse remains include parts of the east and west gables, a section of the south nave wall, and the Precinct Wall (AM). Close by is small St Rule's Church (AM), which was built c1130 and is one of the best of its type in Scotland. The Church's famous square tower, after mounting 158 steps, affords a panoramic view of the town. St Andrews University was founded in 1412 and is the oldest in Scotland. Its Chapel of St Salvator carries an octagonal broach spire and contains the tomb of its founder, Bishop Kennedy. Also to be seen here is the oldest Sacrament House in a Scottish church, and a pulpit from which John Knox preached while leading his Protestant Reformation. St Andrew's Castle (AM) dates from the 13th century and overlooks the North Sea from a craggy eminence. The other reminder of the city's old defences is the West Port, which spans South Street on the course of the town walls. Today St Andrews is a popular summer resort on a cliff-girt coast, close to the four very famous golf courses of St Andrews Bay.

*Leave St Andrews on the A91 SP 'Tay Bridge' and after a short distance pass the Royal and Ancient Golf Course on the right.*

## THE ROYAL AND ANCIENT GOLF COURSE, Fife
Written records of the Old Course, which is the oldest in the world, date back to the 15th century. The Royal and Ancient was founded in 1754 and is the ruling authority on the game throughout the world.

*Continue to Guardbridge.*

## GUARDBRIDGE, Fife
One of the keystones of the attractive old bridge bears the shield of arms and pastoral staff of Bishop Wardlaw, who built it in the 15th century.

*Cross the River Eden and turn right on to the A919 to reach Leuchars.*

## LEUCHARS, Fife
The fine Norman church that stands here was built by the de Quincy family and is one of the best of its type in Scotland. Its chancel and apse are original, and it contains some good monuments.

*Continue for 1¼ miles to St Michael's Hotel and turn right on to the B945 to the port of Tayport.*

## TAYPORT, Fife
This one-time ferry port has a good church that was rebuilt in the 18th century. Some 47 acres of the local countryside have been taken over by the Tentsmuir Nature Reserve, including Morton Lochs.

The collapse of the original Tay railway bridge killed 75 people.

*Leave Tayport on the B946 and drive beneath the new Tay Road Bridge into Newport-on-Tay.*

## NEWPORT-ON-TAY, Fife
A 42-span road bridge, the second longest in Europe, links this busy small town with Dundee – on the north side of the Firth of Tay.

*Continue to Wormit.*

## WORMIT, Fife
The 2-mile railway bridge that spans the Tay here was built in 1885 to replace the famous one that collapsed, with great loss of life, during a freak gale in 1879.

*Continue inland on the B946 and after ¼ mile pass an unclassified right turn that offers a detour to Balmerino Abbey.*

## BALMERINO ABBEY, Fife
Founded in 1226 and built by monks from the great religious centre of Melrose, this abbey was suppressed during the Reformation and is now in ruins (NTS). Among its remains is a 15th-century Chapter House.

*On the main tour, shortly branch left on to an unclassified road SP 'St Andrews' and after another 1 mile meet a roundabout. Take the 2nd exit and in another 1¼ miles turn right on to the A92 to return to St Michael's Hotel. At the crossroads turn right SP 'Cupar' and continue through Balmullo, then after a further 2 miles join the A91 to enter Dairsie. Turn left on to an unclassified road SP 'Pitscottie', in 1 mile cross the River Eden, then turn right with views of Dairsie Castle on the north bank. Continue along the picturesque Dura*

Glen, which is noted for its fossils, to Pitscottie. Turn left and immediately right on to the B939 SP 'Kirkcaldy' and continue to Ceres.

## CERES, Fife
Some call this the prettiest village in Scotland. Old cottages surround a charming green, and the villagescape is completed by a medieval hump-backed bridge and the church.

*After another 1½ miles reach Craigrothie and turn right on to the A916, which passes the entrance to Hill of Tarvit Mansion.*

## HILL OF TARVIT, Fife
Standing in spacious grounds overlooking the Howe of Fife, this fine Edwardian mansion (NTS) contains collections of furniture, paintings, tapestries, and porcelain. It occupies the site of a 17th-century house. On a nearby hill is the ancient Scotstarvit Tower (AM) keys for which are at Hill of Tarvit.

*Continue along the A916 and descend into the Eden Valley to join the A92 for Cupar.*

## CUPAR, Fife
Cupar is a Royal Burgh and the market centre for the fertile Howe of Fife. Its parish church has a good 15th-century tower, and the mercat cross in the town is picturesquely adorned with the figure of a unicorn.

*Follow SP 'Kincardine' to leave Cupar on the A91, and at the end of the town turn right on to the A913 SP 'Perth'. After another 1¾ miles turn right on to an unclassified road SP 'Luthrie'. Meet a junction with the A914 and turn left, then in ½ mile turn right on to another unclassified road for Luthrie. After a further 1 mile bear left with the route, then later meet a T-junction and turn left to follow the Firth of Tay. Meet a junction with the A913 and turn right into Newburgh.*

## NEWBURGH, Fife
Situated on the south shore of the attractive Firth of Tay, this small Royal Burgh is near the ancient remains of Lindores Abbey. Close to the water is 18th-century Mugdrum House, opposite a tiny island which preserves the 1,000-year-old Mugdrum Cross.

*Continue along the A913 to Abernethy.*

Burleigh Castle stands near Loch Leven.

## ABERNETHY, Tayside
One of the main features of this one-time Pictish capital is the remarkable 12th-century round tower (AM) of its parish church. This type of construction is more commonly found in Ireland, and the 74ft-high example standing here is one of only two in Scotland.

*Continue past Aberargie and turn left on to the A912 SP 'Forth Road Bridge'. After 1½ miles turn right on to the B996 and drive through Glen Farg to reach Glenfarg village.*

## GLENFARG, Tayside
Glenfarg is a popular tourist resort in a sheltered position, and makes a good base from which to explore the beautiful scenery of Glen Farg.

*In 2½ miles meet a T-junction and turn right on to the A91, then turn left on to the B919 'Glenrothes' road. In 1¾ miles reach Balgedie and join the A911 for Kinnesswood, with Loch Leven on the right.*

## KINNESSWOOD, Tayside
Poet Michael Bruce was born here in 1746, and his cottage at Portmoak is now a museum containing relics of his life and work. The landscape here is dominated by prominent Bishop Hill and White Craigs.

The Chapel Royal at Falkland Palace was formerly a banqueting hall.

## LOCH LEVEN, Tayside
Romance and beauty mingle with an interesting history to make the very special atmosphere which surrounds Loch Leven. Its 14th- or 15th-century castle (AM), brooding on an island site, was the prison of Mary Queen of Scots until she made a sensational escape. The loch is often the venue for fishing competitions, and in winter its ice provides ideal conditions for curling. Some 300 acres of mixed habitats on the south shore make up the Vane Farm nature reserve, where there are nature trails and an official RSPB observation centre.

*Continue to Scotlandwell.*

## SCOTLANDWELL, Tayside
The springs that give this village its name bubble up into a 19th-century stone cistern at the end of the main street.

*Turn left and continue to Leslie.*

## LESLIE, Fife
A church on the green in this small industrial town is claimed to be the scene of a 15th-century poem entitled *Christ's Kirk on the Green*. Leslie House, a 17th-century seat of the earls of Rothes, stands east of town.

*Pass the church in the main street and after 300 yards reach the Clansman (PH). Turn left on to an unclassified road for Falkland.*

Bishop Hill in the Lomonds rises behind the village of Kinnesswood.

## FALKLAND, Fife
Old weavers' cottages and charming cobbled streets characterize this lovely little Royal Burgh, but it is chiefly known for the historic Falkland Palace (NTS). This was a favourite seat of the Scottish Court from the reign of James V, who made considerable improvements to the building before his death in 1542. The extensive gardens include Britain's oldest tennis court, c 1539.

*Meet a T-junction and turn right on to the A912, and in ¼ mile turn left on to the B936 SP 'Freuchie'. Continue through Newton of Falkland to Freuchie, and at the end of that village meet crossroads. Drive straight across on to an unclassified road and meet a junction with the A92. Turn right here, then turn immediately left on to the 'Kennoway' road. In 4½ miles turn left to enter Kennoway. Meet a main road and turn right, then immediately left SP 'Leven' and continue for 2 miles to reach the outskirts of Leven.*

## LEVEN, Fife
Formerly a weaving village, this resort and maritime town on Largo Bay is well known for its golfing facilities.

*Turn left on to the A915 'St Andrews' road and drive past Lundin Links.*

## LUNDIN LINKS, Fife
Excellent fishing and sea bathing have made this a popular resort. Three prehistoric standing stones can be seen on the western outskirts of the town.

*Continue to Upper Largo.*

## UPPER LARGO, Fife
The 17th-century spire of the church at Upper Largo rests entirely on the arched roof of the chapel and is unique in Scotland.

*Follow the A915 SP 'Crail' and in 1½ miles turn right on to the A917 for Elie.*

## ELIE & EARLSFERRY, Fife
Sailing, fishing, and fine sandy beaches are offered by these twin resorts. They lie between Chapel Ness and Elie Ness, and are known for their good golf courses.

*Follow the A917 'Anstruther' road along the East Neuk coastline, passing St Monans.*

## ST MONANS, Fife
Old houses cluster near the water's edge in this lovely little port, famed for its boat-building. The beautiful Old Kirk of St Monance dating from the 14th century but restored in 1828, stands almost on the foreshore. To the south-west of the village are the ruins of 17th-century Newark Castle.

*Continue to Pittenweem.*

## PITTENWEEM, Fife
Some of the best architecture in this picturesque little Royal Burgh and fishing port has been restored by the National Trust for Scotland. The ruined priory dates back to the 12th century and the tower of the parish church is dated 1592. Some 3 miles north-west of town is Kellie Castle (NTS), a fine example of 16th- and 17th-century architecture.

## ISLE OF MAY, Fife
Many species of sea bird use this isolated lighthouse station as a sanctuary.

## ANSTRUTHER, Fife
Anstruther Easter and Wester, both Royal Burghs in their own right, stand each side of the harbour and make this an attractive resort. At the old harbourside of this fishing port; in a collection of historic buildings, is the Scottish Fisheries Museum. The museum provides a unique record of Scotland's fishing trade which includes examples of some old boats in the harbour.

*Continue on the A917 to Crail.*

## CRAIL, Fife
The oldest Royal Burgh in the East Neuk district, this picturesque fishing town was once the haunt of smugglers. Its many lovely old buildings cluster round quaint streets and the harbour in a way that has attracted artists for generations. A curious weather vane depicting a salmon surmounts the 16th-century Tolbooth, and the mercat cross carries the figure of a unicorn.

*Leave Crail on the A917 and drive through Kingsbarns and return to St Andrews.*

## STIRLING, Central

This Royal Burgh makes an ideal touring base as the 'Gateway to the Highlands', as it is popularly known, but is also worth visiting for its own sake. All round the foot of the rocky crag which carries its imposing castle (AM) are hilly streets of stone buildings, a quaint switchback area where it is difficult to find even the smallest patch of level ground. The castle itself seems to grow from the stone on which it is built. Its 250ft site has been fortified for many centuries, but the oldest parts of the present building date back about 500 years to the reign of James III. Magnificent views can be enjoyed from the viewpoints known as Queen Victoria's Lookout and Lady's Rock, extending far into the rugged Highlands in really good weather. Below the castle ramparts is the King's Knot (AM), one of the earliest ornamental gardens in Scotland, now all grass, but with the outline of the original garden still visible. Down the hill in the Old Town are many good examples of 16th-to 18th-century domestic architecture, interspersed with such fine public buildings as the Guildhall, the Tolbooth of 1701, and the 15th-century and later Chapel Royal where Mary Queen of Scots and the baby James VI were crowned soon after being born. The Argyll Lodgings is a 17th-century mansion that is today a youth hostel. Its exterior (AM) is considered the most impressive of its style and period in Scotland. Unfinished Mar's Wark (AM) in Broad Street was begun in 1570 and intended as a town house for the Regent Mar, and the town's 15th-century Old Bridge (AM) was rebuilt in 1749 after having been blown up during the '45 Rising. About 1 mile east of Stirling are the beautiful ruins of Cambuskenneth Abbey (AM), c1147 and the scene of Robert the Bruce's parliament in 1326. Stirling University (founded in 1967) is Scotland's newest university.

*Leave Stirling on the A811 SP 'Erskine'. In 5¾ miles reach an unclassified road where a left turn can be taken as a short detour to Gargunnock.*

## GARGUNNOCK, Central

Situated in flat countryside traversed by the serpentine course of the River Forth, this village is an attractive little place with a fine 16th- to 18th-century mansion (not open).

*On the main route, continue for 3 miles and turn right on to the B882 SP 'Thornhill'. A short detour can be followed from the main route to visit Kippen by turning left on to the B822.*

## KIPPEN, Central

An unusual aspect of this lovely south-facing village is the fame it attracted by the great Kippen Grape Vine. Claimed to be one of the largest in the world, it clearly liked the sun and soil conditions here and in its 70 years of life managed to cover an area of 50,000 square feet. The reason for its eventual demise is obscure, but before that time it

GATEWAY TO THE HIGHLANDS

Stirling stands in a bend of the River Forth and for years was the battleground of Scottish and English forces. Now it is a peaceful and historic centre from which to tour the beautiful Trossachs, the high country of the Campsie Fells, and the lovely Queen Elizabeth Forest Park.

Stirling Castle, home of Scottish kings, stands on a 250ft crag overlooking the Forth Valley.

managed to produce a staggering 1,000,000 bunches of grapes. A fine old dovecote (NTS) has been preserved in the village, and the local church of 1825 is considered one of the best examples of its period in Scotland. Treacherous Flanders Moss, a wild peat bog that is probably the site of an old forest, lies north of the River Forth.

*On the main drive, continue along the B822 'Thornhill' road and in ½ mile cross the River Forth. Keep left and cross the Goodie Water, then at Thornhill join the A873. Keep forward with the B822 towards Callander, then pass through Torrie Forest and join the A81. Continue to Callander.*

## CALLANDER, Central

Callander's excellent position near the Trossach Hills and Loch Katrine makes it an ideal touring centre and resort. An inscribed sundial of 1753 is an attractive feature of South Church Street, and the Roman Camp Hotel has associations with the author Barrie. Other literary connections exist with Scott, who was a frequent visitor to the town. A road to the north-west leads through the beautiful Pass of Leny, where the River Leny rushes through a narrow gorge in a fine display of natural power. Close by is the Kilmahog Woollen Mill (open), where blankets and tweed cloth are made by hand. Some 3½ miles from the town and easily accessible to climbing enthusiasts is the severe 2,873ft peak of Ben Ledi.

*Follow the A84 'Crianlarich' road and in 1¼ miles turn left on to the A821 SP 'Trossachs'. Cross the River Leny, then drive alongside lovely Loch Venachar with Ben Ledi overlooking Brig O'Turk to the right. Continue to Brig O'Turk.*

## BRIG O'TURK, Central

This particularly beautiful Trossachs village is splendidly situated between Lochs Venachar and Achray, and is a popular base for anglers. The Turk or Finglass Water is spanned here by a rustic old bridge described in Sir Walter Scott's ballad *Glenfinglas*. In the early 19th century Queen Victoria often came here, and during her visits she enjoyed the company of a famous innkeeper called Kate Ferguson. Then, as now, the area attracted many artists who strove to capture the timeless quality of 'typical' Scottish scenery.

*Leave Brig O'Turk and enter the Queen Elizabeth Forest Park by driving alongside Loch Achray. After a short distance reach the romantically-set Trossachs Hotel.*

## THE TROSSACHS, Central

A bewildering combination of mountains, lochs, rivers, and thick woodlands makes up the outstanding landscapes for which this beauty spot is famous. The name means Bristly Country, but the nature of the land is not as unfriendly as this would suggest and has inspired such romantic works as Scott's *Lady of the Lake*. Most of the area is in a wooded gorge between Loch Achray and Loch Katrine.

*Continue for ¾ mile beyond the Trossachs Hotel. A detour can be made from the main tour route to visit Loch Katrine by keeping forward to a pier at the eastern end of the lake.*

## LOCH KATRINE, Central

There are no public roads to disturb the peace of lovely Loch Katrine, but the summer steamer *Sir Walter Scott* which runs from the pier at its east end and gives visitors an appreciation of some of the Trossachs' most secret and beautiful places. After disembarking at Stronachlachar passengers can visit the birthplace of folk hero Rob Roy, but the area will always be most remembered for Scott's *Lady of the Lake*. The lady was Ellen Douglas, her lake was Katrine, and many of the places mentioned in the poem can still be identified. The modern world is not entirely shut out, however, and the 'Silver Strand' that was once opposite Ellen's Isle has been submerged since the water was raised to improve Glasgow's water supply. Ben Venue rises 2,393ft to dominate the whole scene, from Loch Katrine to the Pass of Achray.

*On the main drive, continue on the 'Aberfoyle' road and drive through the Queen Elizabeth Forest Park.*

Wooded Loch Achray leads gently into the mixed landscapes of lakes, rivers, mountains, and woodland which form the picturesque Trossachs.

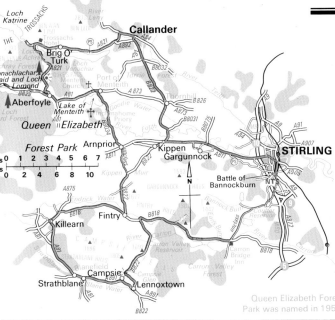

Salmon are sometimes seen jumping the Falls of Leny near Callander.

Queen Elizabeth Forest Park was named in 1953.

## QUEEN ELIZABETH FOREST PARK, Central

This National Forest Park covers 45,000 acres of lovely countryside from Loch Venachar to Loch Lomond, including the lofty summit of Ben Lomond. Both wild and planted areas can be enjoyed best by walking along the numerous marked trails that have been cleared for that purpose, though motorists are well catered for with carparks and stopping areas. A viewing shelter has been built for visitors by the Carnegie Trust.

*Descend to Aberfoyle, passing the AA viewpoint of David Marshall Lodge.*

## ABERFOYLE, Central

The tiny hamlet of Aberfoyle, associated with Rob Roy and Scott's poem of the same name, has little in common with the development of the present village. During the 19th century devotees of Scott's works came here in crowds, and the resort soon eclipsed what was left of its tiny neighbour. A plough coulter hanging from a tree by the old site recalls a scene from the book.

*From Aberfoyle it is possible to take an exceptionally scenic detour along the B829 for Inversnaid, on Loch Lomond: to follow it, drive alongside Lochs Ard and Chon, and 2 miles beyond the head of Loch Chon meet a T-junction. A brief visit can be made to the village of Stronachlachar by turning right here, but the main detour is left.*

## STRONACHLACHAR, Central

A lonely path leads from this village to isolated Glengyle, where Rob Roy was born. This famous freebooter was immortalized by Scott in 1871.

*On the main detour, turn left at the T-junction and continue to Inversnaid along an unclassified road, passing Loch Arklet.*

## INVERSNAID, Central

A fort built here in 1713 was once under the command of General Wolfe, of Quebec Heights fame, but this tiny village is best known for its spectacular surroundings. On the far side of lovely Loch Lomond are the towering summits of 3,318ft Ben Ime, and 3,092ft Ben Vorlich.

*On the main route from Aberfoyle, continue with the A821 'Stirling' road and after 1 mile branch left on to the A81 SP 'Callander'. After another 2¼ miles reach the Lake of Menteith on the right.*

## LAKE OF MENTEITH, Central

Inchmahome Priory (AM) was founded on one of three tiny islands in this lake during the 13th century, and for a time was a refuge for the infant Mary Queen of Scots. The lake itself is the only large expanse of fresh water in Scotland not called a loch, and on its west side it lies peacefully beneath gentle slopes of the 1,289ft Hills of Menteith. The Port of Menteith stands on its shore.

*Drive for 1 mile beyond the lake and turn right on to the B8034 SP 'Arnprior'. After a short distance pass the passenger ferry terminus for Inchmahome Priory, on the right by Menteith Church. Continue to Arnprior.*

## ARNPRIOR, Central

Here there is a fine Georgian mansion set in superb woodland gardens, which are unfortunately not open to the public.

*At Arnprior turn right on to the A811, then turn left on to an unclassified road SP 'Fintry'. After 2 miles cross moorland below the Fintry Hills and turn right on to the B822 to Fintry.*

## FINTRY, Central

Fintry occupies a central position in the ancient territory of Lennox, with the bare Fintry Hills to the north-east. Culchreuch Castle, which stands a little north of the village, dates from the 14th century.

*From Fintry turn right on to the B818 'Killearn' road, then in 5½ miles join the A875 'Glasgow' road to Killearn.*

## KILLEARN, Central

George Buchanan, the historian and scholar who became tutor to James VI, was born here in 1506 and is commemorated by an obelisk. Killearn House is a 19th-century edifice 1½ miles south-west.

*Drive for 2 miles beyond Killearn, keep left on to the A81, and continue through Blanefield to Strathblane.*

## STRATHBLANE, Central

This small resort is charmingly situated on the Blane Water, beneath the Strathblane Hills and the Higher Campsie Fells.

*From Strathblane turn left on to the A891 and proceed to Campsie.*

## CAMPSIE, Strath

Above this Campsie Glen village are the summits of the Campsie Fells, which offer good walking country to the energetic. Excellent views can be enjoyed from the Crow Road, which runs through the glen, and nearby Earl's Seat.

*Continue along the A891 to Lennoxtown.*

## LENNOXTOWN, Strath

Originally known as the Clachan of Campsie, this small industrial town stands in the ancient district that once came under the control of the Lennox family. The local churchyard features the Lennox vault and a number of 17th-century stones.

*At Lennoxtown turn left SP 'Fintry' on to the B822, then climb out of the valley and pass the head of Campsie Glen. Cross the open moorland of the Campsie Fells, reaching a road summit of more than 1,000ft, and descend into the valley of the Endrick Water. Turn right on to the B818 SP 'Denny', then later run alongside the Carron Valley Reservoir. Drive for 1¾ miles beyond the dam and reach the Carron Bridge Inn, then turn left on to an unclassified road SP 'Stirling'. In 1¾ miles pass the small Loch Coulter Reservoir on the right, and after another 2¼ miles meet a T-junction and turn left. Later cross the M9 motorway, then in ¾ mile turn right then left to join the A872. Immediately to the left is the Battlefield of Bannockburn.*

The bronze statue of Robert the Bruce at Bannockburn symbolizes Scotland's rebellion against English monarchy.

## BATTLEFIELD OF BANNOCKBURN, Central

It was this battle, fought in 1314 for the possession of Stirling Castle, that established Robert the Bruce on the Scottish throne. Bruce won against odds of nearly three to one, and earned the fear of his enemy as well as the respect of his people. An open-air rotunda encircles the Borestone, in which a bronze equestrian statue marks Bruce's command post. This site is owned by the NTS.

*Return to Stirling via the A872 and A9.*

# ON THE KINTYRE PENINSULA

*The coast road of Kintyre opens up superb seascapes to the Western Isles and coast of Northern Ireland as it follows the peninsula's dramatic shore to the westernmost point in Scotland. Inland is a spine of rugged little hills scored by fertile valleys and dotted with the relics of ancient man.*

### KINTYRE, Strath
This tour is contained entirely within the Kintyre peninsula, a narrow tongue of wilderness that stretches south towards Ireland from the west coast of Scotland. At one point it is only 12 miles from Ireland's eastern shores. Down the middle of the peninsula is a backbone of rocky hills that culminate near Saddell with 1,491ft Beinn an Tuirc, and at its northern boundary Kintyre is almost completely divided from the Knapdale district by West Loch Tarbert. The farthest point south is the Mull of Kintyre, where there is a lighthouse.

### TARBERT, Strath
Situated on a tiny isthmus between East and West Loch Tarbert, this fishing town and resort, once a centre of the Loch Fyne herring industry, is one of the main towns on the lovely Kintyre peninsula. According to legend the Norse prince Magnus Barefoot dragged his ships overland from loch to loch here, claiming the whole peninsula as one of the Hebridean islands and therefore the property of his father King Olaf. Norse ownership ceased after the Battle of Largs in 1263, and Tarbert later acquired a 14th-century castle that was to become the stronghold of both Robert the Bruce and James II. Remains of the castle still overlook the harbour it once guarded, but the only invasion that threatens the town today, is that of summer holiday-makers in search of the fine beaches and safe bathing.

Tarbert is a good base from which to explore the scenery beyond West Loch Tarbert. The B8024 along the often hilly north shore offers glimpses of the Sound of Jura and Loch Caolisport, and passes impressive Kilberry Castle (not open). This was the seat of the Campbells of Kilberry for 500 years and has fascinating sculpted stones dating form late medieval times. A83 which follows the loch's attractive south shore eventually joins the rugged west coast of Kintyre, affording views across the South of Gigha.

*Leave Tarbert on the A83 'Campbeltown' road and drive alongside West Loch Tarbert to Kennacraig.*

### KENNACRAIG, Strath
Situated on beautiful West Loch Tarbert, Kennacraig is a terminus of car ferries that operate between the mainland and the island of Islay.

*Continue on the Campbeltown road to reach the west coast of Kintyre and Tayinloan.*

### TAYINLOAN, Strath
A passenger ferry crosses the Sound of Gigha from here to the island of Gigha.

### ISLE OF GIGHA, Strath
Although only 6 miles long by 1½ miles wide, this flat little island off the Kintyre coast has an impressive rocky shoreline and several interesting features. Among these is

Achamore House of 1884, whose 50-acre gardens were the inspiration of Sir James Horlick who gave them to the National Trust, and seem to justify Gigha's claim to be the most fertile of all the Scottish Islands. High belts of trees protect azaleas, rhododendrons, hydrangeas, and a host of ornamental shrubs from the destructive Atlantic winds. Also on the island is the 13th-century ruin of Kilchattan Church, and Gigha parish was the birthplace of Gaelic scholar Dr Kenneth MacLeod. Just off the south tip of the island is the tiny islet of Cara, popular with seabirds.

*Continue along the peninsula to Killean.*

### KILLEAN, Strath
Close to the modern church in Killean are the remains of its ancient predecessor, from which it acquired its fine double window.

*Continue to Glenbarr.*

### GLENBARR, Strath
Beyond modernized Glenbarr Abbey the pretty Barr Water meets the sea, and inland the Barr Glen leads deep into isolated hill country.

*Continue along the A83 to Campbeltown.*

### CAMPBELTOWN, Strath
The chief town of southern Kintyre, Campbeltown stands at the head of a sheltered bay and has a rocky shore that is popular with sea anglers. Nowadays it is a resort known for its good facilities and unusually mild climate, but at the end of the 19th century it was a bustling centre of commerce and industry with 30 distilleries and a herring fleet of more than 500 boats. Reminders of the area's very early history, when lone Irish missionaries braved the Atlantic to lead Britain out of the dark ages, are everywhere in place names and ancient religious sites. About 3½ miles south-east near Auchinhoan Head is St Kieran's Cave, which is a mere 25ft above

high-water mark and may be the earliest Christian chapel in Scotland. It is thought that St Kieran, whose name can be recognized in the Kilkerran area of the peninsula, arrived in Scotland even before St Columba. Relics from these and prehistoric times can be seen in the town's museum, and an echo of Celtic culture is in the 16th-century cross standing at Old Quay Head. Offshore from the resort is isolated Davaar Island.

### DAVAAR ISLAND, Strath
Boats can be hired to cover the short distance to this island, which is famous for the Crucifixion scene painted inside a natural cave by the 19th-century artist Archibald Mackinnon. It was designed so that the only illumination required is a shaft of light from a hole in the rock. It was retouched by a local artist in the mid 1950s.

*It is possible to make several detours from the main route in Campbeltown, driving to such places as Machrihanish, Southend, Keil, and the Mull of Kintyre, all of which are worth visiting. Details follow: to visit Machrihanish turn right with the A83 and in 1½ miles go forward on to the B843.*

### MACHRIHANISH, Strath
One of the main attractions in this one-time salt producing village is its beach, which offers 3½ miles of sand on an otherwise rocky coast. Among the resort developments prompted by this natural asset is an excellent golf course that was laid out in 1876. Services from the nearby airport link with Glasgow and the Isle of Islay.

*To visit Southend, Keil, and the Mull of Kintyre, leave Campbeltown on the Machrihanish road A83 and in 1½ miles turn left on to the B842 and drive south to reach Southend.*

The early lighthouse at the Mull of Kintyre is Scotland's closest approach to Ireland.

A small fishing fleet uses Carradale's modern harbour.

## SOUTHEND, Strath

This small resort offers two sandy beaches facing Sanda Island across the narrow waters of Sanda Sound. Pleasantly isolated coastline is accessible by a short walk. direction.

*From Southend follow an unclassified road to Keil.*

## KEIL, Strath

Tradition has it that a ruined chapel here marks the place where St Columba landed to begin his 6th-century mission in Scotland. He and his disciples were pledged to convert the Picts to Christianity; local evidence suggests that this site was a pagan place of sanctity long before the chapel was built. The impressions of two right feet on a flat stone known as St Columba's Footprints, may have been carved to mark the place where pagan chiefs took their initiation vows. Only 100 yards away are the remains of a druidical altar. Sparse remains of Dunaverty Castle, whose 300 occupants were slaughtered by Covenanters, survive in the neighbourhood.

*For the Mull of Kintyre keep forward and in 1 mile turn left on to a narrow road.*

## MULL OF KINTYRE, Strath

The southernmost tip of the peninsula and Scotland's closest point to the Irish coast, this wild headland offers some remarkable views. Rathlin Island rises from the sea a mere 12 miles away, and behind it is the dark line of the Northern Irish coast. On both sides the shore has been torn ragged by the full force of the Atlantic Ocean, and inland the 1,405ft mass of Beinn na Lice isolates the headland from the rest of Kintyre. An early lighthouse built near the South Point in 1788 was later remodelled by Robert Stephenson.

*On the main route, leave Campbeltown on the B842 SP*

'Carradale' and follow the east coast of the peninsula. Continue to Saddell.

## SADDELL, Strath

Interesting remains of an abbey and castle survive in this attractive village. It is thought that the former was founded by Somerled, the first Duke of the Isles, for Cistercian monks in the 12th century. Remains include boundary walls and sculptured Celtic tombstones in the churchyard. One of the recumbent effigies preserved here may be Somerled himself, the ancestor of the Clan Donald. Battlemented Saddell Castle dates from the 16th century and was once the residence of the bishops of Argyll. Lovely Saddell Glen is part of the South Kintyre Forest, a wild and beautiful area that merges with Carradale Forest farther north. To the west the Kintyre Hills are dominated by the peak of 1,491ft Beinn an Tuirc.

*Continue through hill country where open stretches reveal fine views of the hills on the Isle of Arran; particularly prominent is 2,345ft Beinn Bharrain. Skirt the shore of Kilbrannan Sound and later reach the B879 junction*

which can be taken for a short detour to Carradale.

## CARRADALE, Strath

Situated opposite the Isle of Arran, this small resort has a sheltered fishing harbour. Close to the pier are the remains of Aird Castle, and the narrow spit of Carradale Point to the south protecting the sandy Carradale Bay carries an oval vitrified fort. Carradale House has beautiful gardens (open) with flowering shrubs.

*On the main route continue along the B842 to Grogport.*

## GROGPORT, Strath

This small village stands on a secluded little bay in the Kilbrannan Sound, facing the Isle of Arran's mountainous outline.

Continue to Claonaig.

## CLAONAIG, Strath

During the summer this hamlet is the terminus for the Arran car ferry.

*A short detour to Skipness can be taken from the main route by turning right on to the B8001.*

## SKIPNESS, Strath

Features of this charming little place include the remains of an ancient chapel and a large 13th-century castle. Local views extend seaward across the Sound of Bute to the northern part of Arran.

*On the main tour, keep forward on to the B8001 SP 'Tarbert'. Climb, then descend with views of Knapdale and West Loch Tarbert. Continue to Kennacraig and turn right on to the A83 for the return to Tarbert.*

### TARBET, Strath
Situated on a narrow neck of land between Lochs Lomond and Long this resort offers good views eastwards to the magnificent peak of Ben Lomond, 3,192ft.

### LOCH LOMOND, Strath
Popularly known as the Queen of Scottish lakes, 24-mile Loch Lomond is the largest expanse of fresh water in Britain and is sheltered by wooded mountains that climb dramatically from its eastern shores. In the south it is bordered by a gentler landscape of soft green hills, and the isolation of its many beautiful islands was as much of an attraction for 5th-century Irish missionaries as it is for visitors today. One particular example is Inchmurrin, which is believed to have been the site of St Mirren's monastery in the 6th century and now features the ruins of Lennox Castle. Five of the islands in the south-eastern corner of the loch are included in a national nature reserve, and much of the east shore is cloaked by the lovely Queen Elizabeth Forest Park. The famous song *Loch Lomond* is said to have been composed by one of Bonnie Prince Charlie's followers on the eve of his execution.

*Leave Tarbet on the A82 'Crianlarich' road to reach Inveruglas.*

### INVERUGLAS, Strath
Overlooked by 2,785ft A' Chrois and 3,004ft Ben Vane, Inveruglas is the site of a hydro-electric power station that receives its water by tunnel aqueduct from Loch Sloy.

*From Inveruglas continue on the A82 to reach Ardlui.*

### ARDLUI, Strath
Situated at the northern tip of Loch Lomond, this beautiful village stands at the entrance to picturesque Glen Falloch and features a curious pulpit hewn out of the rock face.

*Continue from Ardlui through Glen Falloch, past the Falls of Falloch, to reach Crianlarich.*

### CRIANLARICH, Central
The superb mountain scenery round Crianlarich has made it a natural resort for visiting walkers and climbers. Loch Dochart, with its pretty wooded island enhanced by the picturesque ruins of an old castle, lies to the east.

*In Crianlarich turn left with the A82 'Fort William' road and drive along Strath Fillan. In 2¼ miles reach St Fillan's Chapel.*

### ST FILLAN'S CHAPEL, Central
Fragments of this 14th-century chapel can be seen to the east of Fillan Water. Robert the Bruce dedicated the place as a thanks offering for his victory at Bannockburn.

*Continue on the A82 to reach the resort of Tyndrum.*

## BESIDE LOCH LOMOND
Many centuries ago Irish missionaries were attracted to the enchanting isolation of Loch Lomond's tiny wooded islands. Today the loch, set against a backdrop of gentle hillsides and wooded mountains, is still acknowledged as one of Scotland's loveliest expanses of fresh water.

Beautiful Ben Lomond, seen from the shores of Loch Lomond.

### TYNDRUM, Central
Tyndrum is an angling and climbing resort in Strath Fillan, near its junction with Glen Lochy on the edge of the Grampian mountains. The legendary Brooch of Lorne was reputedly lost by Robert the Bruce during an ambush south-east of the village. It is now kept at the Macdougall mansion of Dunollie, near Oban.

*Leave Tyndrum and turn left on to the A85 'Oban' road. Drive through Glen Lochy to reach Dalmally.*

### DALMALLY, Strath
The River Orchy flows through this Strath Orchy village on its way to Loch Awe. A monument has been erected to the Highland poet Duncan Ban MacIntyre, some 2 miles south-west of Dalmally, near a viewpoint on the old Inveraray road.

*Leave Dalmally and in 1¾ miles turn left on to the A819 'Inveraray' road. For a detour to Kilchurn Castle keep*

Some of the finest views of Loch Lomond can be enjoyed from Tarbet.

*forward on the A85 for ¼ mile to a track on the left of the road.*

### KILCHURN CASTLE, Strath
Beautifully situated in mountainous country at the upper end of Loch Awe, Kilchurn Castle (AM) dates from the 15th century and stands on ground that was once an island. Major additions were made in the 16th and 17th centuries, but in 1879 it was damaged by dreadful gales that also caused the destruction of the Tay Bridge. However, even in its ruined state this former Campbell stronghold is one of the finest baronial castles in Scotland.

*Continue on the A819, following the shore of Loch Awe for 4 miles, then turn inland across open country and ascend before the descent through Glen Aray. Pass Inveraray Castle on the left before entering Inveraray.*

### INVERARAY, Strath
Picturesque woodland provides a backing for this smart Royal Burgh, where white-walled buildings make an attractive cluster on the banks of lovely Loch Fyne. At one time the village site was near the ancient castle that can be seen near by, but after burning down it was replaced by the existing town and castle in the 18th century. The present castle (open), which had to be restored after another fire in 1975, houses many historic relics, including some of Rob Roy's possessions and several fine portraits. Architecturally the building is a very early example of the neo-gothic and Scottish baronial styles. A cannon from the sunken Spanish Armada vessel *Florida* is on display in the grounds. A fine Celtic burial cross, removed to the town from Iona, stands at the junction of Front and Main Streets. In the parish church is an unusual dividing wall which was built to allow simultaneous services in the English and Gaelic languages. The 126ft-high Bell Tower (open) is an excellent viewpoint. South-west of the village at Dalchenna is the comprehensive Argyll Wildlife Park.

*Leave Inveraray on the A83 'Glasgow' road to reach Glen Shira.*

### GLEN SHIRA, Strath
A charming 18th-century ornamental bridge spans the little River Shira at the entrance to this beautiful glen. Although best appreciated on foot, the glen is also accessible by a narrow road that runs through forest past the ruined house of Rob Roy to the Lochan Shira dam.

*Continue on the A83, beside the shores of Loch Fyne and pass the end of Glen Fyne.*

### GLEN FYNE, Strath
Threaded by the River Fyne, this picturesque glen leads north-east from the head of Loch Fyne. On the eastern side is the impressive Eagles Fell waterfall.

*Continue along the shores of Loch Fyne to reach the edge of Cairndow.*

Mighty snow capped summits dwarf Loch Awe and the once-isolated ruins of magnificent Kilchurn Castle.

The 'Rest and Be Thankful' stone.

## CAIRNDOW, Strath

Binnein an Fhidhleir 2,658ft dominates the township of Cairndow. Just outside, near Loch Fyne, is the excellent modern mansion of Ardkinglas House, which was built by the Scottish architect Sir Robert Lorrimer. The gardens (open) of Strone House to the south feature a 190ft tree that is claimed to be the tallest growing anywhere in Britain.

*Leave Cairndow and continue on the A83 to make a long and easy ascent through Glen Kinglas to the 860ft road summit and 'Rest and Be Thankful' stone. An alternative route may be taken from Cairndow to the Rest and Be Thankful summit by leaving the township on the A83 and in 1 mile turning right on to the A815 SP 'Dunoon'. Continue for 2½ miles, then turn left on to the B839 SP 'Lochgoilhead' and drive through Hell's Glen.*

## HELL'S GLEN, Strath

The rocky and lonely glen with this unpleasant name lies between 2,402ft Stob an Eas and 2,001ft Cruach nam Mult and affords views down to the swirling waters of the River Goil.

*Continue the alternative route on the B839 to meet the junction with the B828. A detour from the alternative route to Lochgoilhead and Carrick*

Castle can be taken here by turning right with the B839 and driving to Lochgoilhead.

## LOCHGOILHEAD, Strath

Standing on the shingly shores of Loch Goil, this pleasing little Victorian burgh of whitewashed houses is set against the dark background of the Cowal Hills.

*To continue the detour, leave Lochgoilhead and join the unclassified road which runs west of Loch Goil. In 5 miles reach Carrick Castle.*

## CARRICK CASTLE, Strath

The ruined 14th-century Carrick Castle, once a royal stronghold, was destroyed by fire in 1685.

*From Carrick Castle return to*

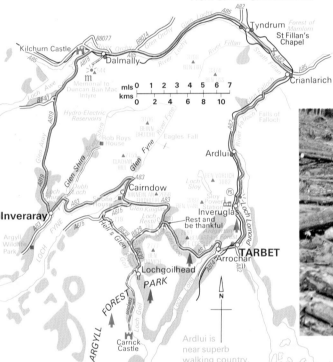

*Lochgoilhead and thence to the junction with the B828 at the foot of Hell's Glen. From here continue the alternative route by keeping forward on the B828 SP 'Glasgow' through a small part of the Argyll Forest Park.*

## ARGYLL FOREST PARK, Strath

The huge forest park of Argyll covers 37,000 acres of beautiful mountain scenery from Ben Ime in the north to the Ben More ridge in the south. It is divided into two distinct areas: the large southern part stretches from Benmore Forest to Glenbranter Forest near Strachur, and the smaller northern section contains the Ardgoil and Ardgartan Forests between Lochgoilhead and Arrochar. The whole area is vast enough to provide an endless variety of gentle rambles, ambitious walks, and difficult climbs. It offers many things, from the pleasures of outdoor activities to the simple seeking out of solitude and peace in the mountains.

*Continue along the B828 to reach Rest and Be Thankful and turn right on to the A83 to rejoin the main tour.*

Forestry is a major industry in Argyll.

## REST AND BE THANKFUL, Strath

Near here the steep old road through Glen Croe, no longer used except for motor trials, reached a 800ft summit marked by a rough stone seat inscribed 'Rest and Be Thankful'. The seat has gone and the reconstructed road has been more gently graded for modern traffic, but the inscribed stone survives. The summit of 3,318ft Ben Ime can be reached by a long climb from the pass.

*From Rest and Be Thankful continue along the A83, descending through Glen Croe and round Loch Long to reach Arrochar.*

## ARROCHAR, Strath

This little yachting and touring centre at the head of Loch Long makes a fine base from which to visit the mountains and forests of the Argyll Forest Park. To the north-west are Beinn Narnain 3,036ft, A'Chrois 2,785ft and Ben Arthur 2,891ft, popularly known as The Cobbler, and to the west above the Ardgarten Forest is The Brack 2,580ft.

*Leave Arrochar and follow the A83 for the return to Tarbet.*

# Key to Town Plans

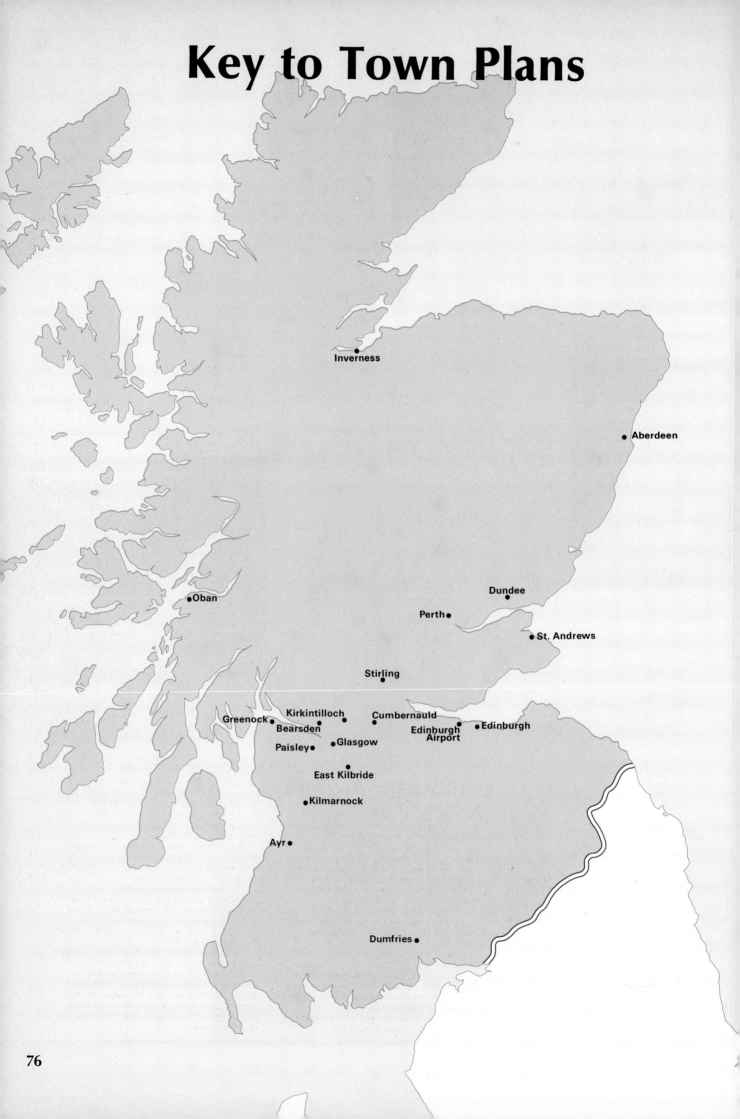

Inverness

Aberdeen

Oban

Dundee

Perth

St. Andrews

Stirling

Greenock   Kirkintilloch   Cumbernauld
        Bearsden              Edinburgh      Edinburgh
Paisley          Glasgow      Airport

East Kilbride

Kilmarnock

Ayr

Dumfries

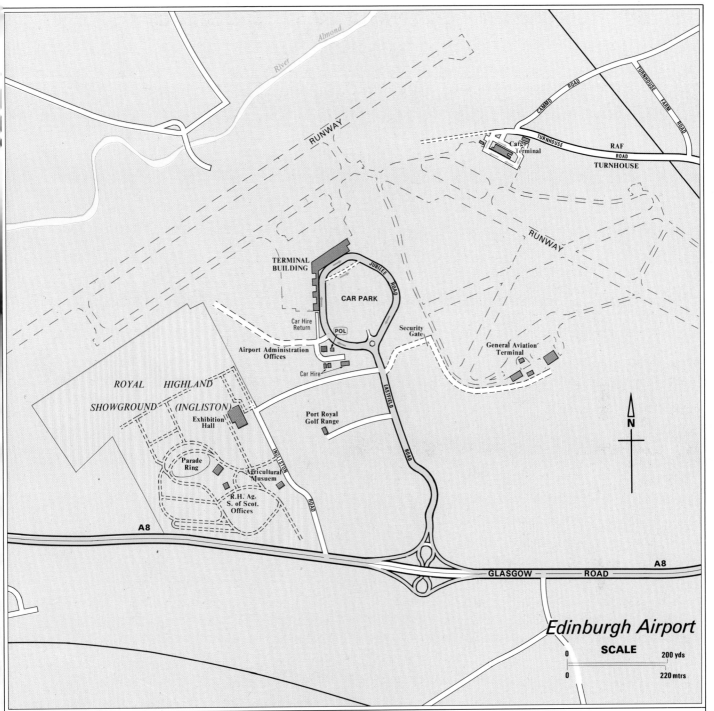

# Edinburgh Airport

Charter flights to international holiday destinations such as Spain, Italy, Corsica and Portugal, business flights to Paris, Amsterdam and Frankfurt and commuter links with the Leeds, Humberside, East Midlands and Norwich Airports are among the services offered by Edinburgh Airport.

Originally known as Turnhouse Aerodrome, it was used by the Royal Flying Corps in World War I, because its closeness to the railway allowed for the delivery of aircraft by rail. The airport remained under military control and in World War II was a fighter station — a period commemorated by the vintage Spitfire which is on display near the cargo terminal.

Next came the very different years of redevelopment, and the British Airports Authority took control in 1971. A new runway and terminal building had been added by 1977, the year in which HM the Queen honoured Edinburgh Airport by coming here to open the new building.

Available for the convenience of passengers and other visitors to the airport today is the

Aerogrill on the first floor. Refreshments are also supplied by the buffet on the ground floor. Alongside each of these is a bar, and to complement the service they provide, the International Departure Lounge also offers the facilities of a bar and buffet.

Ready to deal with any enquiries or problems that arise is the Airport Information Desk, which is situated on the main concourse of the Terminal, and is open from 7am to 11pm.

For those wishing to watch the aeroplanes and the airport at work, a spectators' viewing terrace has been provided. This is accessible by lift and is open to visitors during daylight hours. The terrace runs along the northern side of the second floor of the Terminal.

The airport can be reached by car via the A8 from Edinburgh, and open air car parking is available for 1,025 vehicles. A regular coach service operates between Edinburgh (Waverley Bridge) and the airport, and the journey takes 25 minutes. There is also a coach service to link it with Glasgow Airport, with a pick-up point on the A8 outside the airport.

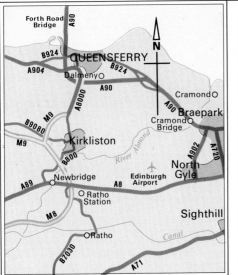

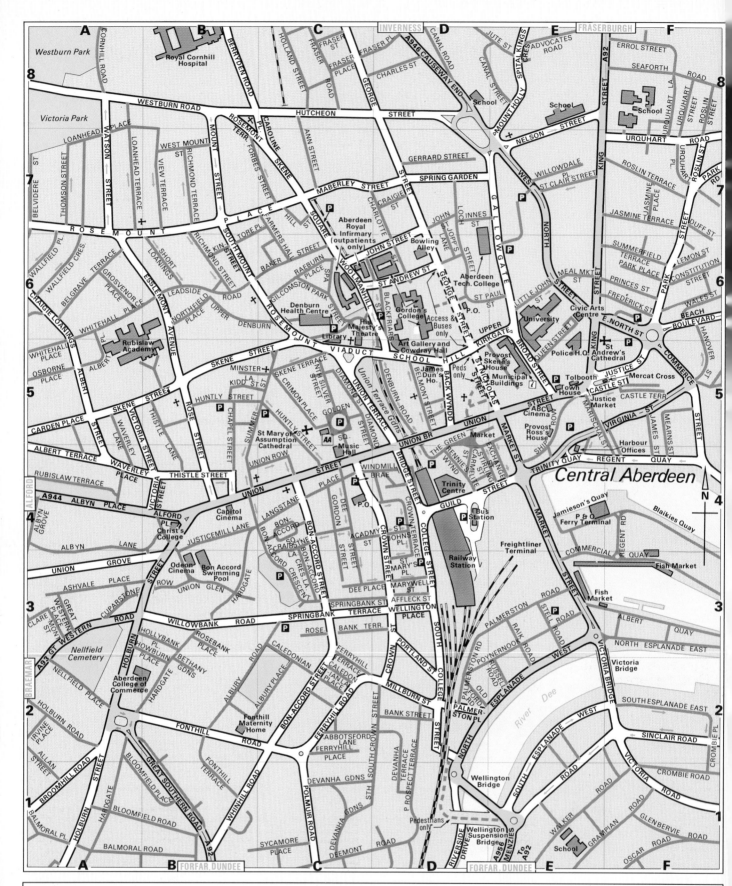

# Aberdeen

Granite gives Aberdeen its especial character; but this is not to say that the city is a grim or a grey place, the granites used are of many hues – white, blue, pink and grey. Although the most imposing buildings date from the 19th century, granite has been used to dramatic effect since at least as early as the 15th century. From that time dates St Machar's Cathedral, originally founded in AD580, but rebuilt several times, especially after a devasting fire started on the orders of Edward III of England in 1336. St Machar's is in Old Aberdeen, traditionally the ecclesiastical and educational hub of the city, while 'New' Aberdeen (actually no newer) has always been the commercial centre. Even that definition is deceptive, for although Old Aberdeen has King's College, founded in 1494, New Aberdeen has Marischal College, founded almost exactly a century later (but rebuilt in 1844) and every bit as distinguished as a seat of learning. Both establishments functioned as independent universities until they were merged in 1860 to form Aberdeen University. The North Sea oil boom has brought many changes to the city, some of which threatened its character. But even though high-rise buildings are now common, the stately façades, towers and pillars of granite still reign supreme and Union Street remains one of the best thoroughfares in Britain.

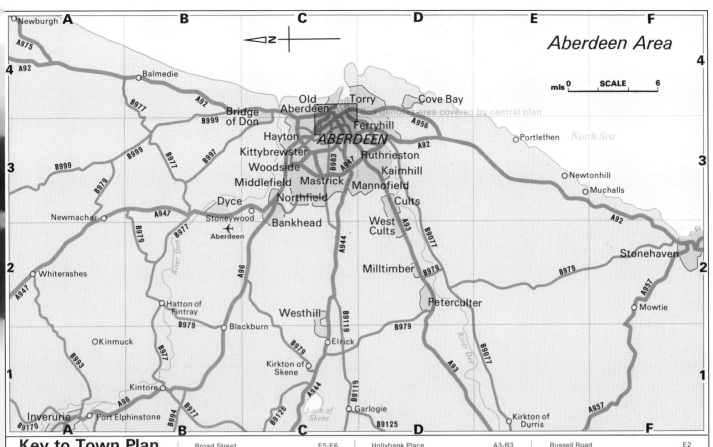

A B C D E F

*Aberdeen Area*

Newburgh

A975

A92

Balmedie

B977

A92

Bridge of Don

B999

Old Aberdeen

Torry

Cove Bay

*denotes area covered by central plan*

Ferryhill

A956

Hayton

**ABERDEEN**

A92

*North Sea*

Portlethen

Kittybrewster

B983

Ruthrieston

A847

Woodside

Kaimhill

Newtonhill

Middlefield

Mastrick

Mannofield

Muchalls

Dyce

Northfield

Cults

Newmachar

A947

Stoneywood

Bankhead

West Cults

A93

B9077

Stonehaven

B979

Aberdeen

A96

A944

Milltimber

B979

B979

A957

Whiterashes

Hatton of Fintray

B979

Westhill

B9119

Peterculter

B979

River Dee

B9077

A93

Mowtie

A947

B979

Blackburn

Elrick

Kinmuck

B977

Kirkton of Skene

A944

B9119

Garlogie

Kirkton of Durris

A957

Kintore

A96

B993

Inverurie

B9170

Port Elphinstone

B994

B977

B9126

Loch of Skene

B9125

SCALE

mls 0    6

# Key to Town Plan and Area Plan

## Town Plan

A A Recommended roads

Other roads

Restricted roads

Buildings of interest    Cinema

Car Parks    P

Parks and open spaces

One Way Streets

Churches    +

## Area Plan

A roads

B roads

Locations    Hattoncrook ○

Urban area

# Street Index with Grid Reference

## Aberdeen

| Street | Grid |
|---|---|
| Abbotsford Lane | C2-D2 |
| Academy Street | C4-D4 |
| Advocates Road | E8 |
| Affleck Street | D3 |
| Albert Quay | E3-F3 |
| Albert Place | A5-A6 |
| Albert Street | A4-A5 |
| Albert Terrace | A4-A5 |
| Albury Place | B2-C2 |
| Albury Road | B2-C2-C3 |
| Albyn Grove | A4 |
| Albyn Lane | A4-A3-B3-B4 |
| Albyn Place | A4-B4 |
| Alford Place | B4 |
| Allan Street | A1-A2 |
| Ann Street | C7-C8 |
| Ashvale Place | A3-B3 |
| Back Wyndd | D5 |
| Baker Street | B6-C6 |
| Balmoral Place | A1 |
| Balmoral Road | A1-B1 |
| Bank Street | D2 |
| Beach Boulevard | F6 |
| Belgrave Terrace | A6 |
| Belmont Street | D5 |
| Belvidere Street | A7 |
| Berryden Road | B8-C8 |
| Bethany Gardens | B2 |
| Blackfriars Street | D6 |
| Bloomfield Place | A2-A1-B1 |
| Bloomfield Road | A1-B1 |
| Bon-Accord Crescent | B4-C4-C3 |
| Bon-Accord Crescent Lane | C3-C4 |
| Bon-Accord Square | C4 |
| Bon-Accord Street | C2-C3-C4 |
| Bridge Place | D4 |

| Street | Grid |
|---|---|
| Broad Street | E5-E6 |
| Broomhill Road | A1-A2 |
| Caledonian Lane | C2 |
| Caledonian Place | C2-C3 |
| Canal Road | D8 |
| Canal Street | D8-E8 |
| Carden Place | A3 |
| Carmelite Street | D4 |
| Caroline Place | B8-B7-C7-C8 |
| Castle Street | E5-F5 |
| Castle Terrace | F5 |
| Causeway End | D8 |
| Chapel Street | B4-B5 |
| Charles Street | C8-D8 |
| Charlotte Street | C7-D7-D6 |
| Claremont Street | A3 |
| College Street | D3-D4 |
| Commerce Street | F4-F5 |
| Commercial Quay | E3-F3 |
| Constitution Street | F6 |
| Cornhill Road | A8 |
| Craibstone Lane | C3-C4 |
| Craigie Loanings | A5-A6 |
| Craigie Street | D7 |
| Crimon Street | C5 |
| Crombie Place | F1-F2 |
| Crombie Road | F1 |
| Crown Street | D2-D3-D4-C4 |
| Crown Terrace | D3-D4 |
| Cuparstone Row | A3-B3 |
| Dee Place | C3-D3 |
| Dee Street | C3-C4 |
| Deemont road | C1-D1 |
| Denburn Road | D5 |
| Devanha Gardens | C1 |
| Devanha Terrace | D1-D2 |
| Diamond Street | C4-D4-C5 |
| Duff Street | F6-F7 |
| East North Street | E6-F6 |
| Errol Street | F8 |
| Esslemont Avenue | A6-B6-B5 |
| Exchange Street | E4-E5 |
| Farmers Hill | C6-C7 |
| Ferryhill Place | C2 |
| Ferryhill Road | C2-D2 |
| Ferryhill Terrace | C2-D2 |
| Fonthill Road | A2-B2-C2 |
| Fonthill Terrace | B1-B2 |
| Forbes Street | B7-C7 |
| Fraser Place | C8-D8 |
| Fraser Road | C8 |
| Fraser Street | C8 |
| Frederick Street | E6-F6 |
| Gallowgate | D7-E7-E6 |
| George Street | C8-D8-D7-D6-D5 |
| Gerrard Street | D7 |
| Gilcomston Park | C6 |
| Glenbervie Road | F1 |
| Golden Square | C5 |
| Gordon Street | C3-C4 |
| Grampian Road | E1-F1 |
| Great Southern Road | A1-B2-B1 |
| Great Western Place | A3 |
| Great Western Road | A2-A3 |
| Grosvenor Place | A6 |
| Guild Street | D4-E4 |
| Hanover Street | F5-F6 |
| Hardgate | A1-A2-B2-B3-B4 |
| Hill Street | C7 |
| Holburn Road | A2 |
| Holburn Street | A1-A2-A3-B3-B4 |
| Holland Street | C8 |

| Street | Grid |
|---|---|
| Hollybank Place | A3-B3 |
| Howburn Place | A3-B3-B2 |
| Huntly Street | B5-C5-C4 |
| Hutcheon Street | B8-C8-D8 |
| Innes Street | D7-E7 |
| Irvine Place | A2 |
| James Street | F4-F5 |
| Jasmine Place | F7 |
| Jasmine Terrace | E7-F7 |
| John Street | C6-D6-D7 |
| Jopp's Lane | D6-D7 |
| Justice Street | E5-F5-F6 |
| Justice Mill Lane | B3-B4 |
| Jute Street | D8-E8 |
| Kidd Street | B5-C5 |
| King Street | E5-E6-E7-E8-F8 |
| Kintore Place | B6-B7-C7 |
| Langstone Place | C4 |
| Leadside Road | B6 |
| Lemon Street | F6 |
| Little John Street | E6 |
| Loanhead Place | A7-A8-B8 |
| Loanhead Terrace | A7 |
| Loch Street | D6-D7 |
| Maberley Street | C7-D7 |
| Marischal Street | E5-F5-F4 |
| Market Street | E3-E4-E5 |
| Marywell Street | D3 |
| Meal Market Street | E6 |
| Mearns Street | F4-F5 |
| Menzies Road | E1-E2-F2 |
| Millburn Street | D2 |
| Minster Holly | B5-C5 |
| Mount Holly | E7-E8 |
| Mount Street | B7-B8 |
| Nellfield Place | A2 |
| Nelson Street | E7-E8 |
| North Esplanade East | E3-F3 |
| North Esplanade West | D1-D2-E2-E3 |
| North Silver Street | C5 |
| Northfield Place | B6 |
| Old Ford Road | D2 |
| Osborne Place | A5 |
| Oscar Road | F1 |
| Palmerston Place | D2 |
| Palmerston Road | D2-D3-E3 |
| Park Place | F6 |
| Park Road | F7 |
| Park Street | F6-F7 |
| Polmuir Road | C1-C2 |
| Portland Street | D2-D3 |
| Poynernook Road | D2-E2-E3 |
| Princes Street | E6-F6 |
| Prospect Terrace | D1-D2 |
| Queen Street | E5-E6 |
| Raeburn Place | C6 |
| Raik Road | E2-E3 |
| Regent Road | F3-F4 |
| Regent Quay | E5-F5 |
| Rennies Wyndd | D4 |
| Richmond Street | B6-B7 |
| Richmond Terrace | B7 |
| Riverside Drive | D1 |
| Rose Street | B4-B5 |
| Rosebank Place | B3 |
| Rosebank Terrace | C3-D3 |
| Rosemount Place | A7-A6-B6-B7-C7 |
| Rosemount Terrace | B7-B8 |
| Rosemount Viaduct | B6-C6-C5 |
| Roslin Street | F7-F8 |
| Roslin Terrace | E7-F7 |
| Rubislaw Terrace | A4 |

| Street | Grid |
|---|---|
| Russell Road | E2 |
| St Andrew Street | C6-D6 |
| St Clair Street | E7 |
| St John's Place | D4 |
| St Mary's Place | D3 |
| St Nicholas Street | D5-E5 |
| St Paul Street | D6-E6 |
| School Hill | D5 |
| Seaforth Road | F8 |
| Ship Row | E4-E5 |
| Short Loanings | B6 |
| Sinclair Road | F2 |
| Skene Square | C6-C7 |
| Skene Street | A5-B5-C5 |
| Skene Terrace | C5 |
| South College Street | D2-D3 |
| South Crown Street | C1-D1-D2 |
| South Esplanade East | F2 |
| South Esplanade West | E1-E2 |
| South Mount Street | B6-B7 |
| Spa Street | C6 |
| Spital Kings Crescent | E8 |
| Spring Garden | D7 |
| Spring Bank Street | C3-D3 |
| Spring Bank Terrace | C3-D3 |
| Stell Road | E3 |
| Stirling Street | D4-E4 |
| Summer Street | B4-B5-C5 |
| Summerfield Terrace | E6-F6 |
| Sycamore Place | B1-C1 |
| The Green | D4-D5 |
| Thistle Lane | B4-B5 |
| Thistle Street | B4 |
| Thomson Street | A7 |
| Trinity Quay | E4 |
| Upper Denburn | B6-C6 |
| Upper Kirkgate | D5-D6-E5-E6 |
| Urquhart Lane | F7-F8 |
| Urquhart Place | F7 |
| Urquhart Road | F7 |
| Urquhart Street | F7-F8 |
| Union Bridge | D4-D5 |
| Union Glen | B3 |
| Union Grove | A3-B3 |
| Union Row | B4-C4 |
| Union Street | B4-C4-D4-D5-E5 |
| Union Terrace | C5-D5 |
| Victoria Bridge | E3-E2-F2 |
| Victoria Road | F1-F2 |
| Victoria Street | A5-B4-B5 |
| View Terrace | B7 |
| Virginia Street | E5-F5 |
| Wales Street | F6 |
| Walker Road | E1-F1 |
| Wallfield Crescent | A6 |
| Wallfield Place | A6-A7 |
| Watson Street | A7-A8 |
| Waverley Lane | A4-A5 |
| Waverley Place | A4-B4 |
| Wellington Place | D3 |
| West Mount Street | B7 |
| West North Street | E6-E7-E8 |
| Westburn Road | A8-B8 |
| Whinhill Road | B1-C1-C2 |
| Whitehall Place | A5-A6-B6 |
| Willow Bank Road | B3-C3 |
| Willowdale Place | E7 |
| Windmill Brae | C4-D4 |
| Woolmanhill | C6-D6-D5 |

**79**

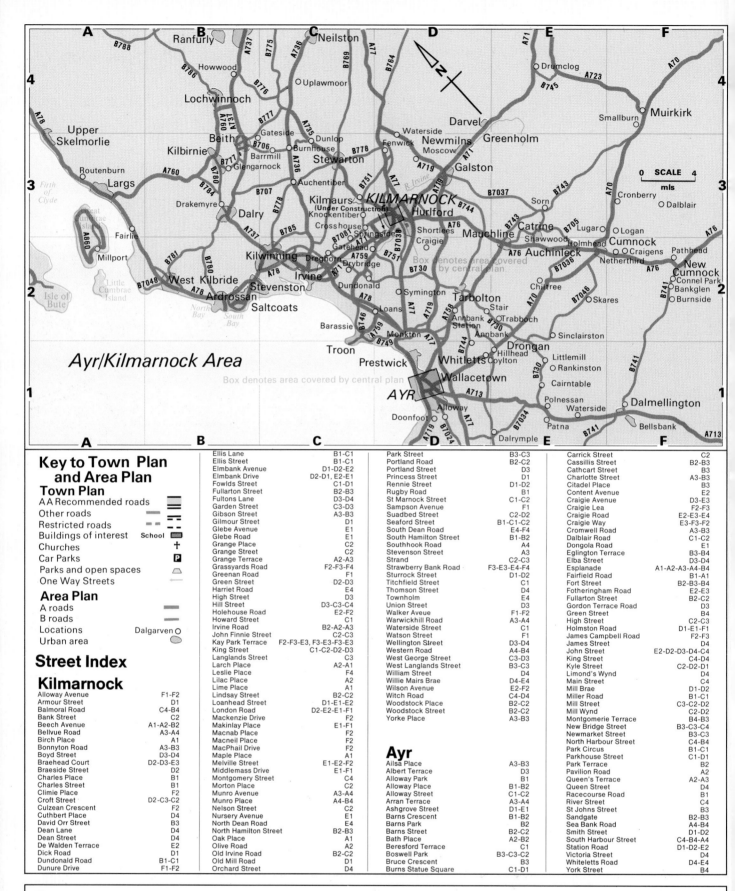

## Key to Town Plan and Area Plan

### Town Plan
- A A Recommended roads
- Other roads
- Restricted roads
- Buildings of interest — School
- Churches
- Car Parks — P
- Parks and open spaces
- One Way Streets

### Area Plan
- A roads
- B roads
- Locations — Dalgarven
- Urban area

## Street Index

### Kilmarnock

| | |
|---|---|
| Alloway Avenue | F1-F2 |
| Armour Street | D1 |
| Balmoral Road | C4-B4 |
| Bank Street | C2 |
| Beech Avenue | A1-A2-B2 |
| Bellvue Road | A3-A4 |
| Birch Place | A1 |
| Bonnyton Road | A3-B3 |
| Boyd Street | D3-D4 |
| Braehead Court | D2-D3-E3 |
| Braeside Street | D2 |
| Charles Place | B1 |
| Charles Street | B1 |
| Climie Place | F2 |
| Croft Street | D2-C3-C2 |
| Culzean Crescent | F2 |
| Cuthbert Place | D4 |
| David Orr Street | B3 |
| Dean Lane | D4 |
| Dean Street | D4 |
| De Walden Terrace | E2 |
| Dick Road | D1 |
| Dundonald Road | B1-C1 |
| Dunure Drive | F1-F2 |
| Ellis Lane | B1-C1 |
| Ellis Street | B1-C1 |
| Elmbank Avenue | D1-D2-E2 |
| Elmbank Drive | D2-D1, E2-E1 |
| Fowlds Street | C1-D1 |
| Fullarton Street | B2-B3 |
| Fultons Lane | D3-D4 |
| Garden Street | C3-D3 |
| Gibson Street | A3-B3 |
| Gilmour Street | D1 |
| Glebe Avenue | E1 |
| Glebe Road | E1 |
| Grange Place | C2 |
| Grange Street | C2 |
| Grange Terrace | A2-A3 |
| Grassyards Road | F2-F3-F4 |
| Greenan Road | F1 |
| Green Street | D2-D3 |
| Harriet Road | E4 |
| High Street | D3-C3-C4 |
| Holehouse Road | E2-F2 |
| Howard Street | C1 |
| Irvine Road | B2-A2-A3 |
| John Finnie Street | C2-C3 |
| Kay Park Terrace | F2-F3-E3, F3-E3-F3-E3 |
| King Street | C1-C2-D2-D3 |
| Langlands Street | C3 |
| Larch Place | A2-A1 |
| Leslie Place | F4 |
| Lilac Place | A2 |
| Lime Place | A1 |
| Lindsay Street | B2-C2 |
| Loanhead Street | D1-E1-E2 |
| London Road | D2-E2-E1-F1 |
| Mackenzie Drive | F2 |
| Makinlay Place | E1-F1 |
| Macnab Place | F2 |
| Macneil Place | F2 |
| MacPhail Drive | F2 |
| Maple Place | F2 |
| Melville Street | E1-E2-F2 |
| Middlemass Drive | E1-F1 |
| Montgomery Street | C4 |
| Morton Place | C2 |
| Munro Avenue | A3-A4 |
| Munro Place | A4-B4 |
| Nelson Street | C2 |
| North Dean Road | E1 |
| North Hamilton Street | B2-B3 |
| Oak Place | A1 |
| Olive Road | A2 |
| Old Irvine Road | B2-C2 |
| Old Mill Road | D1 |
| Orchard Street | D4 |
| Park Street | B3-C3 |
| Portland Road | B2-C2 |
| Portland Street | D3 |
| Princess Street | D1 |
| Rennie Street | D1-D2 |
| Rugby Road | B1 |
| St Marnock Street | C1-C2 |
| Sampson Avenue | F1 |
| Suadbed Street | C2-D2 |
| Seaford Street | B1-C1-C2 |
| South Dean Road | E4-F4 |
| South Hamilton Street | B1-B2 |
| Southhook Road | A4 |
| Stevenson Street | A3 |
| Strand | C2-C3 |
| Strawberry Bank Road | F3-E3-E4-F4 |
| Sturrock Street | D1-D2 |
| Titchfield Street | C1 |
| Thomson Street | D4 |
| Townholm | E4 |
| Union Street | D3 |
| Walker Aveue | F1-F2 |
| Warwickhill Road | A3-A4 |
| Waterside Street | C1 |
| Watson Street | F1 |
| Wellington Street | D3-D4 |
| Western Road | A4-B4 |
| West George Street | C3-D3 |
| West Langlands Street | B3-C3 |
| William Street | D4 |
| Willie Mairs Brae | D4-E4 |
| Wilson Avenue | E2-F2 |
| Witch Road | C4-D4 |
| Woodstock Place | B2-C2 |
| Woodstock Street | B2-C2 |
| Yorke Place | A3-B3 |

### Ayr

| | |
|---|---|
| Ailsa Place | A3-B3 |
| Albert Terrace | D3 |
| Alloway Park | B1 |
| Alloway Place | B1-B2 |
| Alloway Street | C1-C2 |
| Arran Terrace | A3-A4 |
| Ashgrove Street | D1-E1 |
| Barns Crescent | B1-B2 |
| Barns Park | B2 |
| Barns Street | B2-C2 |
| Bath Place | A2-B2 |
| Beresford Terrace | C1 |
| Boswell Park | B3-C3-C2 |
| Bruce Crescent | B3 |
| Burns Statue Square | C1-D1 |
| Carrick Street | C2 |
| Cassillis Street | B2-B3 |
| Cathcart Street | B3 |
| Charlotte Street | A3-B3 |
| Citadel Place | B3 |
| Content Avenue | E2 |
| Craigie Avenue | D3-E3 |
| Craigie Lea | F2-F3 |
| Craigie Road | E2-E3-E4 |
| Craigie Way | E3-F3-F2 |
| Cromwell Road | A3-B3 |
| Dalblair Road | C1-C2 |
| Dongola Road | E1 |
| Eglinton Terrace | B3-B4 |
| Elba Street | B3-C3 |
| Esplanade | A1-A2-A3-A4-B4 |
| Fairfield Road | B1-A1 |
| Fort Street | B2-B3-B4 |
| Fotheringham Road | E2-E3 |
| Fullarton Street | B2-C2 |
| Gordon Terrace Road | D3 |
| Green Street | B4 |
| High Street | C2-C3 |
| Holmston Road | D1-E1-F1 |
| James Campbell Road | F2-F3 |
| James Street | D4 |
| John Street | E2-D2-D3-D4-C4 |
| King Street | C4 |
| Kyle Street | C2-D2-D1 |
| Limond's Wynd | D4 |
| Main Street | C4 |
| Mill Brae | D1-D2 |
| Miller Road | B1-C1 |
| Mill Street | C3-C2-D2 |
| Mill Wynd | C2-D2 |
| Montgomerie Terrace | B4-B3 |
| New Bridge Street | B3-C3-C4 |
| Newmarket Street | B3-C3 |
| North Harbour Street | C4-B4 |
| Park Circus | B1-C1 |
| Parkhouse Street | C1-D1 |
| Park Terrace | B2 |
| Pavilion Road | A2 |
| Queen's Terrace | A2-A3 |
| Queen Street | D4 |
| Racecourse Road | B1 |
| River Street | C4 |
| St Johns Street | B3 |
| Sandgate | B2-B3 |
| Sea Bank Road | A4-B4 |
| Smith Street | D1-D2 |
| South Harbour Street | C4-B4-A4 |
| Station Road | D1-D2-E2 |
| Victoria Street | D4 |
| Whiteletts Road | D4-E4 |
| York Street | B4 |

# Ayr

Set on the lovely coastline of the Firth of Clyde, Ayr enjoys a well-deserved reputation as one of Scotland's most attractive seaside resorts. Its fine natural assets of sandy beaches and pastoral river scenery have been augmented by extensive parks and gardens, as well as a host of leisure amenities.

However, some of Ayr's visitors are drawn to the town by its associations with Scotland's beloved national poet – Robert Burns. He was born at the nearby village of Alloway and many of the places immortalised in his poems can be seen in Ayr. These include the medieval Auld Brig, one of the famous 'twa brigs' that span the River Ayr. The thatched Tam O'Shanter Inn in the High Street, now a museum devoted to Burns, and an imposing statue, are further reminders that this was 'Rabbie's' town.

Ayr has been a prosperous fishing port for centuries and its harbour provides a particularly charming focal point to the town. Surprisingly, few buildings pre-date the 19th century, but one exception is Loudon Hall – a fine 16th-century town house now open to the public. Several handsome Georgian edifaces surround Wellington Square, overlooked by the soaring steeple of the Town Buildings. A statue here commemorates another son of Ayr, John Macadam, who invented the road surface that bears his name.

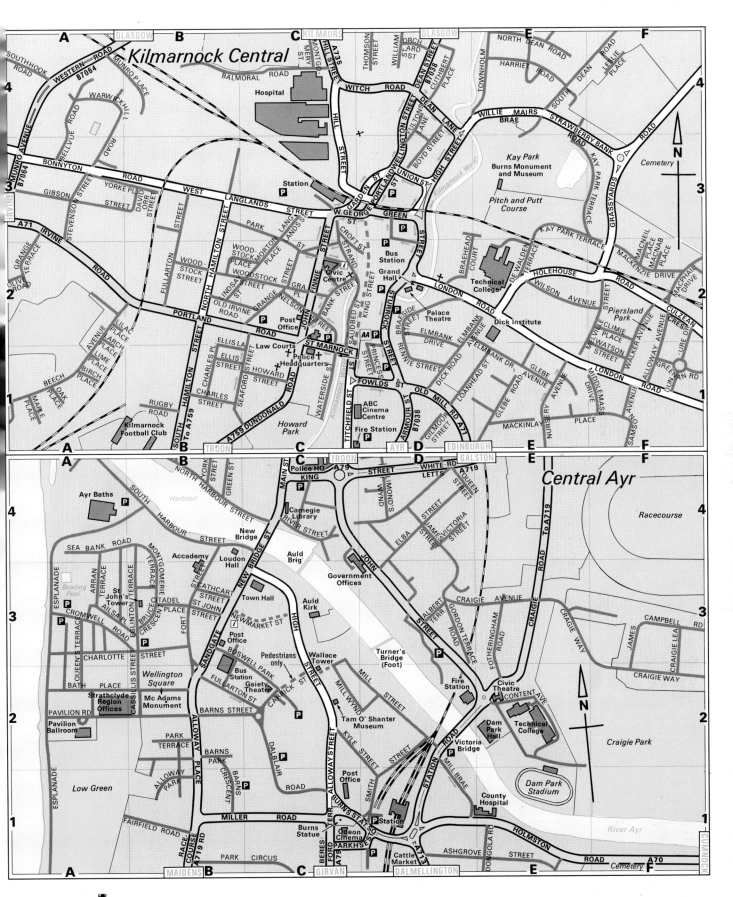

# Kilmarnock Central

A B C D E F

**GLASGOW** **KILMAURS** **GLASGOW**

SOUTHHOOK ROAD
WESTERN ROAD
B7064
MUNRO PLACE
BALMORAL ROAD
ORCHARD ST
NORTH DEAN ROAD
WARWICKHILL
WITCH ROAD
DEAN STREET
CUTHBERT PLACE
TOWNHOLM
NORTH DEAN ROAD
HARRIET ST
SOUTH DEAN ROAD
LESLIE PLACE

Hospital

MUNRO AVENUE
BELLVUE ROAD
BONNYTON ROAD
GIBSON STREET
STEVENSON STREET
YORKE PL
DAVID ORR STREET
HILL STREET
MONTGOMERY ST
PORTLAND ST
WELLINGTON STREET
FULTONS LANE
BOYD STREET
DEAN LANE
UNION ST
HIGH STREET
WILLIE MAIRS BRAE
STRAWBERRY BANK
KAY PARK TERRACE
GRASSYARDS ROAD
Cemetery

**N**

IRVINE
B7064
A71 IRVINE ROAD
GRANGE TERRACE
OLIVE ROAD
FULLARTON STREET
WOODSTOCK PLACE
WOODSTOCK STREET
West Langlands Street
PARK
LANG ST
LANDS ST
MORTON PLACE
LINDSAY STREET
GRANGE STREET
OLD IRVINE ROAD
NELSON STREET
Station
W. GEORGE
GREEN STREET
STRAND
CROFT ST
BANK STREET
FINNIE STREET
KING STREET
SAUDBED ST
Civic Centre
Bus Station
Grand Hall
LONDON ROAD
BRAEHEAD COURT
Technical College
DE WALDEN TERRACE
HOLEHOUSE ROAD
WILSON AVENUE
KAY PARK TERRACE
MACNEIL PLACE
MACNAB PLACE
MACKENZIE DRIVE
MACPHAIL DRIVE
CULZEAN CRESC

PORTLAND ROAD
LILAC AVENUE
LARCH PLACE
LIME PLACE
ELLIS LANE
CHARLES PL
ELLIS STREET
Post Office
JOHN STREET
ST MARNOCK STREET
PRINCESS ST
Palace Theatre
Dick Institute
ELMBANK DRIVE
ELMBANK AVENUE
DICK ROAD
ELMBANK DR
LOANHEAD ST
GLEBE ROAD
GLEBE AVENUE
Piersland Park
CLIMIE PLACE
WATSON STREET
WALKER AVENUE
LONDON ROAD
ALLOWAY AVENUE
MIDDLEMASS DRIVE
GREENAN RD
URE ST

BEECH PLACE
OAK PLACE
MAPLE PLACE
BIRCH PLACE
RUGBY ROAD
Kilmarnock Football Club
SOUTH HAMILTON STREET
CHARLES PL
SEAFORD STREET
HOWARD STREET
CHARLES STREET
Law Courts
Police Headquarters
WATERSIDE
ST MARNOCK
FOWLDS
TITCHFIELD ST
ABC Cinema Centre
Fire Station
ARMOUR ST
OLD MILL RD
B7038
GILMOUR STREET
A71
MACKINLAY PLACE
NURSERY AVENUE
SAMSO

**TROON** **AYR** **EDINBURGH GALSTON**
A759 To A759
A759 DUNDONALD RD
Howard Park

# Central Ayr

A B C D E F

**TROON** **AYR**
**A79** Police HQ
A719 WHITE RD
LETTS

Ayr Baths
NORTH HARBOUR STREET
GREEN ST
MAIN ST
KING STREET
LIMOND'S WYND
QUEEN STREET
Racecourse

SOUTH HARBOUR STREET
YORK STREET
Carnegie Library
RIVER STREET
New Bridge
ELBA STREET
JAMES STREET
VICTORIA STREET

SEA BANK ROAD
ESPLANADE
ARRAN TERRACE
MONTGOMERIE TERRACE
Academy
Loudon Hall
Auld Brig'
JOHN STREET
Government Offices
CRAIGIE AVENUE
CAMPBELL RD

Boating Pool
St John's Tower
BRUCE CRESCENT
CITADEL PLACE
ST JOHN STREET
FORT STREET
SCATHCART STREET
NEWMARKET ST
Post Office
Town Hall
Auld Kirk
HIGH STREET
Turner's Bridge (Foot)
ALBERT TERR
GORDON TERRACE
FOTHERINGHAM ROAD
CRAIGIE ROAD
CRAIGIE WAY
JAMES ST
CRAIGIE LEA
CRAIGIE WAY

CROMWELL ROAD
QUEEN'S TERRACE
CHARLOTTE STREET
BATH PLACE
EGLINTON STREET
Wellington Square
CASSILLIS STREE
Mc Adams Monument
BOSWELL PARK
FULLARTON ST
Bus Station
Gaiety Theatre
CARRICK ST
Wallace Tower
MILL WYND
MILL STREET
Fire Station
Civic Theatre
Technical College
CONTENT AVE
Craigie Park

Pavilion Ballroom
PAVILION RD
STRATHCLYDE REGION OFFICES
PARK TERRACE
BARNS STREET
DALBLAIR ROAD
Tam O' Shanter Museum
KYLE STREET
Dam Park Hall
Victoria Bridge
STATION ROAD
MILL BRAE
Dam Park Stadium

**N**

Low Green
ESPLANADE
ALLOWAY PLACE
ALLOWAY PARK
BARNS PARK
BARNS CRESCENT
Post Office
SMITH STREET
County Hospital
River Ayr

FAIRFIELD ROAD
MILLER ROAD
Burns Statue
Odeon Cinema
BURNS STAT SQ
PARK HS
Station
Cattle Market
ASHGROVE STREET
DONGOLA RD
HOLMSTON ROAD
Cemetery
A70

RACE COURSE A719 RD
PARK CIRCUS
BERESFORD TERR
A79
A713

**MAIDENS** **GIRVAN** **DALMELLINGTON** **CUMNOCK**

## AYR
The town has been an important fishing port on the Firth of Clyde for several hundred years. Today, Ayr is a major seaside resort and tourist centre and the harbour is as busy as ever, with yachts and leisure craft.

81

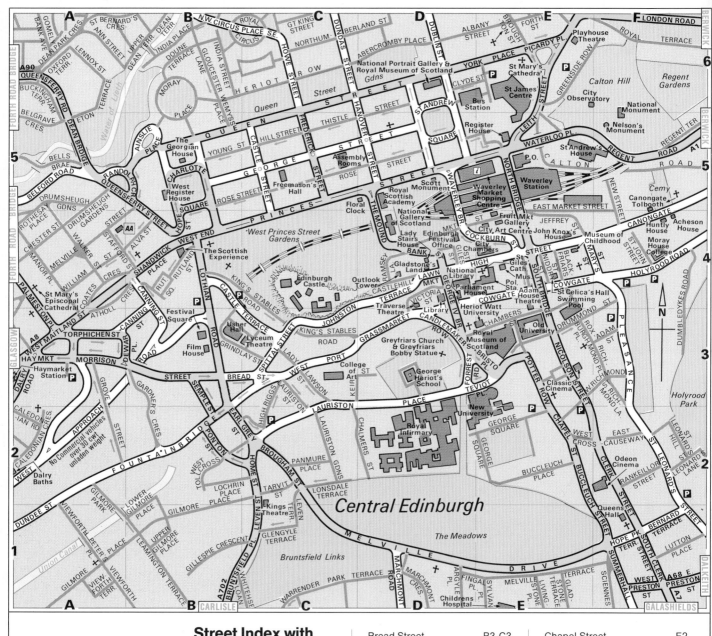

## Key to Town Plan and Area Plan

### Town Plan
A A Recommended roads
Other roads
Restricted roads
Buildings of intrest      Gallery
Car Parks                 P
Parks and open spaces
A A Service Centre        AA
Churches                  +

### Area Plan
A roads
B roads
Locations                 Newcraighall O
Urban area

## Street Index with Grid Reference

### Edinburgh

# Edinburgh

Scotland's ancient capital, dubbed the "Athens of the North", is one of the most splendid cities in the whole of Europe. Its buildings, its history and its cultural life give it an international importance which is celebrated every year in its world-famous festival. The whole city is overshadowed by the craggy castle which seems to grow out of the rock itself. There has been a fortress here since the 7th century and most of the great figures of Scottish history have been associated with it. The old town grew up around the base of Castle Rock within the boundaries of the defensive King's Wall and, unable to spread outwards, grew upwards in a maze of tenements. However, during the 18th century new prosperity from the shipping trade resulted in the building of the New Town and the regular, spacious layout of the Georgian development makes a striking contrast with the old

hotch-potch of streets. Princes Street is the main east-west thoroughfare with excellent shops on one side and Princes Street Gardens with their famous floral clock on the south side.

As befits such a splendid capital city there are numerous museums and art galleries packed with priceless treasures. Among these are the famous picture gallery in 16th-century Holyroodhouse, the present Royal Palace, and the fascinating and unusual Museum of Childhood.

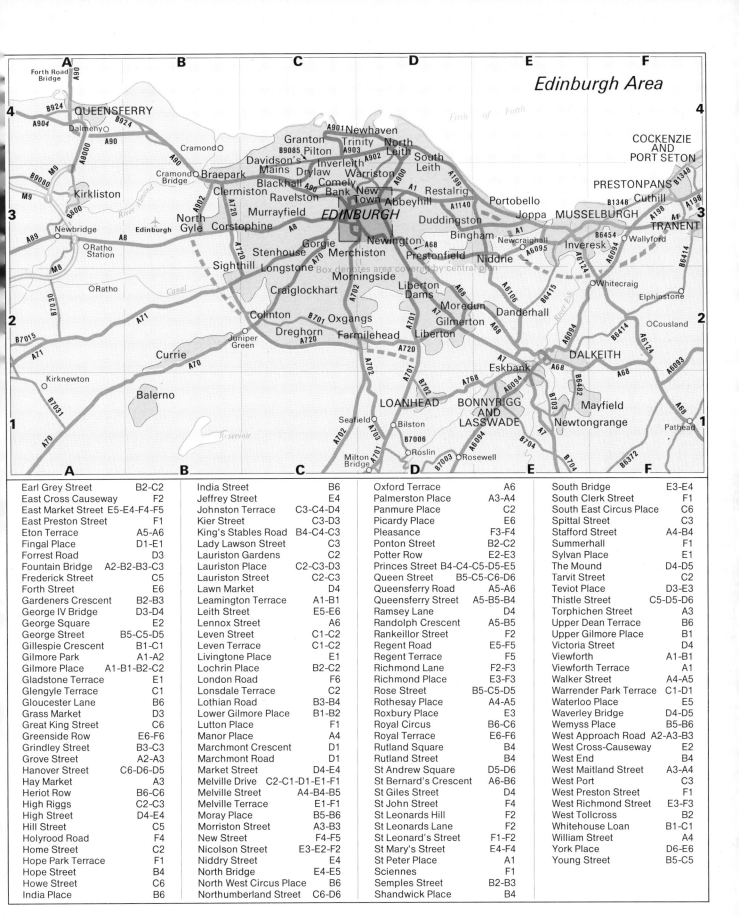

**Edinburgh Area**

|  |  | |  |  |
|---|---|---|---|---|
| Earl Grey Street | B2-C2 | | India Street | B6 |
| East Cross Causeway | F2 | | Jeffrey Street | E4 |
| East Market Street | E5-E4-F4-F5 | | Johnston Terrace | C3-C4-D4 |
| East Preston Street | F1 | | Kier Street | C3-D3 |
| Eton Terrace | A5-A6 | | King's Stables Road | B4-C4-C3 |
| Fingal Place | D1-E1 | | Lady Lawson Street | C3 |
| Forrest Road | D3 | | Lauriston Gardens | C2 |
| Fountain Bridge | A2-B2-B3-C3 | | Lauriston Place | C2-C3-D3 |
| Frederick Street | C5 | | Lauriston Street | C2-C3 |
| Forth Street | E6 | | Lawn Market | D4 |
| Gardeners Crescent | B2-B3 | | Leamington Terrace | A1-B1 |
| George IV Bridge | D3-D4 | | Leith Street | E5-E6 |
| George Square | E2 | | Lennox Street | A6 |
| George Street | B5-C5-D5 | | Leven Street | C1-C2 |
| Gillespie Crescent | B1-C1 | | Leven Terrace | C1-C2 |
| Gilmore Park | A1-A2 | | Livingtone Place | E1 |
| Gilmore Place | A1-B1-B2-C2 | | Lochrin Place | B2-C2 |
| Gladstone Terrace | E1 | | London Road | F6 |
| Glengyle Terrace | C1 | | Lonsdale Terrace | C2 |
| Gloucester Lane | B6 | | Lothian Road | B3-B4 |
| Grass Market | D3 | | Lower Gilmore Place | B1-B2 |
| Great King Street | C6 | | Lutton Place | F1 |
| Greenside Row | E6-F6 | | Manor Place | A4 |
| Grindley Street | B3-C3 | | Marchmont Crescent | D1 |
| Grove Street | A2-A3 | | Marchmont Road | D1 |
| Hanover Street | C6-D6-D5 | | Market Street | D4-E4 |
| Hay Market | A3 | | Melville Drive | C2-C1-D1-E1-F1 |
| Heriot Row | B6-C6 | | Melville Street | A4-B4-B5 |
| High Riggs | C2-C3 | | Melville Terrace | E1-F1 |
| High Street | D4-E4 | | Moray Place | B5-B6 |
| Hill Street | C5 | | Morriston Street | A3-B3 |
| Holyrood Road | F4 | | New Street | F4-F5 |
| Home Street | C2 | | Nicolson Street | E3-E2-F2 |
| Hope Park Terrace | F1 | | Niddry Street | E4 |
| Hope Street | B4 | | North Bridge | E4-E5 |
| Howe Street | C6 | | North West Circus Place | B6 |
| India Place | B6 | | Northumberland Street | C6-D6 |

|  |  | |  |  |
|---|---|---|---|---|
| Oxford Terrace | A6 | | South Bridge | E3-E4 |
| Palmerston Place | A3-A4 | | South Clerk Street | F1 |
| Panmure Place | C2 | | South East Circus Place | C6 |
| Picardy Place | E6 | | Spittal Street | C3 |
| Pleasance | F3-F4 | | Stafford Street | A4-B4 |
| Ponton Street | B2-C2 | | Summerhall | F1 |
| Potter Row | E2-E3 | | Sylvan Place | E1 |
| Princes Street | B4-C4-C5-D5-E5 | | The Mound | D4-D5 |
| Queen Street | B5-C5-C6-D6 | | Tarvit Street | C2 |
| Queensferry Road | A5-A6 | | Teviot Place | D3-E3 |
| Queensferry Street | A5-B5-B4 | | Thistle Street | C5-D5-D6 |
| Ramsey Lane | D4 | | Torphichen Street | A3 |
| Randolph Crescent | A5-B5 | | Upper Dean Terrace | B6 |
| Rankeillor Street | F2 | | Upper Gilmore Place | B1 |
| Regent Road | E5-F5 | | Victoria Street | D4 |
| Regent Terrace | F5 | | Viewforth | A1-B1 |
| Richmond Lane | F2-F3 | | Viewforth Terrace | A1 |
| Richmond Place | E3-F3 | | Walker Street | A4-A5 |
| Rose Street | B5-C5-D5 | | Warrender Park Terrace | C1-D1 |
| Rothesay Place | A4-A5 | | Waterloo Place | E5 |
| Roxbury Place | E3 | | Waverley Bridge | D4-D5 |
| Royal Circus | B6-C6 | | Wemyss Place | B5-B6 |
| Royal Terrace | E6-F6 | | West Approach Road | A2-A3-B3 |
| Rutland Square | B4 | | West Cross-Causeway | E2 |
| Rutland Street | B4 | | West End | B4 |
| St Andrew Square | D5-D6 | | West Maitland Street | A3-A4 |
| St Bernard's Crescent | A6-B6 | | West Port | C3 |
| St Giles Street | D4 | | West Preston Street | F1 |
| St John Street | F4 | | West Richmond Street | E3-F3 |
| St Leonards Hill | F2 | | West Tollcross | B2 |
| St Leonards Lane | F2 | | Whitehouse Loan | B1-C1 |
| St Leonard's Street | F1-F2 | | William Street | A4 |
| St Mary's Street | E4-F4 | | York Place | D6-E6 |
| St Peter Place | A1 | | Young Street | B5-C5 |
| Sciennes | F1 | | | |
| Semples Street | B2-B3 | | | |
| Shandwick Place | B4 | | | |

**EDINBURGH**
Holyrood Palace orginated as a guest house for the Abbey of Holyrood in the 16th century, but most of the present building was built for Charles II. Mary Queen of Scots was one of its most famous inhabitants.

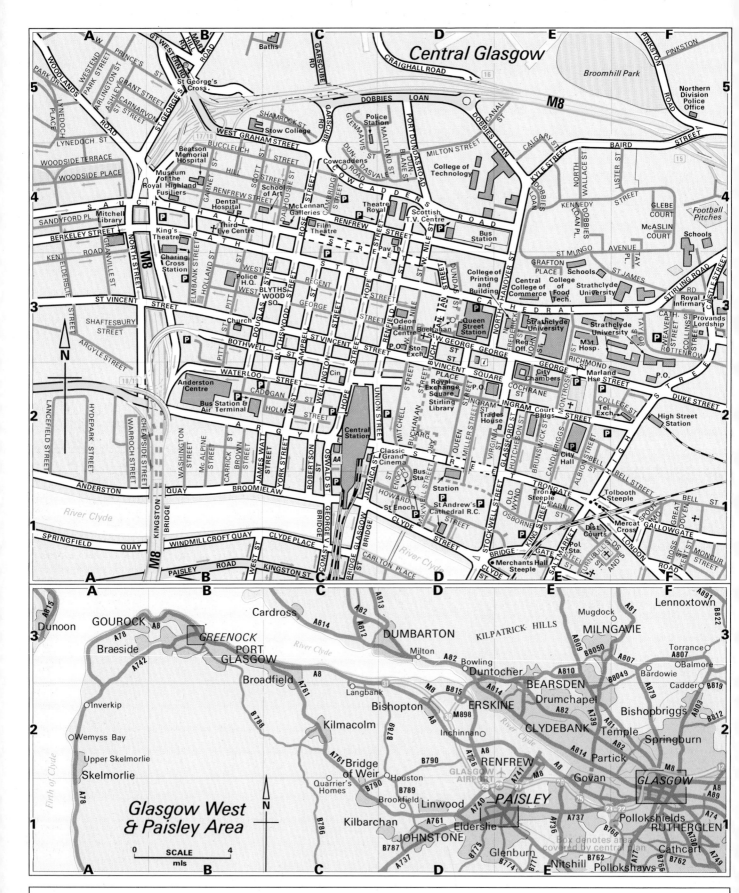

# Glasgow

Although much of Glasgow is distinctly Victorian in character, its roots go back very many centuries. Best link with the past is the cathedral; founded in the 6th century, it has features from many succeeding centuries, including an exceptional 13th- century crypt. Nearby is Provand's Lordship, the city's oldest house. It dates from 1471 and is now a museum. Two much larger museums are to be found a little out of the centre – the Art Gallery and Museum contains one of the finest collections of paintings in Britain, while the Hunterian Museum, attached to the University, covers geology, archaeology, ethnography and more general subjects. On Glasgow Green is People's Palace – a museum of city life. Most imposing of the Victorian buildings are the City Chambers and City Hall which was built in 1841 as a concert hall but now houses the Scottish National Orchestra.

*Paisley* is famous for the lovely fabric pattern to which it gives its name. It was taken from fabrics brought from the Near East in the early 19th century, and its manufacture, along with the production of thread, is still important.

*Greenock* has been an important port and shipbuilding centre since as early as the 16th century. Its most famous son is James Watt, the inventor of steam power, born here in 1736. The town has numerous memorials to the great man.

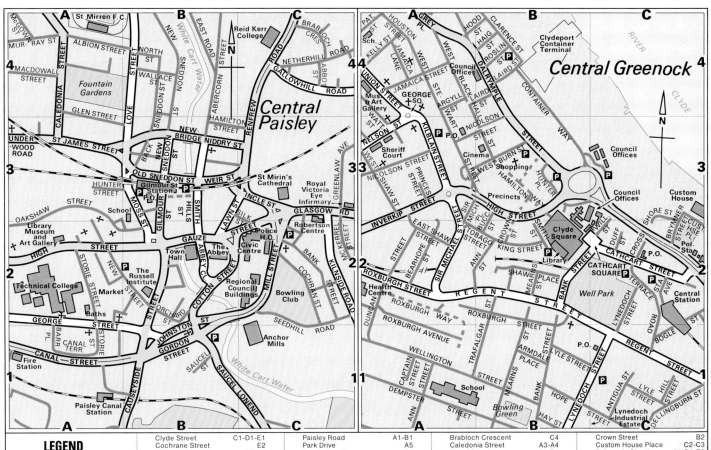

**Central Paisley**     **Central Greenock**

## LEGEND

**Town Plan**

AA recommended route
Restricted roads
Other roads
Buildings of interest   Station ■
Car parks   P
Parks and open spaces
One way streets

**Area Plan**

A roads
B roads
Locations   Garvock ○
Urban area

## Street Index with grid reference

### Glasgow

| | |
|---|---|
| Albion Street | E1-E2 |
| Anderston Quay | A2-A1-B1 |
| Argyle Arcade | D2 |
| Argyle Street | A3-A2-B2-C2-D2-D1-E1 |
| Arlington Street | A5 |
| Ashley Street | A5 |
| Baird Street | E4-E5-F5-F4 |
| Bath Street | B4-C4-C3-D3 |
| Bell Street | E2-E1-F1 |
| Berkeley Street | A4 |
| Blythswood Square | B3-C3 |
| Blythswood Street | C2-C3 |
| Bothwell Street | B3-C3-C2 |
| Bridgegate | D1-E1 |
| Bridge Street | C1 |
| Broomielaw | B1-C1 |
| Brown Street | B1-B2 |
| Brunswick Street | E2 |
| Buccleuch Street | B4-C4 |
| Buchannan Street | D3-D4 |
| Cadogan Street | B2-C2 |
| Calgary Street | E4-E5-E4 |
| Canal Street | D5-E5 |
| Candleriggs | E1-E2 |
| Cambridge Street | C4 |
| Carlton Place | C1-D1 |
| Carnarvon Street | A5-B5 |
| Carrick Street | B1-B2 |
| Castle Street | F3 |
| Cathedral Street | D3-E3-F3 |
| Cheapside Street | A1-A2 |
| Clyde Place | B1-C1 |
| Clyde Street | C1-D1-E1 |
| Cochrane Street | E2 |
| College Street | E2-F2 |
| Collins Street | F3 |
| Commerce Street | C1 |
| Cowcaddens Road | C4-D4-E4 |
| Craighall Road | C5-D5 |
| Dalhousie Street | C4 |
| Dobbies Loan | C5-D5-E5-E4-D4 |
| Dobbies Loan Place | E4 |
| Douglas Street | B3-C3 |
| Duke Street | F2 |
| Dunblane Street | D4-D5 |
| Dundas Street | D3 |
| Dundasvale Road | C4-D4 |
| Elderslie Street | A3-A4 |
| Elmbank Street | B3-B4 |
| Gallowgate | E1-F1 |
| Garscube Road | C4-C5 |
| Garnet Street | B4 |
| George V Bridge | C1 |
| George Square | D3-E3-E2-D2 |
| George Street | E3-E2-F2 |
| Glasgow Bridge | C1 |
| Glassford Street | E2 |
| Glebe Court | F4 |
| Glenmavis Street | C5-C4-D4 |
| Grafton Place | E3 |
| Grant Street | A5-B5 |
| Granville Street | A3-A4 |
| Great Dovenhill | F1 |
| Great Western Road | A5-B5 |
| High Street | E1-E2-F2-F3 |
| Hill Street | B4-C4 |
| Holland Street | B3-B4 |
| Holm Street | C2 |
| Hope Street | C2-C3-C4-D4 |
| Howard Street | C1-D1 |
| Hutcheson Street | E1-E2 |
| Hyde Park Street | A1-A2 |
| Ingram Street | D2-E2-F2 |
| Jamaica Street | C1-C2-D2 |
| James Watt Street | B1-B2-C2 |
| John Street | E3 |
| Kennedy Street | E4-F4 |
| Kent Road | A3-A4 |
| Kent Street | F1 |
| King Street | E1 |
| Kingston Bridge | B1 |
| Kingston Street | B1-C1 |
| Kyle Street | E4 |
| Lancefield Street | A1-A2 |
| Lister Street | F4 |
| London Road | E1-F1 |
| Lyndoch Place | A5 |
| Lyndoch Street | A4-A5 |
| McAlpine Street | B1-B2 |
| McAslin Court | F4 |
| Maitland Street | C5-D5-D4 |
| Maryhill Road | B5 |
| Maxwell Street | D1-D2 |
| Miller Street | D2 |
| Milton Street | D4-D5 |
| Mitchell Street | D2 |
| Moncur Street | F1 |
| Montrose Street | E2-E3 |
| North Street | A3-A4 |
| North Frederick Street | E3 |
| North Hannover Street | D3-E3-E4 |
| North Wallace Street | E4 |
| Old Wynd | E1 |
| Osborne Street | E1 |
| Oswald Street | C1-C2 |

| | |
|---|---|
| Paisley Road | A1-B1 |
| Park Drive | A5 |
| Parnie Street | E1 |
| Pinkston Drive | F5 |
| Pinkston Road | F5 |
| Pitt Street | B2-B3-B4 |
| Port Dundas Road | D4-D5 |
| Queen Street | D2 |
| Renfield Street | D4-D3-C3-C2-D2 |
| Richmond Street | E3-E2-F2 |
| Robertson Street | C1-C2 |
| Rose Street | C3-C4 |
| Ross Street | F1 |
| Rottenrow | F3 |
| St Andrew's Square | E1-F1 |
| St Enoch Square | D1-D2 |
| St George's Road | A4-B4-B5 |
| St James Road | E3-F3 |
| St Mungo Avenue | E3-E4-F4 |
| St Vincent Place | D2-D3 |
| St Vincent Street | A3-B3-C3-D3-D2 |
| Saltmarket | E1 |
| Sandyford Place | A4 |
| Sauchiehall Street | A4-B4-C4-C3-D3 |
| Scott Street | B4-C4 |
| Shaftesbury Street | A3 |
| Shamrock Street | B5-C5-C4 |
| Spoutmouth | F1 |
| Springfield Quay | A1 |
| Steel Street | E1 |
| Stirling Road | F3 |
| Stockwell Street | D1-E1 |
| Taylor Place | F4 |
| Taylor Street | F3 |
| Trongate | E1 |
| Turnbull Street | E1 |
| Union Street | C2-D2 |
| Virginia Street | D2-E2 |
| Warroch Street | A1-A2 |
| Washington Street | B1-B2 |
| Waterloo Street | B2-C2 |
| Weaver Street | F3 |
| Wellington Street | C2-C3 |
| West Street | B1 |
| West Campbell Street | C2-C3 |
| West George Street | B3-C3-D3 |
| West Graham Street | B5-C5-C4 |
| West Nile Street | D3-D4 |
| West Prince's Street | A5-B5 |
| West Regent Street | B3-C3-D3 |
| Westend Park Street | A5 |
| Windmill Croft Quay | B1 |
| Woodlands Road | A4-A5 |
| Woodside Place | A4 |
| Woodside Terrace | A4 |
| York Street | C1-C2 |

### Paisley

| | |
|---|---|
| Abbey Close | B2 |
| Abbot Street | C4 |
| Abercorn Street | B3-B4 |
| Albion Street | A4-B4 |
| Back Sneddon Street | B3-B4 |
| Bank Street | C2 |
| Barr Place | A1 |

| | |
|---|---|
| Brabloch Crescent | C4 |
| Caledonia Street | A3-A4 |
| Canal Street | A1-B1 |
| Canal Terrace | A1 |
| Causeyside Street | A1-B1-B2 |
| Cochran Street | C2 |
| Cotton Street | B2 |
| East Road | B4 |
| Gallowhill Road | C4 |
| Gauze Street | B2-C2-C3 |
| George Street | A1-B1-B2-A2 |
| Gilmour Street | B2-B3 |
| Glasgow Road | C3 |
| Glen Street | A4-A3-B3 |
| Gordon Street | B1 |
| Greenlaw Avenue | C3 |
| Hamilton Street | B3-C3 |
| High Street | A2-B2 |
| Hunter Street | A3-B3 |
| Incle Street | C3 |
| Johnston Street | B1-B2 |
| Kilnside Road | C2-C3 |
| Lawn Street | B2-B3-C3 |
| Love Street | B3-B4 |
| Macdowall Street | A4 |
| McGown Street | A4 |
| McKerrel Street | C2-C3 |
| Mill Street | C2 |
| Moss Street | B2-B3 |
| Murray Street | A4 |
| Netherhill Road | C4 |
| Newbridge | B3 |
| New Sneddon Street | B3-B4 |
| New Street | A2-B2 |
| Niddry Street | B3-C3 |
| North Street | B4 |
| Oakshaw Street | A2-A3-B2 |
| Old Sneddon Street | B3 |
| Orchard Street | B2 |
| Renfrew Road | C3-C4 |
| St James Street | A3 |
| Saucel Lonend | B1-C1 |
| Saucel Street | B1 |
| Seedhill Road | C1-C2 |
| Silk Street | B3-C3-C2 |
| Smith Hills Street | B2-B3 |
| Storie Street | A1-A2 |
| Underwood Road | A3 |
| Wallace Street | B4 |
| Weir Street | B3-C3 |

### Greenock

| | |
|---|---|
| Ann Street | A1 |
| Ann Street | A2-B2 |
| Antigua Street | C1 |
| Argyll Street | A4 |
| Armdale Place | B1 |
| Bank Street | B1-B2-C2 |
| Bearhope Street | A2 |
| Bogle Street | C1-C2 |
| Brymner Street | C2-C3 |
| Buccleugh | B2-B3 |
| Captain Street | A1 |
| Cathcart Square | B2-C2 |
| Cathcart Street | C2 |
| Clarence Street | B4 |
| Container Way | B3-B4 |
| Cross Shore Street | C2-C3 |

| | |
|---|---|
| Crown Street | B2 |
| Custom House Place | C2-C3 |
| Dalrymple Street | A4-B4-B3 |
| Dellingburn Street | C1 |
| Dempster Street | A1-B1 |
| Duff Street | C2 |
| Duncan Street | A1-A2 |
| East Shaw Street | A2-A3 |
| George Square | A3-A4 |
| Grey Place | A4 |
| Haig Street | B4 |
| Hamilton Way | B3 |
| Hay Street | B1 |
| High Street | A3-B3-B2 |
| Hill Street | C1 |
| Hood Street | A4-B4 |
| Hope Street | B1-C1 |
| Houston Street | A4 |
| Hunter Place | B3 |
| Inverkip Street | A2-A3 |
| Jamaica Lane | A4 |
| Jamaica Street | A4 |
| Kelly Street | A4 |
| Kilblain Street | A3 |
| King Street | B2 |
| Laird Street | A4-B4 |
| Lyle Street | B1-C1 |
| Lynedoch Street | B1-C1-C2 |
| Mearns Street | B1-B2 |
| Nelson Street | A3 |
| Nicolson Street | A3-B3 |
| Patrick Street | A4 |
| Princes Street | A3 |
| Regent Street | A2-B2-C2-C1 |
| Roslin Street | B4 |
| Roxburgh Avenue | A1-A2 |
| Roxburgh Street | A2-B2-B1 |
| Roxburgh Way | A1-A2 |
| Shaw Place | B2 |
| Sir Michael Place | A2-A3 |
| Sir Michael Street | A2-A3 |
| Smith Street | B2 |
| Station Avenue | C2 |
| Terrace Road | C1-C2 |
| Tobago Street | A2-B2 |
| Trafalgar Street | A1-B1-B2 |
| Union Street | A4 |
| Watt Street | A3-A4 |
| Wellington Street | A1-B1 |
| West Blackhall Street | A4-A3-B3 |
| West Burn Street | A3-B3 |
| West Shaw Street | A3 |
| West Stewart Street | A4-A3-B3 |
| William Street | C2-C3 |

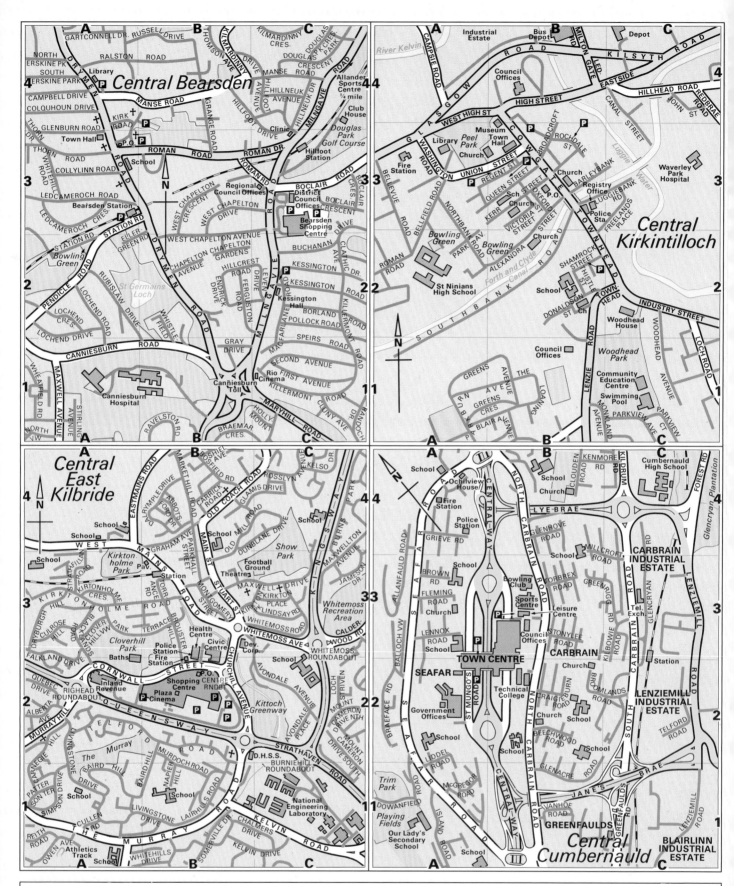

# Glasgow environs

**Cumbernauld** is a New Town — built during the 1950s and '60s, it was specially designed to provide easy access for both motorists and pedestrians. A multi-level shopping area, a sports centre and a thriving local theatre are some of the amenities it enjoys, and amongst the many parks and open spaces in the area, Palacerigg Country Park (1½ miles to the south-east) covers over 600 acres.

**Bearsden** is noted for its public parks and woodland areas. It became established as a residential area in the 19th century, but a number of Georgian buildings are used by the community: Kilmardinny House, for instance, is an Arts Centre with a small theatre.

**East Kilbride** was well-known for its shoemaking and weaving in the 18th century. Its designation as a New Town shortly after the end of World War I boosted its expansion, and today, it is noted for

the good integration of new buildings with old. Popular attractions among the modern buildings are the arcaded shopping precinct and the Dollan Swimming Pool, lying beneath an unusually deep roof within the town's central park.

**Kirkintilloch** Once a station on the old Roman wall, Kirkintilloch in recent years has suffered from the decline of a good many local industries. The former Parish Church of St Mary has been converted into a local history museum.

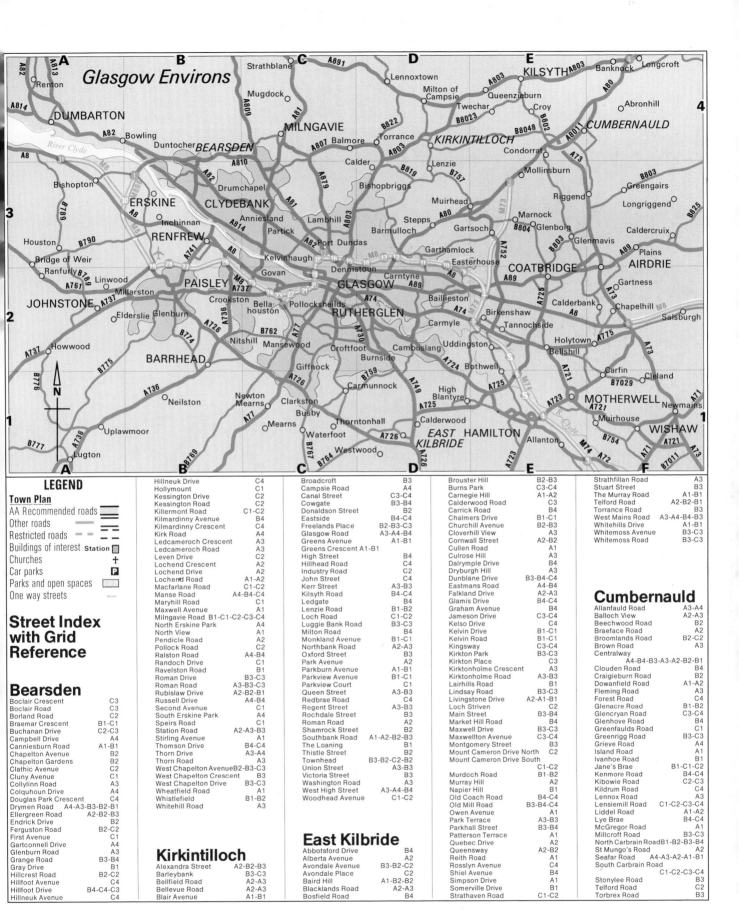

## LEGEND

**Town Plan**

- AA Recommended roads
- Other roads
- Restricted roads
- Buildings of interest   Station
- Churches
- Car parks
- Parks and open spaces
- One way streets

# Street Index with Grid Reference

## Bearsden

| | |
|---|---|
| Boclair Crescent | C3 |
| Boclair Road | C3 |
| Borland Road | C2 |
| Braemar Crescent | B1-C1 |
| Buchanan Drive | C2-C3 |
| Campbell Drive | A4 |
| Canniesburn Road | A1-B1 |
| Chapelton Avenue | B2 |
| Chapelton Gardens | B2 |
| Clathic Avenue | C2 |
| Cluny Avenue | C1 |
| Collylinn Road | A3 |
| Colquhoun Drive | C2 |
| Douglas Park Crescent | C4 |
| Drymen Road | A4-A3-B3-B2-B1 |
| Ellergreen Road | A2-B2-B3 |
| Endrick Drive | B2 |
| Ferguston Road | B2-C2 |
| First Avenue | C1 |
| Gartconnell Drive | A4 |
| Glenburn Road | A3 |
| Grange Road | B3-B4 |
| Gray Drive | B1 |
| Hillcrest Road | B2-C2 |
| Hillfoot Avenue | C4 |
| Hillfoot Drive | B4-C4-C3 |
| Hillneuk Avenue | C4 |
| Hillneuk Drive | C4 |
| Hollymount | C1 |
| Kessington Drive | C2 |
| Kessington Road | C2 |
| Killermont Road | C1-C2 |
| Kilmardinny Avenue | B4 |
| Kilmardinny Crescent | C4 |
| Kirk Road | A4 |
| Ledcameroch Crescent | A3 |
| Ledcameroch Road | A3 |
| Leven Drive | C2 |
| Lochend Crescent | A2 |
| Lochend Drive | A2 |
| Lochend Road | A1-A2 |
| Macfarlane Road | C1-C2 |
| Manse Road | A4-B4-C4 |
| Maryhill Road | C1 |
| Maxwell Avenue | A1 |
| Milngavie Road | B1-C1-C2-C3-C4 |
| North Erskine Park | A4 |
| North View | A1 |
| Pendicle Road | A2 |
| Pollock Road | C2 |
| Ralston Road | A4-B4 |
| Randoch Drive | C1 |
| Ravelston Road | B1 |
| Roman Drive | B3-C3 |
| Roman Road | A3-B3-C3 |
| Rubislaw Drive | A2-B2-B1 |
| Russell Drive | A4-B4 |
| Second Avenue | C1 |
| South Erskine Park | A4 |
| Speirs Road | C1 |
| Station Road | A2-A3-B3 |
| Stirling Avenue | A1 |
| Thomson Drive | B4-C4 |
| Thorn Drive | A3-A4 |
| Thorn Road | A3-A4 |
| West Chapelton Avenue | B2-B3-C3 |
| West Chapelton Crescent | B3-C3 |
| West Chapelton Drive | B3-C3 |
| Wheatfield Road | A1 |
| Whistlefield | B1-B2 |
| Whitehill Road | A3 |

## Kirkintilloch

| | |
|---|---|
| Alexandra Street | A2-B2-B3 |
| Barleybank | B3-C3 |
| Bellfield Road | A2-A3 |
| Bellevue Road | A2-A3 |
| Blair Avenue | A1-B1 |
| Broadcroft | B3 |
| Campsie Road | A4 |
| Canal Street | C3-C4 |
| Cowgate | B3-B4 |
| Donaldson Street | B2 |
| Eastside | B4-C4 |
| Freelands Place | B2-B3-C3 |
| Glasgow Road | A3-A4-B4 |
| Greens Avenue | A1-B1 |
| Greens Crescent | A1-B1 |
| High Street | B4 |
| Hillhead Road | C4 |
| Industry Road | C2 |
| John Street | C4 |
| Kerr Street | A3-B3 |
| Kilsyth Road | B4-C4 |
| Ledgate | B4 |
| Lenzie Road | B1-B2 |
| Loch Road | C1-C2 |
| Luggie Bank Road | B3-C3 |
| Milton Road | B4 |
| Monkland Avenue | B1-C1 |
| Northbank Road | A2-A3 |
| Oxford Street | B3 |
| Park Avenue | A2 |
| Parkburn Avenue | A1-B1 |
| Parkview Avenue | B1-C1 |
| Parkview Court | C1 |
| Queen Street | A3-B3 |
| Redbrae Road | C4 |
| Regent Street | A3-B3 |
| Rochdale Street | B3 |
| Roman Road | A2 |
| Shamrock Street | B2 |
| Southbank Road | A1-A2-B2-B3 |
| The Loaning | B1 |
| Thistle Street | B2 |
| Townhead | B3-B2-C2-B2 |
| Union Street | A3-B3 |
| Victoria Street | B3 |
| Washington Road | A3 |
| West High Street | A3-A4-B4 |
| Woodhead Avenue | C1-C2 |

## East Kilbride

| | |
|---|---|
| Abbotsford Drive | B4 |
| Alberta Avenue | A2 |
| Avondale Avenue | B3-B2-C2 |
| Avondale Place | A2 |
| Baird Hill | A1-B2-B2 |
| Blacklands Road | A2-A3 |
| Bosfield Road | B4 |
| Brouster Hill | B2-B3 |
| Burns Park | C3-C4 |
| Carnegie Hill | A1-A2 |
| Calderwood Road | C3 |
| Carrick Road | B4 |
| Chalmers Drive | B1-C1 |
| Churchill Avenue | B2-B3 |
| Cloverhill View | A3 |
| Cornwall Street | A2-B2 |
| Cullen Road | A1 |
| Culrose Hill | A3 |
| Dalrymple Drive | B4 |
| Dryburgh Hill | A3 |
| Dunblane Drive | B3-B4-C4 |
| Eastmans Road | A4-B4 |
| Falkland Drive | A2-A3 |
| Glamis Drive | B4-C4 |
| Graham Avenue | B4 |
| Jameson Drive | C3-C4 |
| Kelso Drive | C4 |
| Kelvin Drive | B1-C1 |
| Kelvin Road | B1-C1 |
| Kingsway | C3-C4 |
| Kirkton Park | B3-C3 |
| Kirkton Place | C3 |
| Kirktonholme Crescent | A3 |
| Kirktonholme Road | A3-B3 |
| Lairhills Road | B1 |
| Lindsay Road | B3-C3 |
| Livingstone Drive | A2-A1-B1 |
| Loch Striven | C2 |
| Main Street | B3-B4 |
| Market Hill Road | B4 |
| Maxwell Drive | B3-C3 |
| Maxwellton Avenue | B1 |
| Montgomery Street | B3 |
| Mount Cameron Drive North | C2 |
| Mount Cameron Drive South | C1-C2 |
| Murdoch Road | B1-B2 |
| Murray Hill | A2 |
| Napier Hill | B1 |
| Old Coach Road | B4-C4 |
| Old Mill Road | B3-B4-C4 |
| Owen Avenue | A1 |
| Park Terrace | A3-B3 |
| Parkhall Street | B3-B4 |
| Patterson Terrace | A1 |
| Quebec Drive | A2 |
| Queensway | A2-B2 |
| Reith Road | A1 |
| Rosslyn Avenue | C4 |
| Shiel Avenue | B4 |
| Simpson Drive | A1 |
| Somerville Drive | B1 |
| Strathaven Road | C1-C2 |
| Strathfillan Road | A3 |
| Stuart Street | B3 |
| The Murray Road | A1-B1 |
| Telford Road | A2-B2-B3 |
| Torrance Road | B3 |
| West Mains Road | A3-A4-B4-B3 |
| Whitehills Drive | A1-B1 |
| Whitemoss Avenue | B3-C3 |
| Whitemoss Road | B3-C3 |

## Cumbernauld

| | |
|---|---|
| Allanfauld Road | A3-A4 |
| Balloch View | A2-A3 |
| Beechwood Road | B2 |
| Braeface Road | A2 |
| Broomlands Road | B2-C2 |
| Brown Road | A3 |
| Centralway | A4-B4-B3-A3-A2-B2-B1 |
| Clouden Road | B4 |
| Craigieburn Road | B2 |
| Downfield Road | A1-A2 |
| Fleming Road | A3 |
| Forest Road | C4 |
| Glenacre Road | B1-B2 |
| Glencryan Road | C3-C4 |
| Glenhove Road | B4 |
| Greenfaulds Road | C1 |
| Greenrigg Road | B3-C3 |
| Grieve Road | A1 |
| Island Road | A1 |
| Ivanhoe Road | B1 |
| Jane's Brae | B1-C1-C2 |
| Kenmore Road | B4-C4 |
| Kibowie Road | C2-C3 |
| Kildrum Road | C4 |
| Lennox Road | A3 |
| Lensiemill Road | C1-C2-C3-C4 |
| Liddel Road | A1-A2 |
| Lye Brae | B4-C4 |
| McGregor Road | A1 |
| Millcroft Road | B3-C3 |
| North Carbrain Road | B1-B2-B3-B4 |
| St Mungo's Road | A2 |
| Seafar Road | A4-A3-A2-A1-B1 |
| South Carbrain Road | C1-C2-C3-C4 |
| Stonylee Road | B3 |
| Telford Road | C2 |
| Torbrex Road | B3 |

**EAST KILBRIDE**
A fine modern Civic Centre symbolises the forward-looking approach of East Kilbride — an agricultural town of just 2,400 people in 1946, but now one of Britain's biggest new towns.

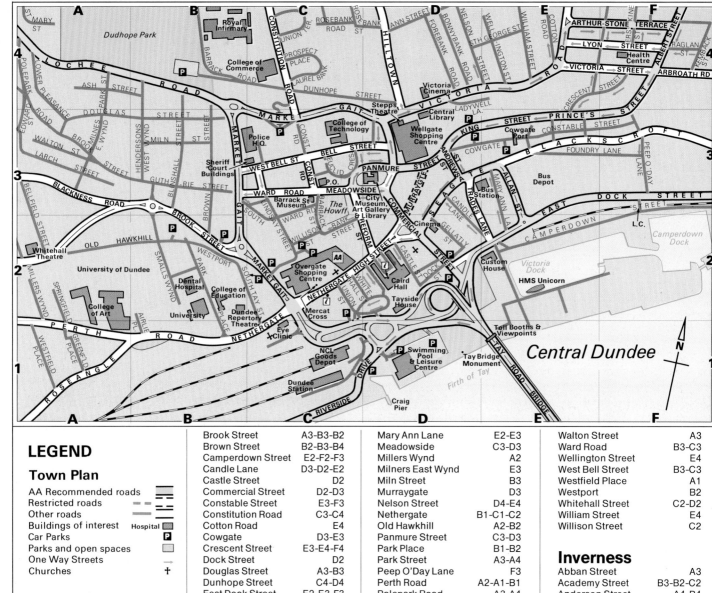

Central Dundee

## LEGEND

### Town Plan

| | |
|---|---|
| AA Recommended roads | |
| Restricted roads | |
| Other roads | |
| Buildings of interest | Hospital ▮ |
| Car Parks | ▯ |
| Parks and open spaces | ▯ |
| One Way Streets | → |
| Churches | ✝ |

## STREET INDEX- with grid reference

### Dundee

| | | | | | |
|---|---|---|---|---|---|
| Airlie Place | B1-B2 | Brook Street | A3-B3-B2 | Mary Ann Lane | E2-E3 |
| Albert Street | F4 | Brown Street | B2-B3-B4 | Meadowside | C3-D3 |
| Allan Street | E2-E3 | Camperdown Street | E2-F2-F3 | Millers Wynd | A2 |
| Ann Street | D4 | Candle Lane | D3-D2-E2 | Milners East Wynd | E3 |
| Arbroath Road | F4 | Castle Street | D2 | Miln Street | B3 |
| Arthur-Stone Terrace | E4-F4 | Commercial Street | D2-D3 | Murraygate | D3 |
| Ash Street | A4-B4 | Constable Street | E3-F3 | Nelson Street | D4-E4 |
| Bank Street | C2 | Constitution Road | C3-C4 | Nethergate | B1-C1-C2 |
| Barrack Road | B4-C4 | Cotton Road | E4 | Old Hawkhill | A2-B2 |
| Barrack Street | C2-C3 | Cowgate | D3-E3 | Panmure Street | C3-D3 |
| Bellfield Street | A2-A3 | Crescent Street | E3-E4-F4 | Park Place | B1-B2 |
| Bell Street | C3-D3 | Dock Street | D2 | Park Street | A3-A4 |
| Blackness Road | A3-B3 | Douglas Street | A3-B3 | Peep O'Day Lane | F3 |
| Blackscroft | E3-F3 | Dunhope Street | C4-D4 | Perth Road | A2-A1-B1 |
| Blinshall Street | B3-B4 | East Dock Street | E2-E3-F3 | Polepark Road | A3-A4 |
| | | Edward Street | A3-A4 | Prince's Street | E3-E4-F4 |
| | | Erskine Street | F4 | Prospect Place | C4 |
| | | Euclid Crescent | C3 | Raglan Street | F4 |
| | | Forebank Road | D4 | Reform Street | C3-C2-D2 |
| | | Foundry Lane | E3-F3 | Riverside Drive | C2-D2 |
| | | Gellatly Street | D2 | Roseangle | A1-B1 |
| | | Greenfield Place | A1 | Rosebank Road | C4 |
| | | Guthrie Street | B3 | Rosebank Street | C4-D4 |
| | | Hendersons West Wynd | B3-B4 | St Andrews Street | D3 |
| | | High Street | C2-D2 | St Mary Street | A4 |
| | | Hilltown | D4 | Seagate | D2-D3-E3 |
| | | Kemback Street | F4 | Smalls Wynd | B2 |
| | | King Street | D3-E3 | South George Street | D4-E4 |
| | | Ladywell Lane | D4-E4 | South Tay | B2-C2-C1 |
| | | Larch Street | A3 | South Ward Road | B3-C3-C2-C3 |
| | | Laurel Bank | C4 | Springfield | A1-A2 |
| | | Lindsay Street | C2-C3 | Tay Bridge Road | D2-D1-E1 |
| | | Lochee Road | A4-B4 | Trades Lane | D3-D2-E2 |
| | | Lower Pleasance | A3-A4 | Union Street | C2 |
| | | Lyon Street | E4-F4 | Union Terrace | C4 |
| | | Market Gait | D3-C3-C4-B4-B3-B2-C2 | Victoria Road | D3-D4-E4 |
| | | | | Victoria Street | E4-F4 |

| | |
|---|---|
| Walton Street | A3 |
| Ward Road | B3-C3 |
| Wellington Street | E4 |
| West Bell Street | B3-C3 |
| Westfield Place | A1 |
| Westport | B2 |
| Whitehall Street | C2-D2 |
| William Street | E4 |
| Willison Street | C2 |

### Inverness

| | |
|---|---|
| Abban Street | A3 |
| Academy Street | B3-B2-C2 |
| Anderson Street | A4-B4 |
| Annfield Road | C1-D1 |
| Ardconnel Street | C1-C2 |
| Ardross Street | B1 |
| Ardross Terrace | B1-B2 |
| Argyle Street | C1 |
| Bank Street | B2-B3 |
| Beaufort Road | D2 |
| Bishop's Road | A1-B1 |
| Bridge Street | B2-C2 |
| Broadstone Park | D1-D2 |
| Bruce Gardens | A1 |
| Burnett Road | C3-C4 |
| Carse Road | A3 |
| Castle Road | B1-B2 |
| Castle Street | C1 |
| Cawdor Road | D2 |
| Chapel Street | B3 |
| Charles Street | C2 |
| Church Street | B2-B3 |
| Coronation Park | A4 |
| Cromwell Road | B4 |
| Crown Avenue | C2-D2 |

**Dundee** Third largest city of Scotland and capital of Tayside, Dundee is a major port with a long and colourful maritime history, and it was also central to the 19th-century textile boom. But with its setting of moors, lochs and mountains, Dundee has become a centre for tourists. The city has a fine landmark in St Mary Tower, also known as Old Steeple, and the Mills Observatory has a refracting telescope and other displays dealing with astronomy and space exploration. Two top-flight football teams are based in the city and complement its fine sports facilities.

**Inverness** has long been called the 'Capital of the Highlands' and stands at the eastern end of the Great Glen, on the banks of the River Ness. Amongst the many places of interest that draw visitors to the town, Aberstaff House dates from the 16th century and has a rare, good example of an old turnpike stair. St Andrew's Cathedral has fine carved columns.

**Perth** Sir Walter Scott's 'Fair Maid of Perth' lived in a 14th-century house which still stands in this historic old Tayside town. St John's Kirk is a magnificent example of 16th-century Gothic architecture and notable as the scene of John Knox's fiery sermon against church idolatry in 1599 — a sermon which is now regarded as one of the major milestones of the Reformation. Also of interest are the Caithness Glass Factory (open to visitors) and the Perth Museum and Art Gallery.

## Central Inverness

## Central Perth

**INVERNESS**
Crowding the skyline with its battlements and towers, Inverness Castle commands an imposing site above the town — but was only built in the last century.

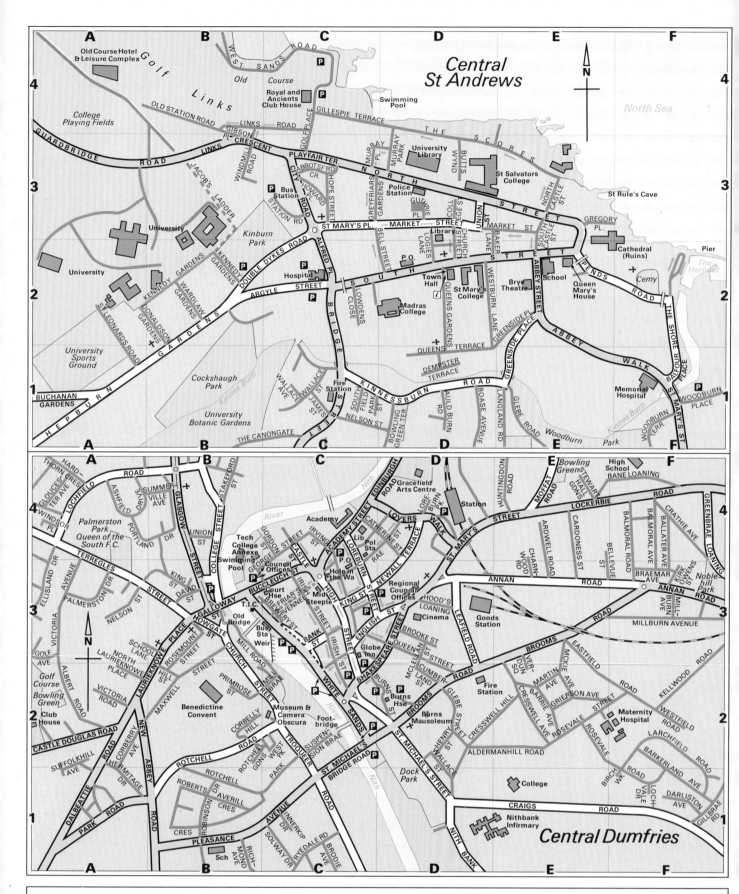

**Central St Andrews**

**Central Dumfries**

**St Andrews** is synonymous with golf. There are no less than 15 golf courses in the vicinity, and the Royal and Ancient Golf Club, founded in the 18th century, has come to be regarded as the international headquarters of the game. But the town's links with the past go back even further: it has a distinguished university which was founded in 1411, its castle is 13th-century and the cathedral dates from the 12th century.

**Stirling** lies just north of Bannockburn, where Robert the Bruce inflicted a swingeing defeat on the armies of England in 1314, and twelve years later he held his first parliament in the town's Cambuskenneth Abbey, which can still be seen. The castle dates back to the 13th century and its Landmark Centre provides an exciting audio-visual display. The Wallace Memorial offers fine views.

**Oban** has been a popular desination for tourists since the 19th century, not least because of its ferry links with the Hebrides. Visitors can see paperweights being made at the local glassworks, and other attractions are the fine views of the town and its surroundings to be seen from McCaig's Tower and Pulpit Hill.

**Dumfries** is Walter Scott's 'Queen of the South': a fine country town and market centre of old sandstone and spacious parks. Robert Burns spent the last years of his life here, and Burns House, where he died in 1796, is now a museum. His Mausoleum stands in St Michael's Churchyard.

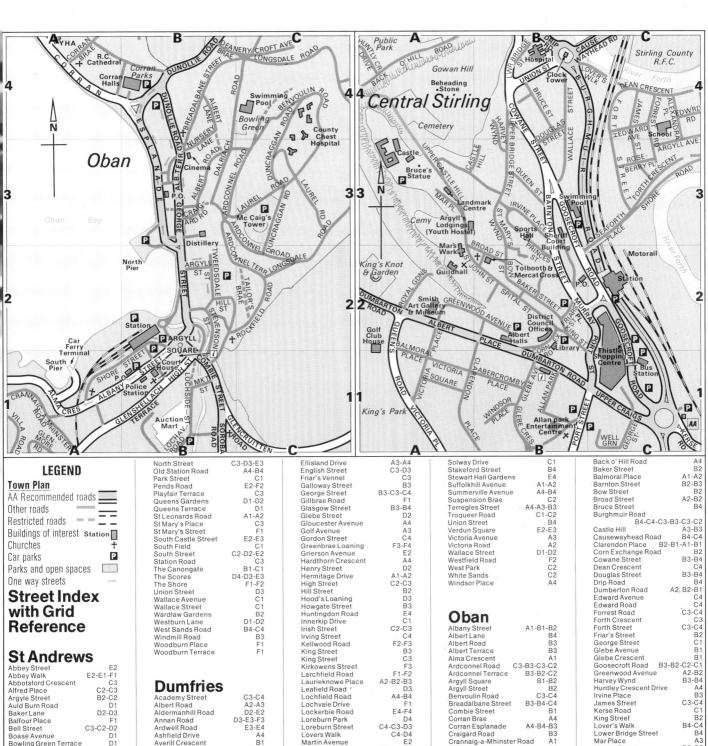

Oban

Central Stirling

## LEGEND

### Town Plan

| | |
|---|---|
| AA Recommended roads | ▬▬▬ |
| Other roads | ▬ ▬ ▬ |
| Restricted roads | ╌╌╌ |
| Buildings of interest | Station ▪ |
| Churches | ✝ |
| Car parks | 🅿 |
| Parks and open spaces | ▢ |
| One way streets | → |

## Street Index with Grid Reference

91

# Legend to Atlas

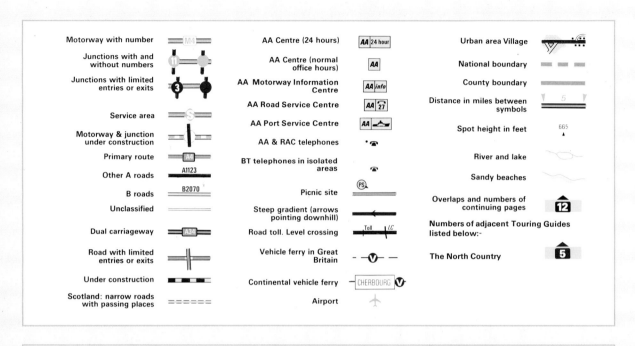

| | | | |
|---|---|---|---|
| Motorway with number | AA Centre (24 hours) | Urban area Village | |
| Junctions with and without numbers | AA Centre (normal office hours) | National boundary | |
| Junctions with limited entries or exits | AA Motorway Information Centre | County boundary | |
| Service area | AA Road Service Centre | Distance in miles between symbols | |
| Motorway & junction under construction | AA Port Service Centre | Spot height in feet | |
| Primary route | AA & RAC telephones | | |
| Other A roads | BT telephones in isolated areas | River and lake | |
| B roads | Picnic site | Sandy beaches | |
| Unclassified | Steep gradient (arrows pointing downhill) | Overlaps and numbers of continuing pages | |
| Dual carriageway | Road toll. Level crossing | Numbers of adjacent Touring Guides listed below:- | |
| Road with limited entries or exits | Vehicle ferry in Great Britain | The North Country | |
| Under construction | Continental vehicle ferry | | |
| Scotland: narrow roads with passing places | Airport | | |

| | | |
|---|---|---|
| Abbey or Cathedral | Coastal Launching Site | Nature Trail |
| Ruined Abbey or Cathedral | Surfing | Wildlife Park (mammals) |
| Castle | Climbing School | Wildlife Park (birds) |
| House and Garden | County Cricket Ground | Zoo |
| House | Gliding Centre | Forest Drive |
| Garden | Artificial Ski Slope | Lighthouse |
| Industrial Interest | Golf Course | Tourist Information Centre |
| Museum or Collection | Horse Racing | Tourist Information Centre (summer only) |
| Prehistoric Monument | Show Jumping/Equestrian Centre | Long Distance Footpath |
| Famous Battle Site | Motor Racing Circuit | AA Viewpoint |
| Preserved Railway or Steam Centre | Cave | Other Place of Interest |
| Windmill | Country Park | Boxed symbols indicate tourist attractions in towns |
| Sea Angling | Dolphinarium or Aquarium | |

## The National Grid

The National Grid provides a system of reference common to maps of all scales. The grid covers Britain with an imaginary network of 100 kilometre squares. Each square is identified by two letters, *eg* TR. Every 100 kilometre square is then sub-divided into 10 kilometre squares which appear as a network of blue lines on the map pages. These blue lines are numbered left to right ⓪-⑨ and bottom to top ⓪-⑨. These 10 kilometre squares can be further divided into tenths to give a place reference to the nearest kilometre.

# Key to Road Maps

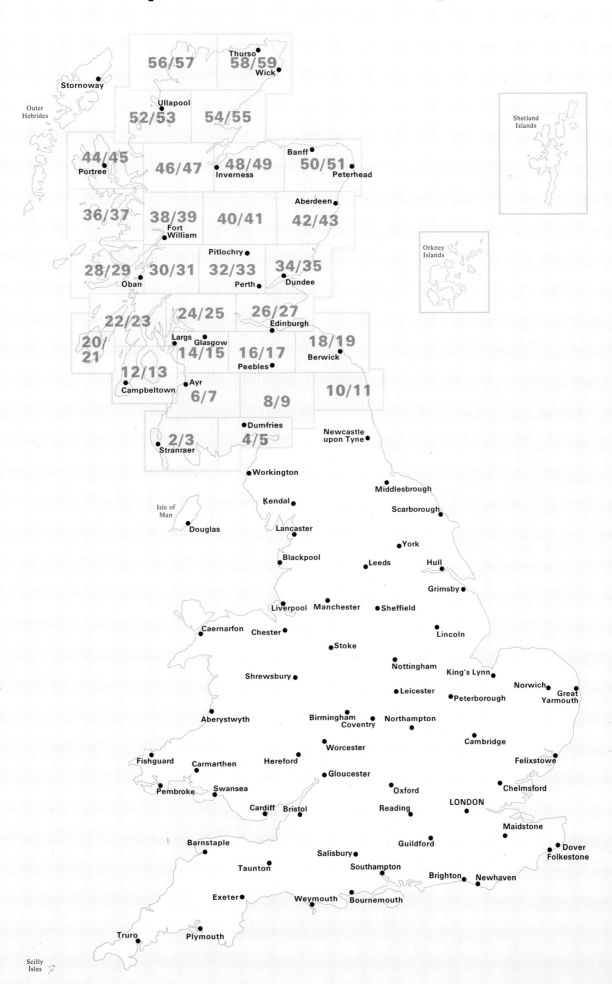

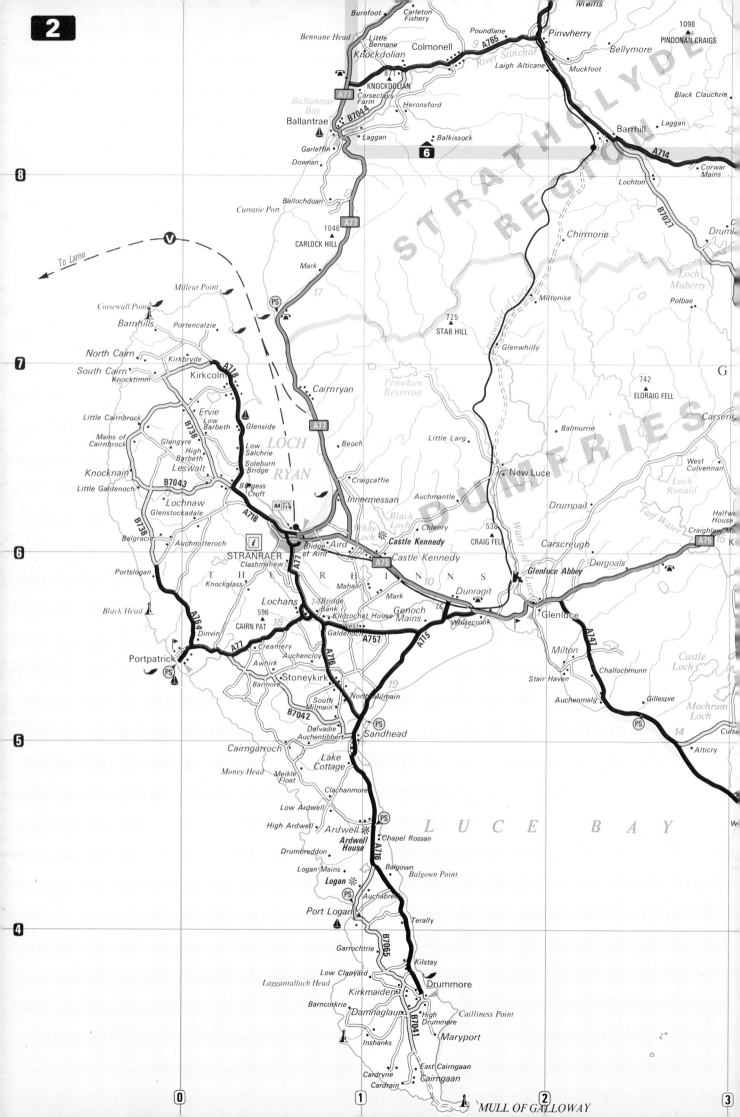

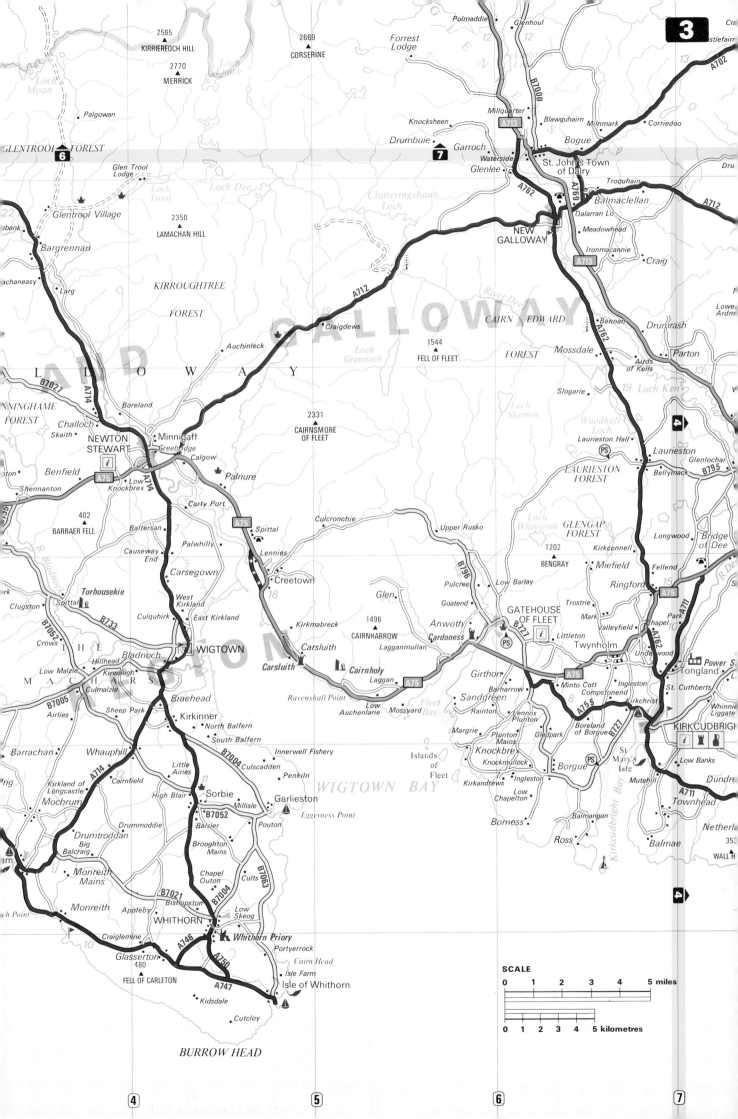

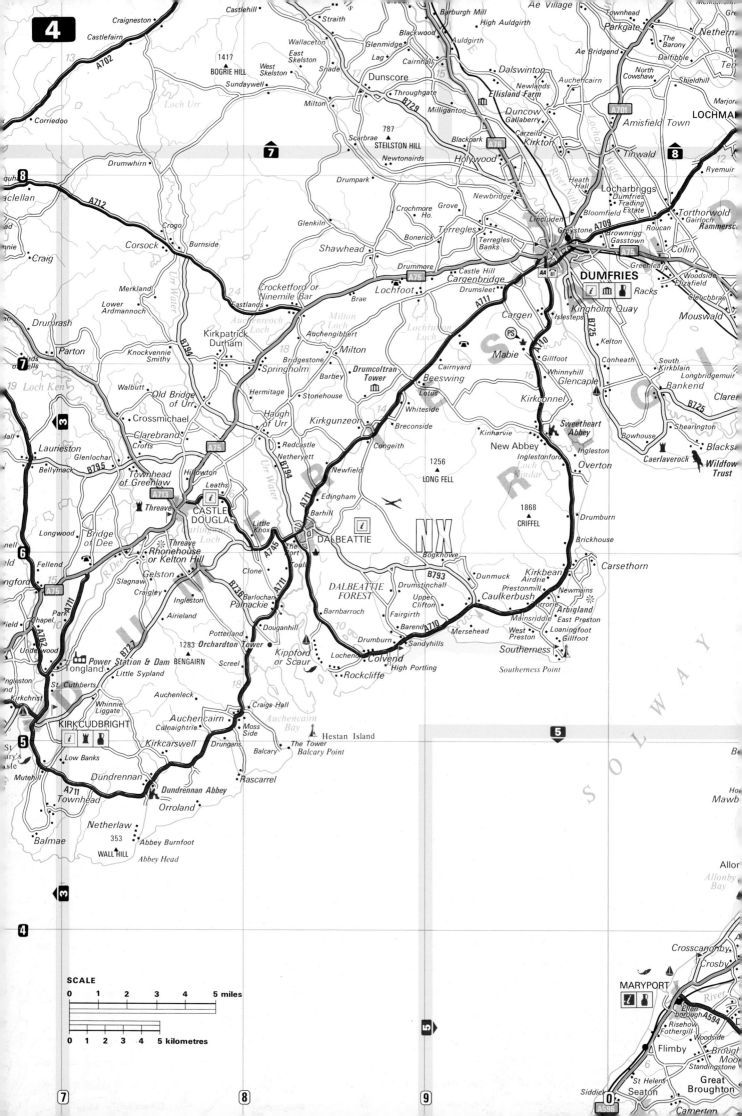

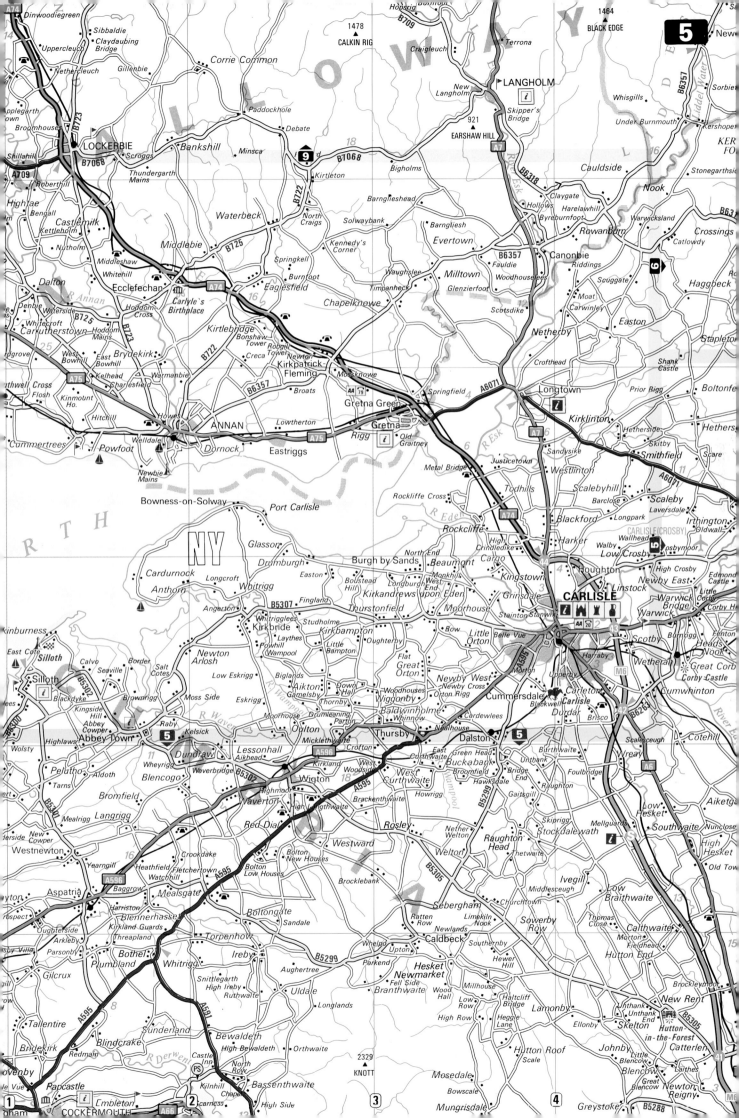

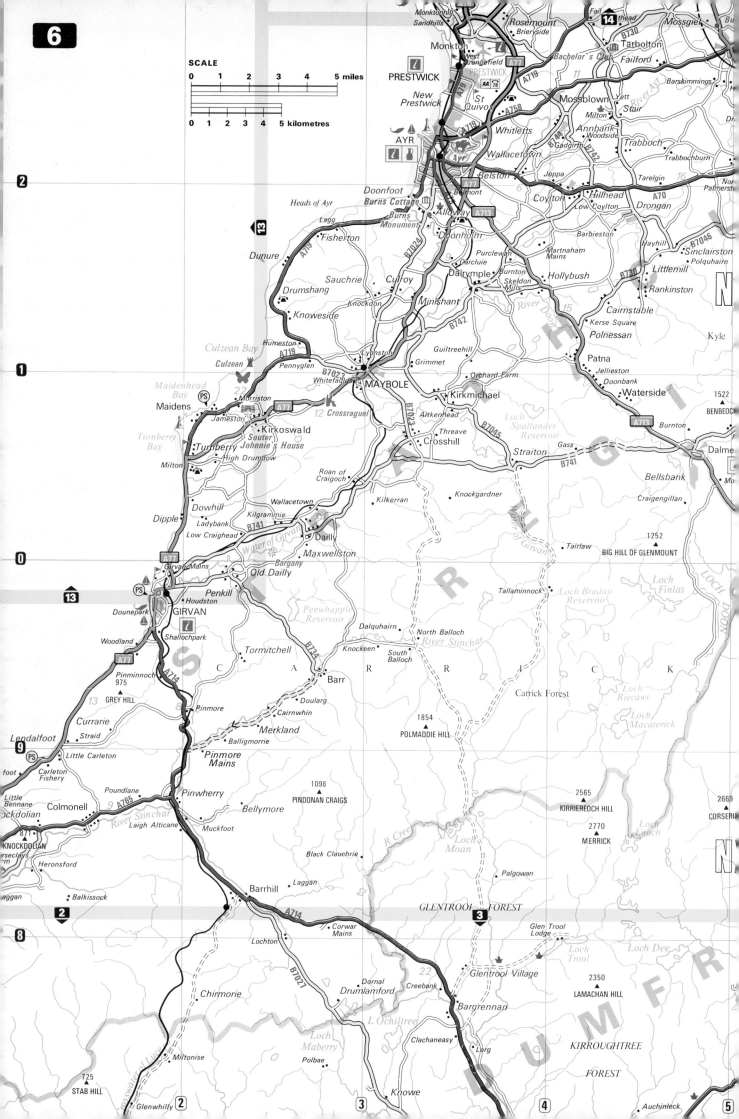

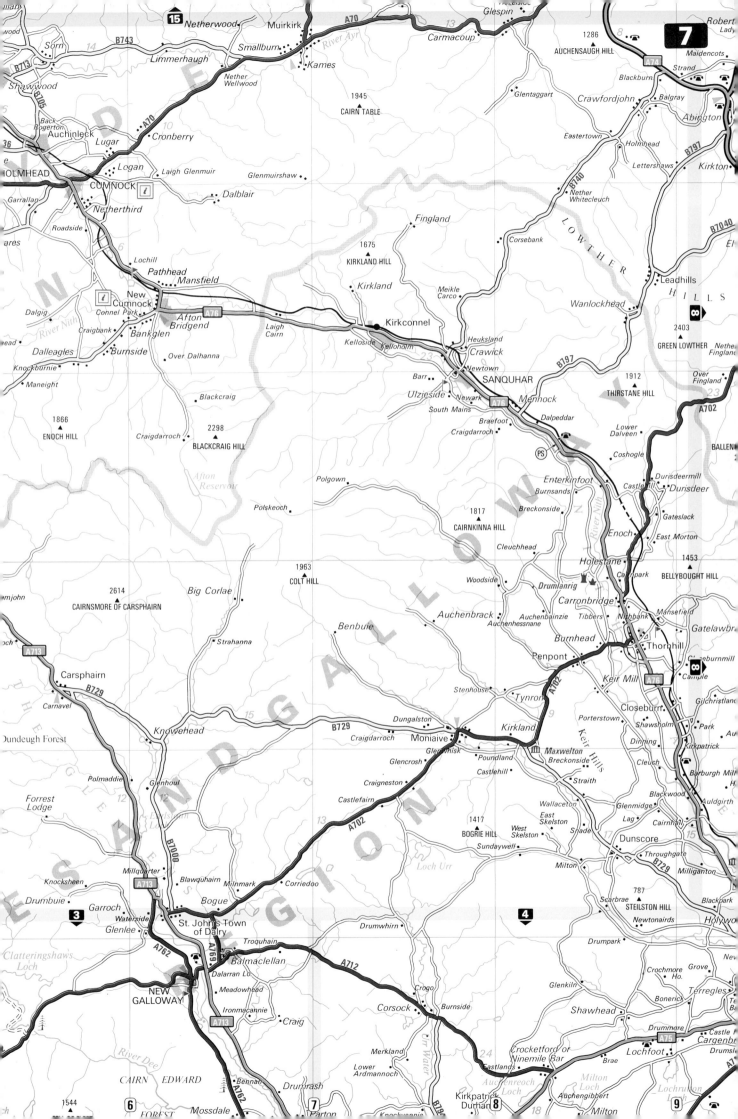

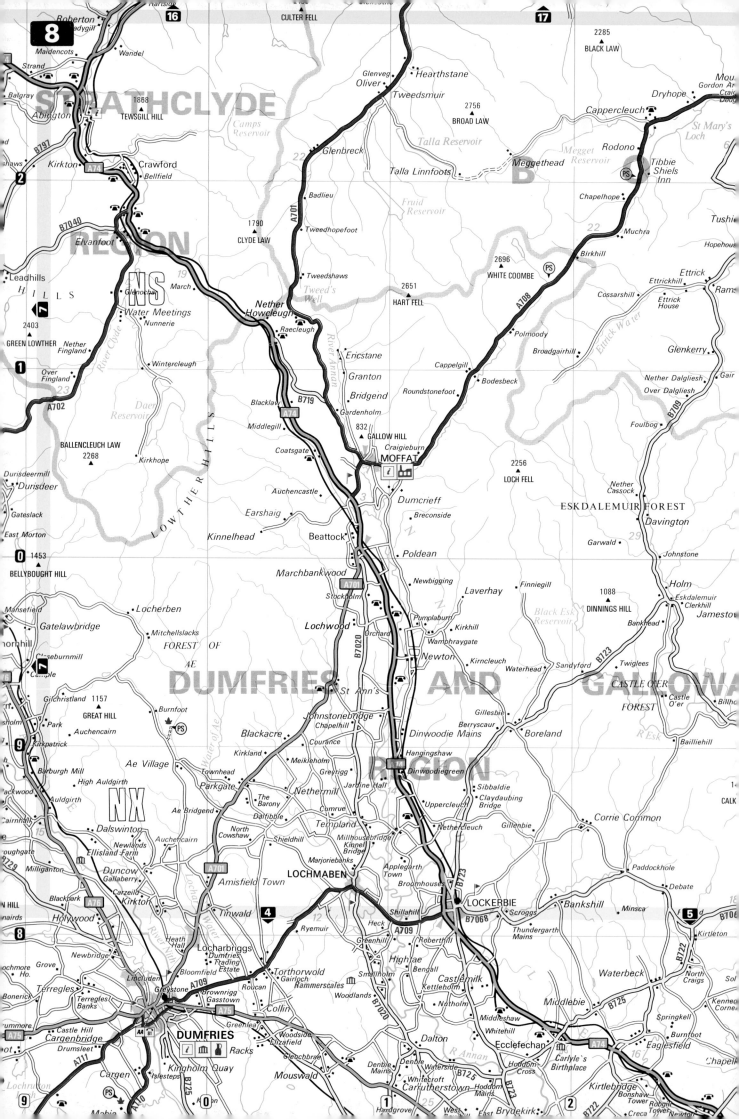

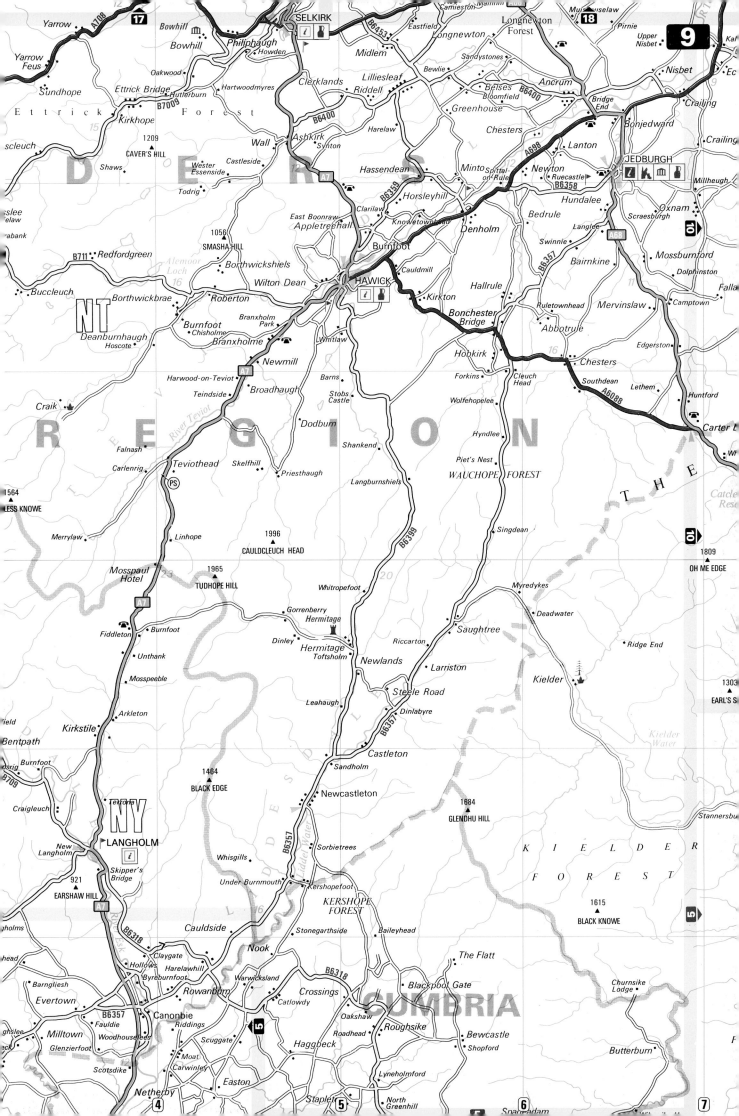

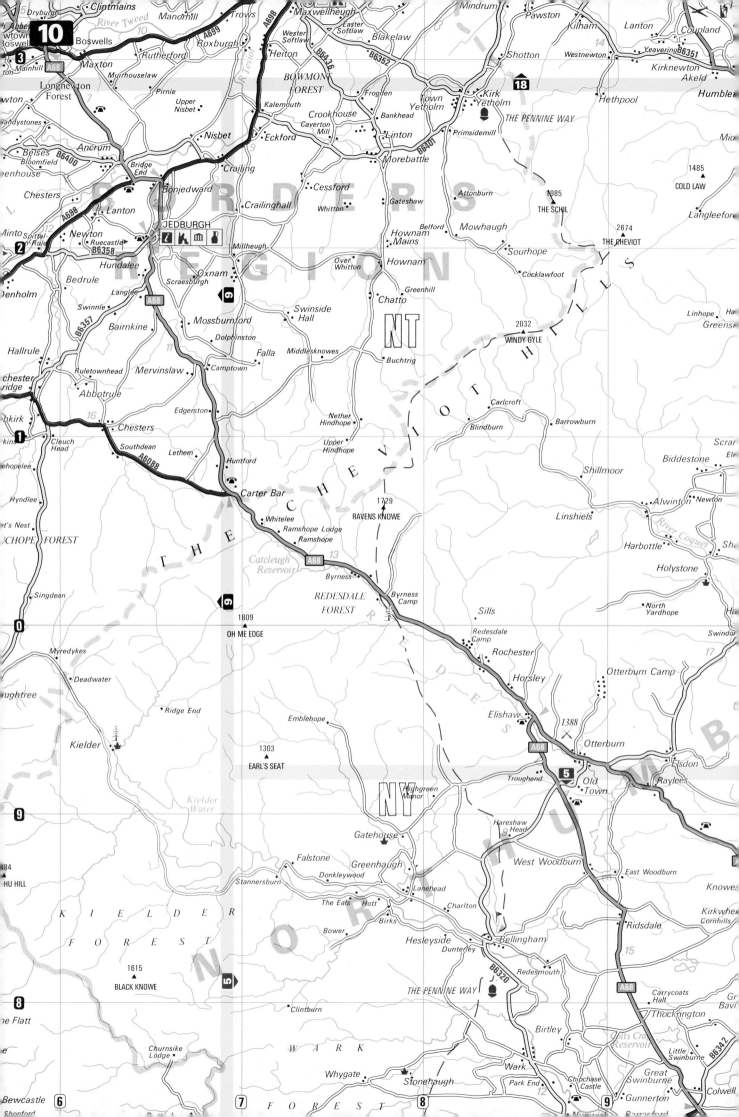

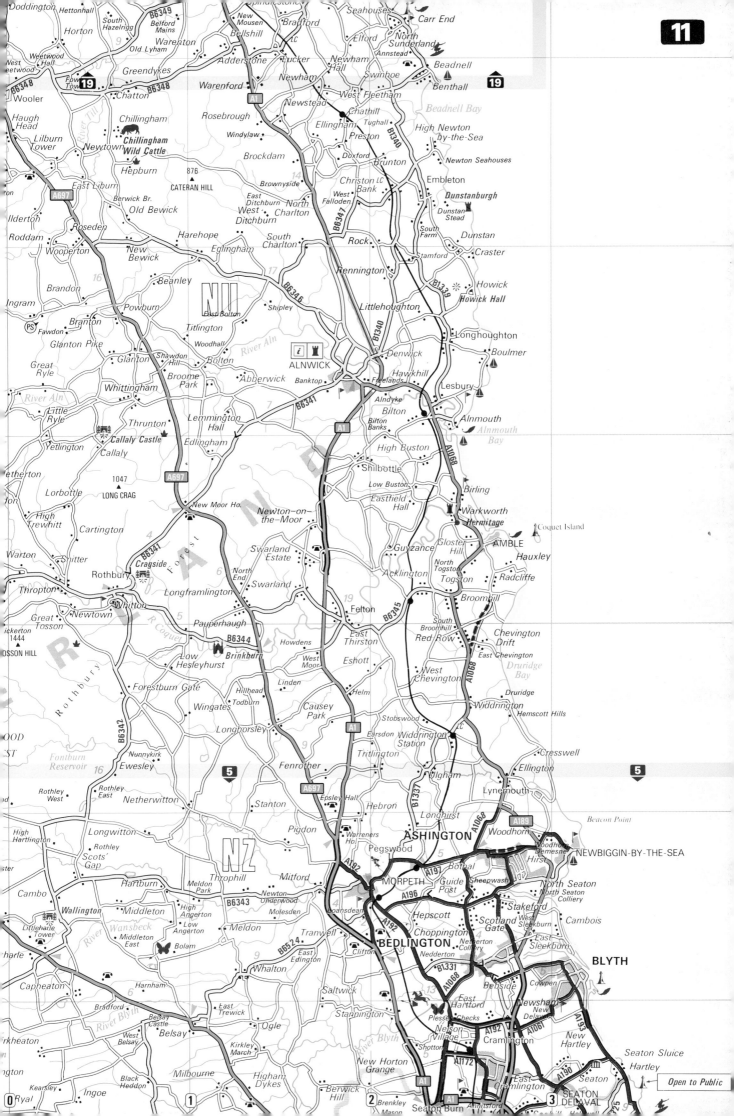

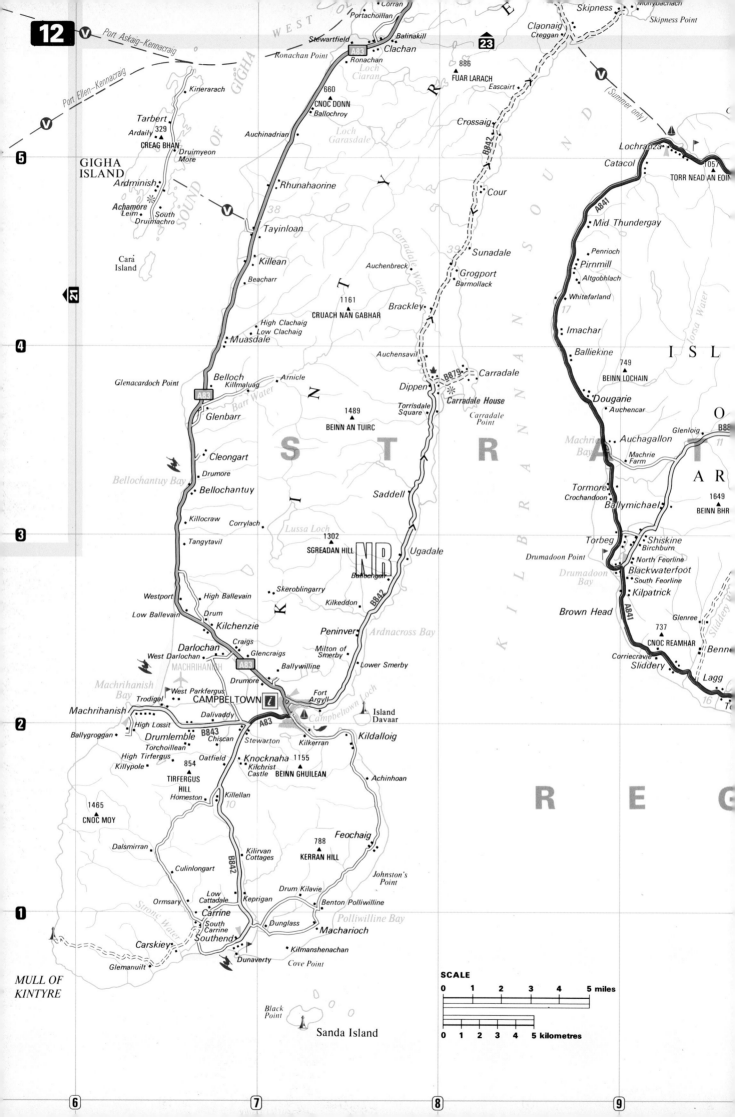

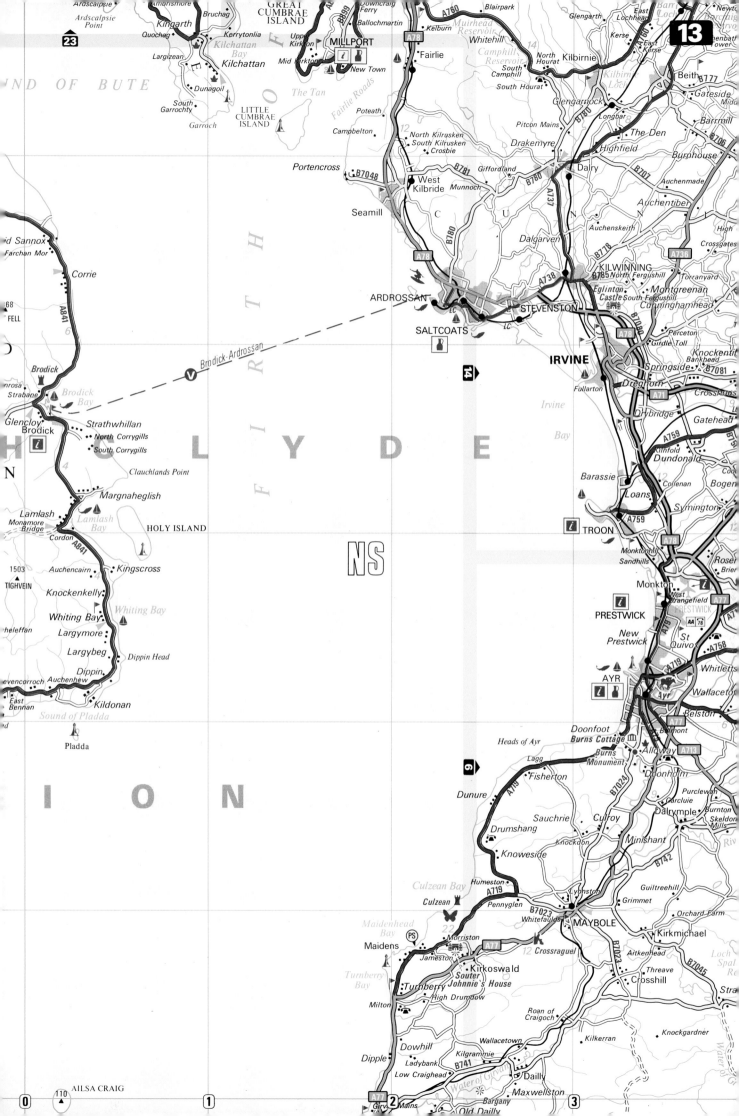

**SCALE**

0  1  2  3  4  5 miles

0  1  2  3  4  5 kilometres

NU

ST ABB'S HEAD

Northfield

St Abbs

...ham

Whitecross

Acredale

Cairncross

EYEMOUTH

Biglawburn

Gunsgreenhill

Reston  A1

Ayton

Burnmouth

Prenderguest

...auseywaybank

Whitering

Edington

Foulden

B6355

Lamberton

Clappers  A1

1333

Conundrum

Foulden
Newton

Hutton

A6105

Meadowhill

...ondykes

Paxton

High Letham

Hutton

Hutton
Mains

B6461

BERWICK-UPON-TWEED

Sunwick

...kegatehead

Tweedmouth

Spittal

...ome

Fishwick

Loanend

East Ord

B6461

Horndean

Horncliffe

West Longridge

Borewell

13

...dykirk

Thorntonpark

A698

Murton

Scremerston

Unthank

Norham

...6470

Norham

Newburn

Thornton

West
Allerdean

Cheswick

West
Newbi...gin

Shoreswood

Shoresdean

Ancroft

Goswick

...k Ho.

Grindon

Felkington

B6525

A1

New
Haggerston

Haggerston

CAUSEWAY
FLOODED
AT HIGH TIDE

HOLY ISLAND

15

Shellacres

Grindonrigg

Berrington

Beal

Holy
Island

Castle Point

...Twizel Bridge

...uth Park

Duddo

West Mains

15

Fenhamhill

Lindisfarne Priory

...kington

Castle
Heaton

Bowsden

Kentstone

Fenham

Burrows Hole

...hill
...eed

B6354

Etal

Heatherslaw Mill

B6353

Kyloe

Fenwick

Staple
Sound

FARNE ISLANDS

...arelees

Cropkham

The Lady Waterford Hall

Ford

Lowick

Buckton

Branxton

Brownridge

Smeafield

Elwick

Ross

1513

Kimmerston

Holburn

Detchant

Low Middleton

Inner
Sound

Budle
Bay

Flodden

14

NORTHUMBERLAND

Middleton

Easington

Budle

Bamburgh

Waren
Mill

Glororum

Bamburgh

...ham

Howtel

A697

Milfield

Fenton
Town

Nesbit

Hetton Steads

Hettonlaw

North
Hazelrigg

Belford

B1342

Spindlestone

Burton

Open to Public

...ton

B6352

Lanton

Coupland

Newtown

Doddington

Hettonhall

South
Hazelrigg

Sionside

B6349

Belford
Mains

New
Mousen

LC

Bradford

Seahouses

Carr End

9

...stnewton

Kirknewton
Akeld

B6351

Bendor

West
...twood

Weetwood
Hall

Greendykes

Horton

Warenton

Old Lyham

Adderstone

Lucker

Newham
Hall

Bellshill

Elford

Newham

North
Sunderland

Annstead

Beadnell

0

1

2

11

...inhoe

11

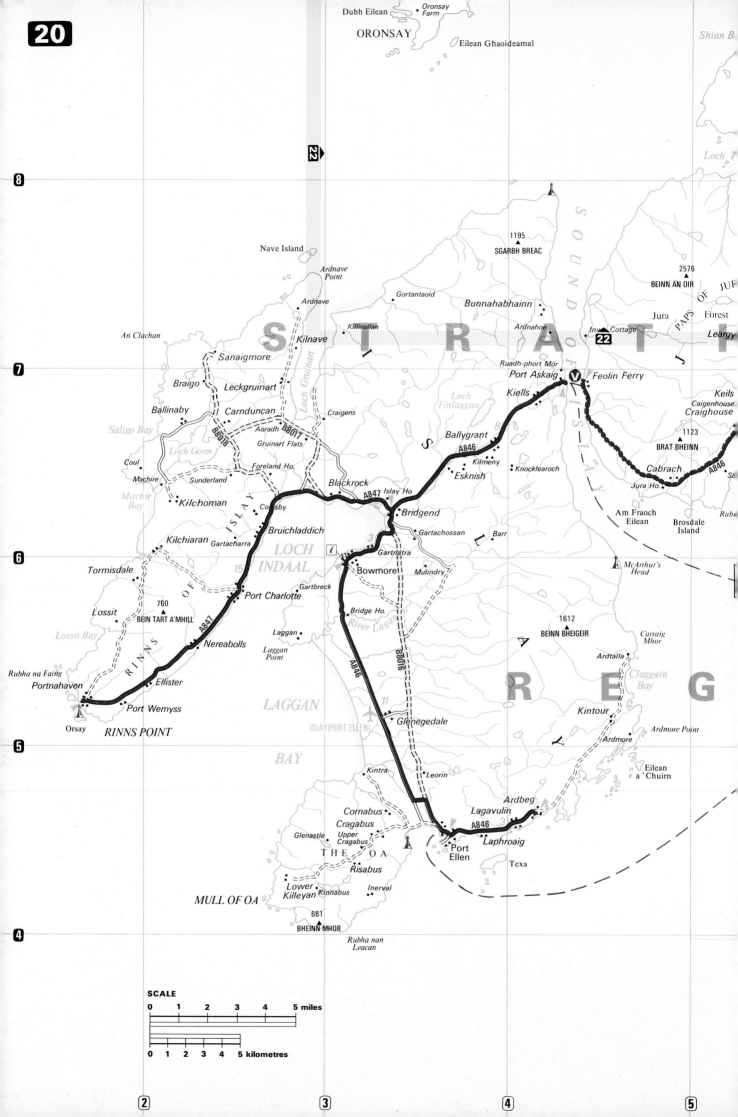

Dubh Eilean
Oronsay Farm
ORONSAY
Eilean Ghaoideamal
Shian B

22

8

Nave Island
Ardnave Point
Ardnave
SGARBH BREAC 1195
BEINN AN OIR 2576
BEINN AN OIR

An Clachan
Kilnave
Gortantaoid
Bunnahabhainn
Jura
PAPS OF JU
Forest
Leargy

Sanaigmore
Killinallan
Ardnahoe
22
Keils

7

Braigo
Leckgruinart
Craigens
Ruadh-phort Mór
Port Askaig
Feolin Ferry
Caigenhouse
Craighouse

Ballinaby
Carnduncan
Kiells

Saligo Bay
B8018
B8017
Aoradh
Loch Finlaggan
Ballygrant
A846
1123
BRAT BHEINN

Coul
Loch Gorm
Gruinart Flats
Foreland Ho.
Kilmeny
Cabrach

Machire
Sunderland
Esknish
Knocklearoch
Jura Ho.
A846

Machir Bay
Kilchoman
Blackrock
Islay Ho.
Am Fraoch Eilean
Brosdale Island
Ru

A847
Coulsby
Bridgend
Gartachossan

6

Bruichladdich
Gartnatra
Barr
McArthur's Head

Kilchiaran
Gartacharra
LOCH INDAAL
i
Bowmore
Mulindry

Tormisdale
BEIN TART A'MHILL 760
Gartbreck
BEINN BHEIGEIR 1612
Ardtalla

Lossit
Port Charlotte
A847
Bridge Ho.
River Lagan
B8016
Carraig Mhor

Lossit Bay
RINNS
Nereabolls
Laggan
Laggan Point
A846
Claggain Bay

Rubha na Faing
Ellister
15
Kintour

Portnahaven
Port Wemyss
LAGGAN
11
Glenegedale
Ardmore
Ardmore Point

Orsay
RINNS POINT
ISLAY (PORT ELLEN)
Eilean a' Chuirn

5

BAY
Kintra
Leorin

Cornabus
Ardbeg
Lagavulin

Cragabus
Upper Cragabus
A846
Laphroaig

Glenastle
THE OA
Port Ellen
Texa

Risabus

Lower Killeyan
Kinnabus
Inerval

MULL OF OA
BHEINN MHOR 661

4

Rubha nan Leacan

SCALE

0 1 2 3 4 5 miles

0 1 2 3 4 5 kilometres

2
3
4
5

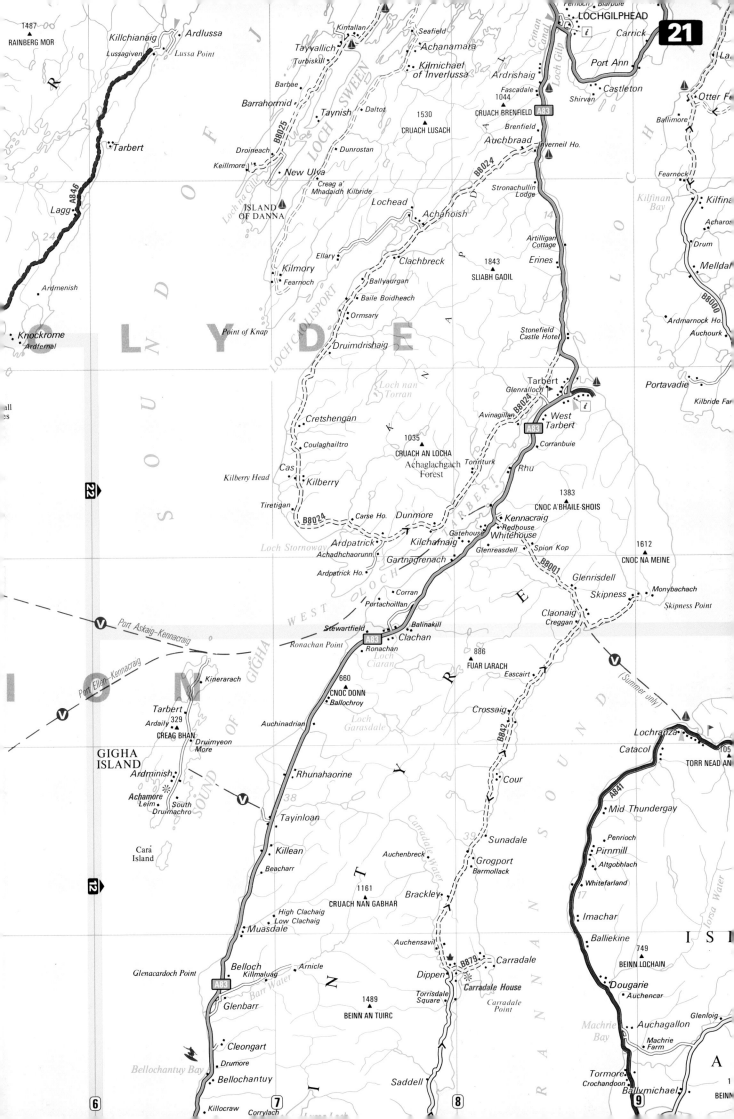

RAINBERG MOR
1487

Killchianaig • Ardlussa
Lussagiven • • Lussa Point

A846

• Tarbert

Ardmenish •

Lagg •

24

Knockrome •
Ardfernal •

C L Y D E

Kintallan •
Tayvallich •
Turbiskill •
Barbae •
Barrahormid •
Taynish • • Daltot
Droineach •
Keillmore •
New Ulva •
Creag a'
Mhadaidh Kilbride •

Seafield •
Achanamara •
Kilmichael
of Inverlussa •
1530
CRUACH LUSACH •

Lochgilphead
Carrick •
i
Port Ann •
Ardrishaig •
Castleton •
Fascadale •
1044
CRUACH BRENFIELD A83
Brenfield •
Auchbraad •
Shirvan •
Otter F
Ballimore •
Inverneil Ho. •

Crinan Canal
Loch Gilp
Loch Gilp

Otter F
Ballimore •

Ardmarnock Ho. •
Auchourk •

B8000

Kilfinan Bay
Kilfina
Acharos •
Drum •
Melldal •

S O U N D

O F

J

B8025

Loch na Cille

ISLAND
OF DANNA

Loch Sween

Lochead •
Achahoish •
Ellary •
Clachbreck •
Kilmory •
Fearnoch •
Ballyaurgan •
Baile Boidheach •
Ormsary •
Point of Knap •
Druimdrishaig •

Stronachullin
Lodge •
14
Artilligan
Cottage •
1843
SLIABH GAOIL •
Erines •
Stonefield
Castle Hotel •

Loch Caolisport

Loch nan
Torran

Cretshengan •
Coulaghailtro •
Cas •
Kilberry Head
Kilberry •
Tiretigan •
B8024
Carse Ho. •

1035
CRUACH AN LOCHA •
Achaglachgach
Forest
Torinturk •
Dunmore •

K

N

Tarbert •
Glenralloch •
i
Avinagillan •
B8024
A83
West
Tarbert
Corranbuie •
Rhu •

Portavadie •
Kilbride Far

L O C H

F Y N E

1383
CNOC A'BHAILE-SHOIS •
1612
CNOC NA MEINE •

22

S O U N D

O F

G I G H A

Port Askaig–Kennacraig
V

Port Ellen–Kennacraig
V

V

GIGHA
ISLAND
Kinerarach •
Tarbert •
Ardaily • 329
CREAG BHAN
Druimyeon
More •
Ardminish •
Achamore
Leim • South
Druimachro •

Cara
Island

12

Loch Stornoway
Ardpatrick •
Achadhchaorunn •
Ardpatrick Ho. •

Corran •
Portachoillan •
Stewartfield •
Ronachan Point
Ronachan •
A83
Clachan •
Balinakill •
Clachan
Loch
Ciaran

660
CNOC DONN •
Ballochroy •
Auchinadrian •

Kilchamaig •
Gatehouse •
Kennacraig •
Redhouse •
Whitehouse
Gartnagrenach •
Glenreasdell •

Spion Kop •

W E S T

L O C H

T A R B E R T

886
FUAR LARACH •
Eascairt •

B8001
Glenrisdell •
Skipness •
Monybachach •
Skipness Point
Claonaig •
Creggan •

K I N T Y R E

Rhunahaorine •

Loch
Garasdale

38

Tayinloan •

Killean •
Beacharr •

1161
CRUACH NAN GABHAR •

High Clachaig •
Low Clachaig •
Muasdale •

Belloch •
Killmaluag •
Glenacardoch Point
A83
Glenbarr •

Cleongart •

Drumore •

Bellochantuy Bay
Bellochantuy •

Killocraw •
Corrylach

Arnicle •

1489
BEINN AN TUIRC •

Carradale Water

Auchenbreck •

Sunadale •
Grogport •
Barmollack •

Brackley •

Auchensavil •
B8879
Torrisdale
Square •
Dippen •
Carradale •
Carradale House
Carradale
Point

Saddell •

S O U N D

O F

K I L B R A N N A N

Crossaig •
Cour •

Lochranza •
Catacol •
TORR NEAD AN
105

A841
Mid Thundergay •
Penrioch •
Pirnmill •
Altgobhlach •
Whitefarland •
Imachar •
Balliekine •
749
BEINN LOCHAIN •
Dougarie •
Auchencar •

Machrie
Bay
Auchagallon •
Machrie
Farm •
Tormore •
Crochandoon •
Ballymichael •

Torr Rosa Water

17

I S L

I S L

A

Glenloig •

BEINN

V
(Summer only)

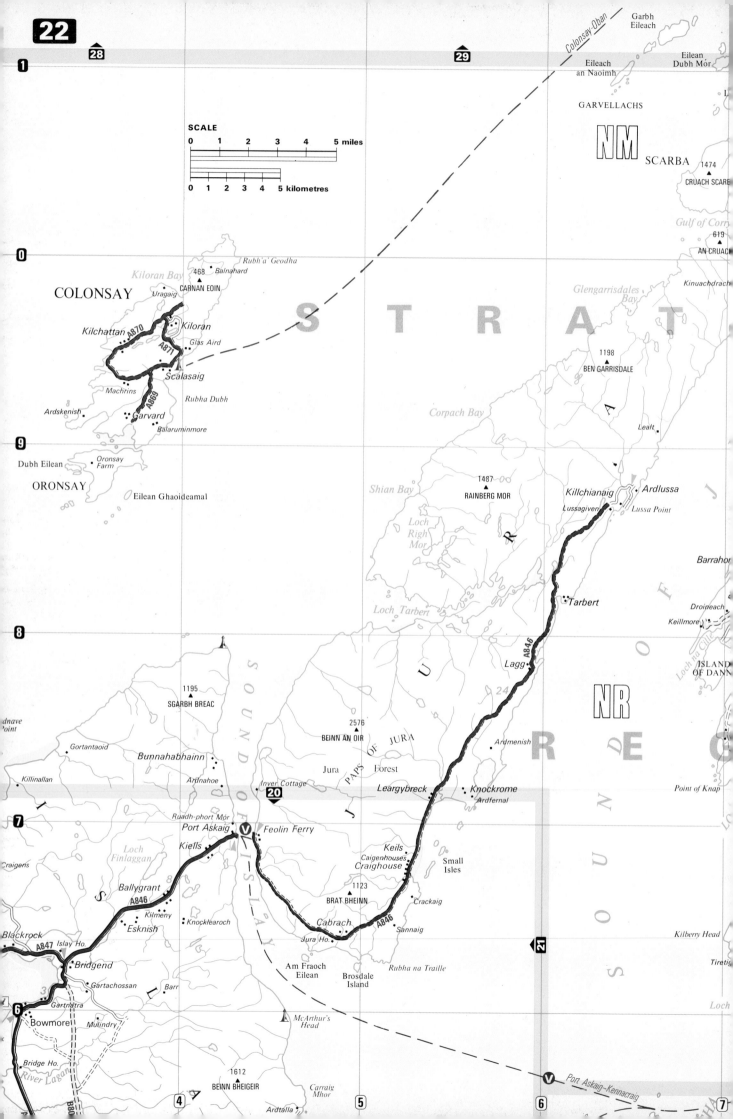

SCALE

0    1    2    3    4    5 miles

0  1  2  3  4  5 kilometres

Garbh
Eileach

Colonsay–Oban

Eileach
an Naoimh

Eilean
Dubh Mór

L

GARVELLACHS

**NM**

SCARBA

1474
▲
CRUACH SCARE

Gulf of Corr

619
▲
AN CRUAC

Rubh'a' Geodha

468  • Balnahard
▲
• CARNAN EOIN

Kiloran Bay

Glengarrisdales
Bay

Kinuachdrach

COLONSAY

Uragaig

Kilchattan
A870
A871

Kiloran

Glas Aird

Scalasaig

Machrins
A869

Rubha Dubh

Corpach Bay

Ardskenish

Garvard

Balaruminmore

1198
▲
BEN GARRISDALE

A

Lealt

Dubh Eilean

Oronsay
Farm

Shian Bay

1487
▲
RAINBERG MOR

Killchianaig • Ardlussa

ORONSAY

Eilean Ghaoideamal

Lussagiven

Lussa Point

Loch
Righ
Mór

Barrahor

Droineach
Keillmore

R

Loch Tarbert

• Tarbert

U

Loch na Cille

ISLAND
OF DANN

**NR**

1195
▲
SGARBH BREAC

A846

Lagg •

24

R

E

Point of Knap

dnave
Point

Gortantaoid

Bunnahabhainn

Ardnahoe

2576
▲
BEINN AN OIR

Jura  PAPS  Forest

Ardmenish

Killinallan

Inver Cottage

**20**

J

Knockrome
Ardfernal

Leargybreck

Ruadh-phort Mór

**7**

Port Askaig

Kiells

Feolin Ferry

Keils

Caigenhouses
Craighouse

Small
Isles

Craigens

Loch
Finlaggan

S

Ballygrant
A846

Kilmeny

Knocklearoch

Esknish

1123
▲
BRAT BHEINN

Cabrach

A846

Crackaig

Sannaig

Kilberry Head

Blackrock

A847

Islay Ho.

Bridgend

Gartachossan

Barr

Jura Ho.

Am Fraoch
Eilean

Brosdale
Island

Rubha na Traille

**21**

Tiretig

**6**

Bowmore

Mulindry

Gartnatra

L

Bridge Ho.

River Lagan

1612
▲
BEINN BHEIGEIR

McArthur's
Head

Ardtalla

Carraig
Mhor

Port Askaig–Kennacraig

Loch

B80

**4**

**5**

**6**

**7**

**28**

**29**

**1**

**0**

**9**

**8**

**7**

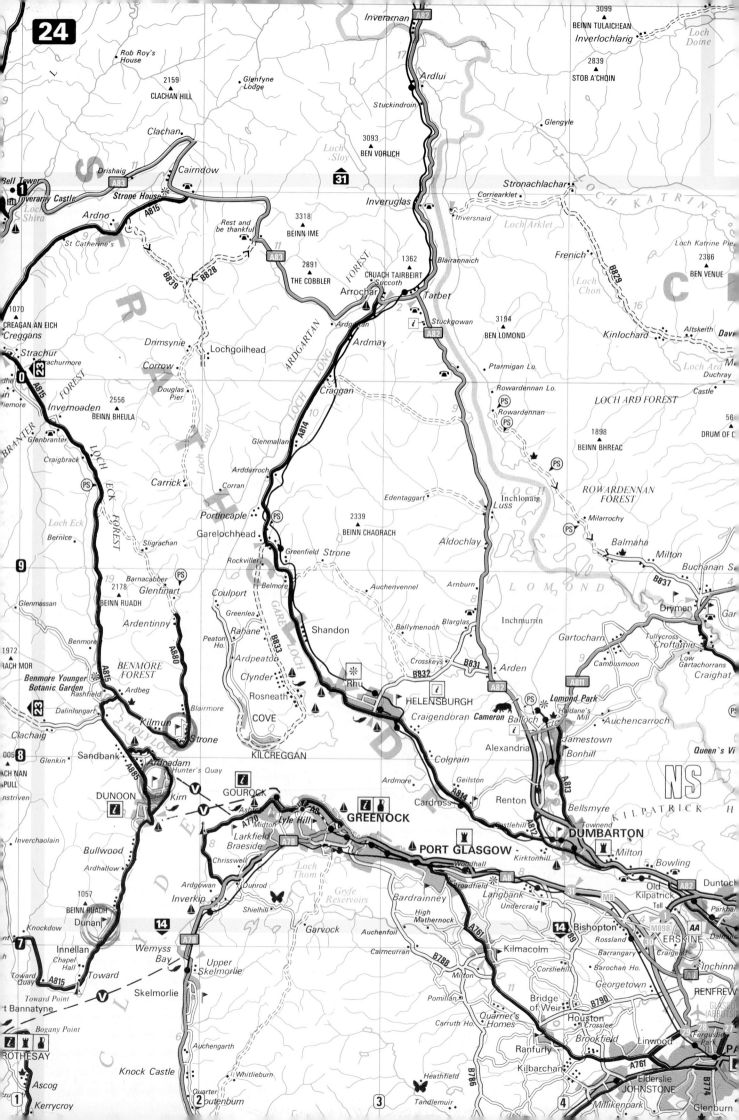

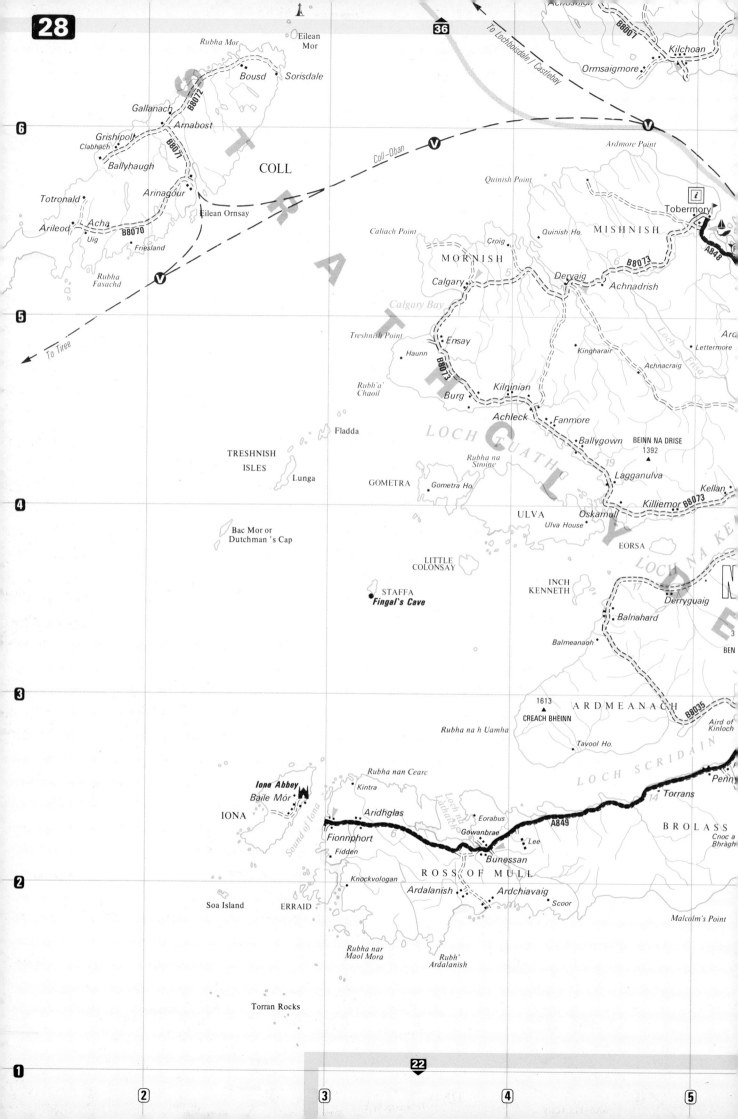

To Lochboisdale / Castlebay

36

B8007

Kilchoan

Ormsaigmore

Rubha Mor

Eilean Mor

Bousd    Sorisdale

Gallanach

Arnabost

B8072

Grishipoll

Clabhach

B8071

Ballyhaugh

COLL

Coll–Oban

Ardmore Point

Totronald

Arinagour

Quinish Point

Tobermory

i

Arileod    Acha

Uig

B8070

Eilean Ornsay

MISHNISH

Friesland

Caliach Point

Croig

Quinish Ho.

Rubha
Fasachd

Calgary

Dervaig

Achnadrish

A848

B8073

To Tiree

MORNISH

Calgary Bay

5

Loch Frisa

Ard

Lettermore

Treshnish Point

Ensay

Kingharair

Achnacraig

Haunn

B8073

Rubh 'a'
Chaoil

Burg

Kilninian

Fladda

Achleck    Fanmore

LOCH  TUATH

Ballygown

BEINN NA DRISE
1392

TRESHNISH

ISLES

Lunga

Rubha na
Stroine

Lagganulva

19

Kellan

GOMETRA    Gometra Ho.

Killiemor    B8073

Bac Mor or
Dutchman 's Cap

ULVA

Oskamull

Ulva House

EORSA

LOCH NA KE

Derryguaig

M

LITTLE
COLONSAY

INCH
KENNETH

Balnahard

STAFFA
Fingal`s Cave

Balmeanaoh

BEN

1613
CREACH BHEINN

ARDMEANACH

B8035

Aird of
Kinloch

Rubha na h Uamha

Tavool Ho.

LOCH SCRIDAIN

Rubha nan Cearc

Penn

Iona Abbey

Baile Mór

Kintra

Aridhglas

Loch na
Làthaich

Torrans

14

A849

IONA

Fionnphort

Eorabus

Gowanbrae

Lee

BROLASS

Cnoc a
Bhràgh

Fidden

Bunessan

Sound of Iona

ROSS  OF  MULL

Soa Island    ERRAID

Knockvologan

Ardalanish    Ardchiavaig

Scoor

Malcolm's Point

Rubha nar
Maol Mora

Rubh'
Ardalanish

Torran Rocks

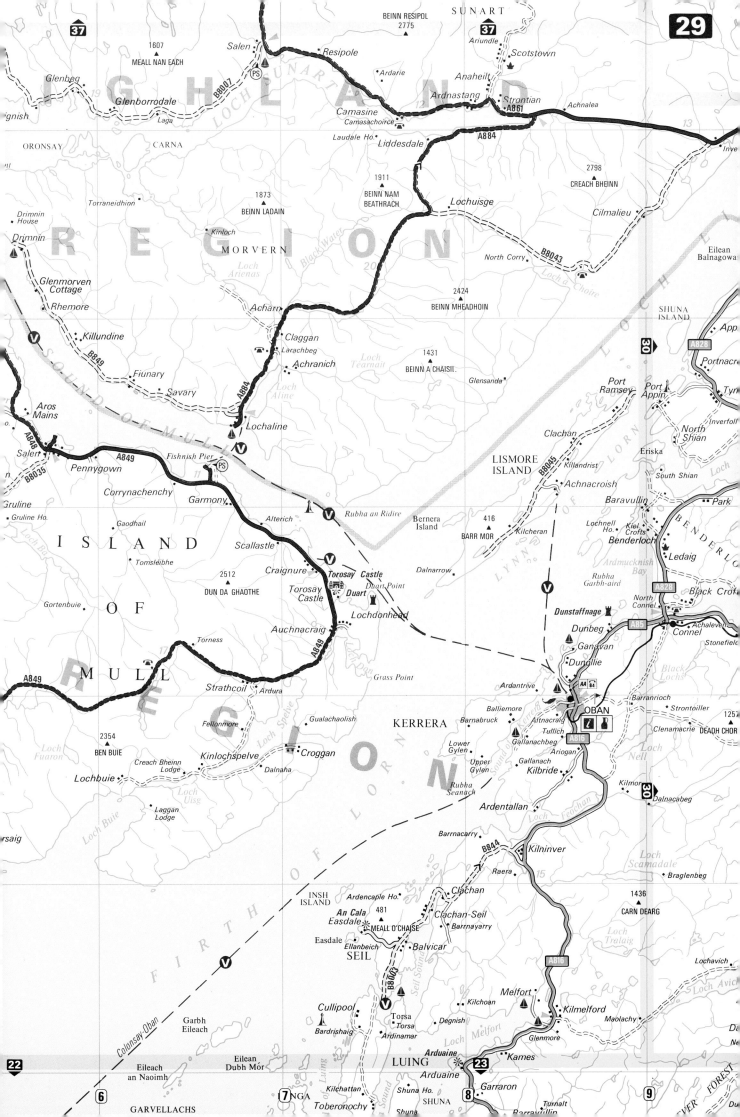

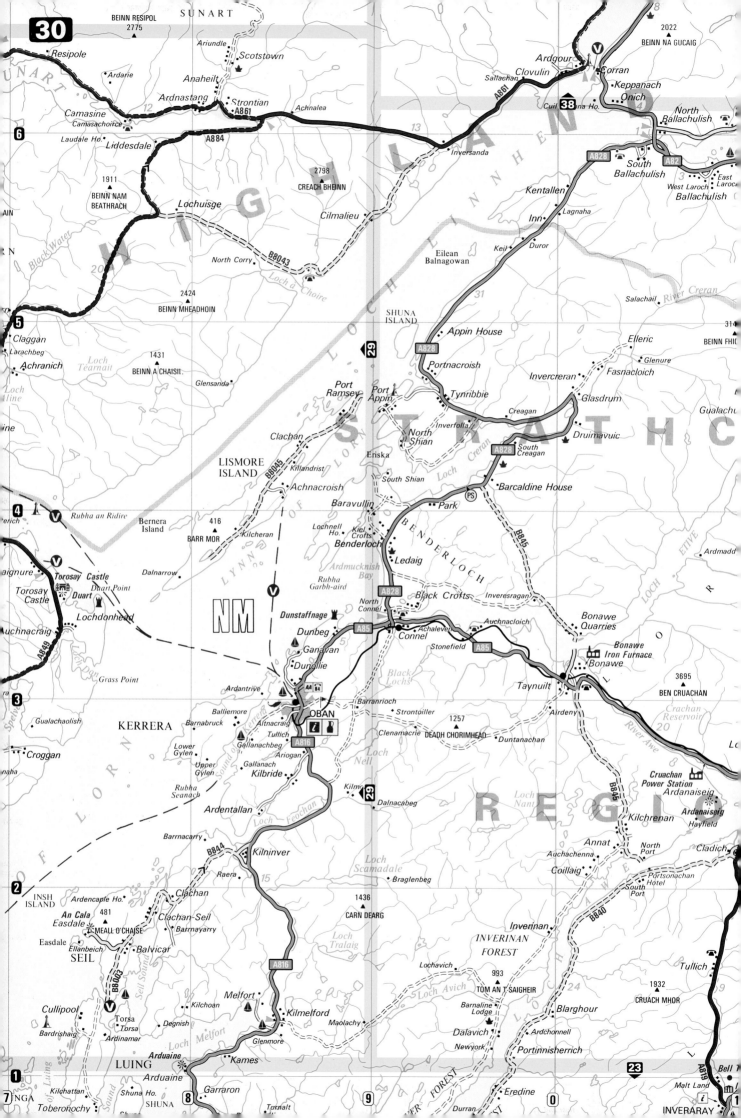

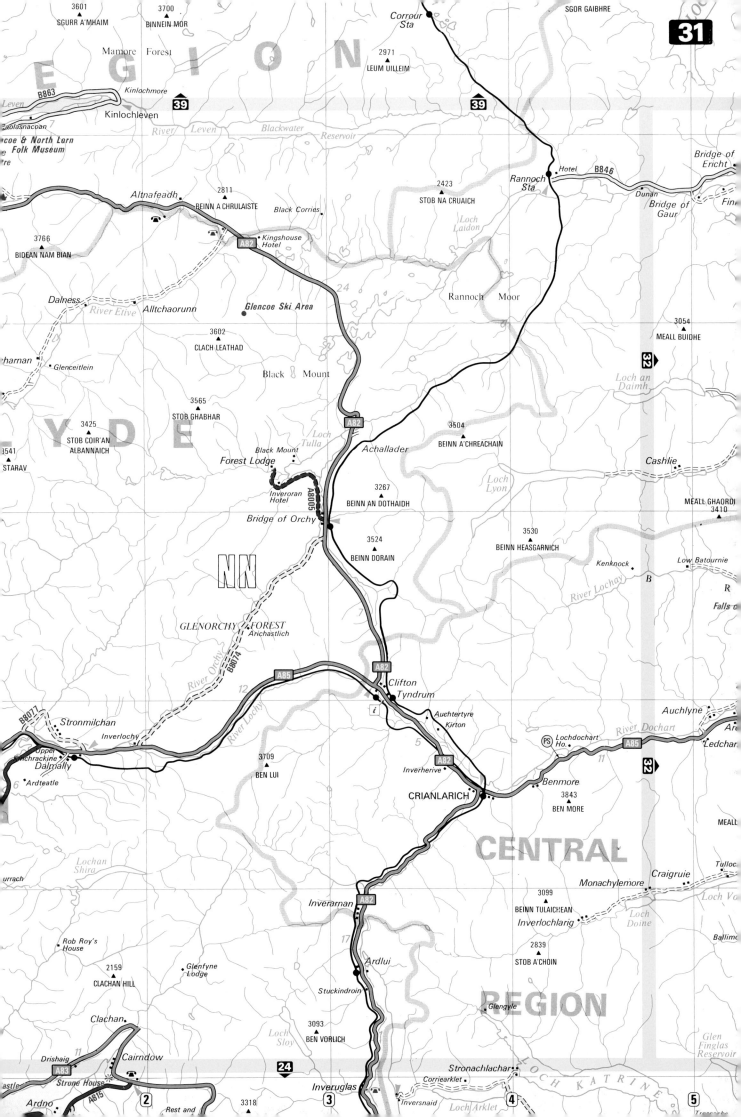

SGURR A'MHAIM  3601
BINNEIN MOR  3700
SGOR GAIBHRE

Corrour Sta

Mamore Forest

LEUM UILLEIM  2971

E G I O N

Kinlochmore

B863

39

39

Hotel  B846

Rannoch Sta

Bridge of Ericht

Kinlochleven

River  Leven  Blackwater  Reservoir

Dunan

Bridge of Gaur

Fin

oe & North Lorn
Folk Museum

Altnafeadh

BEINN A CHRULAISTE  2811

Black Corries

STOB NA CRUAICH  2423

Loch Laidon

3766
BIDEAN NAM BIAN

Kingshouse Hotel

A82

24

Rannoch Moor

MEALL BUIDHE  3054

Dalness

Alltchaorunn

River Etive

Glencoe Ski Area

32

harnan

Glenceitlein

CLACH LEATHAD  3602

Black  Mount

Loch an Daimh

YDE

STOB GHABHAR  3565

A82

3504
BEINN A'CHREACHAIN

Cashlie

3425
STOB COIR'AN
ALBANNAICH

Black Mount

Achallader

Loch Lyon

MEALL GHAORDI  3410

3541
STARAV

Forest Lodge

Loch Tulla

Inveroran Hotel

A8005

3267
BEINN AN DOTHAIDH

3530
BEINN HEASGARNICH

Kenknock

Low Batournie  B

Bridge of Orchy

Falls o

R

NN

3524
BEINN DORAIN

River Lochay

GLENORCHY  FOREST
Arichastlich

B8074

River Orchy

7

A82

Auchlyne

A85

12

Clifton

Tyndrum

Auchtertyre
Kirton

River Dochart

A85

32

B8077

Stronmilchan

i

PS  Lochdochart
Ho.

Ledchar

Inverlochy

5

Upper
Inchrackine

3709
BEN LUI

A82

A82

Benmore

Dalmally

Ardteatle

River Lochy

Inverherive

CRIANLARICH

3843
BEN MORE

11

6

CENTRAL

Lochan Shira

Craigruie

Tulloc

Monachylemore

urrach

Inverarnan

A82

3099
BEINN TULAICHEAN

Loch Vo

Inverlochlarig

Loch Doine

17

Ballim

Rob Roy's House

2839
STOB A'CHOIN

2159
CLACHAN HILL

Glenfyne Lodge

Ardlui

REGION

Stuckindroin

Glengyle

Clachan

3093
BEN VORLICH

Loch Sloy

Glen Finglas Reservoir

Drishaig

Cairndow

A83

11

24

Stronachlachar

Ardno

A815

Strone House

2

Rest and

3318

Inveruglas

3

Inversnaid

Corriearklet

4

Loch Arklet

LOCH KATRINE

5

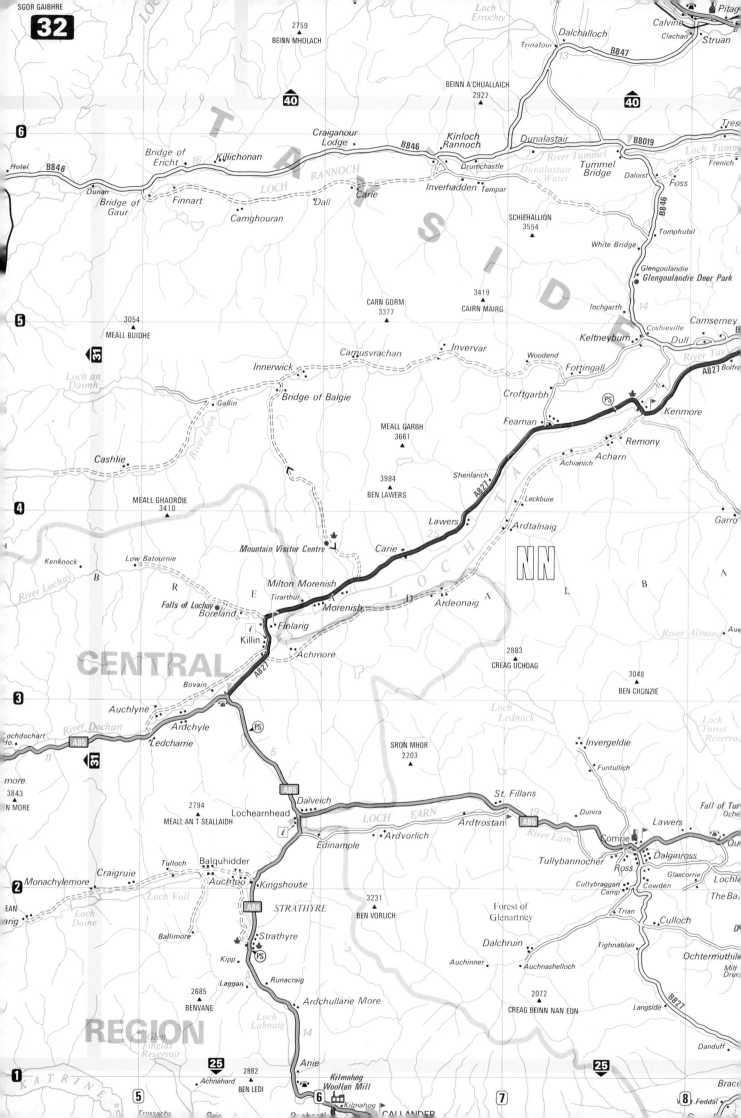

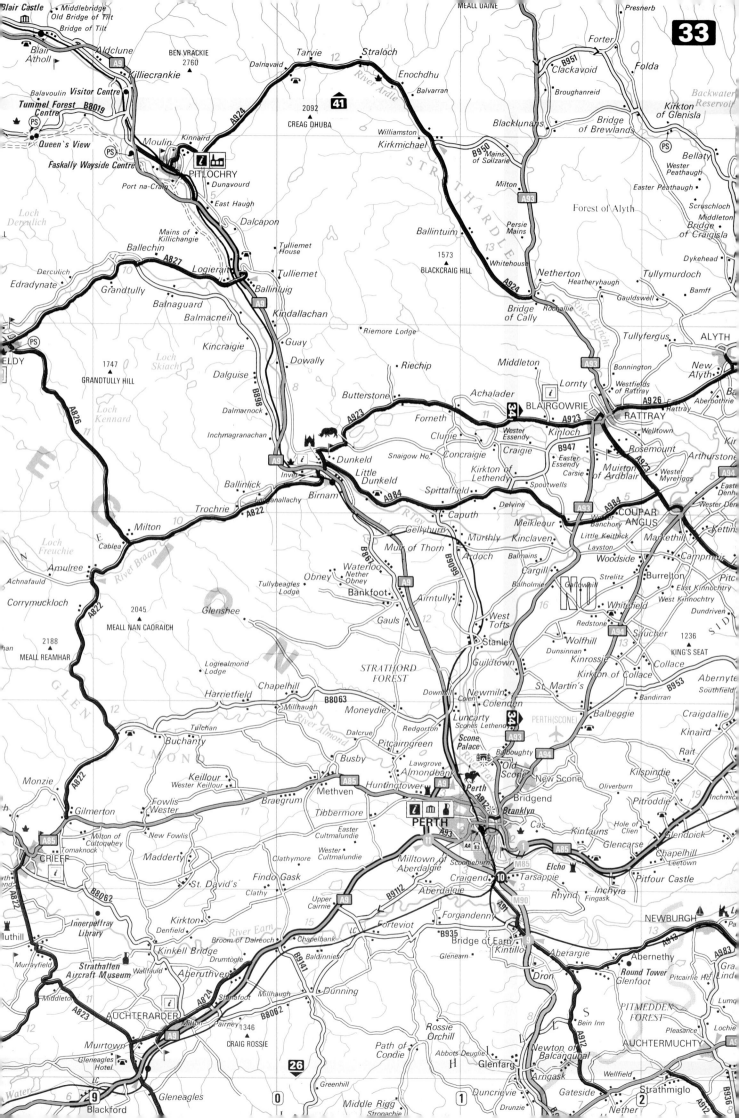

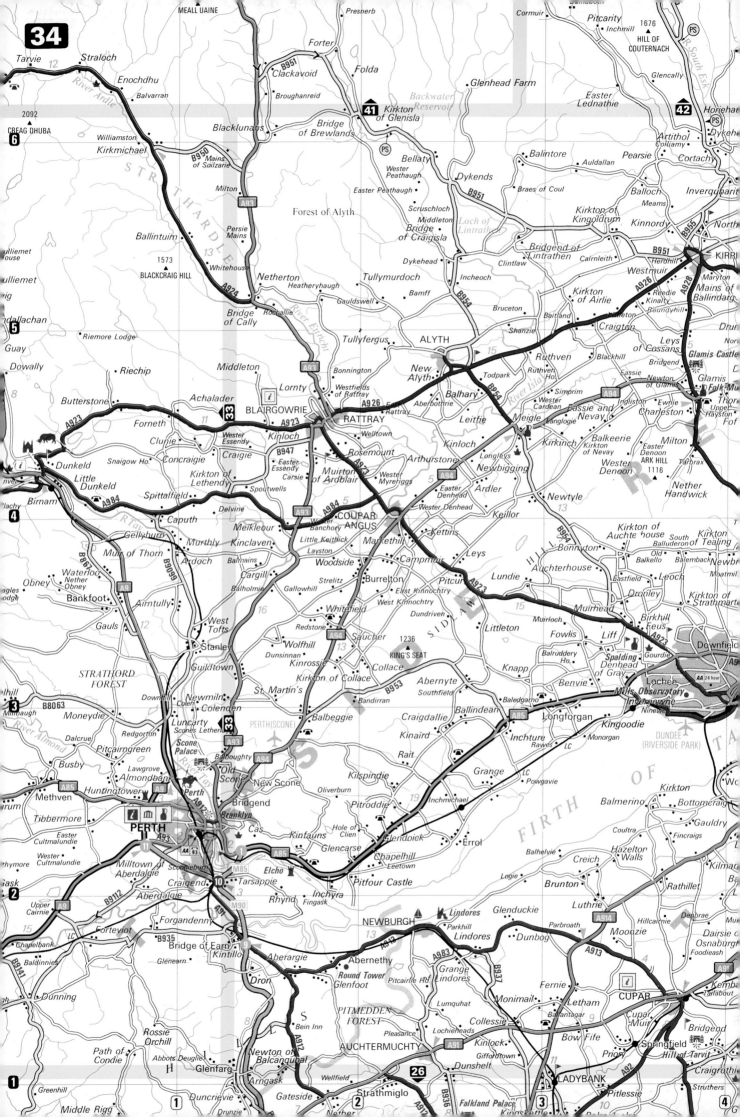

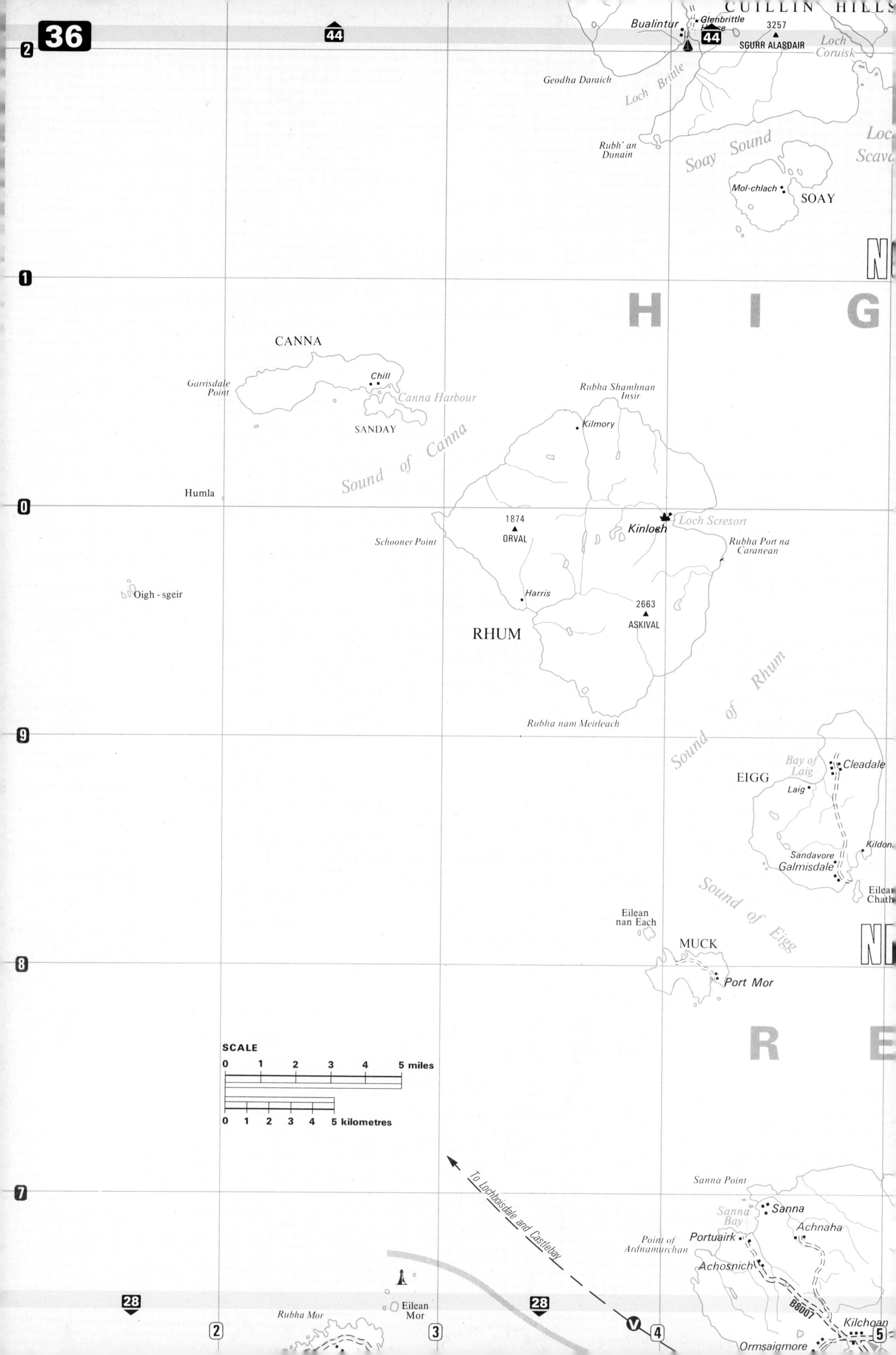

CUILLIN HILLS

Bualintur
Glenbrittle
House
3257
**44**
SGURR ALASDAIR
Loch
Coruisk

Geodha Daraich

Loch Brittle

Rubh' an
Dunain

Soay Sound

Loch
Scava

Mol-chlach

SOAY

N

**1**

H I G

CANNA

Garrisdale
Point

Chill

Canna Harbour

Rubha Shamhnan
Insir

SANDAY

Sound of Canna

Kilmory

Humla

**0**

1874
ORVAL

Kinloch

Loch Scresort

Schooner Point

Rubha Port na
Caranean

Oigh - sgeir

Harris

2663
ASKIVAL

RHUM

Rubha nam Meirleach

Sound of Rhum

**9**

Bay of
Laig

Cleadale

EIGG

Laig

Kildon

Sandavore
Galmisdale

Eilea
Chath

Eilean
nan Each

Sound of Eigg

N

MUCK

**8**

Port Mor

R

E

SCALE

0    1    2    3    4    5 miles

0  1  2  3  4  5 kilometres

**7**

To Lochboisdale and Castlebay

Sanna Point

Sanna
Bay
Sanna

Achnaha

Point of
Ardnamurchan
Portuairk

Achosnich

B8007

**28**

Rubha Mor

Eilean
Mor

**28**

V
**4**

Kilchoan

Ormsaigmore

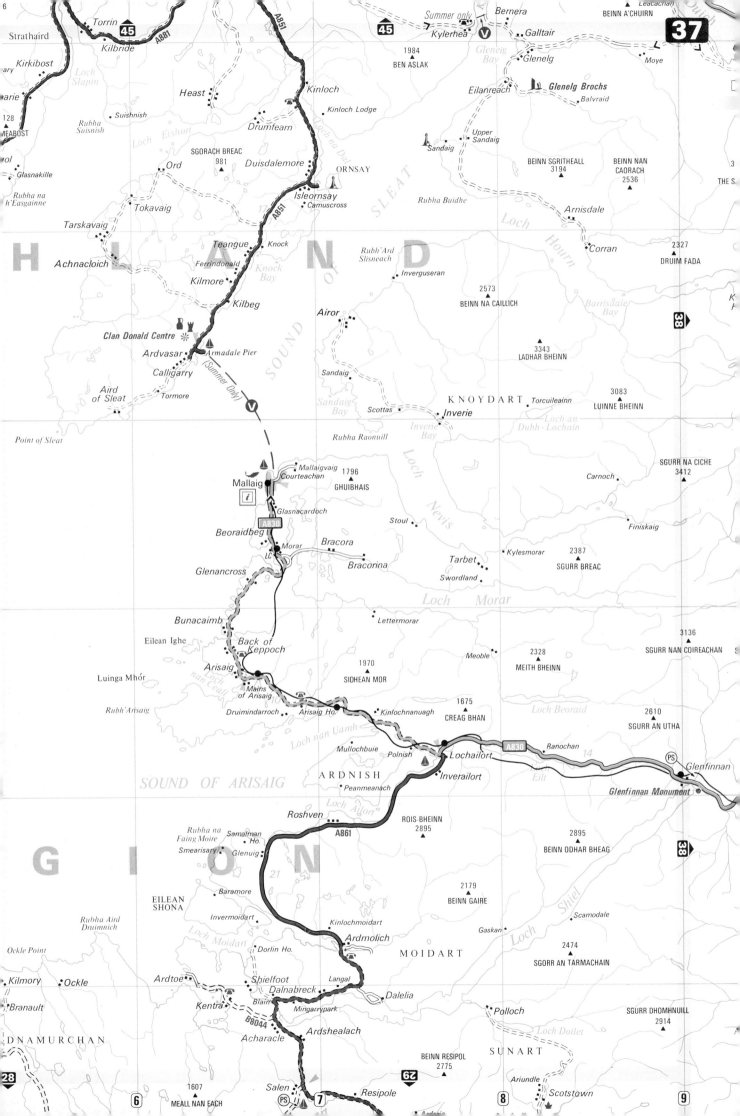

Balvraid

anreac
andaig

BEINN SGRITHEALL
3194

BEINN NAN
CAORACH
2536

3319
THE SADDLE

Arnisdale

Corran

Loch Hourn

2327
DRUIM FADA

Kinlochourn Forest

**NG**

Shiel Bridge

BEINN FHADA
OR
BEN ATTOW

3505
SGURR FHUARAN

**46**

Five Sisters 33

River Shiel

A87

MULLACH
FRAOCH CHOIRE
3614

3218
CISTE DHUBH

Cluanie Inn

A'CHRALAIG
3673

3634
SGURR NAN
CONBHAIREAN

Cluanie Lodge

Loch Cluanie

2901
AONACH SHASUINN

**46**

Lundie

A87

2573
na CAILLICH

Barrisdale Bay

**37**

3343
LADHAR BHEINN

Kinloch
Hourn

3365
SGURR A MHAORAICH

3342
AONACH AIR CHRITH

Alltbeithe

3394
GLEOURAICH

Glenquoich Forest

Loch Loyne

Glen

DART

Torcuileainn

Loch an
Dubh-Lochain

3083
LUINNE BHEINN

**0**

Loch Quoich

**H I G H**

Coille
Mhorgil

River Garry

Tomdoun

Inchlags

Glen

Carnoch

3412
SGURR NA CICHE

Finiskaig

3290
SGURR MOR

SGURR MHURLAGAIN
2885

Loch
Blàir

2154
MEALL BLAIR

1825
GLAS BHEINN

Kylesmorar

2387
SGURR BREAC

Glendessary

Strathan

Murlaggan

Loch Arkaig

Caonich

Ardechive

Morar

**9**

Loch Beoraid

2328
MEITH BHEINN

le

3136
SGURR NAN COIREACHAN

3164
SGURR THUILM

2610
SGURR AN UTHA

**NM**

Achnasaul

Inver Mallie

Achnacarry

B8005

Bunarkaig

2612
BEINN BHAN

2533
MEALL A PHUBUILL

Gairlochy

Mucomir

Brackletter

A830

Ranochan 14

Loch
Eilt

PS

Glenfinnan

Glenfinnan Monument

Strone

Highbridge

River Lochy

**8**

Kinlocheil

Lochellside
Sta

Fassfern

12

Muirshearlich

Torcastle

A82

**R F G**

8

A830

Drimsallie

Garvan A861

Duisky

Blaich

Loch Eil

B8004

Corpach

Banavie

Caol

Inverlochy

Torlundy

2895
BEINN ODHAR BHEAG

**37**

Achaphubuil

Camusnagaul

2

i

Killiechona

Scamodale

Trislaig

**FORT WILLIAM**

AA 112

2474
SGORR AN TARMACHAIN

Corrlarach

2528
STOB COIRE
A'CHEARCAILL

Stronchreggan Ho.

21

Auchintore

Achenadain

Roaring Mill Falls

Glen
Nevis Ho.

4406
BEN NEVIS

AONA

**7**

Polloch

Loch Doilet

SGURR DHOMHNUILL
2914

Druimarbin

PS

Blarmachfoldach

Achriabhach

3601
SGURR A'MHAIM

Loch Shiel

ARDGOUR

Conaglen
Ho.

Aryhoulan

Inverscaddle Bay

8

Coruanan Lodge

Blàr a'
Chaorainn

SUNART

Ariundle

Scotstown

Anaheilt

astang

Strontian

Achnalea

A861

13

**9**

A861

V

Ardgour

Clovulin

Sallachan

2022
BEINN NA GUCAIG

Cuilchea Ho.

**30**

**0**

Corran

Keppanach

Onich

4

North
Ballachulish

**1**

Callert
Cottage

9

B863

Caolasnacoan

Kinloch

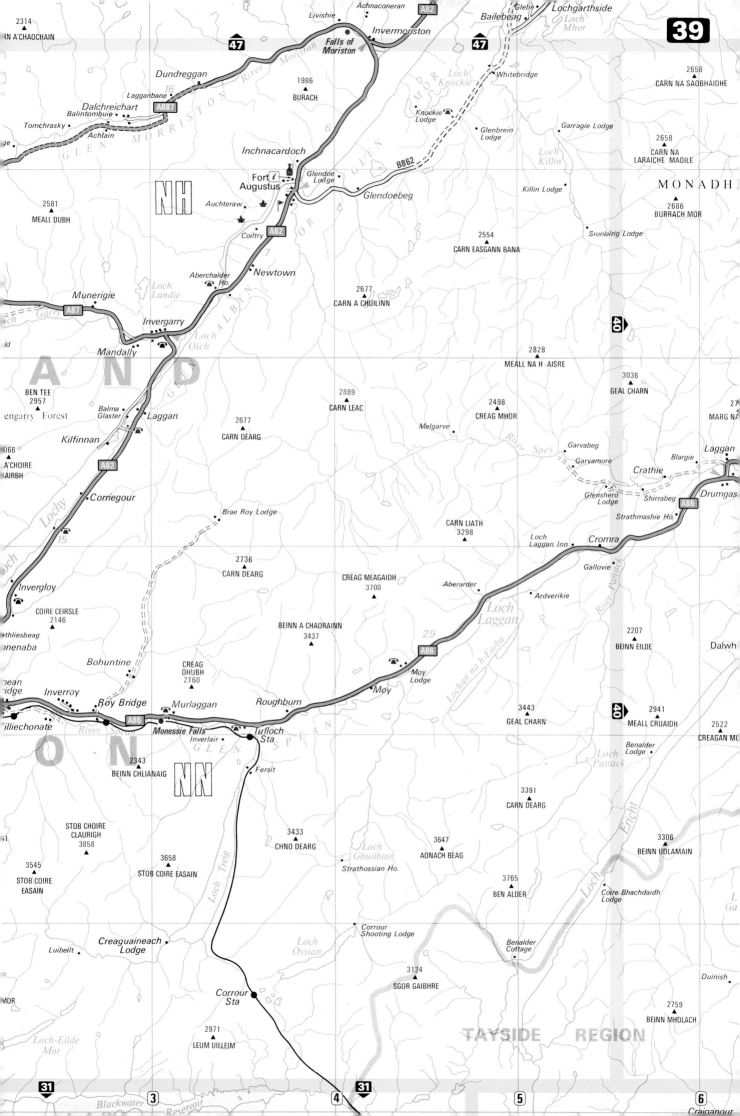

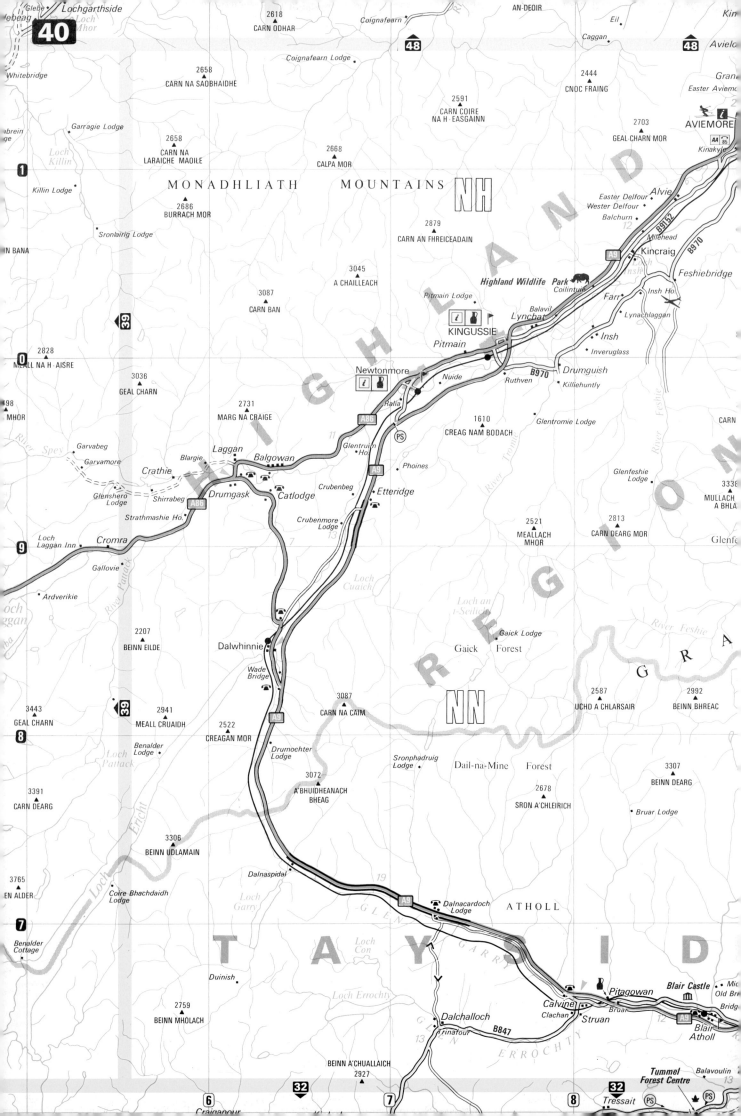

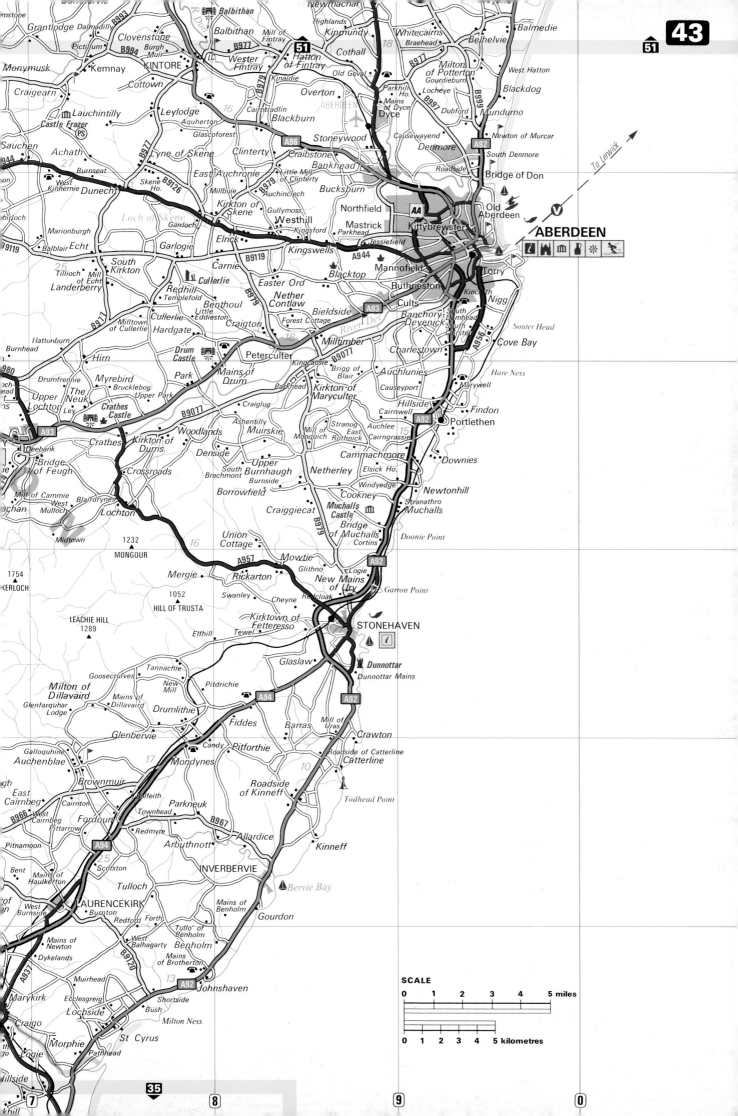

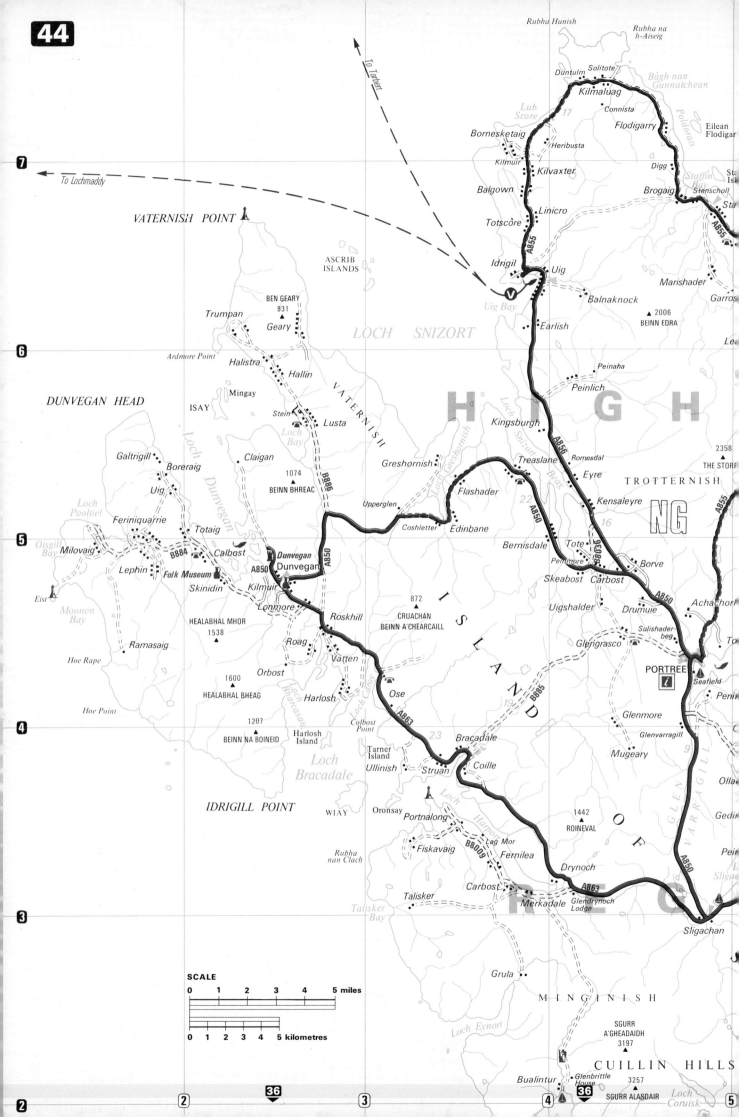

Rubha Hunish
Rubha na h-Aiseig

To Tarbert

Bàgh nan Gunnaichean

Duntulm  Solitote
Kilmaluag
Connista
Flodigarry
Bornesketaig
Heribusta
Kilmuir
Kilvaxter
Balgown
Linicro
Totscore
Idrigil  Uig
Digg
Brogaig  Stenscholl  Sta
Staffin Bay  St Isl
Eilean Flodigar

Poldorais

Lub Score  17

A855

To Lochmaddy
7

VATERNISH POINT

ASCRIB ISLANDS

Uig Bay

Marishader
Balnaknock
Garros
2006
BEINN EDRA
Le

BEN GEARY 931
Geary
Trumpan

LOCH    SNIZORT

Earlish

Peinaha
Peinlich

H I G H

6
Ardmore Point  Halistra
Hallin
ISAY  Mingay
Stein  Lusta
Claigan
DUNVEGAN HEAD
1074
BEINN BHREAC

VATERNISH

Loch Bay

B806

Greshornish
Upperglen
Coshletter  Edinbane
Flashader

Kingsburgh

A856

Treaslane
Romesdal
Eyre
Kensaleyre

2358
THE STOR
TROTTERNISH
NG

A850

16
22
A850

Galtrigill  Boreraig
Uig
Feriniquarrie
Totaig

Loch Pooltiel

Milovaig
B884  Calbost
Lephin  Folk Museum
Skinidin
Dunvegan
Dunvegan
A850  Kilmuir
Lonmore
Roskhill
Oisgill Bay
Eist

Moonen Bay

Ramasaig

HEALABHAL MHOR 1538
872
CRUACHAN
BEINN A'CHEARCAILL
ISLAND
Bernisdale
Tote
Penmore
Skeabost  Carbost
Uigshalder
Sulishader-beg
Drumuie
Borve
Achachor
To

5

Hoe Rape
Hoe Point

1600
HEALABHAL BHEAG
Roag
Vatten
Orbost
Harlosh
Ose

Glengrasco

PORTREE
i
Seafield
Peni

Glenmore
Glenvarragill
Mugeary

4
1207
BEINN NA BOINEID
Harlosh Island
Colbost Point
Tarner Island
Ullinish
Struan
Bracadale
Coille

B885
19
23

Loch Bracadale

IDRIGILL POINT
WIAY
Oronsay
Portnalong
Fiskavaig
B8009
Lag Mor
Fernilea
Rubha nan Clach
Talisker Bay
Talisker
Carbost
Merkadale
Drynoch
Glendrynoch Lodge

1442
ROINEVAL
O F

GLEN VARRAGIL

A850

Sligachan
Peir
Olla
Gedi

A863

RE C

3
Grula
MINGINISH

SCALE
0  1  2  3  4  5 miles
0  1  2  3  4  5 kilometres

Loch Eynort

SGURR A'GHEADAIDH 3197

Bualintur  Glenbrittle House
CUILLIN HILLS
3257
SGURR ALASDAIR

Loch Coruisk

2

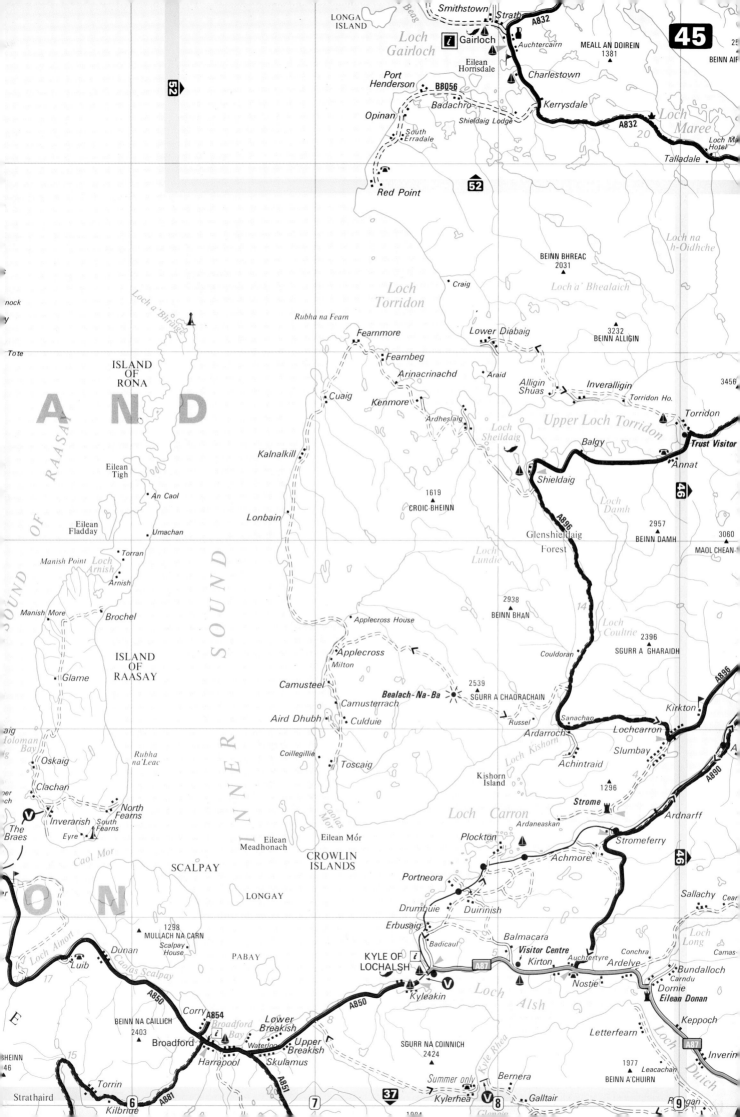

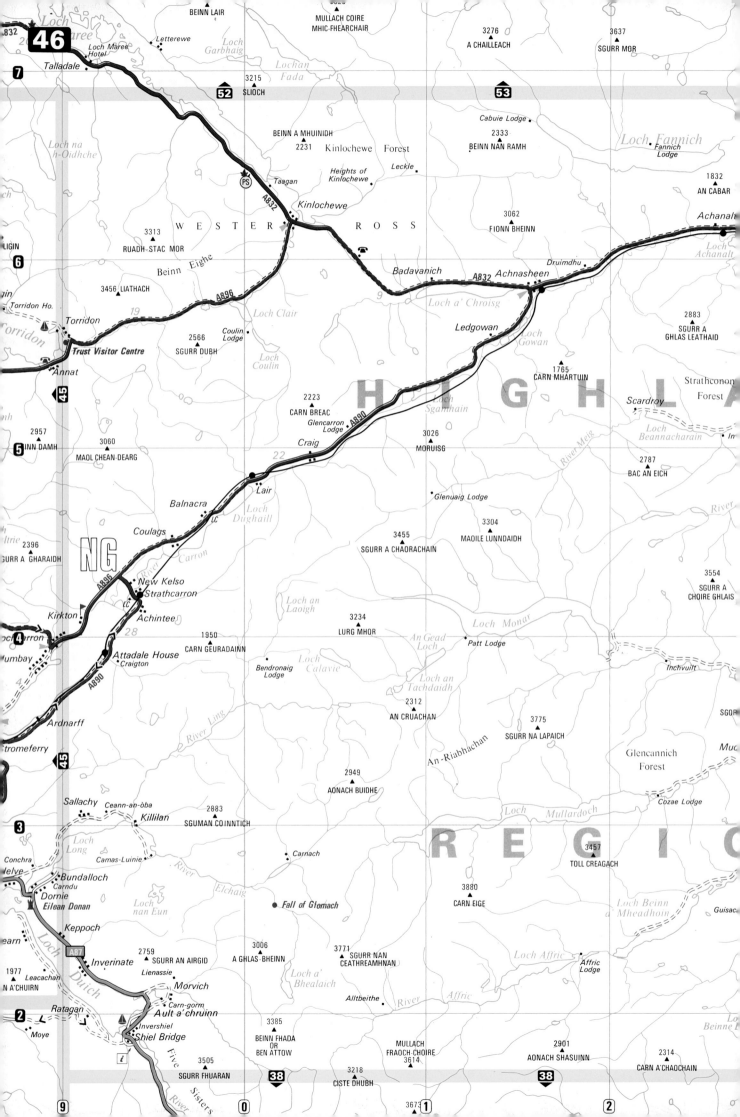

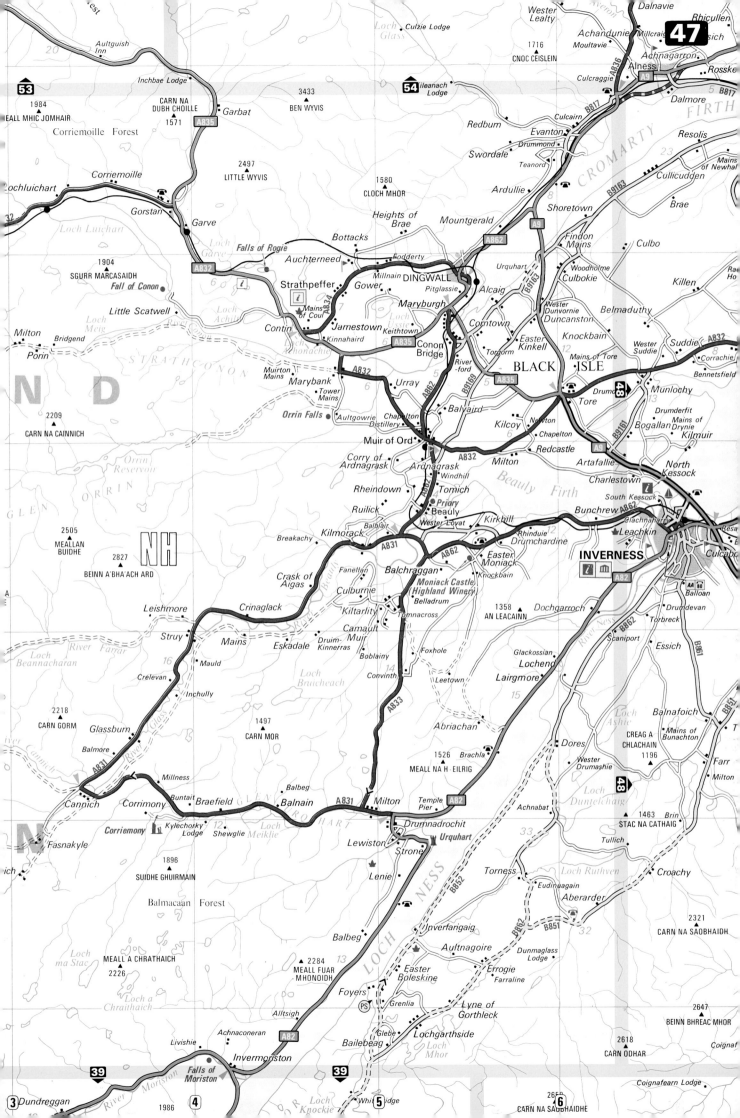

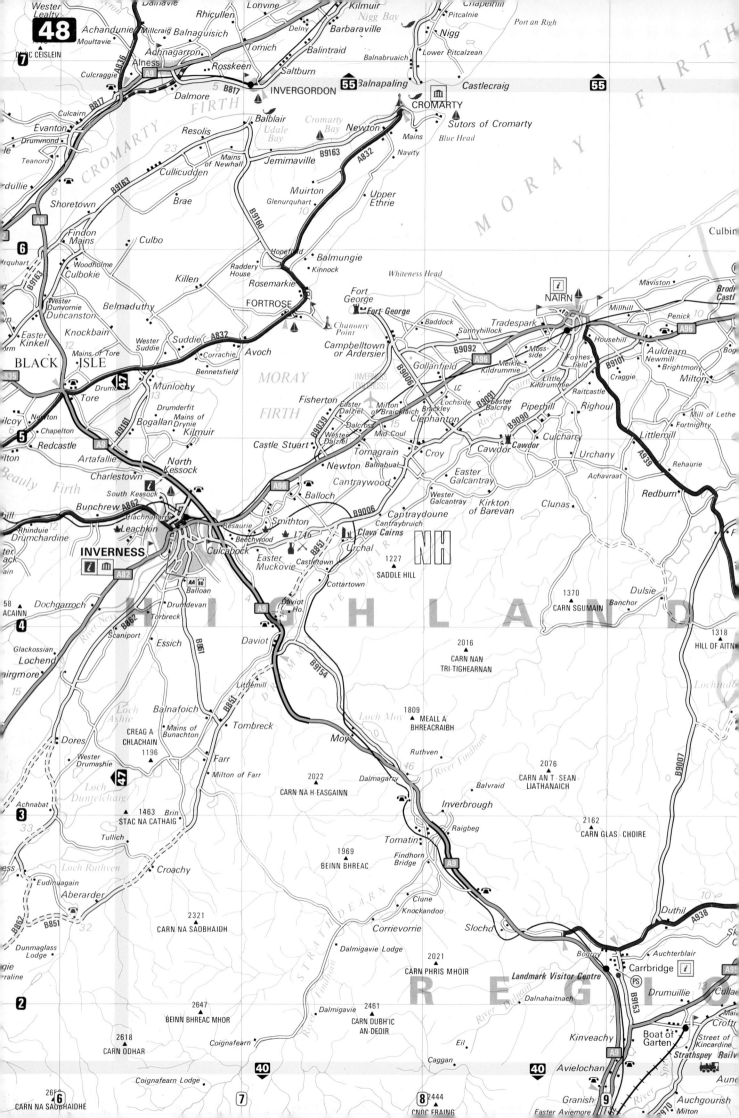

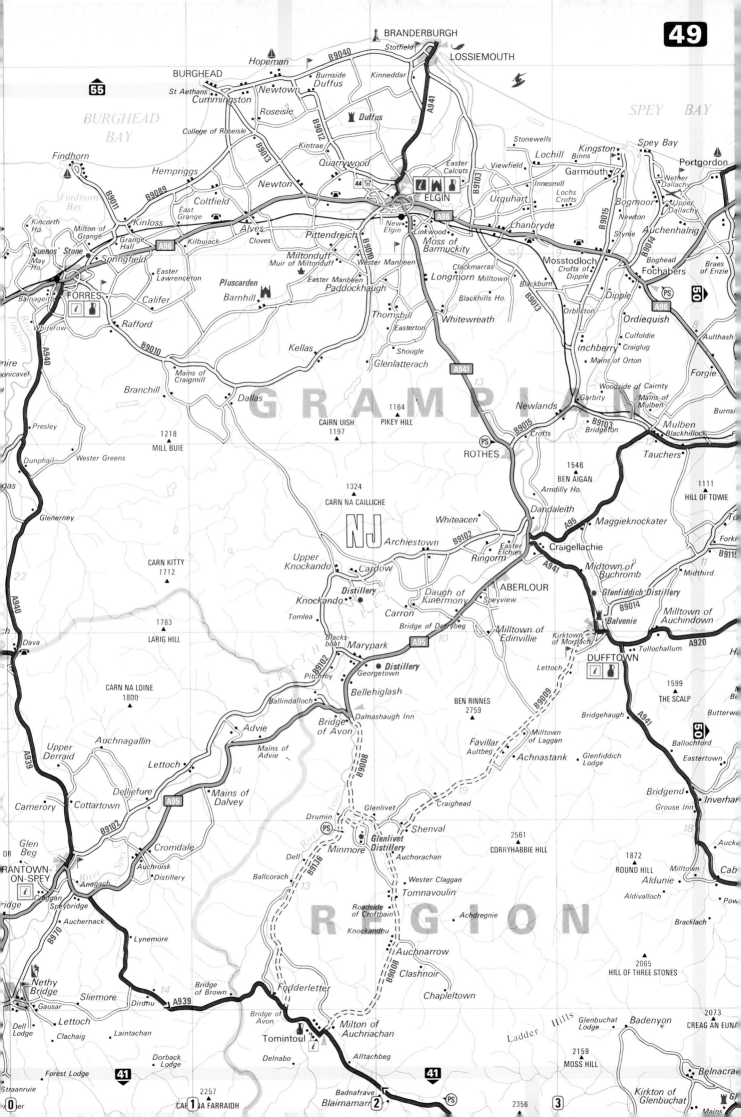

7

Y BAY

PORTKNOCKIE

FINDOCHTY

Logie Head

Cullen Bay

Redhythe Point

Sandend Bay

CULLEN

Knock Head

Boyndie Bay

BUCKIE

A942

Poctessie

Moor of Scotstown

Buckpool

Bauds of Cullen

Rathven

Sandend

PORTSOY

Easter Whyntie

Whitehills

Inverboyndie

MACDUFF

Head of Garness

Bay

Portgordon

A990

Mains of Buckie

Rannas

Westerside

Bogside

Lintmill

Tochieneal

Birkenbog

Bogtown

A98

B9139

Auds

BANFF

Duff

Silverhillocks

Mains Silver

Upper Dallachy

A98

Slackhead

Cairnfield Ho.

Broadley

Drybridge

Farnachty

Kirktown of Deskford

12

Milton

Nicholsonpark

Fordyce

Auchmillie

Lintmill of Boyne

Boyndie

Cairnton

Blairshinnoch

Wester Culbeuchly Crofts

Tipperty

Mains of Montcoffer

Gellyhill

Netherwood

Keilhill

Cairnandrew

Millhow

A98

Longr

Crowhillo

henhalrig

Clochan

6

Braes of Enzie

abers

Craibstone

Langlanburn

Mid Skeith

Berryhillock

Greenhill

Toux

Drochedlie

Tillynaught

Drakemires

Ordens

Newhills of Boyne

Culphin of Park

Oldtown of Ord

B9025

Kirktown of Alva

Ella

Fattahead

Balchers

Gorrach

Balmau

Deerhill

Burn of Aultmore

Goukstone

Nethertown of Windyhills

Mains of Edingight

Gordonstown

Berrydrum

KNOCK HILL

1412

Park

Cornhill

Middle Witchyburn

The Pole of Itlaw

Peatknowe

Auchinderran

Finnygaud

Deuchries

Mountblairy

Hill of Mountblairy

Nether Muirden

Muirden

Denhead

Plaidy

Slackadale

Kinbate

Croft of Danshillock

Castleton

Aulthash

Broadrashes

Garralburn

Grange Crossroads

Crannach

Berryhillock

Sillyearn

Bracobrae

Upper Fowlwood

Knowhead

Newton of Auchintoul

Cranna

Bogton

Slack of Scotston

B9025

Knockiemill

Meikle Hilton

Kirkton

Croft of Mu

Forgie

Aultmore

Forgieside

Guilyknowes

Newmill

Auchinhove

Davoch of Grange

Braco

Knock

Drumnagorrach

Bunervie

Old Crombie

ABERCHIRDER

Clunie

Carnousie

TURRIFF

Mulben

Burnside

Fife Keith

A95

KEITH

Farmtown

Knauchland

Tillydown

Marnoch

Mill of Muiresk

Bridgend

Colp

Blackhillock

Retanach

Greenfold

5

chers

A95

Auldtown

Tullochs

Rothiemay

Eastertown of Mayen

B9117

Hillbrae

Auchininna

Ardmiddle Mains

Darra

1111

HILL OF TOWIE

B9014

Poolside

Edintore

Ruthven

Yonder Bognie

Inverkeithny

Parkdargue

Westfield

Auchininna

Fotrie

Birkenhills

Mains of Towie

Towiemore

Little Pitlurg

Coachford

Cairnie

Bogniebrae

Chapelhill

Drumblair Ho.

Carlincraig

Upper Pitglassie

A947

Dykeside

Stei

Forkins

B9115

Mains of Davidston

Botary Mains

Corse of Kinnoir

Cairnton

B9024

Placemill

Easter Aucharnie

NJ

Balgaveny

Mains of Hatton

New Mill

Kirktown of Auchterless

17

Midthird

Mains of Blairmore

A96

Westerton

Bogie

Meikleton

Aucharnie

Nether Lenshie

Thornybank

Gordonstown

tillery

Milltown of Auchindown

A920

HUNTLY

Huntly

Lessendrum

Drumblade

Affleck

Loangarry

Corse

Newton Auchaber

Glenmellan

Logie Newton

Badenscoth

Redhill

Rothiebrisbane

Torry

Cairnborrow

Invermarkie

Upper Cairnargat

Glen

PS

Upper Pirriesmill

Slioch

Brideswell

Crofts of Heathfield

Wells of Ythan

B992

Newseat

A920

Haugh of Glass

STRATHBOGIE

Lower Gordonsburn

Bothwellseat

Denend

Agricultural Museum

Thomastown

Bainshole

Fisherford

Auchintender

Rothienorman

Overhill

Folla Rule

Cro

Jac

THE SCALP

1599

Dumeath

Mains of Beldorney

Bailiesward

Bridgend

Crofts of Shanquhar

Newtongarry Croft

A96

Skares

Colpy

Newton of Rothmaise

Rothmaise

Ja

Butterwards

Succoth

Tillathrowie

Dunscroft

Kirkstile

Crofts of Blackburn

Largie

Kirkton of Culsalmond

Cairnhill

Tocher

Ballochford

Easterton

Tomnaven

Coynachie

Tillyminnate

Kirkney

Gartly

Knockandy Hill

1425

Cults

Wrangham

Kirkton of Rayne

Meikle Wartle

Auchentarph

Whiteinches

Daviot

Mel

dgend

Inverharroch

rouse Inn

Clashindarroch

Newnoth

Smithston

Leith Hall

Aulton

Insch

Dunnydeer

B992

Pitmachie

Old Rayne

Ardoyne

3

18

Auckmair

Milton of Lesmore

Milton of Noth

Kennethmont

Earlsfield

Oldtown Ardlair

B9002

LC

Ladywell

Westhall

Mill of Carden

Whiteford

A96

B900

Balhalga

Milltown

Cabrach

Belhinnie

Rhynie

Druminnor Castle

Duncanston

Christskirk

Kirkton

Old Westhall

Oyne

Pittodrie

PS

Pitcaple

Inveramsay

nie

Wheddlemont

Craik

Cottown

Auchmenzie

Clatt

Mill of Leslie

Leslie

Auchleven

Chapel of Garioch

Bogmill

Burgh Muir

Alton

INVERUR

B9002

Newton

Powneed

Coldwells Croft

Millburn

GARIOCH

Bracklach

2366

THE BUCK

Todstone

Clova

Knockespock Ho.

Dubston

Bogend

Muckletown

1733

BENNACHIE

Bennachie

House of Aquahorthies

Bograxie

i

Lumsden

Littlemill

Newmill

North Warrackston

Cardensbrae

Broadmire

Westhaugh

Keig

Rorandle

Ramstone

Burnhervie

2

2073

CREAG AN EUNAN

on

Mossat

A944

Scotsmill

Cullyblean

Tullynessle

Montgarrie

River Don

Rorandle

Pitfichie

Grantlodge Dalmadilly

B9993

Clov

Rinmore

Glencuie

Kildrummy

Upper Balfour

Bithnie

Bridge of Alford

42

Auchintoul

Ardgathen

Gateside

Pitfichie

Monymusk

7

Belnacraig

Mains

4

5

Milltown of Buck

A97

Upper

Asloun

Alford

42

Meikle

Whitehouse

6

Pitmunie

Kemnay

Kenmay

B99

of Gl..buchat

Wellhouse

Craigeo

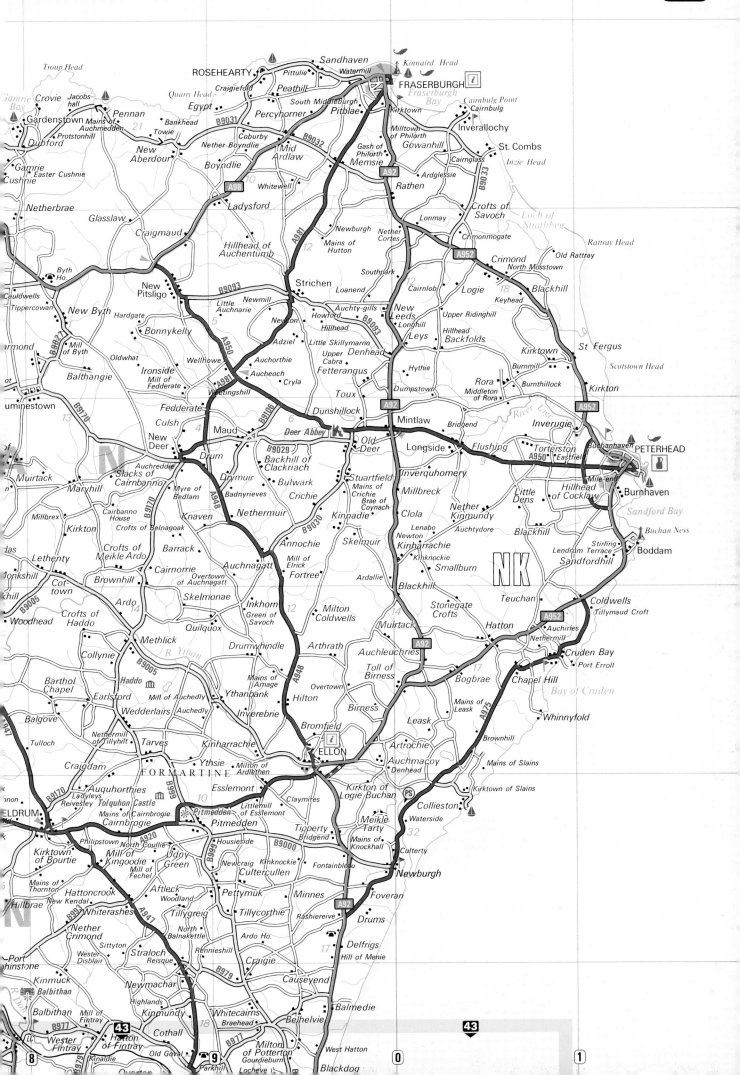

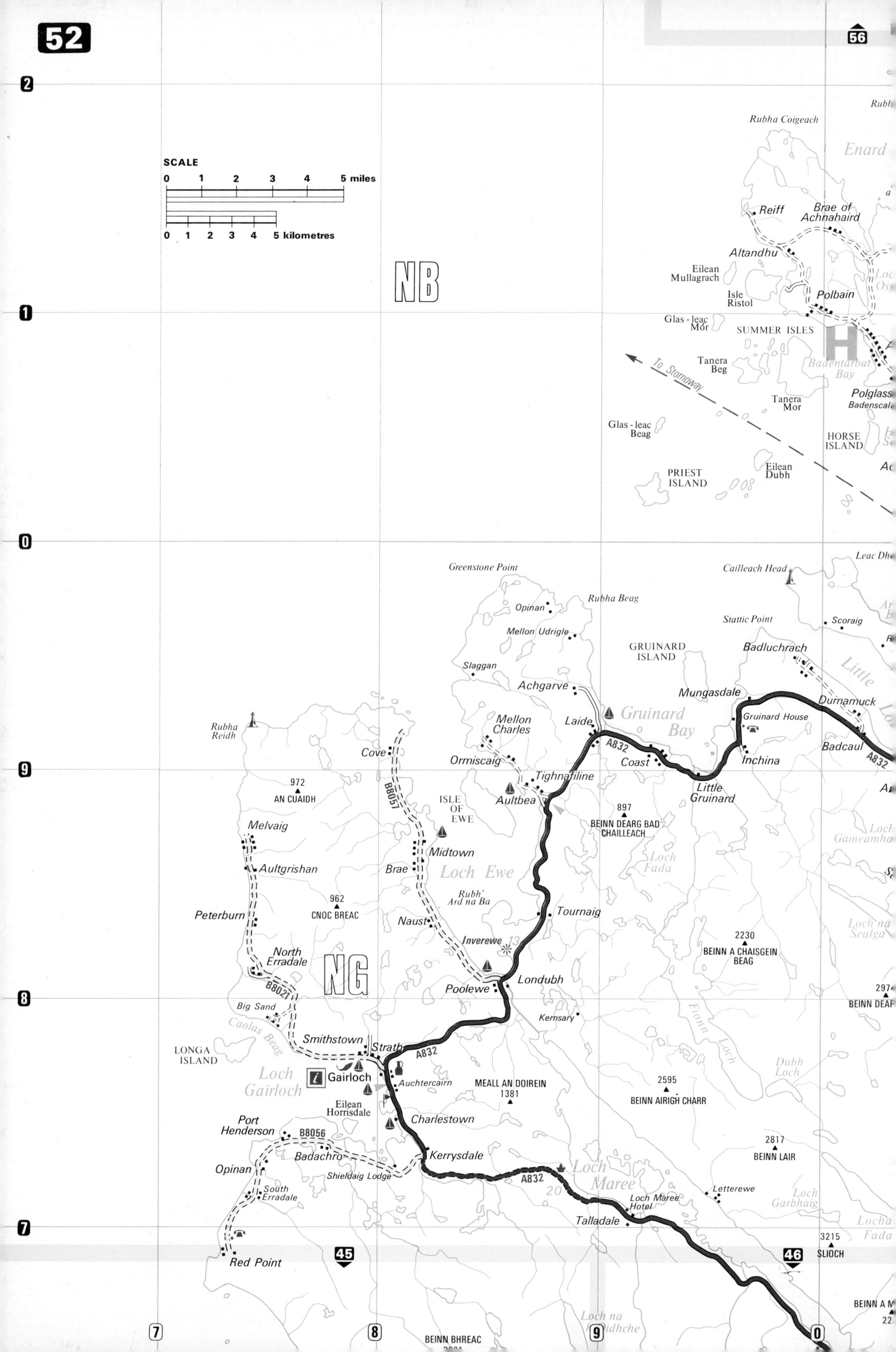

NB

SCALE

| 0 | 1 | 2 | 3 | 4 | 5 miles |

| 0 | 1 | 2 | 3 | 4 | 5 kilometres |

Rubha Coigeach

*Enard*

Reiff · Brae of
Achnahaird

Altandhu

Eilean
Mullagrach

Isle
Ristol

Polbain

Glas - leac
Mór

SUMMER ISLES

*Badentarbat
Bay*

Polglass
Badenscal·

To Stornoway

Tanera
Beg

Tanera
Mór

HORSE
ISLAND

Glas - leac
Beag

PRIEST
ISLAND

Eilean
Dubh

Leac Dh

Greenstone Point

Cailleach Head

Rubha Beag

Opinan

Stattic Point

Scoraig

Mellon Udrigle

GRUINARD
ISLAND

Badluchrach

Slaggan

Achgarve

Mungasdale

Durnamuck

Rubha
Reidh

*Gruinard
Bay*

Gruinard House

Badcaul

Mellon
Charles

Laide

Gruinard

Coast

Inchina

A832

Cove

Ormiscaig

Tighnafiline

Little
Gruinard

A832

972
AN CUAIDH

ISLE
OF
EWE

Aultbea

897
BEINN DEARG BAD
CHAILLEACH

B8057

Melvaig

Midtown

*Loch
Fada*

Aultgrishan

Brae

*Loch Ewe*

Loch
Gaineamha

Peterburn

962
CNOC BREAC

*Rubh'
Ard na Ba*

Tournaig

2230
BEINN A CHAISGEIN
BEAG

Naust

Loch na
Sealga

North
Erradale

NG

Inverewe

297
BEINN DEA

B8021

Poolewe

Londubh

Kernsary

Big Sand

*Caolas Beag*

Smithstown

Strath

A832

*Fionn
Loch*

*Dubh
Loch*

LONGA
ISLAND

*Loch
Gairloch*

Gairloch

Auchtercairn

MEALL AN DOIREIN
1381

2595
BEINN AIRIGH CHARR

Eilean
Horrisdale

Charlestown

Port
Henderson

B8056

Kerrysdale

2817
BEINN LAIR

Opinan

Badachro

*Loch
Maree*

Letterewe

Loch
Garbhaig

South
Erradale

Shieldaig Lodge

A832

Loch Maree
Hotel

*Locha
Fada*

Talladale

3215
SLIOCH

Red Point

BEINN A M
22

BEINN BHREAC

*Loch na
idhche*

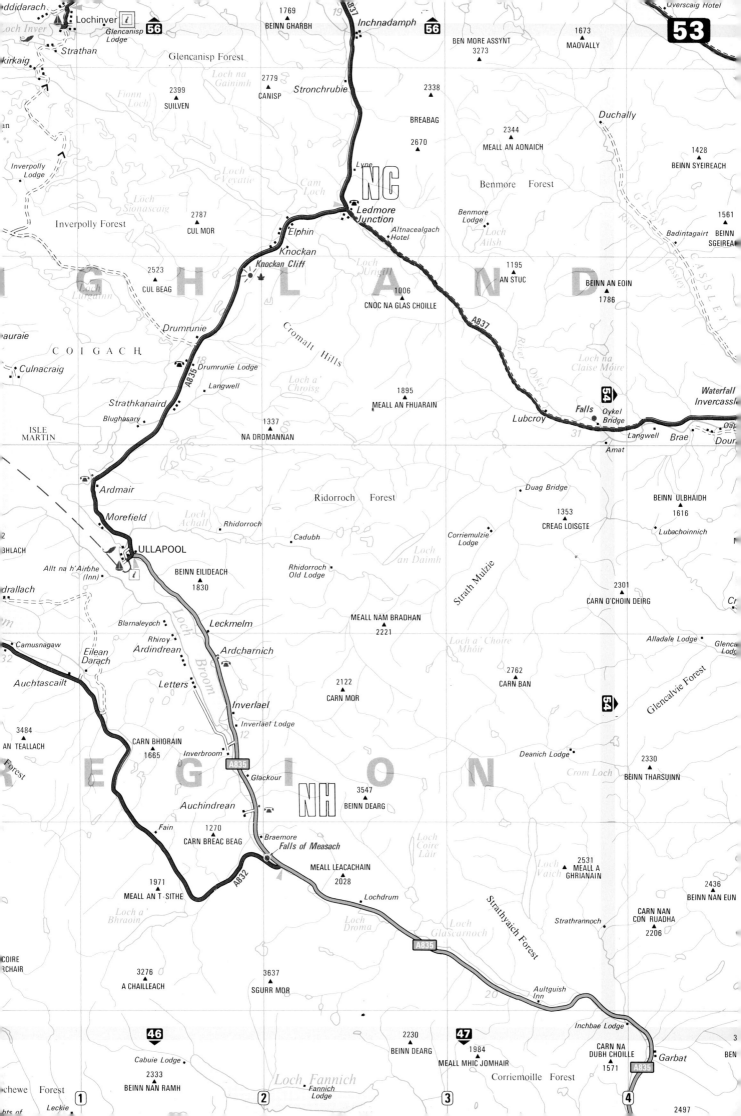

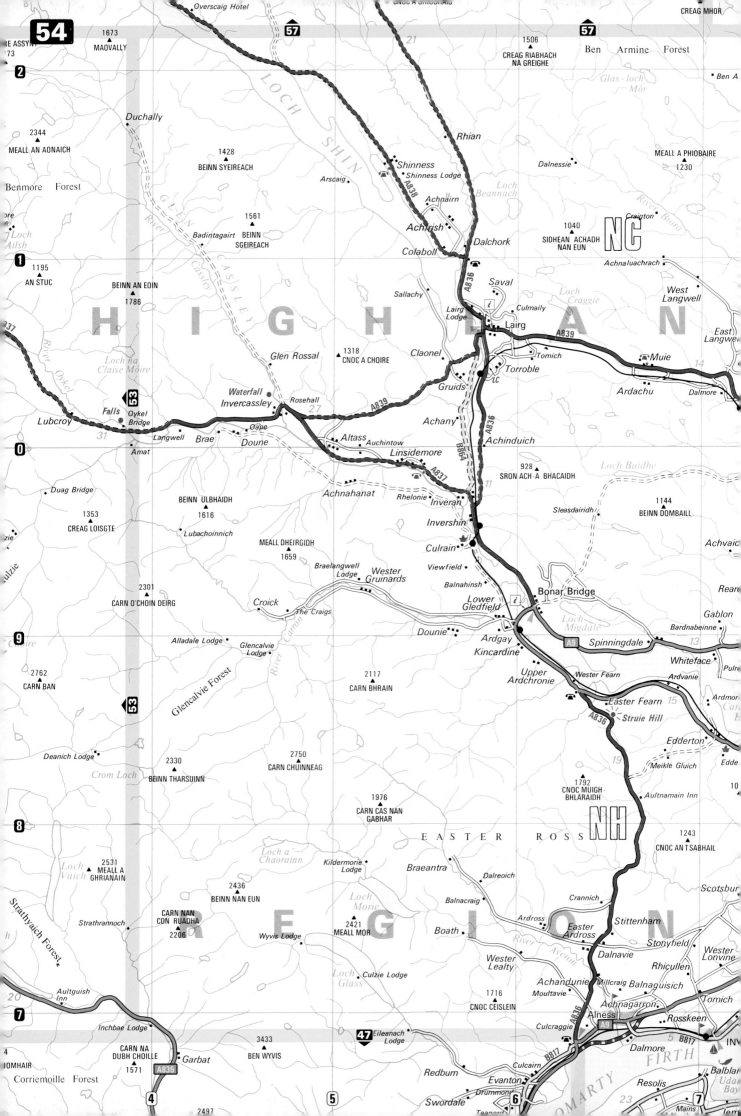

**54**

**2**

**1**

**0**

**9**

**8**

**7**

CREAG MHOR

Overscaig Hotel

**57**

**57**

1673
MAOVALLY

E ASSYNT
73

2344
MEALL AN AONAICH

1506
CREAG RIABHACH
NA GREIGHE

Ben Armine Forest

Glas-loch
Mór

Ben A

MEALL A PHIOBAIRE
1230

Duchally

1428
BEINN SYEIREACH

Arscaig

Shinness

Shinness Lodge

Rhian

Dalnessie

Benmore Forest

ore

Loch
Ailsh

1561
BEINN
SGEIREACH

Badintagairt

Achnairn

Achfrish

Loch
Beannach

1040
SIDHEAN ACHADH
NAN EUN

Crainton

River Brora

**NC**

1195
AN STUC

BEINN AN EOIN
1786

Colaboll

Dalchork

Achnaluachrach

H     I     G     H

Glen Rossal

1318
CNOC A CHOIRE

Sallachy

Lairg
Lodge

Saval

West
Langwell

837

River Oykel

Loch na
Claise Móire

**53**

Waterfall
Invercassley

Rosehall

A839

Claonel

Lairg

Culmaily

A839

East
Langwe

Muie

14

Falls

Oykel
Bridge

27

Gruids

Torroble

Tomich

Ardachu

Lubcroy

31

Langwell
Brae

Oape

Doune

A837

Achany

Achinduich

Dalmore

Amat

Altass

Auchintow

Linsidemore

B864

Duag Bridge

BEINN ULBHAIDH
1616

Achnahanat

Rhelonie

Inveran

SRON ACH·A·BHACAIDH
928

Loch Buidhe

1144
BEINN DOMBAILL

1353
CREAG LOISGTE

Lubachoinnich

Invershin

Sleasdairidh

Achvaic

2301
CARN O'CHOIN DEIRG

MEALL DHEIRGIDH
1659

Braelangwell
Lodge

Wester
Gruinards

Culrain

Viewfield

Balnahinsh

Bonar Bridge

Bardnabeinne

Gablon

Rear

**9**

Croick

The Craigs

Lower
Gledfield

Loch
Migdale

2762
CARN BAN

Alladale Lodge

Glencalvie
Lodge

River Carron

Dounie

Ardgay
Kincardine

A9

Spinningdale

Whiteface

Pulre

**53**

Deanich Lodge

2330
BEINN THARSUINN

2750
CARN CHUINNEAG

2117
CARN BHRAIN

Upper
Ardchronie

Wester Fearn

Ardvanie

Ardmor
Can

Glencalvie Forest

Crom Loch

A836

Easter Fearn

Struie Hill

15

Edderton

Edde

1792
CNOC MUIGH-
BHLARAIDH

Meikle Gluich

19

Aultnamain Inn

**NH**

**8**

1976
CARN CAS NAN
GABHAR

E   A   S   T   E   R       R   O   S   S

1243
CNOC AN T SABHAIL

Loch a'
Chaorainn

Kildermorie
Lodge

Braeantra

Dalreoich

Crannich

Scotsbur

2531
MEALL A
GHRIANAIN

Loch
Vaich

2436
BEINN NAN EUN

Loch
Morie

Balnacraig

Ardross

Stittenham

Wester
Lonvine

Strathvaich Forest

Strathrannoch

CARN NAN
CON RUADHA
2206

Wyvis Lodge

2421
MEALL MOR

Boath

Easter
Ardross

Dalnavie

Stonyfield

Rhicullen

R    E    G    I    O    N

Culzie Lodge

Wester
Lealty

River Averon

Achandunie

Moultavie

Millcraig Balnaguisich

Tomich

**7**

20

Aultguish
Inn

Loch
Glass

1716
CNOC CEISLEIN

Achnagarron

Alness

A836

Rosskeen

IN

Inchbae Lodge

CARN NA
DUBH CHOILLE
1571

Garbat

3433
BEN WYVIS

**47**

Eileanach
Lodge

Culcraggie

A9

B817

5

B817

Dalmore

JOMHAIR

Corriemoille Forest

**4**

2497

**5**

Redburn

Evanton

Drummont

Swordale
Teanord

Culcairn

**6**

Resolis

Udale
Bay

FIRTH

OMARTY

23

Balbla

Mains

**7**

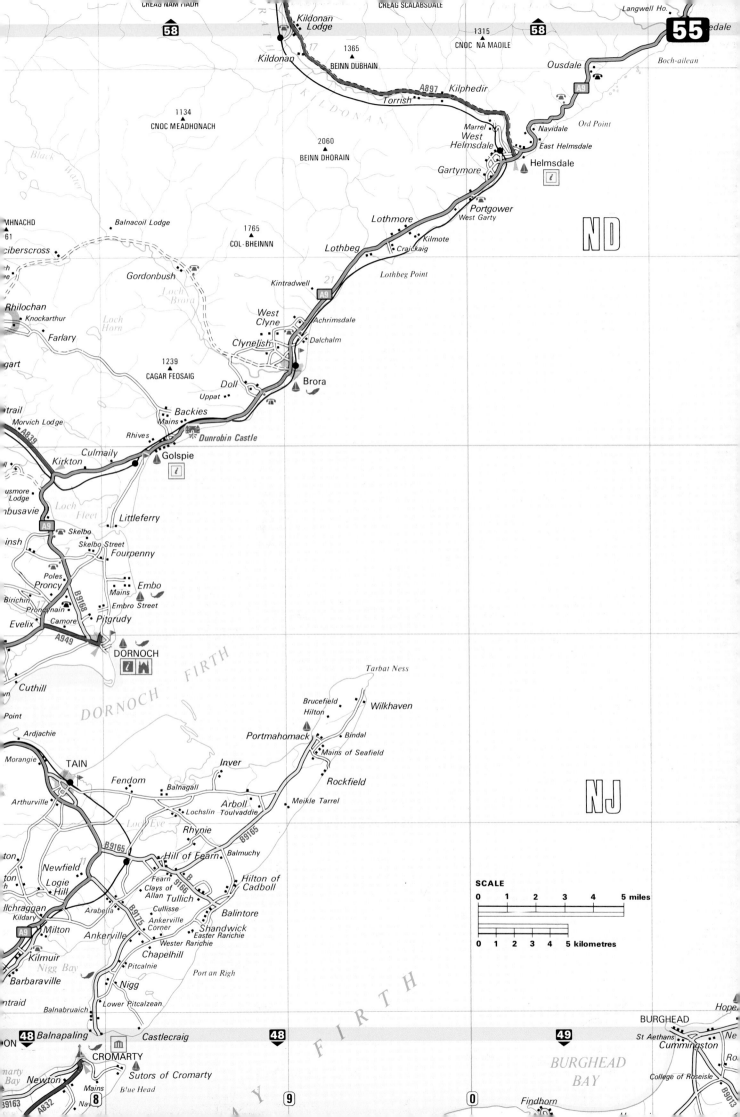

CREAG NAM FIADH
CREAG SCALABSDALE
Langwell Ho.

Kildonan Lodge
1315
CNOC NA MAOILE
dale

17
Kildonan
1365
BEINN DUBHAIN
A897  Kilphedir
Torrish
Ousdale
Boch-ailean

A9

1134
CNOC MEADHONACH
Marrel
West
Helmsdale
Navidale
East Helmsdale
Ord Point

2060
BEINN DHORAIN
Gartymore
Helmsdale
i

NMHNACHD
61
Balnacoil Lodge
Portgower
West Garty

ciberscross
1765
COL-BHEINNN
Lothmore

Gordonbush
Lothbeg
Kilmote
ND

Loch
Brora
Kintradwell
Craickaig
Lothbeg Point

Rhilochan
Loch
Horn
21

Knockarthur
West
Clyne
Achrimsdale
A9

Farlary
Clynelish
Dalchalm

gart
1239
CAGAR FEOSAIG
Doll
Brora

trail
Uppat

A839
Morvich Lodge
Backies
Mains

Rhives
Dunrobin Castle

Kirkton
Culmaily
Golspie
i

usmore
Lodge
Loch
Fleet
Littleferry

busavie
A9
Skelbo

insh
Skelbo Street
Fourpenny

Poles
Pronncy
Mains
Embo

Birichin
Proncynain
Embro Street

Evelix
Camore
Pitgrudy

A949
DORNOCH
i

Cuthill
Tarbat Ness

Point
Brucefield
Hilton
Wilkhaven

Ardjachie
Bindal

Morangie
Portmahomack
Mains of Seafield

TAIN
Inver
Rockfield
NJ

Fendom
Balnagall

Arthurville
Arboll
Toulvaddie
Meikle Tarrel

Lochslin
B9165
Rhynie

Newfield
Hill of Fearn
Balmuchy

ton
B9165
Fearn
Hilton of
Cadboll
SCALE

Logie
Hill
Clays of
Allan
Tullich
0    1    2    3    4    5 miles

llchraggan
Kildary
Arabella
Cullisse
Balintore

A9
Milton
Ankerville
Corner
Shandwick
0  1  2  3  4  5 kilometres

Kilmuir
Ankerville
Wester Rarichie
Easter Rarichie
Chapelhill

Nigg Bay
Pitcalnie
Port an Righ

Barbaraville
Nigg
BURGHEAD

ntraid
Lower Pitcalzean
Hope

Balnabruaich
BURGHEAD
St Aethans
Ne

Balnapaling
Castlecraig
Cummingston

ON
CROMARTY
BURGHEAD
BAY
College of Roseisle

marty
Bay
Newton
Mains
Nay
Sutors of Cromarty
Blue Head
Findhorn
B9013

9163
A832

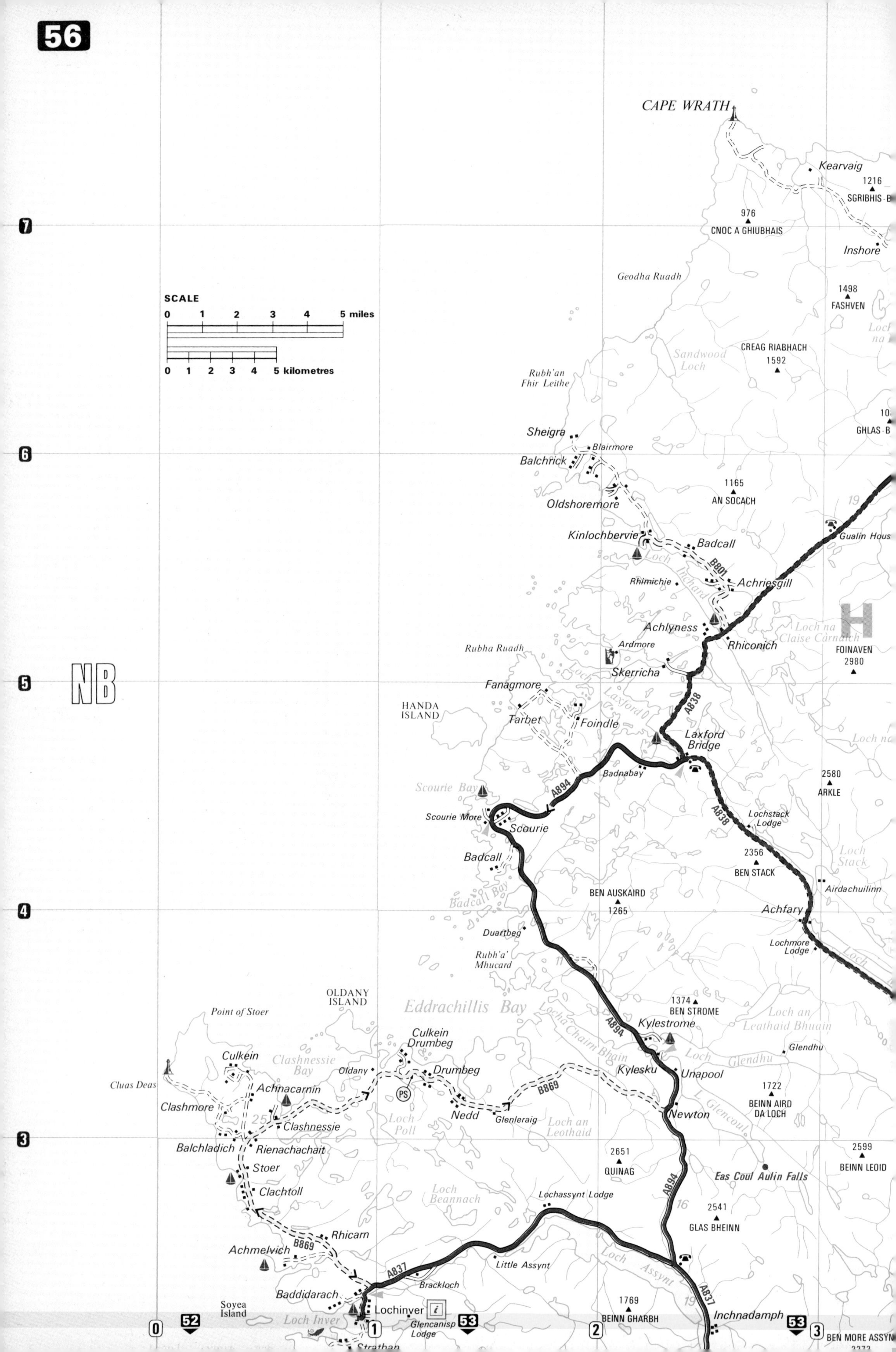

CAPE WRATH

Kearvaig

1216
SGRIBHIS·B

976
CNOC A GHIUBHAIS

Inshore

Geodha Ruadh

1498
FASHVEN

Loch
na

SCALE

0   1   2   3   4   5 miles

0   1   2   3   4   5 kilometres

Sandwood
Loch

CREAG RIABHACH
1592

Rubh'an
Fhir Leithe

Sheigra

Blairmore

Balchrick

1165
AN SOCACH

19

10
GHLAS·B

Oldshoremore

Kinlochbervie

Badcall

B801

Gualin Hous

Rhimichie

Achriesgill

Loch Inchard

Achlyness

Loch na
Claise Carnach

Rhiconich

FOINAVEN
2980

NB

Rubha Ruadh

Ardmore

Skerricha

HANDA
ISLAND

Fanagmore

Tarbet

Foindle

Loch Laxford

A838

Laxford
Bridge

Loch na

2580
ARKLE

Scourie Bay

Badnabay

A894

Lochstack
Lodge

A838

Scourie More

Scourie

2356
BEN STACK

Loch
Stack

Badcall

Airdachuilinn

Badcall Bay

BEN AUSKAIRD
1265

Achfary

Duartbeg

Rubh'a'
Mhucard

11

Lochmore
Lodge

Loch

OLDANY
ISLAND

Eddrachillis Bay

Locha Chairn Bhain

A894

1374
BEN STROME

Kylestrome

Loch an
Leathaid Bhuain

Point of Stoer

Culkein
Drumbeg

Glendhu

Culkein

Clashnessie
Bay

Oldany

Drumbeg

B869

Kylesku

Unapool

Glendhu

Cluas Deas

Achnacarnin

Loch
Poll

PS

Nedd

Glenleraig

Loch an
Leothaid

Newton

1722
BEINN AIRD
DA LOCH

Clashmore

Clashnessie

25

L. Glencoul

Balchladich

Rienachachait

2651
QUINAG

2599
BEINN LEOID

Stoer

Loch
Beannach

Lochassynt Lodge

A894

Eas Coul Aulin Falls

Clachtoll

2541
GLAS BHEINN

16

Rhicarn

B869

Achmelvich

Little Assynt

Loch Assynt

A837

Baddidarach

A837

Brackloch

1769
BEINN GHARBH

Inchnadamph

19

## 52

Soyea
Island

Lochinver

i

Glencanisp
Lodge

53

2

53

3

BEN MORE ASSYN

Loch Inver

Strathan

0

1

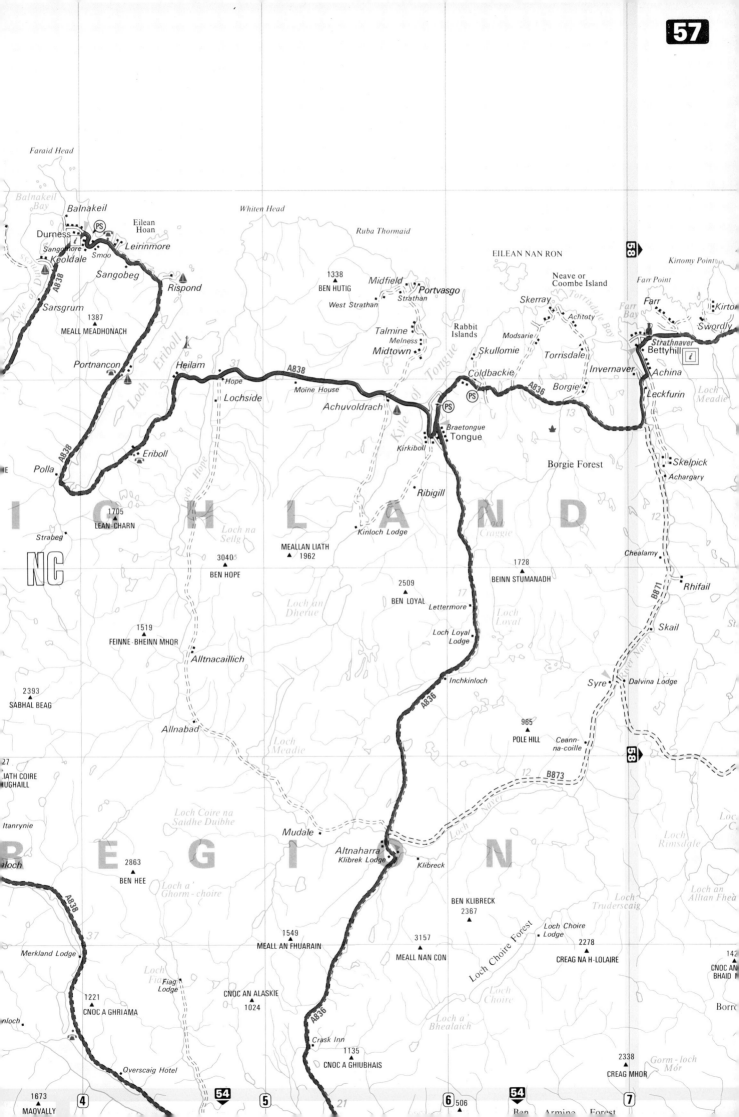

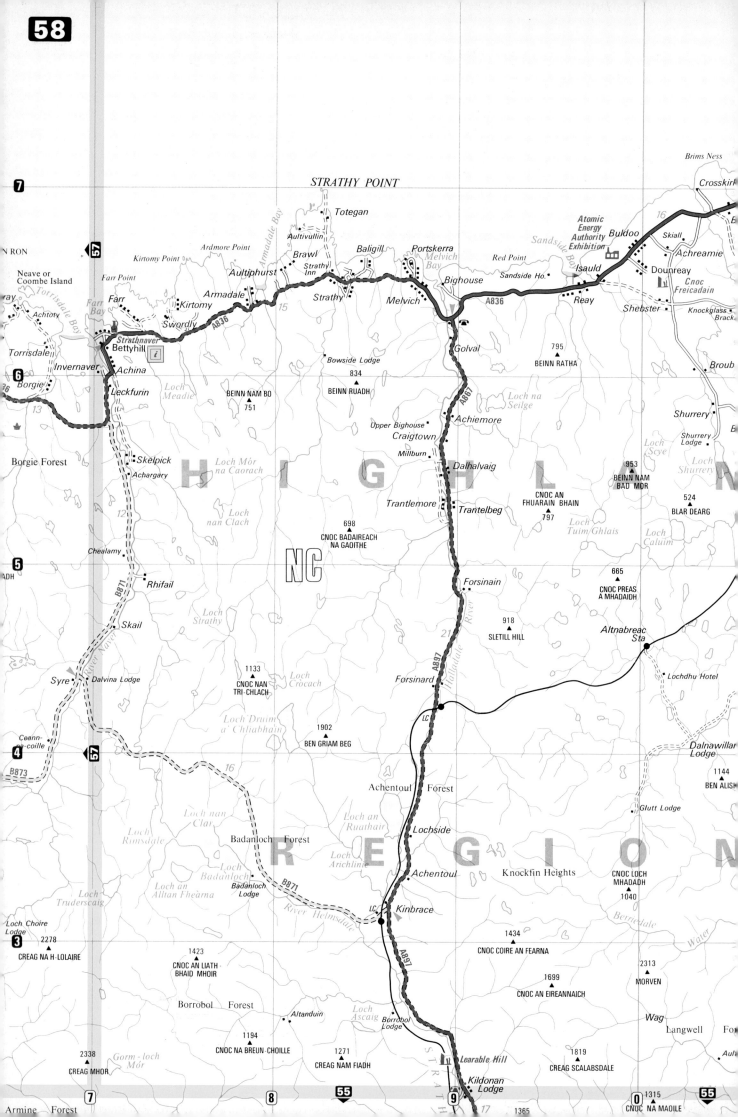

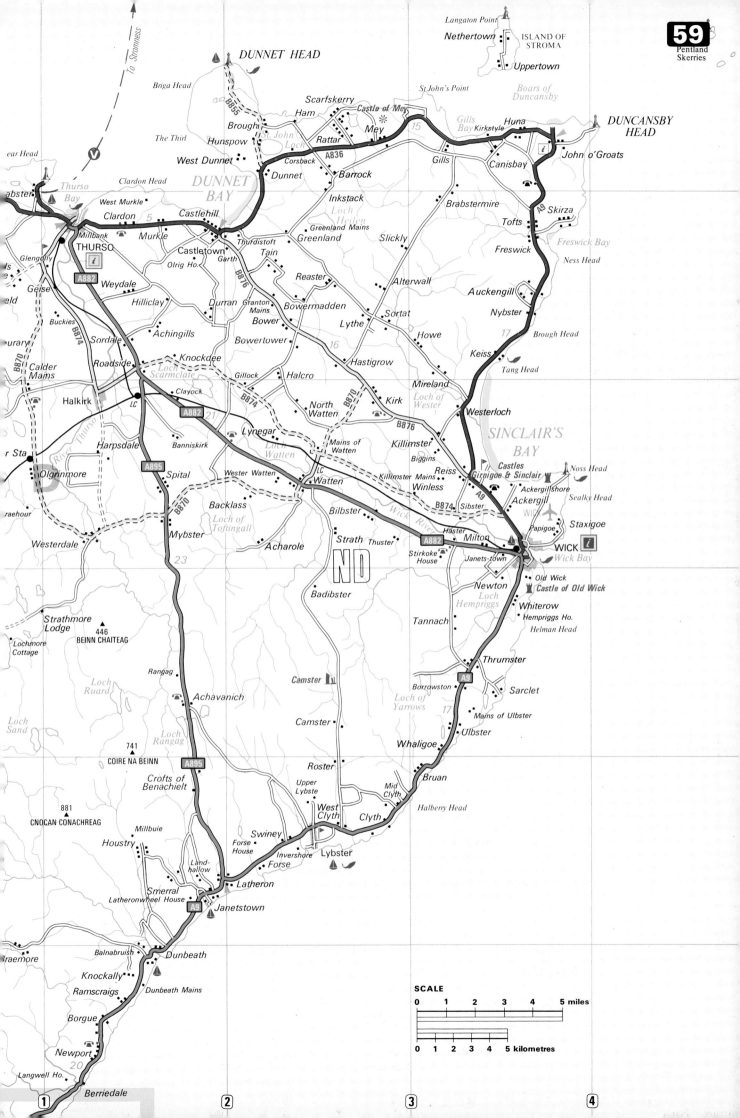

# INDEX

As well as the page number of each place name the index also includes an appropriate atlas page number together with a four figure map reference (see National Grid explanation on page 92).

In a very few instances place names appear without a map reference. This is because either they are not shown on the atlas or they lie just outside the mapping area of the guide. However, each tour does include a detailed map which highlights the location of all places mentioned on the route.